ATHERS: The Authorised Biography of Michael Atherton

David Norrie has been cricket correspondent for the *News of the World* for many years. He is the author of several books, among them *The Authorised Illustrated Biography of Will Carling* (Headline, 1995). He lives in Surrey with his family.

For Helen, Alasdair, Jack, Eleanor
and Freya – my inspiration

Athers

*The Authorised Biography
of Michael Atherton*

David Norrie

HEADLINE

First published in 1997
by HEADLINE BOOK PUBLISHING

First published in paperback in 1998
by HEADLINE BOOK PUBLISHING

10 9 8 7 6 5 4 3 2 1

ISBN 0 7472 5446 X

Typeset by
Letterpart Limited, Reigate, Surrey

Printed and bound in Great Britain by
Mackays of Chatham PLC, Chatham, Kent

HEADLINE BOOK PUBLISHING
A division of Hodder Headline PLC
338 Euston Road
London NW1 3BH

Contents

Acknowledgements

My grateful thanks go to all those who helped so generously in the preparation of this book. Wendy and Alan (Michael's Mum and Dad), Neil Fairbrother, David Lloyd, Peter Martin, Peter Lever, Ray Illingworth, John Emburey, Paul Allott, Mark Nicholas, Graham Gooch, David Graveney, Bob Bennett, Angus Fraser, Michael Henderson, Jon Holmes, Bob Wilson, Ian Marshall and all at Headline, my tour buddies (Reggie, Bonker, the Count, Toff, Stan, the Iguana, Crash, Leepy, Scoop and others of the Fourth Estate), Richie Benaud, the sports department at the *News of the World* and, of course, the lad himself, for giving freely of his time and recollections of some pretty memorable years and incidents.

Bibliography

A Test of Cricket: Know the Game, Mike Atherton (Hodder & Stoughton); *Atherton's Progress*, Keith Booth (Clifford Frost Publications); *One-Man Committee*, Ray Illingworth and Jack Bannister (Headline); *Tampering with Cricket*, Don Oslear and Jack Bannister (Collins Willow); *Winning Ways*, Dermot Reeve (Boxtree); *Uncorked*, Dominic Cork (Richard Cohen Books); *Wisden Cricketers' Almanack*, Matthew Engel (John Wisden); *Playfair Cricket Annual*, Bill Frindall (Headline); *The Cricketers Who's Who*, Chris Hawkes (Queen Anne Press); various issues of the *Cricketer* and *Wisden Cricket Monthly*, national daily and Sunday newspapers.

Introduction

Michael Atherton was always expected to captain England. He fulfilled his cricket destiny at Edgbaston against Australia on 5 August, 1993 at the age of 25. Atherton began the 1997 summer having led England in all 40 Tests since being appointed to the position by Ted Dexter after Graham Gooch's resignation, a total that left him one behind Peter May's record. The 1997 Ashes series brought Atherton full circle. His four years in charge have made him one of the most famous sporting personalities in the land. Atherton has enjoyed and endured an extremely bumpy roller-coaster ride as captain, being exalted and worshipped, or condemned and vilified with equal passion. Atherton has treated 'those two impostors' with equal disdain, rarely reacting in public to the fickle ways of sport and life. The gummy, toothy George Formby smile is usually only revealed in private moments. Yet his distinctive northern cackle has become a familiar sound round the international cricket circuit. Only with his team, his close friends, in a cricket dressing-room or out in the middle with a bat in his hand, does Atherton feel truly at home.

Michael Andrew Atherton is the professional sportsman with the traditional Establishment education – public school and Oxbridge. On the way to the England job, Atherton picked up the three initials once believed essential for high cricket office. 'FEC' was soon daubed on his cricket 'coffin' in boot whitener by a member of the Lancashire dressing-room. At the time Atherton was regarded more as a F****** Educated C*** than a Future England Captain. He has since emerged as both, living easily with that double identity. The English Establishment believed that Atherton's Manchester GS and Cambridge University upbringing makes him a paid-up member of the ruling class. Yet, Atherton is much more Player than Gentleman, a proud northern lad who loves his Mancunian roots (the 'Ath' in Atherton is soft, not hard) and the life of a professional cricketer. He would just as happily have dined with Harold Larwood as Douglas Jardine on the Bodyline tour. Such dexterity can make for a lonely life, as does the captain's duties. Atherton has never had problems with his own company, though he is not a loner. Atherton has his father's reserve. Alan, on Manchester United's books in the early sixties, has been a major influence. Atherton's brother, Chris, is much more like his mum, Wendy, who is gregarious and outgoing.

Cricket has dominated Atherton's life. His interests are varied, but cricket has been the constant factor. His skill with a cricket bat has taken him to the very top of his chosen profession. It has brought him fame and some fortune. The England captaincy has brought him notoriety, plenty of controversy and a less glowing verdict on his leadership abilities. Atherton's vision of a brave new world was dismantled after a few months by the incoming chairman of selectors, Ray Illingworth. For the next two and a half years, Atherton's power and influence were curtailed and England's captain, along with his team, has continued to operate while the English game's governing body has made feeble attempts to provide the players with some sort of competitive domestic structure. Atherton has often been caught in the crossfire, largely because the England captain is the recognisable face of cricket in this country.

Atherton knew that territory came with the job. What he does loathe is any intrusion into his private affairs. His love life has featured only once in the headlines to any extent, during the 1994 West Indies tour. The story of his split with Suzie Carman, whom he had met at Cambridge University, was actually three months old. Atherton had already met Isabelle de Caires, daughter of a Guyanan newspaper publisher, in the Sidewalk Cafe in Georgetown. They have been together ever since. Atherton is hopeless at the social graces. Isabelle and Atherton's parents were both at the Old Trafford Test that followed that tour. For five days the Lancashire chairman, Bob Bennett, nagged Atherton to introduce them. In the end, Bennett had to do it himself, while Atherton was lying on the physiotherapist's couch. The press have tracked down the courting couple twice, on holiday in Tobago at the end of that 1994 tour and in the Lake District after the Lord's ball-tampering incident that summer. Since then Atherton has been careful not to give the press any reason for following him. Atherton has found the photographer's lens just as intrusive. The Old Trafford dressing-room is now in almost permanent darkness after Atherton's bare bottom was put on the back of the *Sun* under the headline 'Silly Arse'. Atherton was furious and sought legal advice, while the club organised the tinting of the windows. England's captain has never understood the fascination to click away with cameras every time he drops his trousers to get padded up or changed.

Public appearances are not another favourite. Walking out in front of a packed Lord's, MCG or Wanderers with a bat in his hand is no problem, yet Atherton does not enjoy public speaking. Even thanking the tea ladies at Manchester GS was beyond him. He was only 19 when he turned up at Blackpool Cricket Club expecting to hand out some prizes. Atherton was horrified those assembled were expecting a speech. He is not an 'off-the-cuff' man. With nothing prepared, Atherton managed a few sentences before escaping the embarrassment of the situation, a feeling that lingers still when such circumstances arise. For all his education and subsequent high sporting profile, Atherton lacks self-confidence in some of the more frivolous places, like a dance-floor, disco or singing. It goes by the name of Atherton's Barmy Army, but the likes of Stewart, Gough and Croft are more comfortable in its company, especially when it requires standing on a bar stool or table to lead the singing. Atherton likes drinking and being one of the lads – just that, one of the lads. His friends know how embarrassed he can get. His chums from university made it to the city bookshop where he was signing copies of his book *A Test of Cricket* just to see how he'd cope. There was more embarrassment on Noel Edmonds' 'Gotcha' when England's captain thought he was dealing with eskimos. His discomfort was obvious. Most of his friends come from his Cambridge days and you can tell how close he is to his cricket mates, like Neil 'Harvey' Fairbrother and Angus Fraser, by the amount of time they spend arguing.

There can be few modern sportsmen who have failed so convincingly to cash in on all the money that goes with a high sporting profile in today's world. Cricket has always come first to Atherton. Atherton is fully aware of the opportunities; so is the man who now looks after this aspect of his career, Jon Holmes. For a brief spell at the start of his Test career, Atherton signed up with Ted Markwick and the CarPhone Group, as did Robin Smith. That commercial operation was not for him, and he feels more at home in the Holmes stable which includes Gary

Lineker, Will Carling, David Gower and Dominic Cork. It is not just because he is England captain that Atherton resents those who chase money at the expense of their talent. He hates talking about money, as if mentioning it will lead to the conclusion that it has played some part in his cricketing journey. That has also made life difficult for his benefit chairman, Bob Wilson, in 1997, although Atherton ended up with a record total of £307,000.

His main non-playing commercial activities are writing for the *Sunday Telegraph* and he is on the board of *Wisden Cricket Monthly*. Even these deals do not distract him from the real job. His university training came in handy in Georgetown in 1994 when the magazine rang up, saying it was going to press in an hour and where were his 1,000 words on the tour so far. When Jonathan Agnew was about to join the editorial board of the magazine for the December 1996 issue, Atherton was rung up again, to see if he had any objections. Atherton and Agnew have not been bosom buddies since the latter called for Atherton to quit during the 1994 ball-tampering row. It would not be in Atherton's nature to object in such circumstances, though he did threaten to resign from the board after a racial article on some of his team. He remained only when it was made clear that was not editorial policy.

As for endorsements, his bats are made by Gray Nicholls. A rare excursion into the big-time came in 1994 when he did a photo session for a Scottish Life advertisement, but it never appeared. His contract had a 'death or disgrace' clause and the company regarded his involvement in the Lord's ball-tampering affair as the latter. Many thought it would lead to the former as far as his captaincy future was concerned. Atherton also has a deal to wear Henri Lloyd clothes, though some in cricket joke that another clothing manufacturer, like Armani, pays him to wear them, for England's captain is, without doubt, one of the scruffiest sportsmen around.

Atherton admits: 'I'm the type of bloke who can wear the most expensive suit and still look a mess.' It is not Bob Geldof scruffy, more university untidy. It is not just Atherton, but wherever he goes or has been: his flat, his corner in the Lancashire dressing-room, his car and his hotel room on tour. All have entered cricket legend. His Didsbury flat, bought in 1989, has also housed for varying periods Lancashire and England's David Lloyd, Paul Allott and Peter Martin. Allott remembers picking up the keys and finding unwashed dishes in the sink and milk and cheese in the fridge. Not that unusual, except Atherton had left for a four-month tour of Australia the week before and had not known Allott would be staying. The dishes and milk would have been waiting for Atherton's return. Martin remembers trying to tidy the flat when he heard Atherton's mum, Wendy, was coming round to clean it. Nor can he forget the time Atherton melted his bowling boots, which he had put in the oven to dry. His mum still does his washing and ironing. There are piles and piles of shirts and tops still in their cellophane. His mum cannot understand why he wants to wear the same things all the time.

The 'rat's nest' is the name for his dressing-room spot. It is piled to the ceiling with gear, most of it still in the wrapper and given away at the end of the season. There is method in his untidiness. Atherton knows immediately when one of his socks goes walkabout. And that is not by smell, for Atherton has no sense of smell. During last winter's tour, runs were not the only things hard to come by – the fish in Zimbabwe and New Zealand were not biting. One was hidden in his room with a note saying: 'This is what a brown trout looks like'. It was wasted on Atherton. With no sense of smell, he never found it. The absence of that faculty might be an advantage in a cricket dressing-room, but close friends like Neil Fairbrother are on hand outside to warn him if his shirt has been on too long. They cannot be everywhere. Atherton was spotted in the lobby of a posh Caribbean hotel with his swimming trunks on inside out. While his favourite pair of Timberland shoes, bought for £40, have been going for almost as long as his Test career.

Atherton is not the only England captain whose stubble had brought him strife. The obsession of cricket hierarchy with razors and clean-shaven players is overwhelming. After England lost three consecutive Tests in India and one in Sri Lanka at the start of 1993, the emergency meeting at Lord's castigated Graham Gooch and his team for not shaving and for their untidy appearance. After England's dismal one-day showing in South Africa and in the 1996 World Cup, the chairman of the TCCB, Dennis Silk, had a similar message for Atherton: 'He cannot neglect self-discipline like shaving every day and dressing in a manner that will not offend either his opponents or his hosts. I hated wearing a suit, but as a headmaster I had to wear one every day of my working life. I had to have my hair cut, I had to shave every day and I had to be polite to people.' Atherton's stubble has never made the long journey to fully fledged beard. But shaving can be a hassle on tour, especially under the baking sun and block cream. If it annoys the hierarchy as well, so be it.

His sense of humour is sometimes lost on others and inappropriate. The morning after the ball-tampering fracas, Atherton walked down the Pavilion steps with his hands in his pockets. Under the glare of the television lights, England's captain denied that gesture was intentional. It was, but the £2,000 fine and threat of losing his job advised Atherton this was not the time to admit levity. His critics will point this out as another example of his failure to tell the truth that weekend.

As chaotic and shambolic as Atherton outwardly appears, England's captain has one of the most organised minds in sport. He has always arranged his time effectively; Atherton sets time aside for tasks. Most people do, but Atherton's strength is that he does them when scheduled. His homework was completed when set, not when due. Cricket tours meant Atherton was left to his own devices to catch up at Cambridge. Even during term time, his day was organised into three sections – work in the morning, cricket in the afternoon and out to play in the evening. And he stuck to it. Atherton hates wasting time. He hardly attended a lecture at university and studied from books. Atherton has been an avid reader all his life, although the sports pages have been mainly given a miss in recent years.

Atherton does tend to categorise and compartmentalise people. He is too trusting of those very close and too wary of those outside. Atherton is extremely loyal to all things Lancashire and all things Cambridge. Able to work things out, he does not always think them through, often erring on the side of intelligence over common-sense. Not everything you need to know is in books. Atherton is much more street-wise after four years of the England captaincy, although the instinct for survival, not self-interest, has always been there. Passing examination by the world's fastest bowlers means more to Atherton than success in any scholastic test.

The 'Iron Mike' tag, which took over from his first nickname 'Iceman' (one of the characters in the movie *Top Gun*), does not sit uneasily with him. Cricket allows him to keep the physical and intellectual worlds apart. When Atherton is being brave, there is no time to think. There are Hamlet tendencies in Atherton – the intellectual who hankers to follow his gut feelings. His brain tells him cricket is only a game, his heart knows how much it hurts when Australia are tramping all over England and aches for revenge, terrible revenge. Atherton is patriotic, not nationalistic, and would never blindly follow any flag. He wants the pride to come from within, not through outside expectations. Sadly, his England team have all too often been guilty of talking a good game.

No one can doubt Atherton's loyalty, to his team, his players and those who have managed and coached him. To start and finish the Ray Illingworth era as captain is an achievement that is near the peak of sporting endurance – no other player came close to matching his record of playing in every Test. Even now, the grudges Atherton holds are not personal ones. It would be unnatural if Atherton had not fallen out with a few: Dermot Reeve and Phil DeFreitas are not on his Christmas card list. His remark about Steve Waugh 'wetting himself' at The Oval came back to haunt him on the next Ashes tour. Since then, England's captain has been more circumspect. In those late bar-room discussions round the world, Atherton can often be dismissive of other arguments. He will respond for effect, or if he has had enough, yet Atherton does not miss much. The next day the argument might be countered or he might concede a point, though only after sleeping on it. Atherton loves games, challenges, tests and does not like being beaten, at golf or even by an electronic chess game. He learns by his mistakes. One of the most frustrating aspects of being captain of England's cricketers for him has been their failure to do the same.

His pugnacious character was never more evident than at The Wanderers in late 1995 when he battled for a seemingly lost cause, but Atherton was just as defiant and determined during his troubles in Zimbabwe and New Zealand last winter. Atherton has rarely made excuses or complained about his troublesome back, his inconsistent charges, an indiscreet chairman, crazy schedules or the many other hindrances that affect the effectiveness of England's cricket captain. Yet, for all his national heroics, Atherton was not honoured by cricket-loving John Major during his term as Britain's prime minister, although the likes of Warwickshire's Dermot

Reeve did receive a 'gong' in the 1996 New Year's Honours List, along with TCCB chief executive Alan Smith. Perhaps Atherton's troubles in the second half of the 1994 summer had not been forgotten. It was an oversight which was corrected by the Labour government last June. But Atherton had been far more interested in regaining the Ashes. His hopes, and the nation's, were raised after England's winning start at Edgbaston. Four Tests and two months later the Ashes were back in Australian hands and Atherton's future as England's captain had become cricket's main talking point again. His second victory at The Oval over Australia as captain helped change his mind, and he was reappointed for the 1997-98 tour of the West Indies. After the abandoned first Test at Sabina Park, England threw away the first Trinidad Test in typical style and it appeared the tourists were heading for self-destruction as so often in the past. But England held their nerve to win the most tense cricket match Atherton had ever experienced to level the series a week later at the Queen's Park Oval. Atherton could not complain about such a nerve-jangling roller-coaster ride as he contemplated his decision to stay on as England captain. The first of two very hazy nights at the Pelican in the Port-of-Spain ended with Atherton falling over when he went to lean on a bar that wasn't there. He lay on his back unable to get up. When asked what he was doing, England's defeated captain replied: 'Getting a Test match out of my system.' Eight nights later at the opposite end of the sporting spectrum, having triumphed by three wickets, Atherton was in exactly the same condition, celebrating victory in much the same way he had coped with agonising defeat.

CHAPTER ONE

The Trouble with Illy

Michael Atherton emerged from his 1996-97 Zimbabwe nightmares with a battling 83 against New Zealand in Auckland, only to be denied a desperately needed Test victory by a batsman who has scored a record number of Test ducks. Immediately, Atherton's captaincy replaced his batting as the issue of the day, and he wondered what England's chairman of selectors, Raymond Illingworth, would make of it all. Atherton had a fair idea and reckoned that the verdict would not be long in coming. He had long ago given up any thoughts of a reassuring phone-call from a chairman to his captain in time of trouble, for that was not Illingworth's way. Yet not even Atherton was prepared for this death sentence: 'Mike Atherton must take much of the blame for England's unbelievable failure to beat New Zealand yesterday. If this carries on, there will be no alternative to replacing him as England captain.'

The message, as ever, was a public one, in the sports pages of the *Daily Express*. And the messenger was the man who had picked his squad, worked closely with the captain for nearly three years and declared more than once that 'The buck stops with me.' Atherton just shook his head in despair. Illingworth just could not keep his mouth shut, and this was a problem Atherton knew was not going to disappear during the Ashes summer as Illingworth retired as chairman and returned to newspaper duties.

Whether Illingworth was technically still chairman of selectors or not during the 1996-97 winter tour was an unimportant though not an irrelevant point. Either way, Atherton felt the comments were way out of order. Illingworth knew precisely what the team were going through. He had been in charge of them as they struggled through the sub-continent during the World Cup the winter before and had seen the problems and the need to pull together. There was no grovelling apology a few weeks later after Atherton had revived England to a 2-0 victory in the New Zealand series. Atherton did not expect one – that too is not this Yorkshireman's way. Uncompromising is the word. Most people believe that Atherton has suffered more than anyone at Illingworth's hands, though England's captain does not agree. He is convinced that the main casualty of the Illingworth years was the young England team that fought back bravely in the Caribbean in 1994 only to be dismantled by the new chairman of selectors on its return.

Illingworth has often acted in ways that seem almost designed to make Atherton's life a misery over the past three years (and occasionally succeeded), for reasons which have not been especially apparent. Atherton has battled on, venting his annoyance and frustration in the way he knows best, scoring runs for England. His public outbursts have been extremely rare, and not just because of the 'gagging' powers of Lord's. Illingworth has interfered with his captain in a way he himself would never have tolerated or expected in his days as England leader. The secrets of selection meetings have frequently entered the public domain, especially when an Atherton 'pick' has not proved successful. By contrast, many of the chairman's mistakes have stayed locked away behind closed doors. It was Illingworth who sent Devon Malcolm home the day before the 1994 New Zealand Lord's Test, against his captain's wishes, yet the buck did not stop with Illingworth as it was left to Atherton to tell his fast bowler the bad news. Atherton has never had any desire to join those who wash his team's dirty linen in public, but since Illingworth took over as England's chairman of selectors early in 1994, the team and their captain have endured a series of humiliating public lashings with no right of reply.

Whatever respect Atherton has or had for Illingworth, as a cricketer and former Test captain, is now heavily outweighed by the damage he feels the chairman has done to England's spirit and fortunes over the past three years. Atherton believes that had Illingworth not abandoned the youth policy instigated in the Caribbean in 1994, English cricket would be in far better shape today. Only when Illingworth's power base was weakened in 1996, and David Lloyd took over as coach, were England able to start building again. The war of the Roses, Atherton's Lancashire Red and Illingworth's Yorkshire White, made for easy copy and good headlines, but Illingworth's infatuation with all things east of the Pennines was certainly clear.

Illingworth banned the players from writing columns and diaries on the 1995-96 tour of South Africa, yet the team flew out just as a three-part series of articles by Illingworth appeared in the *Sun*. The squad left for Zimbabwe the following winter in exactly the same circumstances. The secrets of selection meetings were not sacred to Illingworth, nor was the dressing-room a holy place. Indeed, Atherton's biggest mistake was in allowing Illingworth into the dressing-room at all. Illingworth seemed to set up home there, often hanging his jacket up first thing and staying there all day. It took Atherton a while to realise that his players resented Illingworth's permanent presence, not only because they felt unable to let off steam but because things said and observed could make their way to the outside world. A cricket dressing-room is the one safe refuge of the players, and Illingworth, more than anyone, should have understood that. Atherton could have controlled that particular situation; the rest was out of his hands.

When the England squad returned from the Caribbean in 1994 (minus Atherton, who had stayed on for a well-earned holiday), they were greeted by Illingworth's views on the tour. He had beaten MJK Smith for the chairman of selectors post while the team were in Guyana. England had battled back to become the first side to win in Barbados for 59 years after going 3-0 down in the series, and even Brian Lara's 375 in the drawn final Test could not dampen English spirits and their sense of a real revival. But Illingworth did what Lara could not. Angus Fraser, Graeme Hick, Chris Lewis, Mark Ramprakash and Jack Russell, among others, arrived back to be confronted by a less than glowing end-of-tour report from the new chairman. It set the trend for the Illingworth reign.

There was never any consideration given, or even lip-service paid, to sticking with Atherton's youth policy. Illingworth had made up his mind from the television pictures. In the curious world of cricket, the chairman was able to mark his preferred candidates in the list of prospective selectors that was sent to the counties. His two choices, Fred Titmus and Brian Bolus, were duly elected, giving him a 3-2 majority in meetings (and a 182-75 advantage in years). Illingworth was in charge and Atherton was left in no doubt that his days of influence were over – Illingworth knew better, especially where the team line-up was concerned. Ignoring the preference of Atherton (not to mention the West Indies and Australia) for having six front-line batsmen, Illingworth wanted an all-rounder at No. 6. Atherton's protests at the selection meetings were brushed aside. In fact, the over-60s felt that England's captain had rather too much to say for himself.

Atherton has never been allowed to forget that Illingworth 'saved his neck' after the ball-tampering incident against South Africa at Lord's in 1994. Illingworth has perpetuated that myth. The truth is that the chairman aggravated that situation with a series of tactical blunders for which Atherton suffered badly. Illingworth left the ground while the captain was being interrogated by ICC referee Peter Burge, and Atherton's failure to tell Burge about the dirt in his pocket only came to light after a discussion between Illingworth and Burge on Saturday night. The following day, Illingworth decided that the only way to save Atherton was to fine him £2,000 and present him to the media at the close of play that evening. Atherton had little say in the process, or in the statement he was to read out. But crucially, Illingworth did nothing to change those arrangements when it became obvious that England were going to lose badly. As a result, a dejected Atherton was in no state to cope with the press conference. Illingworth stood by while his captain was roasted alive.

That began a month of enormous turmoil for Atherton. The fuss after his 'gutter press' remark at Headingley and his fine for dissent at The Oval would have crushed weaker spirits. At Leeds, England did actually field the six batsmen line-up that Atherton had wanted at the start of the summer, and drew the match. Atherton hoped that that performance, and England's recovery at The Oval when Devon Malcolm blitzed the South Africans, might encourage Illingworth to adopt a power-sharing attitude. No chance. Illingworth insisted that *his* choices go to Australia in 1994-95 and overruled the captain on the final batting and bowling places. Martin McCague went instead of Fraser and Mike Gatting rather than Ramprakash. History proved the chairman wrong and the captain right. Yet by the start of the following summer, Illingworth was England's first cricket 'supremo' and Atherton was kept dangling for weeks over the captaincy.

Illingworth's part in that Ashes defeat was immense. His fast-pitches strategy was flawed, as Atherton always knew it would be. McCague lasted one Test and showed little stomach for the fight, while Gatting, his Adelaide century apart, was exposed for his years and fitness. Before the first Test at Brisbane, England's captain was coming to terms with the loss of Malcolm because of chickenpox when, back in England, Illingworth went 'public' again – only on this occasion the chairman must have been feeling guilty because he rang Atherton and told him his remarks had been taken out of context. Illingworth had been speaking at an on-the-record Sports Writers' Association lunch. 'I saved Mike's neck' was the general theme, with the chairman apparently aggrieved that Atherton had not thanked him properly or phoned him from Australia. Atherton did not worry for himself but for his team, going into the opening Test of an Ashes series.

Illingworth flew in for the Melbourne and Sydney Tests and again was extremely critical. This time Atherton got his own back by stating that the abandonment of his youth policy had proved costly in Australia, that he had not got the squad he wanted and the selectors needed to be more in touch. He did not say that the captain should pick the England team, but Illingworth did not enjoy a taste of his own medicine and Atherton was called for a showdown. Titmus wanted him sacked. Back home again, Illingworth told the *Sun*: 'This modern trend of not shaving makes me angry. The captain is the worst culprit. He's going to be clean-shaven this coming summer, I can tell you.' Atherton and England responded in the best possible way, with a win in Adelaide.

The weakness of Illingworth's selection and strategy, a tour plagued by injury and an outdated itinerary were ignored as the knife went into Keith Fletcher, the England coach and whipping-boy for the tour, who was sacked. Illingworth was given full powers and Atherton's reappointment as captain was put on hold after his outburst in Australia. 'It is really not a captain's job to be going around criticising selectors,' Illingworth scolded. 'When I was England captain, I would not have thought of criticising Alec Bedser or Don Kenyon. If he has anything to say, he should say it in the privacy of the selectors' meeting.' He did not add that, likewise, Bedser and Kenyon would never have criticised the captain, nor that it was he who had taken the secrets of selection meetings onto the sports pages. The one consolation for the younger generation was the arrival of David Graveney as a selector instead of Bolus.

Illingworth's treatment of Atherton over the first weeks of the summer of 1995 kept the pressure on him. Atherton wondered about chucking it in. The key question, as it had been during the ball-tampering row, was whether he would be quitting for the right reasons. Illingworth had made no secret to Atherton, and publicly, that Gatting would have been his chosen captain in 1994. The Australian tour had scotched that alternative. Alec Stewart, who had captained England twice in 1993, was the only other contender. Atherton tried as best he could to shut out Illingworth and the captaincy issue. He was not going to quit. If Illingworth sacked him, so be it.

In the end, Atherton was appointed for half the summer. (There was never any doubt that that would be the decision. If Stewart had been brought in and failed, Illingworth would have been left with nowhere to turn. If Atherton flopped, then Illingworth had given him his chance and was justified in making a change. If Atherton succeeded, three cheers for the new supremo being magnanimous and getting it right. Illingworth could not lose.) Atherton was subsequently confirmed for the whole summer when England beat the West Indies at Lord's, though before that Test there were reports of him resigning, that he had had enough of Illingworth's meddling. Despite his great show of being the supremo, Illingworth tended to create problems by delegating at the wrong times. He had got Fletcher to ask Graham Gooch whether he was happy batting No. 5 in Australia. The wrong answer was relayed back and it had a serious impact. He now got Atherton to ask Stewart whether he would open and keep wicket at Lord's. Again, an incomplete answer came back. The error was then compounded by Illingworth taking two days to speak to Stewart. The day before the Test, the original choice as wicket-keeper, Steven Rhodes, was sent home by Illingworth and talk started of the captain throwing in the towel. Atherton claims that was not the case. More confusion followed at Edgbaston when Illingworth failed to look at the wicket and sent Titmus. By the time Illingworth and Atherton turned up, England had no option but to perform on a wicket that was tailor-made for the West Indies.

Illingworth's bluff was called once and for all on the winter tours to South Africa and the World Cup in India and Pakistan. Illingworth announced that he would be in sole charge of selection in South Africa – 'My reputation is on the line. My success as manager and chairman of selectors will probably be judged by this winter's tour' – but it was his views which appeared in the *Sun* as England flew out that angered Atherton and the team. 'Atherton is so stubborn, inflexible and narrow-minded' was rich coming from any Yorkshireman and hardly conducive to tour harmony. Atherton's friendship with Fraser, his disagreements with Phillip DeFreitas and his problems with Phil Tufnell were all chewed over by Illingworth and Geoff Boycott. The comments about players and selection were bad enough. What really annoyed the squad was that the players' tour letter had contained the following: 'The chairman stipulates that players will not be allowed to write columns or diaries.' The official reason was that such public outpourings could harm the team (so what about Illingworth's?). But it wasn't that at all. Any articles had to be approved and cleared by the tour management anyway, and it appeared that the management of this tour simply did not want to be bothered. The Board had to backtrack as some players' contracts with newspapers pre-dated the tour contract. The Board was offered the chance of compensating the players concerned, but backed down. That made it even more unfair, as it meant some players could make money writing while others could not. Atherton was not happy. England needed to be a team, not a bunch of individuals, some more privileged than others.

Illingworth's forthright style of management was not too evident as the Devon Malcolm affair blew up in Johannesburg in late October. Atherton handled the first run-in with Malcolm when the fast bowler failed to appear at Springs. The captain maintains that it was no big deal, although Malcolm was left in no doubt about the level of commitment Atherton expected from all his players. By and large, that incident was a one-day wonder as far as the press were concerned. But when Illingworth, with a little help from fast-bowling coach Peter Lever, got to work, the whole business became a public relations disaster. Matters were not finally settled until Illingworth was cleared of bringing the game into disrepute at the end of the following summer. Atherton had little sympathy for either protagonist. To him, anything that diverted attention away from England winning the Test series was disruptive.

Even in Atherton's hour of triumph, when he almost single-handedly saved The Wanderers Test, the captain found himself in conflict with the boss. The squad flew to Cape Town and travelled by coach to Paarl. Atherton took a well-deserved break, visiting local wineries and experiencing fly-fishing for the first time. When he returned to the team hotel that night to cook his own supper, Atherton learnt that Illingworth had ended the four-day game a day early and the England captain was required for duty in a hastily arranged limited-overs match. It was man-management at its worst – until it was surpassed after the final Test in Cape Town. Having lost the Test and the series inside three days, Atherton was not in the best frame of mind at the presentation ceremony. His dejection turned to fury when it was announced that England would now play a one-day game against Western Province on the scheduled final day of the Test. Atherton stormed into the dressing-room – his question about who had agreed to the switch was purely rhetorical. Yet Illingworth laid into the batsmen and Malcolm before he started choking and left the dressing-room red-faced. No one was more upset than Atherton by what had happened at Cape Town, especially in the '40 minutes of madness' – yet Illingworth had to have his say at the most inappropriate time.

Atherton does not believe this incident explains England's inept showing in the seven one-day internationals in South Africa and the World Cup. He blames that on the end-of-tour South African itinerary. But England, Atherton and Illingworth were never the same again. That weekend, Illingworth wrote off seven of the England tour squad. Of these, only Stewart has played since. It was obvious to Atherton that Illingworth suffered physically under the demands of running a tour. That put more strain and responsibility on him as captain, something of which Illingworth seemed totally unaware.

Atherton was not sure that he was going to last out the Illingworth era, but was determined that things could not continue as they were. He returned to Manchester, changed his telephone number and then headed off to Jamaica with Lancashire to ponder his future. If he was going to carry on as captain, he was not going to put himself in a position where Illingworth was calling all the shots. But Lloyd's appointment as coach, with Gooch joining Graveney as the other selector, meant that the old generation had been ousted and Illingworth would not be able to dictate matters again. He was no longer the supremo and his final season would be only as chairman of selectors. He spent most of that summer in conflict with the TCCB over the Malcolm affair. Atherton had no desire to see Illingworth leave the game with a disrepute charge against his name, but once Illingworth's appeal was successful, Atherton was happy for him to retire. The chairman's final tour-selection meeting was a lot less confrontational than the first. Atherton was back to where he had been when Illingworth came in.

Atherton felt less upset at the usual series of Illingworth articles that marked England's winter departure. The headline on the first – 'The Day I Saved Your Skin, Mike' – was reasonably familiar. The chairman continued: 'Michael now looks likely to break Peter May's record of captaining England in 41 Tests. His record, though, is fairly forgettable.' It was a harsh judgement from the man who had picked him to lead his country in 33 of those Tests. At no time did Illingworth ring the captain during his difficult trot last winter. Their selection battles over, it might have been a conciliatory gesture. Instead, the Illingworth view was again being conveyed through the sports pages. The stinging comments after the Auckland draw said it all.

It is doubtful whether Illingworth ever understood Atherton, or took much trouble to try. England's captain found the chairman's assessment that Fraser's inclusion owed much to his friendship with Atherton as offensive. Personal likes and dislikes have played a smaller part in Atherton's captaincy than most; the careers of Lewis and Tufnell have been turbulent for other reasons. Lewis was kicked out of the Texaco squad at the end of 1996 not for turning up late, but for turning up late with a story that even Inspector Lestrade would have found difficult to believe. Tufnell has suffered several off-the-field problems, yet Atherton has been happy to take him on tour three winters out of four. He has been careful to write off nobody and has been loyal, too loyal at times – but not to Fraser. If anything, the Middlesex fast bowler appears to have suffered, rather than benefited, from Atherton's presence as captain. That is just Atherton trying to get it right. He stuck with Hick time and again because he believed in his talent. The same was true of Ramprakash. Neither was with England last winter. Nasser Hussain was. Only when Atherton held the balance of power was Hussain brought back. The captain had been pressing for him in vain for most of 1995. When Atherton banged on Jack Russell's bedroom door in Harare, England's wicket-keeper looked through the spy-hole and knew what was coming – another winter of carrying the drinks and paints. That was tough for Atherton; exactly a year earlier, the pair had embraced at The Wanderers after defying South Africa. Atherton has taken the rough and tough decisions when the need has arisen. The toughest, though – seeing his Caribbean experiment aborted a few weeks after the first signs of success – had nothing to do with him. But he has still had to live with it.

ATHERTON
Strange as it might seem, Illy and I got on very well on a personal level. We had our differences on the way and I think we were suspicious of each other at the start – a lot

had been written before we met of how we would react to each other. I had my dream of the way the England cricket should go, Illingworth had another vision. It was a great blow to me that much of the hard work in the Caribbean was put to one side.

We gradually developed a working relationship, though it was never warm. My biggest gripe was his public utterances. I don't care what's said within four walls of the dressing-room or selection meeting, but that's where it must begin and end. It should not finish up on the back pages of the tabloids. Illy did not seem to understand the damage he did. It upset me, though not as badly as some others who got really narked. There was no great sense of collective responsibility. I always felt that Illy was too available to the media. I know he's been one of them, but it seemed to me that he got led up the garden path on occasions. He was certainly less than happy over some of my statements in Australia.

Illy appeared less in the dressing-room last summer. He was not asked to stay away or anything like that, it just seemed to happen. We knew he was going anyway and no one wanted to upset him. I know it gets his goat if I don't shave or I put my jeans on in the dressing-room. There's been a fair bit of mickey-taking between us. From my side, it has always been good-natured.

When Illy rang me at the end of the World Cup and said he was considering his position, I told him I was happy for him to carry on as chairman, but we had to have a full-time coach. The demands on the captain are considerable and there's not enough time to organise the tasks that Fletch used to. I felt sorry when Fletch went, not because of the extra workload but because he had been very supportive of me and diverted much of the flak away from the team. Bumble [David Lloyd] has been a great help in the same way, and I really believe that we made good progress last winter.

23

CHAPTER TWO

A Head's Start

Michael Andrew Atherton has always had a passion for cricket. That love affair began with a Ladybird book, a cricket ball hanging from a tree and a back-garden path which doubled as an artificial wicket. This love was fostered and encouraged by his parents, who made many sacrifices in dual pursuit of his sporting and scholastic excellence. Atherton's studious and serious nature was evident from the start. Only at Cambridge University did his interests begin to develop beyond the classroom and sports field. His prodigious cricket achievements brought him national attention while at Manchester Grammar School, where a professional career and international success were predicted. Atherton was not convinced that he would make the grade. Only after his ability and temperament were tested against Essex's Test-class, first-class bowling attack at Cambridge, did Atherton feel confident that his future was a professional sporting one.

Atherton's childhood was spent in the same house in Warwick Road in Failsworth, where his parents, Alan and Wendy, still live. They married a year before Michael Andrew arrived on 23 March, 1968. A younger brother,

Chris, came along three years later. Alan's father was a professional boxer, Wendy's brother, David, was a professional golfer and Alan himself had been on Manchester United's books before a back injury forced a change of career. The nearest Alan came to the famous first-team was as substitute man against Burnley. In the early sixties, the replacement was only there for problems before the kick-off. Once the match had started, his chance had gone. Alan played in the same youth team as Nobby Stiles.

Atherton's mum and dad met at a tournament at Northern Lawn Tennis Club, both were Manchester tennis champions. Wendy's father was a butcher, who had fought in North Africa in the war. He retired to a village called Woodhouses, where the future England captain played his club cricket in his teens. Alan showed familiar Atherton determination after those displaced vertebrae. He finished with football in 1961, and undertook a three-year teaching course in history and physical education, and began his first job in Wythenshaw in 1965. He taught soccer, history and physical education at Wright Robinson, then moved to North Manchester High School as deputy head before taking the headship at the Harper Green in Bolton, where he has stayed for 15 years. Wendy, who had been a secretary in an accountant's office, stopped work while the boys were growing up and now works part-time in the local magistrates court.

The first important decision they took regarding Atherton's education was to send him to Briscoe Lane Primary School in Newton Heath. That meant a long bus journey on a No. 76 for the youngster, although there was a local primary school at Failsworth. Briscoe's reputation persuaded Atherton's parents that the extra travel and effort would be worth it. The school had an outstanding sporting record, as well as one for concentrating on the basics and old-fashioned teaching methods. His mother knew her offspring would not be overawed. 'Michael was very independent as a baby. He never laughed and joked and smiled, but was always very serious. He was happy in his own company and knew what he wanted. If you read him a story, he would sit there, not budging or reacting. And he would read, read, read – he was very advanced for his age. We would go out in the evening and when we came back, he would still be sitting up in bed reading, probably that Ladybird cricket book.' That Ladybird book was one of his most cherished possessions. Briscoe Lane lived up to its Wild West-sounding name, for it was a tough school in a rough area. When Atherton was made England captain, one of the national newspapers reproduced the Briscoe Lane cricket team which included Atherton. Very few had gone on to become solicitors, accountants and doctors, most had learnt to live by their wits. Other former pupils include Judy Finnigan of TV's *Richard and Judy* fame and Michael Le Veil (then Turner) of *Coronation Street*. Briscoe Lane was not an integral part of the feeder system for public schools in the area; no one had ever gone from there to Manchester Grammar School. Atherton took extra lessons with Ted Parrett to prepare for the entrance exams, which he passed.

They were his first exams, as pupils did not sit them at Briscoe Lane, instead they took home term reports. Most afternoons were spent playing sport. The school had a swimming pool, as well as a successful soccer and cricket team. Atherton was part of both sides, although cricket brought him more individual success. Alan had spotted a budding cricket star from the earliest days in the back garden. As Wendy explains: 'It all started with us hanging an old grey sock from the washing line. We put a cricket ball in a sock, tied it to the line with a piece of rope and left him to it. It was just the right height for him to hit with a bat and he would practise his shots until it got dark.' Eventually the path became his pitch and the dustbin his wicket. Atherton's first experience of cricket was watching his father. 'Later, I would take him with me to Woodhouses when I was playing. You would expect kids of that age to spend the afternoon running around. Not Michael. He would sit and watch and never used to move. He was always very serious and very sensible. I'd bowl at him and he'd hit it back, with no power. I remember him playing for Manchester Under-11s as an eight-year-old. He didn't get many runs, but they couldn't get him out. He got hit on the head when he was about eight playing for Woodhouses Under-15s. I walked round the field afterwards, but it never bothered him.' The youngster had a simple technique and played straight, sticking to the way that worked for him rather than progressing to the cross-batted swipes and extravagant flourishes of most budding stars. Briscoe were runners-up in the Flanagan Trophy, the Manchester Schools Cricket Championship, in 1977 and winners the following summer.

Atherton played for Manchester Under-12s at the start of the 1978 season, scoring 50 out of 70 for 9 v North Manchester High School. That brought him a trial with the Lancashire Under-13s and a quote from Manchester manager Tony Cox in the local paper: 'Technically Mike's batting is very straight and correct, and if he develops as well as we hope, he will be one to watch.' Still only 10, Atherton played for Lancashire Under-13s against Yorkshire at Bolton School, eventually playing five matches in all. Cox's end-of-season report concluded: 'Of all the players in all the squads, there is only one who consistently plays straight in defence and he is Mike Atherton. The Junior teams did remarkably well to avoid the worst of the weather and they provided some glittering performances. Heading the list was Mike Atherton's selection for the Lancashire Under-13 team while he was still attending junior school. I hope he can continue to develop into the outstanding player he promises to be and is able to overcome the setbacks that occur from time to time.' He topped the batting averages for both the Under-13s and Under-12s and was named the Outstanding Junior Batsman.

Atherton's England cricket connection began in 1980 when he was sent on a national Under-13 coaching course. That Easter he was requested to report to 'the junior pros dressing-room in the pavilion' at Old Trafford and provided with a Complimentary Junior Pass by Lancashire secretary Chris Hassell, now chief executive at Yorkshire.

Atherton's next stop was when he captained the Manchester GS Under-12s, a side that also featured Mark Crawley and Gary Yates. Atherton and Crawley struck up a friendship from the first day at the school and between them, they scored over 6,000 runs for the first XI. Later the pair were opposing captains in the 1989 Varsity Match, the first time that two from the same school had done this since 1905. Their parents got on well and shared a box at Lord's on that occasion. Atherton's leg-spin bowling attracted as much praise as his batting in his first year at MGS.

In 1981 Atherton helped the Manchester SCA Under-15s to victory over Bradford with 7 for 33 and 48 not out at Newton Heath. He also appeared for the county Under-13 XI for the third successive season. More significantly, Atherton made his debut for the Manchester GS first XI against Bangor, the first second-former in the school's history to be selected. He bowled 22 overs, with figures of 3 for 45, then hit the winning runs in an innings of 8 not out with two balls to spare. Atherton's promotion was down to David Moss, the master in charge of cricket. The following year, Moss promoted Crawley as well. Atherton's Under-13s won all their fixtures, apart from one game being abandoned. The margins of victory were huge, three by over 100 runs, three by 10 wickets, three by nine. The closest was a revenge seven-wicket win against William Hulme, who had beaten them the previous year in which Atherton took 7 for 20. Even at such a gentle age, Atherton took part in several beer matches, because of the early finishes, with the batting orders reversed. Atherton's 474 runs for the Under-13s came at 94.8, while his record 49 wickets were taken at an average of 3.63. The school magazine reported that 'as a batsman he seems in the Boycott mould, both in his tremendous concentration and his refusal to take risks. Even the occasional running out of his partner is reminiscent of the Master! His accurate and good-length leg-breaks are not to be found in the senior game. Opponents were often mesmerised and only a handful knew how to play him. He was deservedly promoted to the first XI for a couple of games.'

Atherton was a permanent member of the first XI in his last four years at Manchester GS. An early indication of his reliability can be judged by the comment that 'extraordinary events have already taken place', referring to the first XI early season report in 1982. One of those events was 'Mike Atherton has played and missed'. Atherton topped the batting averages with over 500 runs in that first full season, 1982, and was fifth in the bowling, receiving his full colours. He also played for South Manchester, Manchester Under-15s, Northern England, the North and for GH Doggart's XI v the ESCA, opposition which included Nasser Hussain, Trevor Ward and Mike Roseberry. More significantly in the Atherton household, his dad was dropped to allow him a place in the Woodhouses first XI. Atherton now held a Young Amateurs pass at Old Trafford. His exploits were well known and he was regarded as one of the most exciting cricket prospects in the country, although it was Michael Afferton who represented the

North in the United Friendly Cricket Festival in 1983.

Atherton played for England Under-15s, scoring 60 against Wales at Formby Cricket Club. At the end of the summer, Atherton received the Sir John Hobbs Jubilee Memorial prize from EW Swanton as the most promising Young Colt in English schools cricket. Previous winners included Mike Gatting, Chris Cowdrey, Tim Robinson, Kim Barnett and Robin Bailey. It was a double celebration for Lancashire: Neil 'Harvey' Fairbrother was named the Most Promising Player.

The following summer, Atherton scored over 1,000 runs for MGS 7 and represented England Schools. His leg-spin embarrassed a visiting MCC side as he claimed 6 for 27. *Wisden Cricketers' Almanack* recorded his remarkable progress: 'Outstanding for Manchester GS was the captain and England Schools representative M. A. Atherton, who also played for Lancashire Second XI. His aggregate of 1,013 runs and five centuries were both school records. Bowling leg-spin he captured 61 wickets, taking six in an innings on three occasions.' Atherton was one of eight schoolboys who passed 1,000 runs that season. Others included Hussain and Mike Roseberry. Atherton also spent two winters working with Peter Lever's group of promising youngsters. Lever recalls:

> He didn't have a lot to say for himself, but when he opened his mouth, it was worth listening. He was mature beyond his years, head and shoulders above the rest. I recall his mother calling at the start of the second winter to say that they thought it might be better if he stopped coming. 'All he thinks about is cricket and doing his homework,' his mum said. 'He's not taking part in family affairs.' I replied: 'Mrs Atherton, do you realise how good your son is? He'll play for England.' I wasn't shooting a line. I genuinely believed that if I had ever seen an England

prospect, it was him. He was the only player to treat the sessions as a match. He had the desire to go all the way. I remember in one session with the quicks bowling at him one night. His poles went over, the next was nicked, his poles went over again, he nicked another, he played and missed. He looked at me and we both burst out laughing. He had that confidence. This was just a bad night. From the very start, Athers wanted to talk about the mental approach to the game rather than the technical aspects.

Atherton was part of the Lancashire Under-16 team that won the Texaco County Championship and then toured the Isle of Wight with the Under-19 squad, his three matches putting him top of the batting averages and second in the bowling. He also made a trip to Cambridge as a member of the Lancashire Federation and experienced the delights of cider for the first time. Representative honours were coming thick and fast, including the Headmasters' Conference Schools XI against the ESCA. He was chosen for the MCC Schools and hit 62 at Lord's, his first appearance at the home of cricket.

Although he failed to reach 1,000 runs for MGS in 1985, Atherton did average 187.00. *Wisden Cricketers' Almanack*: 'For Manchester GS, who were undefeated, the captain M. A. Atherton was outstanding, scoring four successive unbeaten centuries in June v Hulme GS Oldham, Royal GS Lancaster, Arnold and William Hulme GS. He played for MCC Schools and captained England Schools, as well as travelling with North of England Under-19 to Bermuda.' David Moss remembers Atherton for his shyness as much as his cricket ability. 'The ritual after the cricket tea was for the captain to go and thank the tea ladies. Michael was so shy he couldn't bring himself to do it. It became a standing joke. As the boys sat down to tea, they would say: "Have you thanked the tea ladies, Michael?" and collapse into laughter. On the field, though, he was the natural leader.' Atherton's selection as England Schools captain merely confirmed that fact.

Atherton, who had flown to La Manga before the start of the 1985 season with senior Lancashire coaching staff and promising youngsters, played only two matches for Lancashire's second XI.

Atherton was selected for the North in an International Youth Tournament in Bermuda in July. Atherton's postcard home explained the bad start: 'Arrived 2.30am after a good flight. Our accommodation is dreadful as we are staying in Army barracks. The manager has complained and we are shortly to move out into apartments following the decision by Lord's to send $10,000 to help us. So far the organisation has been poor and no nets have been arranged even though our first match starts tomorrow against the Dutch.' Typically, the postcard spent a considerable time in Atherton's bag before being sent. He was able to add the results of the first three matches before it was sent home.

That winter Atherton went to the ESCA course at Gateshead. The coach's report stated: 'A fine player – probably the best in the country at his age. Now that he is stronger, I managed to get him to drive with full extension of his arms, particularly against the spinners and it worked.' Atherton headed off to La Manga again, this time as a member of the Lancashire touring squad. Atherton lost his MGS record aggregate of runs in his final season to Mark Crawley, but he led MGS to another unbeaten season, scoring 627 runs and taking 50 wickets. In all, Atherton played 82 matches for the first XI, 50 of them as captain. In 76 innings, he scored 3,462 runs at 65.32, with nine centuries. His leg-spin brought him 170 wickets at 16.65, including seven five-wicket hauls.

Chris Hassell wrote in early September offering him a

playing contract for the following summer, at a basic salary of £130 a week. Gray Nicholls had been in touch a couple of months earlier to sponsor him and Atherton uses their bats to this day. The final honour before his undergraduate days came when Atherton was selected to lead Young England Cricketers to Sri Lanka that winter, with Tim Lamb, the ECB's new chief executive, as manager. That was going to interfere considerably with Atherton's first year at Cambridge, a problem that was to repeat itself during his university days. The tour itself was not a huge personal success for him, though *Wisden* reported that 'he had impressed experienced observers with his captaincy'.

Atherton had been in seventh heaven at Manchester GS. The intense sporting and academic environment brought out the best in him, as his father had hoped. Alan and Wendy made a serious financial commitment to send him there. At one stage over a quarter of Alan's wage packet went on his education. There was also the moral dilemma of the headmaster of a comprehensive sending his son to a private school. 'I don't believe in selection. But you do the best for your children. I was not going to sacrifice my kids for political theory. I was worried about Michael's trek to school at first. He wasn't a very big lad, but he's very independent. He's also very competitive. I remember going over Latin with him. It was a real slog, but he wasn't going to be beaten. He was aware of other people and their marks. That competitive edge was always there. Michael loved it there with his mates playing football and cricket.' The school had a fast-track system that allowed the brightest pupils to take their O-levels in the fourth form and begin the two-year A-level course in the fifth. Neither Atherton nor his father saw any need to rush; his grades – nine As and a B – at O-level suggest his studies were not being affected by cricket. His A-levels were English, History and German.

ATHERTON

We were a close-knit family. Earliest memories included going to my grandparents every weekend, holidays in Wales and Dad's light blue Anglia. Briscoe was great – class in the morning, games in the afternoon. Towards the end of my time there, I started extra lessons with Ted Parrett for those entrance exams. Ted was held in awe and fear by the lads. I never questioned the extra work; I always believed my folks were acting in my best interests. In soccer, I was just one of the team, but I was aware that I was a better cricketer than the rest.

My first day at MGS was rather daunting. The school seemed so far away. I was there from 1979-86 and had a wonderful time. The facilities were fantastic and the teachers were keen. I will always be grateful to my mum and dad for sending me there. With games after school, often I wouldn't get home until 6.30 and there was always a fair amount of homework. I did it that night. I never waited until it was due. Dad instilled that discipline into me. It went out the window at university. There were a few tears early on with Latin, I hadn't done it at primary school. I struggled at maths – I'm hopeless with figures and chemistry equations – but I didn't quit. O-levels are just a test of memory, which came easy to me.

I was in trouble a few times, talking in assembly and so on, but nothing serious. Foreign trips were out because of the cricket season, though I did go on a French exchange when I was 14. We had a great football team and went 95 games without defeat, our first defeat was in the fifth form. I used to miss quite a lot of school once I got in the first XI, as well as Manchester and Lancashire Schools. MGS took preference and that was a source of debate – school v representative sides – that rumbles on even today. I kept moving teams, out of my age group, but I never found that a problem; it was good for me; it tested me. I was happy with that. My whole life revolved round the school. We went on cricket tours to Cambridge, the Isle of Man and Bermuda.

Cricket filled my summer holidays, although we still went away as a family. Those trips, I'm sure, were organised around cricket. I never got in a fight. I read a lot, anything that was under my nose. I had nothing stuck on my bedroom walls. I didn't get into music until university. I don't remember going to watch Manchester United, although I went to see the trophy room with Dad and met Jimmy Murphy, Sir Matt Busby's right-hand man. I occasionally went with Dad to Old Trafford to see one-day games. Mostly, I went to watch Dad. And I did, intently, even when quite young. Generally, I preferred playing rather than watching. At that stage, though, it never struck me that I would be good enough to play professional cricket. I've never been overly confident. I was well aware that I was privileged to be attending a special institution, although it didn't stimulate my mind much beyond sport and schoolwork. I would say that I had a fairly sheltered upbringing. I must have been a rather serious young man and that was governed a little bit by the school. I went with it at the time. The girls' high school was across the road. There was female contact through school dances. Mine was very minimal. I had no regular girlfriend, so I had to fend off the usual questions from Mum. I think she hoped I might blossom a bit at Cambridge.

While Atherton worked to find his feet at Cambridge, he also had to establish himself in the Old Trafford dressing-room. As with MGS, Atherton revelled in both environments to such an extent that he graduated to the full England side a few weeks after leaving university. Atherton travelled down to Downing College for his interview in November 1985. He passed the entrance exam and interview, after being advised not to make too much of his sporting prowess in the meeting with Admission

Tutor John Hopkins. That was it. He was in. His A-level requirements were simply two Es. Atherton achieved two As and a B – despite the distraction of a full summer of cricket and knowing that he could do very little work and still go to Cambridge. His pride and his respect for his parents' sacrifices did not allow him to give it away at the final hurdle. Poor grades would not have helped his request to miss much of the second term to go on the Young England tour to Sri Lanka. Atherton stayed at college during the Easter break to make up for lost time.

His summer term was hectic, too, with the university team's first-class fixture list. It was during the match against Essex, his first-class debut, that Atherton first genuinely believed that he could make a professional cricketer after all. Cambridge were beaten by 249 runs, but Atherton scored 73 not out, though at one stage Cambridge were 20 for 7, and 33 against the bowling of Hugh Page, Neil Foster, John Lever, John Childs and Geoff Miller. 'That's when it hit me that I was good enough to make a living out of this.' Eighteen days later, Atherton scored his maiden first-class century at Fenner's against Derbyshire, when he carried his bat for 109, only the third occasion a Cambridge opener had achieved this feat against county opposition. Atherton appeared for the Combined Universities in the Benson and Hedges Cup and scored 43 for an Oxbridge side that played the Pakistan tourists. Lots of talented schoolboy sportsmen go to university to find themselves exposed. Many eyes were on Atherton. *Wisden* commented that he 'lived up to his advanced billing right from the start' and that 'he impressed his colleagues to such an extent that they took the unusual step of electing him as captain in the second year'.

A few weeks later Atherton made his championship debut for Lancashire against Warwickshire at Southport. The first of many Atherton–Fairbrother partnerships

helped Lancashire recover from 16 for 2 to 144 for 3, after
the visitors had been bowled out for 116. Atherton made
53 in Lancashire's 10-wicket victory. In 11 championship
matches, Atherton made safe and steady progress, scoring 602 runs at an average of 35.61. His highest score was
76 not out, the lowest, a pair against Sussex. Atherton had
found himself part of the most successful Lancashire side
for over a decade. There had been sweeping changes at
the end of the 1986 season. Team manager Jack Bond and
coach Peter Lever were replaced by Alan Ormrod, who
took over both roles, and David Hughes was installed as
captain from the second XI in place of Clive Lloyd, who
retired. Finally, Cedric Rhoades was forced to resign as
chairman in February 1987 and Bob Bennett took over.
The changes paid off as Lancashire left the bottom six of
the county championship for the first time in a dozen
years. They won their final six matches to finish only four
points behind champions Nottinghamshire, the best Old
Trafford finish for 27 years.

Just as at Briscoe Lane, Atherton had entered another
intimidating environment when he took up residency in
the Lancashire dressing-room. The two senior pros were
Paul Allott and Graeme Fowler. In their England days,
they mixed with the Botham/Lamb/Gower set. No
longer international stars, Allott and Fowler still ruled the
roost at Old Trafford. Atherton found that out the hard
way during the Roses match in Leeds. The newcomer
showed little respect for the established order when he
dumped Allott's gear out of the tumble dryer to use it
himself. Allott was not impressed when he returned, but
said nothing. Allott recalls his reaction:

> I didn't say anything at the time. Later on, I invited
> him for a drink with me and Foxy [Fowler] that
> night. When Athers got in the car, we told him we
> were heading back to Manchester for a party and

would be back about four in the morning, or would
check in to a Manchester hotel and get up early next
morning. He looked petrified. He'd just come into
the side and would be batting the next day. I'm sure
if there hadn't been child locks on the back doors,
he'd've been out of there. He was mumbling 'I've got
no money, I need a meal, I've got to bat tomorrow.'
We got on the car phone and started making imaginary arrangements. Eventually, someone rang us
back and we agreed to 'meet the girls' in the Bradford Novotel. We got there and told Athers to wait in
the bar while we went up to room 305 for a while.
Foxy and I wandered off for a drink somewhere else.
We came back after an hour. He was still sitting at the
bar, with a glass in front of him, a complete gibbering
wreck. We got in the car, still heading for Manchester.
By now he was pleading to go back to Leeds. We
pretended to take pity on him and headed back.
Then we burst out laughing. I turned to him and
said: 'Don't ever do that to my kit again, boy!' He
was so relieved to be going back, I don't think he
cared that it was all a set-up.

That was Athers – strong-willed. He still is. He
found his feet quickly. That Novotel incident apart,
he was fairly unflappable. That Southport game was
a low-scoring contest. All you have to do as a young
lad is play well. That's the quickest way of gaining
respect. He was obviously determined to be his own
man. After that Yorkshire incident, we became firm
friends. The beauty is that he never changes. He's a
bit more reserved in company that he doesn't know.
Athers is happiest with his old university chums.

Old Trafford brought Atherton into contact with his best
cricket friend, Neil 'Harvey' Fairbrother. They had both
received awards from the Cricket Society in 1983 and got

to know each other in La Manga the following year on the schoolboys coaching trip. Fairbrother recalls:

I remember him being quiet. It's about the only time he's ever known his place. My first impression was here was a blocker. He was only a small lad with no strength in his shots. I thought he would make an opening batsman, he was so technically correct. He came into a legendary dressing-room. With all that university education, he was very headstrong, someone who didn't listen. I thought he needed help, but Athers could look after himself. Most young players keep quiet. Not Athers. If he thought the whole dressing-room was wrong, he would speak out. He's still the same. There are 14 lockers in the senior dressing-room, but you can't miss his: it's the rubbish tip.

That debut first-class season, 1,193 runs at 38.38, with Cambridge University and Lancashire had convinced the student that a professional cricket career was not only attainable, but preferable. The Cricket Society agreed. Atherton was named the Most Promising Young Cricketer of the Year.

Atherton was named captain of the England party to take part in the McDonald's Bicentennial Youth World Cup at the start of 1988. That meant more holiday time spent studying at Cambridge. Atherton never abused the freedom and privileges his cricket ability brought, actually enjoying his time at Downing when few others were about. Australia's Youth side included Alan Mullally, later appear under Atherton at Test level; the West Indies captain was Brian Lara; Mushtaq Ahmed, Inzamam-ul-Haq and Aqib Javed were in the Pakistan line-up; and Lee Germon was the New Zealand captain and one of his bowlers was another Atherton used in

1996, Andrew Caddick. England reached the semi-finals, but lost by seven wickets to Australia, the eventual winners. England's leading run-scorer was Hussain and top wicket-taker was Chris Lewis. Atherton provided the tour report published in the May edition of *The Cricketer* magazine. He highlighted a time-keeping problem that was to surface eight years later at The Oval. 'The Lilleshall sessions were attended by the whole squad, including Chris Lewis who arrived eight hours late, after inadvertently ending up in Newport (Wales) rather than Newport (Shropshire)!' Atherton encountered another problem that was to affect England and him in the coming years. 'The dominant reason for our failure to win the competition was our persistent batting failure.'

Back at Cambridge in 1988, Atherton led the way with 665 runs at 60.45 (the second best average was 21.41) and two centuries, although the Varsity Match was another disappointment. Not for any personal failure, the 144th contest was abandoned without a ball being bowled. Atherton scored 151 not out against Middlesex and an undefeated century against Surrey. He experienced the West Indies firepower for the first time when he led the Oxbridge XI. The students were bowled out for 38 in the first innings, but Atherton top-scored with 45 in the second. Because of injuries and examinations, Atherton called up Alastair Scott, who had graduated the previous year, from his City desk. 'Scottie' has remained one of Atherton's great friends, often turning up on England tours to share a glass and to reminisce with the England captain. Atherton's commitment can be judged from *Wisden* notes of that season. 'University cricket in 1988 was played against the continuing threat of the loss of first-class status. This prospect has prompted Cambridge to look seriously at an admissions policy which does not assist young sportsmen to gain places. Although such matters are strictly outside the control of the Cricket

Club, Atherton has made it a priority, following his re-election as captain, to seek a way of opening more academic doors for promising young cricketers.'

ATHERTON

I certainly noticed the difference in those boys who came from the 'big' public schools, such as Eton. They were much more relaxed, more confident. I felt they had a broader experience of life, they had more of a social life. I felt MGS was regarded as rather inferior and I didn't feel instantly at ease. It took me a long time to regard people as friends. It still does. Then again sport always gives you an opening, a status.

One thing was certain. I had to organise my time at Cambridge. MGS had taught me not to waste time, but there was a much less rigid way of working – one essay a week. I never went to lectures as what was in lectures was in the books. I studied in the morning, played sport in the afternoon and was on the razz at night. In my final year, I took a two-week break before the exams. I left everything during those two weeks. The tutor, Dr Christine Carpenter, suggested some extra lectures, but there wasn't time. The subject was the 15th-century gentry and the Black Death.

I spent a lot of time at college. I enjoyed being up there before everyone came back, for Cambridge is such a beautiful place. Most of the friends I've made, I made at Cambridge. University certainly brought me out of my shell. I was a lot more confident, my horizons were expanding. Downing was a very social place. It was a mixed college and lots of time was spent at the local pub, the Prince Regent. I wasn't a tee-totaller when I went there, but you can't not drink. I had a whale of a time. My recovery rate from alcohol was a lot better than it is now. There was the Griffin's Club for sports and the Patricians for drinking. I met Suzie in my final year, she was studying medicine, and that last year was pretty hectic. My finals came two days after the Combined Universities lost by three runs to Somerset in the Benson and Hedges quarter-final, and we had a few drinks that night.

We played cricket for fun at Cambridge. If you can't have fun getting hammered every day, then you'd flip. The FEC thing started in the first year. Because I had captained England Schools, an article built it up. I didn't need it hanging round my neck. I honestly never thought about it.

Atherton returned to Old Trafford after the washed-out Varsity Match at the start of July to find himself at the centre of a cricket controversy for the first time. Despite his position in the top ten of the national batting averages, Atherton was not promoted immediately to the Lancashire first XI. Skipper Hughes did not feel the need to change the side, although Gehan Mendis was the only Old Trafford batsman averaging over 30. The matter caused considerable debate in the county and brought adverse comment in national papers. Once again, it appeared that a promising England talent was being held back and that debate was repeated the following summer, although Atherton was already in Ted Dexter's thoughts for the winter's tours. In 1988 one irate member, Howard Grocott, pinned the national averages to the noticeboard outside the Old Trafford dressing-room while Atherton was away with the second XI in Newark.

Atherton's affray with a nightclub bouncer on that trip might have its origins in his frustrations with the Lancashire situation. Atherton has always shown shrewd tactical appreciation, so calling a 6ft 9in bouncer a 'muppet' was out of character and foolish. Suddenly, Atherton found himself on his back with a big boot pressing down on the larynx that he had intended to use to smooth talk his way out of this confrontation. The most vivid memory came after Atherton was deposited back in the fresh air. 'I looked around for my team-mates, but they had all disappeared!' Off the field, Atherton has tried to avoid all such confrontations since. His wait for promotion to the first XI lasted three championship matches. The folly of Lancashire's policy became evident as Atherton finished top of the Lancashire batting averages. His 456 runs in eight games at 38.00 included his maiden Red Rose century at Hove, 152 not out, and another undefeated hundred, 115 v Derbyshire at Old Trafford. That Sussex effort in his third championship match of the season was all the more impressive as Lancashire were in trouble at 137 for 5. The Derbyshire knock took Atherton past 1,000 runs for the season. Atherton's 1,121 runs at 48.73 in all matches, brought him ninth place in the national averages. He was one of four nominated for the Young Cricketer of the Year award, along with Andy Clarke (Sussex), Angus Fraser (Middlesex) and Matthew Maynard (Glamorgan). It went to Maynard and another two years would pass before Atherton earned that accolade. That did not matter. Atherton's composure and performance over the previous couple of seasons had more than alerted the England selectors that his time was coming.

Atherton's upbringing was not a privileged one, but an undoubted privilege for such a bright lad with a special sporting talent. It is difficult to imagine his parents being able to provide any better sanctuary for their offspring. The combination of Briscoe Lane, Manchester GS and Cambridge University was a rare treble in the educational stakes. Atherton responded to each challenge and passed with flying colours. A less determined student would have settled for a county cricket career straight from school. That never entered Atherton's or his parents' heads. They realised that he needed a spell away from home in a more liberal environment. Cambridge allowed him his initial experience of first-class cricket away from the potentially intimidating and destructive atmosphere of a professional dressing-room. Without being domineering and interfering, Atherton's parents were always there for him. They have enjoyed his successes and coped with the bad days, no more so than during the ball-tampering controversy in 1994 when TV crews and reporters camped outside their house as their son was put on national trial by the media. For his mum that experience remains the worst moment. 'When I first heard, I just laughed. I know my son better than anyone. He would never lie to me. When he was called deceitful, I felt ill.' His parents have also been careful not to concentrate all their efforts on the elder son. Chris found it hard to match up to his brother's sporting and academic achievements, although he played for Lancashire Under-11s and Under-13s and joined the England Schools coaching squad with John Crawley. He went to Radclyffe School in Oldham, leaving after his O-levels. His father admits Chris went through a bad phase in his late teens, not helped by his brother's high-profile success. Atherton believes Chris was more naturally athletic than him and could give a cricket ball a crash. He did play professional cricket in New Zealand and turns out for Woodhouses when he's in England. Chris now has his own joinery business and is working and playing for Manley CC in Australia.

Atherton's parents flew to Australia to see their elder son open the innings in the 1990 Boxing Day Ashes Melbourne Test, one of cricket's most famous events. His dad remembers the silence as Atherton walked back without disturbing the scorers that first morning. He made amends with a century at Sydney, by which time his parents were on the aircraft home. The pilot made the announcement over the tannoy and the cabin crew presented the proud parents with a bottle of champagne. Alan's lowest point is the same as Wendy's:

The South Africa ball-tampering period was when I came into my own as a supportive parent. He was hurt; I was very aggrieved and upset. Michael is an honourable person, tradition is important to him. I feel he was unfairly treated. Afterwards, I realised he was foolish and naive. He should have been totally honest immediately. It was a natural reaction. The holier-than-thou reaction of people like Boycott and Agnew really got to me. Everyone was taking the moral high ground. You try to be dispassionate, but it was our son and he was being murdered in the press. I'm sorry, but there shouldn't be that sort of pressure on any one individual, especially someone who's just a professional sportsman. We chatted a fair bit that week. I said to him, if you've had enough, fair enough. I don't blame you. But do you feel you have done something wrong? He didn't have a good reason for going. It was still a rotten time. Reporters knocked on the door. We'll pay you or a charity of your choice for the Atherton story. Lancashire were very good to Michael and us. I wrote a letter afterwards thanking them for their forthright support. I'm not one for mixing with committees, but Bob Bennett and the Lancashire officials went up in my estimation after that.

Bennett has been an important ally and protector for Atherton, ensuring England's captain has not been distracted unnecessarily by county matters. Atherton has needed a friend in high places at Old Trafford and, more recently, Lord's. Bennett has been that friend. They first met on the La Manga trip, when Bennett took manager Jack Bond's place. They talked at length when MGS toured the Isle of Man the following year. When Atherton became a cricket professional, it was Bennett who ensured that Lancashire's best long-term interests would be served by the young star focusing on his international future.

ATHERTON

Lancashire have been a great help to me throughout my cricket career. I was fortunate to turn professional just as the club was turning round. Bob Bennett was made chairman at the same time. He has been very caring and loyal to his players, especially me. He's always been around in times of crisis and trouble. Bob is also very concerned that you do things right – by the club and by yourself. He's been a paternal figure for me. When there's been trouble, even when it's been on England duty, it's been my county, not the country, which has come to my aid. They organised the second press conference after the 'soil-in-the-pocket' incident. Bumble [David Lloyd] just happened to bump into me in the Lake District in the midst of all the trouble. That's typical of the way the club is and treats its own. Then Bob came down to The Oval after my dissent fine two Tests later just to show his support. Bob got stick when he was manager of the England tour to India and Sri Lanka in 1993, but it was a well-run trip. Bob has ruffled a few feathers and people in cricket don't forget. With his business background, Bob's ideal for a job in cricket and I'm delighted that he's involved with the new England management committee. Bob is a former cricketer who loves the game and cares about the players. Lancashire have been lucky to have had him in charge for the past decade. And I'm positive I would not have coped with all the trials and tribulations of the England captaincy as well if I hadn't had the full backing of the Old Trafford set-up.

And there's lads like Gary Yates, Peter Martin, Graham Lloyd and Warren Hegg that I've known and played with since schooldays. And there's 'Harvey',

who thought I'd need looking after when I first appeared
at Old Trafford. That's not been the case. If anyone's
needed looking after on numerous occasions, it's been
'Harvey'. The great thing is that I can be myself with
them. No fuss. And if I ever tried the big 'I am' – I'd
soon get my come-uppance. As at MGS and Cambridge,
I can't imagine I could have been happier or more
successful anywhere else. There were rumours in the
early days of me going to captain Somerset. But I can't
see myself playing anywhere else.

CHAPTER THREE

A False Start

Atherton's final summer at Cambridge University coincided with yet another new dawn in English cricket. At least, that was the masterplan when Ted Dexter took over from Peter May as chairman of selectors. In April, Dexter unveiled his popular choice as captain, David Gower, with a great fanfare at Lord's. The Test team's future was bright, with the Dexter–Gower combination billed as the 'dream ticket'. Unfortunately, indeed crucially, the partnership had begun with a lie, of which the captain was unaware until towards the end of the summer. Gower was not, after all, the chosen one – Mike Gatting had been the new chairman's preferred captain, a choice strongly influenced by the team manager Micky Stewart, the man working closest with the new skipper.

Gatting had been removed as captain the previous June at the start of the West Indies series over the infamous Rothley Court barmaid incident, but those who believed he had been punished enough for that episode, or rather his row with Pakistan's umpire Shakoor Rana, were wrong. Gatting's return as England captain was vetoed by Ossie Wheatley, the chairman of the cricket committee.

The unveiling of Gower was nothing but a show, one in which all the participants were sworn to secrecy. Gatting was confused because he had been told by Dexter that he was the captain. The truth was only revealed at the end of the Ashes series. It was unfair on Dexter, who spent much of that series defending a captain who had not been his original choice. The man who suffered most, though, was Gower. Whatever the rights and wrongs of Gatting's treatment, Gower should have been made aware of his true position. Instead, he was kept in the dark along with everyone else, and when his position became difficult as England went behind in the series and then lost several senior players to a rebel tour of South Africa, his deliberations on his future were made without the pertinent knowledge that he had been Dexter's second choice in the first place.

That Ashes series had begun with such high hopes. England had regained the little urn under Gower in 1985 and retained it under Gatting in 1986-87. Gatting, Gower, Graham Gooch, Allan Lamb, Robin Smith and Ian Botham were all available to take on an Australian side that was widely acknowledged by general consensus Down Under as one of the worst ever to leave those shores. But before a ball was bowled, things went wrong for England. Allan Border called incorrectly in the first Test at Headingley and Gower invited Australia to bat. Eight years, three captains, four series and 24 Tests later, England had failed to halt the Australian roller-coaster which Gower set in motion that day. The only Test successes have come at The Oval (1993) and Adelaide (1995), both under Atherton. Australia have won 14 Tests in that time.

The 1989 calamity certainly projected Atherton into the Test arena ahead of schedule. His Cambridge season had not been particularly successful. Captain Atherton scored 417 runs in 15 innings with a top score of 79 against Kent.

The Varsity match was spoilt by rain on the final day with Cambridge in a strong position. Atherton scored 56 and 30 and his side were 210 ahead with eight second-innings wickets left. The highlights of Atherton's last year as a student had come in the Benson and Hedges Cup with the Combined Universities. They were in a tough group with Gloucestershire, Surrey, Worcestershire and Middle-sex. Atherton was captain of the side which also featured Nasser Hussain, who was at Durham University. Surrey were defeated at Cambridge in a tie reduced by rain before Middlesex beat the Universities by eight wickets at Oxford with a Gatting century. Atherton's team then beat Worcestershire before losing to Gloucestershire, who won the group, but the students qualified by virtue of their superior run-rate over Middlesex, becoming the first non-championship side to reach the quarter-finals. There, Hussain scored a brilliant century and took the Gold Award as they lost at Taunton by just three runs. Despite needing 144 runs off 22 overs, Hussain and John Longley had taken the combined team to within 30 runs of victory with seven wickets left. Earlier, Atherton's leg-spin had brought him the wickets of Jimmy Cook, Peter Roebuck, Richard Bartlett and Richard Harden.

England were 2-0 down in the Ashes series by the time Atherton returned to play for Lancashire. The rot had started in dramatic fashion at Leeds with a 210-run defeat. After being asked to bat, Border's tourists obliged with 601 for 7 declared in two and a bit days, but England scored 430 and saved the follow-on. At the end of the fourth day, Australia were 158 for 3, a lead of 329, well-positioned but unlikely to force a win in the remaining time. The visitors added 72 runs on the final morning and England had 83 overs to survive. They failed spectacularly by 27 overs, with the new chairman, who had suggested to Gower that the only way to win was to invite the Australians to bat because of the unpredictable weather, nowhere to be seen. At Lord's Australia scored 528 in reply to England's 286 and the home side then slumped to 28 for 3 on the Saturday evening. After play, Gower abruptly left a hostile press-conference to rush off to the theatre to see Cole Porter's *Anything Goes*. He was reprimanded by Dexter and apologised for his behaviour at the traditional eve-of-Wimbledon garden party at the Hurlingham Club on the rest day. Although Gower bounced back with a brave century on the Monday, it was not enough. Australia overcame the rain and an early collapse to win by six wickets. This was Gower's eighth successive defeat as England captain, following the 1986 West Indies 'blackwash' and the defeat against India at Lord's which had cost him his job first time round.

Matters went from bad to worse at Edgbaston, despite the losing sequence being halted as England were helped by 10 hours being lost to rain on Friday and Saturday. Lamb and Botham had been recalled but injury forced Lamb out, along with Smith, Neil Foster and Gatting, who had a family bereavement and did not play again for another five years. Chris Tavaré was brought back after five years and Angus Fraser made his debut, becoming the first bowler to dismiss Steve Waugh in the series, after 393 runs and four innings. Once the rain had ended any chance of a result, Border just batted England into the ground. The fourth Test at Old Trafford saw the end of England's possession of the Ashes as Border became the first Australian captain since Bill Woodfull in 1934 to regain the urn in this country. For England, Smith scored a century in the first innings and Jack Russell in the second, but they received little support. That final day was a bad one for Dexter and England. The morning papers carried the news that an England squad would undertake an unofficial tour of South Africa in the winter. Unlike the 1982 rebels, who had broken no rules and whose three-year bans came later, these players knew they would be out of Test cricket for five years, seven if they went back for a second visit as planned. Three of them were playing in the Old Trafford Test, including Emburey, one of the not-out batsmen that morning. Six others had played in the series. Lord's felt betrayed, having asked all the players about such intentions at the start of the summer.

It was clear-out time. No one in the South African tour party was to be considered. Atherton had not set the world on fire back in the county scene – his best score in half-a-dozen knocks for Lancashire was 90 at Trent Bridge – but by the time the selectors made their deliberations for the fifth Test at Nottingham, the mood was that England and the selectors had nothing to lose by looking ahead. Gooch, whose technique was being exposed by Alderman, told the selectors they would be better choosing some young talent to open the batting. Tim Curtis and Martyn Moxon, the subsequent choices, were not quite what he had in mind. The only gesture to youth and the future was the selection of Michael Atherton. He would be coming into bat for his country first wicket down. Atherton had played against the tourists for a combined Oxbridge side in a one-day game at the end of June. In a match reduced to 33 overs, Australia won by 99 runs and Atherton, who had been hit for three successive sixes by Geoff Marsh, made 20. The other newcomer at Trent Bridge was Devon Malcolm. Both have clear memories of their first moments in Test cricket.

Malcolm's eventual figures were 1 for 166 as England failed to take a wicket on the opening day. Australia, as they had at Headingley, batted until Saturday morning, going one run better as Border declared on 602 for 6 after Taylor's double hundred and Marsh's century. England had taken 744 deliveries to remove an Australian opener – Australia needed just four. Atherton walked in to replace Moxon. Two balls later, he had joined that distinguished group who have begun their Test careers with a duck. He had been trapped lbw by Alderman and England were 1 for 2 at the end of the first over. Atherton's reaction was typical: 'It bothered other people more than it did me. I hadn't suddenly become a bad player with one duck.' Smith salvaged some pride with a magnificent century but England followed on 347 behind on Monday morning. Gower opened, to little purpose, and the only glimmer of hope for England came from Atherton. He batted three hours for his gritty 47, England's top score, before being caught and bowled by Trevor Hohns as England went down to their heaviest-ever defeat by Australia on home soil. It was not the most auspicious of starts, but at least it had given a national audience its first glimpse of Atherton's fighting qualities and spirit. He returned to Old Trafford to be presented with his county cap before the start of the Roses match. England's newest batsman responded to that honour with his first century of the summer, as well as the wickets of Ashley Metcalfe and Richard Blakey, in Lancashire's 181-run victory.

England's selectors took the total of players used in the Ashes series to 29 at The Oval, John Stephenson and Alan Igglesden making their debuts. Gooch returned, but injury kept out Malcolm, DeFreitas and Fraser. England just escaped the follow-on and Australia were frustrated on the final day by Smith's undefeated 77. Atherton, who made 12 and 14, had taken his first Test catch at third slip to remove David Boon, but it had been a tough baptism. England had been on the back foot the entire time Atherton had been on the field, and there had been no fairytale start to his Test career. There was no happy ending to Gower's second reign as captain, either. Incredibly, after all he had been through, Gower told Dexter that he was prepared to carry on. Dexter, having kept Gower in the dark about Gatting's appointment being blocked, ended the series by insisting, 'I am not aware of making any mistakes.' Confusion about Gower's future in charge intensified because of the apparent lack of an alternative. Gooch, who had been the incumbent when Dexter took over, had endured a troubled summer with his technique. Another factor counting against him was that the Caribbean was the winter destination and Gooch had pleaded to come home from the last tour there after comments from Antiguan politician Lester Bird. Besides, Dexter had removed Gooch from the captaincy at the start of the summer. Wheatley might have relented over Gatting, but Gatting was now totally disillusioned and heading for South Africa. Other names in the frame were Worcestershire's Phil Neale, Somerset's Peter Roebuck and Surrey's Ian Greig – though when Greig was mooted as a contender, Surrey were embarrassed to discover that he was not eligible to play for England any longer – but speculation began to suggest that Gower was the only option. That had to be a safer bet than pitching an untried leader into the most hostile environment in the cricket world. Gower entered the meeting with Dexter and Stewart prepared to soldier on.

No one expected the Dexter decision: the selectors were looking elsewhere. Probably. To make matters worse, Gower was told that the selectors might come back to him if the alternative did not accept the job or was not acceptable! Gower was getting used to being second best. In the end, the England management went for the only other player of proven ability at the highest level, Graham Gooch. Although he had suffered against Alderman and similar types of bowlers over the years, his record against real pace was not in doubt and he had lost the job as England captain only because of a change in chairman of selectors. Micky Stewart, who Gower believed was behind his rejection, was happy with Gooch. The nomination went for approval to the TCCB's cricket committee and Gooch was named as captain for the tour to the West Indies.

The squad to tour the Caribbean was picked later on the day that Gooch was unveiled to the press. That same day, the TCCB announced a new sponsorship deal with the City investment firm Whittingdale. To assist the development of some of the most promising youngsters, Whittingdale would pay one batsman and one bowler's summer wages in the winter. Atherton was an obvious candidate, but Patrick Whittingdale, the company chairman and prime mover in the sponsorship, felt it would be defeating the object of the exercise to sponsor a young player who would be making the senior England tour. Enquiries were made the day before the side was selected and the word was that Atherton was going to the Caribbean, so the first two recipients were announced as Essex's Nasser Hussain and Surrey's Martin Bicknell. It proved a double blow for Atherton, because the tour spot never materialised and he missed out on the award and a tour place. Hussain got the jackpot – both. Atherton's consolation was the vice-captaincy of the 'A' tour to Zimbabwe, under Hampshire's Mark Nicholas. It was a blow to his pride. In years to come, Atherton would claim that not touring the Caribbean was a better long-term career move. No one will ever know (it took Hussain seven years to establish himself at Test level). Atherton is not one for ducking challenges, though. Suggestions that the Cambridge graduate had been pitched in too early did not sit easily with him – nor did the idea that his undoubted talent might be harmed by exposure to the fastest bowling attack in the world. The vice-captaincy tag, at least, maintained the FEC (Future England Captain) image.

ATHERTON
The rebels went and that's why I got my chance against Australia. I was the new boy, just out of university and

wet behind the ears. I didn't know a thing. We didn't stand a chance of winning. It was a bit of a shambles. Micky and David weren't seeing eye to eye. David was at the end of his tether. It had been gruelling for him. It wasn't a team, just a group of individuals. I hadn't met half the players before. In all honesty, it was a big let down. You wait for this day all your life and expect it to be something special. Instead you're thrown into a team that's all over the place. It was great to get picked, but I don't think they had much choice after the rebels went.

The England A tour was a great success. The tourists triumphed in the first unofficial Test and drew the other two. The one-day series was also won, 3-0 (a scoreline that was reversed on England and Atherton in the first full tour to Zimbabwe seven years later). England started off in Kenya – the birthplace of one of the party, Derek Pringle – where they beat the Kenyan Cricket Association XI in two one-day matches. The game against the Chairman's XI was cancelled because half the England party had gone down with food poisoning. The three-day games against Young Zimbabwe and Zimbabwe B were not recognised as first-class fixtures, but Atherton's pride in performance was evident with 91 and 5 for 35 in the first game and an undefeated 97 in the second. The opening 'Test' at Harare was Zimbabwe's first five-day game. England gained a first-innings lead of 76 thanks to Atherton's seven-hour, 341-ball century. Zimbabwe were beaten by 10 wickets after being bowled out for 118 with Atherton taking 3 for 4. His bowling was attracting as much praise as his batting. The tourists moved on to Bulawayo for the next 'Test' and Atherton scored another century. After putting on 185 together in Harare, he and Blakey added 154 for the third wicket at Bulawayo, the Yorkshireman stealing the show this time with 221. Zimbabwe's David Houghton matched that double hundred and the game petered out into a draw. Atherton added another century in the next one-day international.

Gooch's side in the Caribbean began the third Test the day before Nicholas's team took on Zimbabwe for the third time, and the timing should have been perfect for Atherton. He was in sparkling form and an opportunity opened up on the main tour when Gooch broke a bone in his hand in Trinidad. As it turned out, the timing could not have been worse. Atherton was forced to miss the third Zimbabwe match because of a groin strain and when the call came from the West Indies, he was indisposed. Instead of flying to Barbados, Atherton could only limp up the aircraft steps for the flight home. Surrey's David Smith, who had played in two Tests in the Caribbean four years earlier, was flown out from England instead. He lasted one game, his thumb broken by Ezra Moseley, the man who had put Gooch out of action. Although Atherton felt frustrated, he has always been philosophical about such setbacks – no 'might-have-beens'. England led 1-0 going into the final two Tests against the West Indies. Unfortunately, the tourists played those matches without their best batsman, Gooch, and best bowler, Fraser. Had Atherton produced anything like his Zimbabwe form and given England some Gooch-like solidity at the top of the order, he might have emerged the hero and England the victors. Instead, the West Indies won in controversial circumstances in Barbados and Antigua to maintain their unbeaten records. Atherton went back to Lancashire for the new season. He was a Test player, and a promising one, but his future at international level was rather uncertain.

CHAPTER FOUR

Open For Business

The summer of 1990 was Atherton's coming of age. In truth, there was no better summer to be a batsman, especially one whose England career was taking off in such dramatic fashion. At the start of June, Atherton was aspiring. By the end of August, he was established as the England captain's right-hand man, with the bat at least. His return to the Test team owed a little to good fortune. Wayne Larkins, Gooch's partner in the Caribbean, damaged a finger, while Gower, who had not toured, failed in the two Texaco Trophy contests. Larkins, the preferred choice, did not recover by the Test series. The selectors turned to Lancashire, and Atherton and Fairbrother.

The pair had enjoyed an eventful start to the season. The county game against Surrey at The Oval gave a clear indication that this was going to be a batsman's summer. Lancashire conceded more runs than they had ever done in an innings as the home side made 707 for 9 declared, with skipper Ian Greig contributing 291 runs. The Surrey plan was to bowl out the visitors twice. They managed it only once as Lancashire hit 863, the highest County Championship score of the century and 14 runs short of Yorkshire's all-time record. Atherton hit his highest first-class score, 191, in a record third-wicket stand with Fairbrother of 364, exactly the number of runs scored by Sir Len Hutton at The Oval against the 1938 Australians. Fairbrother himself beat that Hutton ground record by two to record the third-highest county score of all-time. The Atherton–Fairbrother partnership contributed just 10 runs in the Benson and Hedges Cup game against Hampshire, but that was the second unsuccessful attempt to gain a result in the group match and neither player was very happy when the first was wiped from the record books: Fairbrother had smashed a county record 145 in another record partnership with Atherton (who scored 100 exactly) of 244 in a competition record total of 352 for 6 in 55 overs. It was all to no avail, apart from helping to impress the England selectors. The second attempt saw one of the few occasions when Atherton and Fairbrother have fallen out. After five balls and no runs from Atherton, Fairbrother enquired from the other end rather bluntly what was going on. Atherton hit out next ball and was caught. Fairbrother soon followed and Atherton was waiting at the top of the stairs for him. The argument that ensued started in the dressing-room and finished up in the captain's room.

Alec Stewart's displays in the Caribbean gave him priority over Atherton for the England No. 3 position – that was the background to the formation of one of England's most successful Test opening partnerships of all time. A back injury to Graeme Fowler allowed Atherton to open in Lancashire's pre-Test match at Horsham. He proved to the selectors that he had the temperament and determination for the job with a stodgy 67 runs in 64 overs. So when New Zealand were bowled out for 208 at Trent Bridge on the third day of the first Test (the rain, not the touring batsmen, had kept England in the field for so long), it was Atherton and Gooch who strode out together for the first time just after midday. It was difficult to judge whether the pair had struck up an immediate rapport because Gooch was out first ball, adjudged lbw to Hadlee. Stewart joined Atherton, but the rains came again and play only resumed on the Monday, with England 4 for 1. There was nothing left in the match, other than pride, but Atherton correctly perceived it as an ideal opportunity to get his head down. There was no pressure for quick runs and he had total licence to bat for as long as he wanted, without any recourse to the clock or scoreboard. That might appear the perfect scenario for batting, but it takes a special kind of talent and temperament to shut out the rest of the world and bat in a vacuum. Atherton proved he had that quality in abundance, though his innings of 151 was not played in total isolation – Stewart was soon out, Lamb went for a duck and England were by no means safe at 45 for 3. Atherton batted for over eight hours, hitting 16 boundaries, and was seventh man out at 302, having contributed exactly half of England's total. The inevitable draw followed, as did Atherton's Man of the Match award. England saluted a new cricket star with a bright future. Gooch and Micky Stewart (Alec's father) tried to apply some sort of restraint to the press hype, but to little avail.

Those warnings looked appropriate as the new partnership failed again at Lord's. Atherton was the man with no score against his name this time, being bowled by Danny Morrison in the second over of the match. But when England began their second innings trailing by 128 runs, the Gooch–Atherton pairing finally got out of the blocks. They put on 68 and Atherton went on to score 54 before becoming Andrew Jones's first Test victim. Another draw meant the series would be decided at Edgbaston. That contest, however, went England's way the minute the Kiwi captain John Wright asked the home side to bat. Rain had delayed the start until mid-afternoon but Gooch and

Atherton made up for lost time with a stand of 170 before Atherton was lbw to Snedden. It was England's best start since Bill Athey and Chris Broad's partnership of 223 at Perth in 1986. Gooch finished with 154 as England reached 400 for the first time in 11 Tests. Eddie Hemmings then produced his best England figures of 6 for 58 to give the home side a first-innings lead of 186, but the need for a carefully timed declaration disappeared as England's last seven second-innings wickets fell for 29. Their total of 158, which set New Zealand a target of 345, was largely achieved thanks to Atherton's careful 70. He was the eighth man out. The last two wickets fell to Sir Richard Hadlee and the honour of being his 431st and final Test wicket went to Devon Malcolm, who had the final word with five wickets of his own in England's 114-run victory. Atherton was named England's Man of the Series. Much more important for him, though, was just being part of a winning Test set-up at the fifth attempt.

July turned out to be a great month for Atherton. He headed back to London for his first Lord's final. Apart from those problems in the group match against Hampshire, Lancashire had been all-conquering in the Benson and Hedges Cup – Atherton and Fairbrother, with 74 and 61 not out respectively, were too good for Surrey in the quarter-final; Atherton's undefeated 56 and Fairbrother's 78 accounted for Somerset in the semi-final. Worcestershire were the opponents in the final, but the dynamic duo were not so dominating this time. Atherton scored 40 before being run out and Fairbrother made 11. Runs from Mike Watkinson and Warren Hegg set Worcestershire a target of 242 in 55 overs, but they never coped with Wasim Akram and could not recover from a bad start. Lancashire's winning margin was 69 runs, and this second ever Benson and Hedges Cup win was their first Lord's success for six years. They would only have to wait a couple of months for the next one. After victories over Durham and Derbyshire – the latter giving Atherton his first NatWest Man of the Match award – Lancashire were already in the quarter-finals of the 60-over competition.

Atherton's aptitude and appetite for the fight at the highest level were becoming evident to the England management and he was included in the one-day squad for the first time. England lost that series 2-0 to India. In the second match at Trent Bridge, Atherton scored 59, helping to put on 115 with Robin Smith to rescue England from 62 for 3, but the home side had no answer to the stroke-play of Shastri, Manjrekar, Vengsarkar, Tendulkar and Azharuddin. Gooch and Atherton swapped centuries at Chelmsford before combining again in the first Test against India at Lord's. Atherton missed out on that first-innings run feast as Gooch scored 333, Lamb and Smith added centuries and England declared on 653 for 4. Shastri and Azharuddin – who, like Wright at Edgbaston, had asked England to bat – replied with hundreds, but it still required four consecutive sixes off Eddie Hemmings by Kapil Dev to save the follow-on. Atherton then grabbed some of the action with 72 as England's openers posted their first double-hundred stand. Gooch, who had scored 456 runs, and taken a wicket and a catch, ended the proceedings with a run out that gave England victory by 247 runs.

The second Test was another run feast, producing another half-a-dozen centuries. Atherton's 131 was England's top score in the first innings, and his century on that first day was all the more special for coming on his home patch. Geoff Pullar, incidentally against the same opposition 31 years earlier and with the same number of runs, is the only other Lancastrian to score an England hundred at Old Trafford. Gooch's glorious summer continued and the pair struck another double-century opening stand. Smith added an undefeated 121 as

England passed 500, but India, inspired by the captain Azharuddin's 179, got within 87 runs of England. In the second innings, Gooch failed for once, but Atherton (74) and Lamb (109) allowed England to declare on the final morning. India looked beaten at 183 for 6 with two and a half hours remaining, but a dropped caught-and-bowled by Hemmings when Tendulkar was on 10 was the turning point. He went on to score an unbeaten 119 at the age of 17 years and 112 days, only 30 days older than Pakistan's Hanif Mohammed who became the youngest centurion at Delhi in 1960. It was a masterful display in dire circumstances by a batsman who was obviously destined for greatness (comparisons with Gavaskar were not only noted because he was wearing a pair of the great man's pads). The draw ensured that England could not lose the series.

Atherton remained at Old Trafford for the NatWest semi-final and Roses match. Lancashire, who had demolished Gloucestershire by 241 runs in the quarter-final, took three days to overcome Middlesex. Desmond Haynes's unbeaten 149 was the backbone of the visitors' 296 for 4. Mendis dug in for Lancashire, and with support from Atherton, Fairbrother and Watkinson, the Red Rose was triumphant with more than four overs to spare. Atherton scored his seventh century of the season against the White Rose, then his leg-spin removed Moxon, Blakey and Byas and almost brought Lancashire victory. England and Atherton finished the summer undefeated. In the final Test, England followed on after India had posted 606 for 9 declared, but Gooch and Atherton set England on the road to recovery with a stand of 176, Atherton making 86 in five and a half hours. Gower made the game safe (and ensured winter employment) with 157 not out – he and John Morris had replaced Stewart and Fairbrother for the India series. Atherton's 378 runs in the series at 63.00 was only good enough for fourth place in the England averages. Even Gooch, 752 runs at 125.33, was only runner-up: Smith's 361 runs came at 180.50.

The Atherton–Fairbrother show gave an encore at Lord's in the NatWest final. Northants' 171 was never likely to stretch Lancashire's firepower. The duo put on 114 for the third wicket and Atherton was there at the end on 38 (Fairbrother made 81) as Lancashire won with 14.2 overs to spare. For once, the batsmen did not grab all the honours. The Man of the Match was Phil DeFreitas, whose opening spell of 5 for 19 in eight overs had effectively ended the contest. Lancashire were after a third trophy, the Refuge Assurance Cup. They had lost the opening league game to Middlesex, then won their last six matches to challenge Derbyshire, who would have surrendered the title to Lancashire if they had not beaten Essex on the final Sunday. The top four sides qualified for the Cup, but Lancashire had a rare off-day at Old Trafford and Middlesex made the final, beat Derbyshire and took the trophy. Lancashire's sixth-place finish in the Britannic Assurance Championship was two down on the previous season, but it had still been an impressive year, with Lancashire becoming the first county to take both Lord's finals in a season. In 28 limited-overs matches, they had lost only four.

Atherton was right to feel satisfied with his first full season on the county circuit. Now an England regular, he finished ninth in the national batting averages, 76 runs short of 2,000 with an average of 71.25. Two of his seven hundreds were for England. Atherton also tried his arm with much success at the other end of the pitch. He topped the Lancashire bowling averages, his 45 wickets ranking him number 29 in the country. The Cricket Writers' Club, who had voted Hussain ahead of him as the Young Cricketer of the Year in 1989, made Atherton a clear winner in 1990. When the *Wisden Cricketers' Almanack* was published the following April, Atherton was named as one of its Five Cricketers of the Year. The *Manchester Evening News*'s Brian Bearshaw remembers Atherton's debut season: 'For those of us witnessing him for the first time, it was not just his class which shone through; it was the temperament, his ability to adjust to any situation and play accordingly.' England appreciated those qualities, which was why Atherton was now heading to Australia as an important member of Gooch's Ashes squad.

Just as Atherton was to find as captain four years later, the England party never discovered the spirit and camaraderie of the previous winter's expedition to the Caribbean. Again, injuries played a crucial part. Gooch missed the first Test, Lamb the second and third, and Fraser the third and fifth. Atherton had a mixed time. The biggest blow came when he was made the scapegoat for a one-day defeat at Adelaide against New Zealand. It was to be five years before he completely wiped that stain from his record.

England never recovered from a bad start in the Tests, losing the Ashes and the series 3-0. Atherton went into the opening Test at Brisbane with 59 runs in six first-class knocks and a new opening partner. Gooch had undergone an emergency operation in Adelaide on his infected finger and was out for a month. Atherton walked out with Wayne 'Ned' Larkins. Both went cheaply, Atherton lbw to Bruce Reid. Acting captain Lamb and Gower took England to 117 for 2 before they were bowled out for 194 on a day that was not easy for batting. That was put in perspective when Australia were dismissed for 152. On the second evening, England led by 98 with seven second-innings wickets left. Atherton's off-stump had been removed by a devastating out-swinger from Alderman when he had made 15, after Larkins, struggling with an infected tooth, had gone with the scoreboard bare. Just before the close, Border dropped Lamb and the

Australian captain was convinced that it would prove to be a costly mistake in such a low-scoring game. He admitted he would rather have been in England's position on that second night. Not on the third evening, as he celebrated Australia's 10-wicket win. England had been bowled out for 114, and with the pitch already flattening out, Marsh and Taylor made no mistakes. Worse was to follow for England when newspapers reported that Lamb, who added just four runs to his overnight score, had gone up to the Gold Coast the previous evening and been seen in a casino after midnight. The events of the third day made Lamb's excursion a serious error of judgement and the hard work of the summer dissolved in a matter of weeks. It became imperative that Gooch returned.

Five days after the Brisbane defeat, Atherton's tour took a serious downturn. It is something that he struggles to understand even to this day. England's opening Benson and Hedges World Series Cup game was against New Zealand. The Kiwis made 199 for 6 off the rain-reduced 40 overs after Wright, who had been caught off a rising delivery from Malcolm that was signalled a no-ball, went on to make 67. In England's reply, Gower hit the second ball for six and got out to the fourth, and Atherton took on the anchor role. Only John Morris's 63 in 46 balls took England close. Atherton made 33. It was a shoddy performance all round. A trip to Geoff Merrill's winery the next day was delayed to make way for 'naughty-boy' nets. The finger was pointed at Atherton, to such an extent that he only played in one more of England's eight qualifying matches in the one-day series. England failed to qualify for the best-of-three final, losing the last match to Australia, when a win would have taken them through, by three runs. More importantly for Atherton, that selection policy restricted his opportunities to play himself into form as the second Test approached. He put on 198 with Lamb at Ballarat against Victoria, scoring 76, only for Lamb to tear a calf muscle running back to the hotel and put himself out of the next two Tests.

The Boxing Day Test at Melbourne is one of Australia's great sporting events, and Atherton walked out with Gooch, who had won the toss, in front of a big crowd. Atherton was soon making his way back, after prodding the ball to Boon at short square-leg off Bruce Reid, for 0. Gooch soon followed him. The middle order did well to finish the day at 239 for 4, and Gower completed his century the next day as England made 352. Overnight Australia were 109 for 1. A magnificent spell by Fraser (6 for 82) and six catches by Russell gave the tourists a first-innings lead of 46 runs. Atherton went cheaply again, but Gooch and Larkins took England to 149 ahead. Even a minor collapse did not appear too damaging and with England 147 for 4, Gooch was wondering about a declaration. What took place next was described by Micky Stewart as '50 minutes of madness'. After tea, Reid and Greg Matthews took six wickets in 12 overs for three runs: England 150 all out. Australia had a day and a bit to score 197 for victory. Reid's figures were 6 for 97 and 7 for 51, giving him a match analysis of 13 for 148. England looked devastated. Atherton raised hopes again with two gully catches as Australia closed at 28 for 2, but those were England's last successes. Malcolm was certain Boon was lbw the next morning, and Tufnell was sure he had picked up his first Test wicket when Russell claimed a catch. Umpire Peter McConnell's refusal certainly upset the Middlesex left-arm spinner, but that came late in the day and would not have affected the result. Australia had won the first two Tests by 10 wickets and eight wickets. The contests had been much closer than that, yet there was no escaping Australia's 2-0 advantage and vice-like grip on the Ashes.

Sydney was England's last chance. Australia's 518 on

the opening two days appeared to put paid to that. Atherton, though, recorded his first century against Australia. At 451 minutes, it was the slowest in Ashes history, but no one, least of all Atherton himself, was complaining. He reached three figures with a cracking cover-drive off Carl Rackemann. A few runs earlier, a third umpire might not have given Atherton the benefit of the doubt on a close run-out decision. Gower also hit his first century at Sydney and Stewart's 91 allowed Gooch to declare 49 runs behind Australia. By stumps on day four, England had taken two Australian wickets. It was Rackemann who saved his country by frustrating the tourists for nearly two hours. England's target was 255 in 28 overs, realistically an impossible task. Gooch opened with Gower and the pair rattled along at seven an over until Gower was caught at 84. Larkins and Stewart went cheaply and Gooch was caught by Border for 54. The chase was over; the Ashes had gone. Atherton was named Man of the Match. That was little consolation, although the tourists had shown that there was not a great gap between the teams. Atherton hit another century at Albury against New South Wales, who won by six wickets. The party moved on to Queensland's Gold Coast where England won by 10 wickets, their only first-class victory of the trip. The important winning runs came from Atherton's bat but the match will always be remembered for Gower and Morris joy-riding in a Tiger Moth airplane. That brought the pair a £1,000 fine and failed to lift English spirits, although the management made a real meal of the whole affair.

England once more failed to nail Australia down in the Adelaide Test, although again the tourists almost conjured up an impossible win. The home side were in trouble at 124 for 5 before Mark Waugh, making his debut at the expense of his twin brother Steve, saved his side with an inspired 138. Australia took another first-innings lead of 157. Gooch made 87 and Atherton went for another duck, this time giving Craig McDermott his first Test wicket for a couple of years. Border then batted England into the ground. The visitors were set a victory total of 472 with a day and 35 minutes left. Gooch and Atherton had only reduced the deficit by 19 runs as they walked out for the fifth day, but by lunch, Gooch's intent was obvious with England 115 for 0. By tea, although the openers had gone – Gooch for his first Test century in Australia and Atherton for 87 in a remarkable partnership of 203 – Lamb and Gower had taken the tourists to 267 for 2. It was still a stiff task, but the aroma of adventure was in the air. Lamb went at 287. Gower, unlucky to be adjudged lbw, went at the same score. When Stewart went soon after, the chase was called off. Border did not press for victory, relieved to have stemmed the flow. England's 335 for 5 was still a courageous effort.

England gathered themselves for one last throw in the final Test. They were well placed after two sessions on 212 for 3, but after tea, McDermott took 5 for 17 in 6.4 overs and England were bowled out for 244. McDermott's figures were 8 for 97 and Atherton had been his second victim. England tried to fight back, reducing Australia to 168 for 6 before Ian Healy and Greg Matthews, whose batting had frustrated the tourists all through the series, sapped England's spirit. Matthews remained defiant and Australia had a lead of 63 runs. England's second innings saw Atherton as third-highest scorer with 25 and they were bowled out for 180. After a rest day, the Australians scored the last 81 runs needed for a nine-wicket victory in the morning session. Taking the margin of the three wins, it was eight, nine, ten wickets and out for England. The detour to New Zealand for three one-day games was totally unnecessary and not popular with the players. Atherton was back in the team, which lost the series 2-1 after throwing away match-winning positions.

Atherton had found the whole trip tough and draining. A total of 279 runs in the Tests at 31.00 showed a drop from the summer. He averaged even less in 11 first-class matches. Atherton is not a man to make excuses, but his back had been troubling him for most of the tour and had been getting progressively worse. He hoped a long rest would resolve matters. It did not. As his back deteriorated the following summer, so did his performances.

ATHERTON

Gooch's injury early on set us back and we never recovered. Graham felt a little bit let down. I know what it's like as captain. It's easy to load everything on yourself, thinking 'I'm working my socks off. Look at that lot.' You can worry too much about attitude. There was friction between Graham and David, and Graham and Tuffers. The management response to things not going well was to work us into the ground. That backfired. You can dull players' enthusiasm with practice. I like practice to be intense – short, sharp. That keeps players keen. My attitude in Australia in 1994-95 was tempered by what had happened four years earlier. I tried to do the opposite. I'm not saying one is right and the other's wrong. We had a couple of 'naughty-boy' nets and then fielding practices. In 1994-95 I was aware of how the players would react. Mind you, when we had a day off in Sydney after losing the Melbourne Test, you would have thought I had committed murder by the media reaction.

CHAPTER FIVE

Athers' Back

Atherton began the West Indies series in 1991 as England's vice-captain. Two years later, he succeeded Gooch as captain of his country. His rise to the top cricket job in the land had long been predicted, but those two years were far from an easy ride – they brought Atherton much soul-searching and anguish. The West Indies fast bowlers put him through the mill as he became increasingly troubled by his back, and an operation to correct that problem kept him out of the winter tour and the 1992 World Cup. He returned to the England side midway through the home series against Pakistan, but the next winter tour to India and Sri Lanka found him way down the pecking order and no longer part of the management set-up. Alec Stewart was now Gooch's chosen successor, and Atherton spent much of the tour on the sidelines. His Test future, let alone any captaincy aspirations, looked far from certain. Atherton wonders where those two years fit in with his so-called 'steady rise' to the captaincy.

The 1991 summer had started promisingly for Atherton. He re-established his one-day credentials after the disappointments of Australia, opening with Gooch and being named Man of the Series as England won the Texaco Trophy 3-0. His undefeated 69, the only fifty of the match, guided England to a one-wicket win at Edgbaston in the game that marked Graeme Hick's international debut. Atherton then scored 74 as England's openers put on 156 at Old Trafford, where the tourists fell nine runs short of the 271 target. It was another Lancastrian, Neil Fairbrother, who stole the show in the final game at Lord's, with his maiden century. Atherton felt he had proved a point to Gooch and Micky Stewart. After the Lord's victory, Gooch was seen on the players' balcony with Lamb, who had been vice-captain on England's last two winter tours. Gooch was explaining that Lamb's services in that capacity were no longer required. It was time to look ahead: Atherton was the replacement.

The Test series was a very different affair, and Atherton was not the only batsman to suffer. Hick was dropped after making just 75 runs in four Tests; Lamb, with a good record against Caribbean bowling, went the same way at the same time after 88 runs; and Ramprakash passed 20 seven times in nine innings and never reached 30. Atherton finished 11th in the England batting averages that summer. Gooch and Smith were the England heroes, the captain carrying his bat for 154 in the first Test at Headingley where a 115-run victory was England's first at home against the West Indies for 22 years. Atherton was bowled, playing back to Lancashire's former overseas player Patrick Patterson, for 2 in the first innings and made 6 in the second, the first of Ambrose's six victims as England slumped to 124 for 6. Ambrose was twice on a hat-trick, with Smith and Lamb going first ball. Smith's 148 not out and the rain saved England at Lord's, where Ambrose removed Atherton, who scored 5, and Hick without conceding a run at the start of England's innings. At Trent Bridge, Atherton and Gooch lasted through to the afternoon session on the first day with their sixth

century opening-stand together. That first session, however, was England's best of the Test. The West Indies
manufactured a first-innings lead of 97, then reduced
England to 115 for 8 and levelled the series with a
nine-wicket victory. England then went behind when the
West Indies won at Edgbaston by seven wickets after
being bowled out for 188 early on the second day. That
contest was much closer – the West Indies had been 24 for
3 chasing the 152 victory target. Viv Richards made the
winning hit, a straight six, to ensure that he would finish
his career without losing a series as captain. Atherton had
moved down to No. 3 to accommodate Hugh Morris. The
runs still did not flow. It had been decided that a back
operation could not be avoided, but Atherton delayed
that until after The Oval Test.

Back at Old Trafford on the Sunday between Tests, the
tension between Atherton and DeFreitas erupted into a
'sausage-roll' fight. The pair had never seen eye to eye.
The bowler felt this batsman played for himself. The
batsman thought this bowler pulled up the ladder when-
ever things got tough. Fairbrother was a close friend to
both and 'piggy in the middle'. Lancashire were having a
poor day in the field and DeFreitas was not happy. When
the ball bounced off Fairbrother's knee on the edge of the
circle, the fielder stopped the single, then turned to
remonstrate with someone who was giving him abuse in
the ground. That gave Graham Thorpe the chance to
sneak a single after all. DeFreitas was not best pleased,
and the sight of Atherton doubled-up at the whole farci-
cal situation was the final straw. Atherton had not been
laughing at DeFreitas, but things exploded in the
dressing-room as DeFreitas scooped up some of the tea,
sausage-rolls and all, and hurled them at Atherton. That
was the 'bell' to start a fight that had been brewing for a
long time and soon the pair were rolling around the
dressing-room floor. No serious damage was done,

although it can hardly have been of much benefit to Atherton's back. He lasted four balls in the first innings at The Oval and scored 13 in the second. Botham, Tufnell and Stewart had been recalled. Botham hit the winning runs after Tufnell had taken 6 for 25 as the West Indies crashed from 158 for 3 to 176 all out in the first innings. This was Atherton's second and final Test appearance with Botham, and a much happier occasion than his debut at Trent Bridge two years earlier. England finished the summer in style with a victory over Sri Lanka at Lord's, but Atherton was missing for the first time in 18 months as he went under the knife.

ATHERTON

It was a nightmare series for me after doing well in the Texacos. My back became a real problem. This was my introduction to very quick bowling. Result-wise, I failed, but I've proved myself since. Three of us had nightmares — me, Hickie and Lambie, who had built a great reputation against them. I kept going when I would have been better dropping out earlier and having the operation. I've always felt that series exposed my fitness and technique a little — not my temperament. Going back to county cricket is not the answer, as Hickie and Ramps have found out. That merely exposes the different standards. I kept positive and confident all through the series. I never worried where my next run was coming from. I was getting good deliveries. The edges were going to the fielders and the fielders were catching them. I was not the first to suffer that against the West Indies.

The England selectors aided his recuperation by naming him in the squad to tour New Zealand and then go on to the World Cup. The departure date was late December and Atherton had high hopes of recovering in time, as did another casualty: Angus Fraser had not played since the Adelaide Test, suffering from a hip and back problem which an operation had failed to sort out. In the event, neither Atherton nor Fraser made the winter trips. Atherton took longer than expected to get back to full fitness, and Fraser had an even tougher fight. He did not play Test cricket again until the end of the 1993 summer, by which time Atherton had become England captain.

His back has been a nagging problem ever since. Most of the time it is fine, although Atherton has kept the physios busy, especially Laurie Brown at Old Trafford, and Dave Roberts and Wayne Norton on England tours. Hard as they have worked, it has been Atherton's regular routine that has kept him so free from injury. Twice he has needed injections into the 'hot spots' to enable him to play – Lord's in 1995 and Harare at the end of 1996. He deflects questions about his back as deliberately and purposefully as he executes the pull or cut. As Atherton frequently reminds enquirers, his fitness record is better than anyone in recent years.

ATHERTON
The first time I ever felt it was during the Old Trafford Test against India in 1990. I was getting pains in my legs. The condition got worse during the Ashes tour of 1990-91 and I was often grateful when the ball did not come to me. The most painful time was during the Adelaide Test when I was standing at gully. Lancashire's pre-season tour in 1991 took me back to Perth. The problem was becoming serious, so I had injections and scans while I was out there. The scans were sent back to England and they revealed that I had a stress fracture, so would need an operation. But it was postponed until after the West Indies series. Judging by my run tally, I would have been better off going under the knife a few months earlier. Eventually, I pulled out of the Sri Lanka Test at the end of the season. The operation was carried out by Mr John Webb at Park

75

Hospital in Nottingham. He performed a screwfusion. Bone was taken from elsewhere and screwed on while the vertebrae healed. I was on my back for a week in hospital and another week at home. I could get up after that, but couldn't do anything active for three months. My World Cup hopes were over straightaway. I spent the end of the winter in South Africa, firstly staying with Alan Igglesden in Cape Town and then joining Lancashire on their pre-season tour in Johannesburg.

Since then I've undertaken a daily routine of exercises for strength and flexibility. Well, almost daily. I've needed injections a couple of times. The biggest problem in Zimbabwe was that the pain-killers weren't in my body long enough to do any good. My back is no big deal – it's something I live with. There are millions of back sufferers; many, I'm sure, much worse than me. I can't say whether that will be the reason I finally call it a day. All I can say is that I never intended playing for as long as Goochie anyway!

Atherton was back in the Lancashire side and back at Lord's early in May 1992. He led the Red Rose county for the first time at the end of the month. Derbyshire spoilt the occasion with a five-wicket win after Atherton gave them a sporting lunchtime declaration: 301 to get in 69 overs. The new captain played his part with 140 not out, his first century since the previous August, but he was going to have to wait his turn to regain an England place. In his absence, Gooch's team had taken the three-Test series in New Zealand 2-0 and reached the final of the World Cup, and Alec Stewart had taken Atherton's place at the top of the order and in the line of succession. The Surrey captain consolidated that position with 190 in the first Test of the summer against Pakistan. Only 11 wickets fell in the rain-affected match for a total of 905 runs. The second Test at Lord's was a low-scoring game. Pakistan won by two wickets after a ninth-wicket stand of 46 between Waqar and Wasim. Gooch ran out of bowlers after reducing Pakistan to 95 for 8, with Botham and DeFreitas injured. Atherton, still leading Lancashire, did little to impress Gooch at Chelmsford in the next county game, scoring 9 and 8 as his team lost by an innings and 37 runs in two days after Essex had scored 510 for 2 declared, but the following night Atherton was recalled to England colours, as was David Gower, whose 115th appearance took him clear of Colin Cowdrey's record. Lamb and Botham, two of cricket's more colourful characters, had played for England for the last time.

Atherton was pleased to be back. He had scored two centuries, but the runs had not flowed and the selectors could easily have ignored him had they not seen him as an important part of England's long-term strategy. He was to play a very minor role, however, in the most ill-tempered of matches, failing to trouble the scorers for the fourth time in his Test career as he was caught behind in the same over that Wasim Akram dismissed Stewart. Gower passed Geoff Boycott's record aggregate of runs on the Monday, taking half an hour to score the 34 runs needed to overtake 8,114, but the headlines the next day were not Gower's. Pakistan's captain Javed Miandad and bowler Aqib Javed had been involved in an unsavoury incident with umpire Roy Palmer, standing in his first Test. Palmer had warned Aqib for running through the crease at Devon Malcolm. Pakistan claimed that Palmer had thrown the bowler's sweater at him, but the BBC pictures showed that was not the case. Aqib was fined and the Pakistan manager Intikhab Alam was reprimanded.

Headingley had become the crunch Test for Atherton and England. Gooch's team were 1-0 down in the series and Atherton needed runs. He was helped when the selectors decided to make Stewart wicket-keeper at

Russell's expense again. That meant that the Gooch–Atherton opening partnership was back together for the first time in a year. Picking 'horses for courses', the selectors also gave Neil Mallender his debut and Pakistan were bowled out for 197. England's openers then put on 168, and it took one of Wasim's high-speed leg-breaks to breach Atherton's defence. Gooch's 17th Test century took England to 270 for 1, only for the final nine wickets to fall for 50 runs – England were getting used to the Pakistan bowlers becoming more effective the older the ball got – as Waqar took 5 for 13 in 38 deliveries. Mallender finished with match figures of 8 for 122 as Pakistan were bowled out for 221 and England needed 99 to win. The loss of Atherton and Smith at 27, both removed by Waqar, gave Pakistan hope, and Gooch was lucky to escape a run-out verdict by umpire Ken Palmer. The Pakistan team were exerting pressure both on the batsmen and the umpires. In the end, England reached their target to win by six wickets, with Gower and Ramprakash steadying the nerves.

Such had been the extent of England's collapse in the first innings that Gower had been left stranded on 18 batting at No. 5. It was the same story at The Oval where Pakistan won by 10 wickets and took the series. England had been 182 for 3 forty minutes after tea on the first day; they were all out for 207 three-quarters of an hour later, Wasim having taken 5 for 8 in 22 deliveries. Aqib Javed started the collapse. Atherton was eighth man out, after scoring 60 in four and a half hours, and was Waqar's only victim. Pakistan had then built up a lead of 173 runs by Saturday afternoon and England had lost Gooch, Stewart and Atherton to Waqar by tea. Only Robin Smith offered any resistance and forced Pakistan to bat again. Ramprakash bowled a wide, then was hit to the boundary. England's team manager, Micky Stewart, laid the foundation for a controversial end to the summer by announcing that he knew how the Pakistani bowlers managed to swing the old ball. He did not reveal the secret.

Atherton missed the fun and games of the final three Texaco matches. England's successful one-day squad had been kept together, having won the opening matches at Lord's and The Oval convincingly before the Tests began. England took the one-day series with a 198-run win at Trent Bridge and Pakistan's only success came by three runs at Lord's in the match that sparked the ball-tampering row. The umpires had had to change the ball during the lunch-break, but the ICC ruled the matter closed five days later without a satisfactory explanation. Allan Lamb went public about the allegations and in years to come, the matter twice reached the High Court. Atherton was one of many cricket celebrities who found themselves in the witness box in the summer of 1996.

The other controversy at the end of that summer was the exclusion of David Gower from the party to tour India. It led to a special emergency meeting of the MCC to consider a motion of no confidence in the England selectors. Those present agreed with the motion, 715 to 412. The postal ballot saved the selectors' blushes with 6,135 to 4,600 rejection. The inclusion or otherwise of Gower was an issue even before the squad was selected and announced, and the emotive affair was not helped by Dexter's refusal to explain the reasons behind the decision. Gooch and Gower had had their differences during the 1990-91 Ashes tour, and with no other explanation forthcoming, the media decided that had to be the basis of Gower's exclusion. Fletcher explained that England did not want three batsmen of a certain age – Gooch, Gatting and Gower – and were putting the emphasis on youth. That did not hold water; England supporters expected the best players to be picked. There was also some resentment that the South African rebels, Gatting and Emburey, were being allowed back in the fold at all. Gatting had a reputation of being a good player of spin, but then so had Gower – and it was four years since Gatting had made a significant contribution at Test level.

Atherton, for his part, finished the summer in style with centuries against Warwickshire, Yorkshire and Durham, when he batted for over eight hours and finished one run short of his maiden double-hundred. Atherton's runs came after two Old Trafford stalwarts, Allott and Fowler, were released and coach Alan Ormrod was sacked, Ormrod carrying the can for Lancashire's poor showing in all competitions. David Hughes was named as manager for the next season, with David Lloyd as coach. It was not an easy season for Neil Fairbrother in his first season as captain, as injury restricted his appearances. But he finished seventh in the national averages, 15 places higher than Atherton, and both were in the Indian tour party. Atherton had come back well after his back operation. In all first-class games, he had scored 1598 runs at 51.54 with five centuries. Atherton felt India would be the perfect place to get his Test career moving again with some big runs.

CHAPTER SIX

Out Of Sorts

India turned out to be a disaster – for England and Atherton. New team-manager Keith Fletcher had a nightmare start from which he never recovered, England lost all three Tests to India by large margins, and the last leg in Sri Lanka saw England defeated in the Test and two one-dayers. Gooch, who came home as scheduled after India, failed with the bat for the first time as captain and missed the Madras Test thanks to a 'dodgy prawn'. Alec Stewart led England in two Tests and saw his full-time captaincy prospects diminish. Gower was missed. Gatting did not dominate the Indian spinners as expected, while England's trio – Salisbury joined Emburey and Tufnell – made little impact. England's quick bowlers also struggled. Hick and Lewis scored centuries, but the touring side were always under pressure in the Tests. Smith was tortured by the Indian spinners and Atherton had the worst cricket time of his life. After illness had forced him out of the Calcutta Test on the morning of the match, the expected recall for Madras did not come and Atherton let Gooch know what he thought of that decision. Even when sickness laid Gooch low the next day, Atherton was not required. He finally made it back for the Bombay Test, getting involved in an embarrassing run-out mix-up with Stewart. Another failure in the Colombo Test and his absence from the one-day side there left Atherton confused and completely unsure as to what his England future was.

Most had expected the Test series to be one-sided in England's favour. India were losing badly in South Africa when England landed in the sub-continent, and such were the reports in the local newspapers that it appeared unwise for skipper Mohammad Azharuddin to return home. England had prepared assiduously at Lilleshall, with special mats to try and replicate facing the spinners. But it was the quick bowlers who had Atherton in trouble. For all the times he has faced barrages from Ambrose, Wasim, McDermott, Donald and Pollock, the occasion he remembers being hit was in those Lilleshall nets. Paul Jarvis was the bowler who cracked him on the helmet. Atherton remembers because it affected his confidence. That might have been because of his 1991 experiences against the West Indies and his spell out with his back problem.

ATHERTON

The tour was the second part of my re-establishment. It wasn't like starting over – I had played and scored Test hundreds, I knew what to expect and I knew I could do it. I was fighting to be one of the six or seven who are always written down on the team sheet. I'd been part of an established opening partnership with Goochie. I was keen to get back in the side. I had been vice-captain. They had decided Lambie was not the answer, and Stewie was not in the side. I never felt that I was bound to be the next captain. I did feel that Gower should have gone, but it was nothing to do with me. Age should be no bar to being in an England side.

I got that crack on the helmet at Lilleshall. I don't get hit

*that often and after that, I didn't play the short ball that
well. We prepared well; if anything, we were over-
confident. 'Harvey' [Neil Fairbrother] said to me, 'Who's
going to get Goochie out?' We were guilty of being naive.
India are a much different proposition at home. Fletcher
had been out to watch them. He came back and said,
'Kumble doesn't spin the ball.' He's right – but the whole
tone that we had nothing to fear backfired. Azza's head
was on the block after South Africa, but he got a hundred
on the first day of the series and never looked back. We've
all been through it – can't do no wrong, can't do no right.
So few of us had been to India before. Still, we should have
coped better.*

The tour went wrong from day one. While the tourists
were in the air, the story broke that the Gooch marriage,
believed to be one of the strongest in sport, had broken
up. There were also worries about the safety of the
England cricketers, making their first Test visit since
Gower's trip in 1984-85. The scheduled tour four years
later, also under Gooch, had been cancelled after the
Indians complained about the South African connections
of half the England squad. The civil unrest that greeted
this party had nothing to do with that, but the destruction
of the temple of Ayodhya, which led to rioting all over
India and hundreds of deaths. Just to add to England's
logistical difficulties, the Air India pilots were on strike,
and planes had to be leased from Uzbekhistan and Bul-
garian airlines with Russian-speaking pilots. That did
little to reassure those members of the England party
rather nervous of flying. When one pilot landed his jet at
the wrong airport in Delhi and then turned his plane
upside down on another landing in the fog 36 hours later
some of the England squad felt it was time to head for
home. Tufnell was one who requested to travel by rail.

England's itinerary was a shambles anyway, and

should never have been accepted. Gooch's side were almost stranded in Bhubaneshwar and had to catch an overnight train to Calcutta – and arriving at Calcutta station at the crack of dawn is about as big a culture shock as anyone from the West can receive. Illness and sickness wore the squad down, as did the pummelling from the Indian bowlers. Towards the end of the tour, Lord's met to discuss the calamitous state of the game. The verdict: the players needed to shave more and be smarter.

Atherton's tour started to go wrong in Lucknow, scene of British resistance during the Indian Mutiny. There were soldiers guarding England's hotel, yet locals would frequently wander into the bedrooms looking for tickets and autographs. Atherton was receiving no visitors. He was laid low with what was first thought to be malaria, shivering and sweating isolated in his hotel room. He had top scored with 59 in the tour opener at Faridabad. Gatting opened with Gooch in Atherton's absence at Lucknow and the pair put on 131 in a dull draw. The players, expecting searing heat, did not enjoy the cold conditions. They returned to Delhi to hear that the opening one-day international in Ahmedabad had been cancelled because of the unrest. Atherton played his first first-class game for three weeks at Cuttack after sitting out the one-day matches. He was beginning to resent this idea that he was surplus to limited-overs requirements. After his illness, he needed time at the crease before the Tests started, and that became critical when he was dismissed for 0 on the first morning against the Indian Under-25s. He finally got the practice he needed with an undefeated 80 in the second innings as the match was drawn.

It was all to no avail. Atherton picked up the virus that was doing the rounds from Paul Taylor in Cuttack and dropped out on the morning of the first Test. His opening partner was also struggling. Had this not been Gooch's 100th Test and had Atherton not been indisposed, the captain might well have sat this one out himself. He was never with it. That certainly might explain England's crazy bowling attack. While the Indians picked three spinners, England selected a four-man pace attack plus leg-spinner Ian Salisbury. The folly of ignoring Emburey and Tufnell was best illustrated by Hick's match figures of 5 for 28. Azharuddin, under intense pressure, won the toss and took the game to England, his century establishing a control that India never lost. His 182 not out was almost half India's 371. England failed by nine runs to save the follow-on, with India's spinners taking all but one of the wickets. Gatting's innings forced India to bat again and 25,000 came to watch the last 43 runs scored on the final morning to seal India's eight-wicket win. The declining health of the England party prompted Dexter to cite the 'smog factor' as a reason for the defeat, and England were certainly happy to be heading for Vishakhapatnam on the coast. The game against the Rest of India was another boring draw. Atherton scored 33 and 0, and this was the game that told him just how far down the captaincy pecking order he was. Gooch was rested and Stewart took over. He burst a blood vessel in his finger after nine balls and did not field. Emburey took over the captaincy and the next man up was Fairbrother. Gatting, not playing, was now part of the selection panel, leaving Atherton as sixth choice at best. Tufnell was the centre of attention here, though. The England management had just made a statement in support of the left-arm spinner, who was finding touring India hard work. The next day, he was fined £500 by the England management for 'ungentlemanly conduct towards an umpire'. A session with the team's spiritual adviser, Andrew Wingfield-Digby, calmed Tufnell down and helped his bowling the following morning.

Tufnell was recalled for the Madras Test. Atherton was left out. He was stunned when Gooch read out the line-up at the team meeting the night before the game. That was an eventuality he had not seen coming. Atherton had been picked for the first Test, the side had lost heavily after he was forced to drop out, yet his name was missing for the second Test. He could not understand it. The blow might have been softened if there had been some warning, and the management should have realised that a change in strategy needed some explanation to those who were casualties. Atherton had suffered setbacks in the past, but nothing as devastating as this. In Madras he felt as low as he had ever done personally in a cricket environment. But whatever lack of communication there might have been from the England management, Atherton was not going to be accused of the same crime. His words to Gooch were plain and simple: 'You're wrong.' The level of his hurt and anger was there for all to see.

Gooch did not have a pleasant evening. The England captain, along with Gatting and several others, dined in the hotel's Chinese restaurant. It proved a two-prawned attack on England's chances. Gooch was suffering from sickness and dizziness, and Gatting was struggling too. (It was not just the prawns – Robin Smith had chicken in his room and was having stomach problems.) Gooch had no option but to withdraw, but there was still no place for Atherton. Stewart felt unable to lead the side, open and keep wicket, so Richard Blakey was brought in. The media thought this an astonishing decision, though Atherton was less upset at this rejection than that of the night before – he understood Stewart's reluctance to overburden himself in his first game as England captain. The England dressing-room soon resembled a roadside cafe as tour manager Bob Bennett put his apron on and 'Bob's Bistro' opened for lunch-time business. The menu was not extensive, but at least it was guaranteed to stay down and in. The players queued for corned beef, baked beans and nan bread, dished out by Bennett, Wingfield-Digby and physio Dave Roberts. Four substitutes were used as England's troubled fielders needed spells off the field. The one member of the party not required that day, other than Gooch, was Atherton. Fairbrother has never seen Atherton as miserable as he was that day. He felt that the England management could have offered his Lancashire colleague more of an explanation for his enforced inactivity. The only consolation for Atherton was that another dismal England bowling and batting performance ensured his appearance in the final Test.

ATHERTON

It's a tough trip. There should be a 'no moaning' rule. You have got to muck in and experience India. There were problems, riots, strikes, etc. I'd been ill in Lucknow, then I caught a virus from Paul Taylor just before the first Test. I tried to practise the day before but I had a temperature of 104 on the morning of the match and had to drop out. After the first Test, I chatted to Fletch about my batting because I wasn't happy with it, but it was still a bolt from the blue when they announced the team for the second Test. I can't deny it was one of the great shocks of my life. Maybe I should have thought about it more. I had assumed they would revert to the original line-up, especially after losing the Test. I grabbed hold of Goochie after the meeting and told him I thought it was ridiculous.

Goochie lost his battle with the prawn and dropped out just before the start. Richard Blakey came in. People said I was gutted by that – not true. The night before, I was angry. But this switch was the right thing to do. It was asking Stewie too much to open, keep wicket and captain the side. I congratulated Dick; we were rooming together. Maybe my chat with Fletch had counted against me. Vishakhapatnam was an indication of the way things were

going, but I was much more concerned about the way I
was batting. I didn't need the hassle of being involved in
selection. I enjoyed my chess matches with Embers; I think
I beat him 19-18. He clears the board, I play my chess a bit
like my cricket. In those days, I felt the need to be batting
all the time. I'm easy about missing a match before a Test
now. I am always disappointed missing out. I wasn't even
used as one of the four substitute fielders. I'm not a bad
fielder. I just sat and watched.

India hit their highest score against England on home soil
– 560 for 6 – and England again failed to save the
follow-on, this time by 75 runs. They failed to make India
bat again by 22 runs, despite Lewis's attacking maiden
Test hundred. Smith, opening for the first time, scored 56,
but the other five front-line batsmen contributed a total of
34 runs. The Indian spinners took nine wickets in the first
innings and eight in the second as England crashed to
their heaviest ever defeat against India. It was clear that
the inexperience of most of England's batsmen and bowlers on these wickets was a decisive factor. Because of the
cancellation of the previous tour, only Emburey, Gatting
and Gooch had been on a senior tour to India before.

Now India were on a roll and England were on a
downhill slide. The Bombay Test went to the home side
by an innings and 15 runs, after England batted first and
scored 347, which included Hick's first Test century in his
22nd innings. England had become the first side to lose
every match of a Test series in India. Much was made of
the Atherton–Stewart run-out mix-up in the first session.
Both batsmen had been stranded at the bowler's end, and
there was a rather undignified effort by both to get back
to that crease while the stumps were broken at the other
end. There was an uneasy silence and little eye-contact
between the two as umpire Venkat decided which of
them was out. It was Stewart who went, but Venkat had

got it wrong. Atherton, who had been the non-striker, should have departed. The press had a field day.

England's poor form had not only thrown doubts on Gooch's future as leader but also opened up the captaincy debate again. Alec Stewart was linked closely with Gooch and the 'work ethic', which was going out of fashion as England started losing. Being closely linked with this management set-up was certainly not a charge that could be labelled against Atherton. Gatting, too, was back in the shake-up, the compromise and short-term candidate if the two youngsters did not measure up. The Bombay run-out was perceived as evidence of the tension between Gooch's two vice-captains. Atherton denies this; so does Stewart. It came towards the end of a miserable tour in which nobody had lived up to expectations. All that could go wrong, on and off the field, had. After seven weeks of the worst cricket inactivity of his life, the last thing Atherton needed was a stupid and senseless run-out. India's record score against England at home lasted only 10 days. This time, with a Kambli double hundred, the scoreboard reached 591. Prabhakar quickly removed Stewart, Gooch and Atherton, and England had no way back at 34 for 3. They crumbled on the fourth morning. India's spinners had claimed 46 wickets; England's took 17 and eight of those went to Hick, who topped the England averages and was the only touring bowler to take more than four wickets. England were a beaten side and looked like one at the presentation ceremony. Back at the hotel, Gooch revealed that he was in no state to make a decision about whether he wanted to carry on as captain against Australia in the summer.

ATHERTON
I got picked for the third Test because 'Harvey' was ill. The Bombay run-out was just a cock-up. I shouted 'No' – Stewie was looking at the ball. Suddenly, he gets into view

and we are both at the same end. I was standing outside my ground. The umpire hadn't noticed. I wandered back in. Stewie stretched for it. I don't remember the lack of eye-contact. I have never watched the incident again. We got walloped. They were a much better side than us, but they got ridiculous runs.

England returned to the one-day series, which meant another period on the sidelines for Atherton. There seemed little method to the England madness, and the folly of having selected one-day players for a Test tour was plain for all to see. (Two years later, England were criticised for *not* taking limited-overs specialists to Australia.) Atherton returned to his chess challenge against John Emburey. England took a 3-1 lead in the one-day series, before losing twice at Gwalior. Gooch headed for home as planned. England, under Stewart, headed for Sri Lanka. With Gooch gone, Atherton was the ready-made replacement at the top of the one-day order. He was not called upon – Lewis opened with Smith in the final tour international at Morawatu. The visitors gave one of their most inept performances in recent years, losing by eight wickets with almost 15 overs to spare.

Atherton was relieved to be on an aircraft flying home the next day. Being omitted from that game remains just about the worst cricket indignity he has suffered in his life. Both the one-day games, and the Test in between, were lost. Atherton did at least play in the Test, in which England went down by five wickets after scoring 380 in the first innings. Smith hit a century after opening with Atherton, who only managed 13 and 2. His first-innings lbw looked as though the ball had hit him outside the line, but that was the story of his tour. The TCCB held a two-day meeting into the disastrous tour results. Dexter said: 'We will do what we consider necessary to enhance the team's appearance and image. We have been asked to

Atherton's mum and dad (*left*), Wendy and Alan, on the day of their son's elevation to the England captaincy. Atherton, after posing at Lord's (*previous page*), was soon back at Manchester Grammar School again (*below*) for the cameras (*Allsport/Ben Radford*).

Atherton, aged 12, listens closely to Lancashire coach John Savage at Old Trafford.

Atherton receives the Cricket Writers' Young Cricketer of the Year award from the club's chairman and *Sunday Times* cricket correspondent, Robin Marlar *(Patrick Eagar)*.

Atherton is the proud possessor of one of the safest pairs of hands in cricket. These two catches are from the 1990 Edgbaston victory against New Zealand, Atherton's first success in his fifth Test. Removing John Bracewell (*above*) at third slip off Devon Malcolm and (*below*) diving to dismiss Sir Richard Hadlee in his final Test appearance as Eddie Hemmings collected his best England bowling figures (*both Patrick Eagar*).

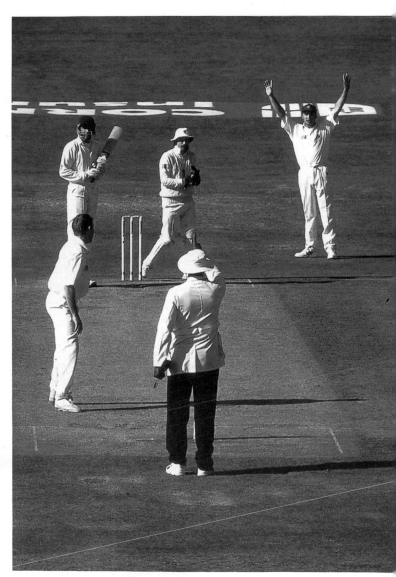

At one time there were high hopes that Atherton's leg-spin bowling would create an impact at international level. His back trouble put paid to that, although Atherton was more than delighted to claim Pakistan captain and sometime Old Trafford team-mate Wasim Akram in the 1996 Headingley Test. It was the first time Atherton had bowled for his country in 50 Tests (*Patrick Eagar*).

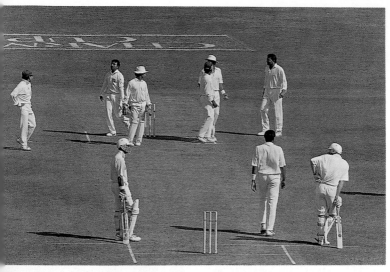

Atherton stranded at the same end as Alec Stewart (*above*) during the Bombay Test and troubled 1992-93 India tour. Wrongly, Stewart was sent on his way. Atherton's gutsiest innings is ended on 99 as South African Brian McMillan (*below*) takes a return catch at Headingley in the Test following the 'dirt-in-the-pocket' uproar (*both Patrick Eagar*).

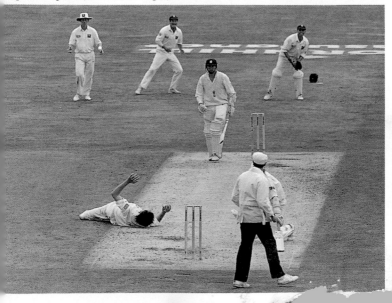

Atherton cannot believe the ball has rolled back and hit his stumps at Lord's in 1993 as Australians Shane Warne and Ian Healy celebrate (*Patrick Eagar*).

Lancashire and Old Trafford have provided Atherton with valuable support over his 20-year connection with the county. Success continues to elude the Red Rose in the championship, although Lancashire are once again English cricket's Cup Kings. Atherton in action during the 1990 Benson and Hedges final *(above, right)*, his first Lord's trophy. Surrey were the victims of Lancashire's fighting spirit at The Oval in 1993 when the home side lost nine wickets for 18 runs when needing 25 for victory in the Benson and Hedges second round clash. Fairbrother and Atherton *(below)* show the smiles of victors *(both Patrick Eagar)* and the pair also look happy *(above, left)* after their 364-run record partnership in 1990, The Oval again the venue, Surrey again on the receiving end.

reconsider the whole matter of the team's dress code. We want to see them smart in appearance at all times. We will be looking at the whole matter of people's facial hair.' Robin Smith had been involved in a bust-up with a photographer who was peering into the England dressing-room to get more pictures of the team looking less than smart. It was publicity pictures which found their way into the national press that had started all the trouble.

ATHERTON
What we should have been copping for was the cricket we were playing. We wore only what had been provided by the Board. The guys riding around on bicycles just given them at the presentation ceremony was wrong. It wasn't fair to criticise us for our appearance on our arrival at Calcutta. After 13 hours on a train and arriving at the station at dawn, you are going to look shabby. It was all part and parcel of losing. If we had won the Test, not too much would have been said. Originally, I understood why I wasn't in the one-day side. I couldn't get going and got out to an indifferent shot in the Sri Lanka Test. Then they opened with Lewis in the one-dayer. What was the point, at that stage? I came back no nearer to doing what I set out to do.

As the team headed for home, the *Sun* back-page head-line said: 'In deepest, darkest Africa, *SunSport* finds a team that England can beat. Hopefully . . .' Underneath was a map of Africa, with Zimbabwe coloured in red. Four winters later, the paper's theory was unsuccessfully put to the test.

Gooch had said at the end of the Indian leg: 'Everyone knows there's going to be a new England captain this year. It's merely a question of whether it's now or at the end of the summer.' When Fletcher had been asked who

Stewart's main rivals to succeed Gooch were, he cited Gatting and the 'A' team captain Martyn Moxon. The tour which Atherton had hoped would consolidate his return to the Test scene had merely left an enormous question mark over his international future.

CHAPTER SEVEN

Out Of The Ashes

Michael Atherton's life changed for ever on Wednesday 28 July 1993. Ted Dexter rang him in the Lake District to tell him that the job of England cricket captain was his. This was the day many believed to be his sporting destiny. He was 25 years and 124 days old. Atherton had lived with the prediction that he would one day lead his country for nearly a decade. Two years after his Test debut, this Lancastrian was made vice-captain to Graham Gooch. But his apparently effortless rise to the top job began to go wrong at the end of that summer, and when England lost the opening Ashes Test of 1993 on Atherton's home patch, his scores of 19 and 25, on top of what had happened in India and Sri Lanka almost cost him his place. One Test later, he had re-established himself as the man to take over from Gooch; and a month later, Atherton was the new England captain.

England went into the Ashes series having lost five Tests – against Pakistan, India and Sri Lanka – in a row. Gooch's personal achievements no longer motivated and inspired the side as they had in his early days as captain. To no one's surprise, Atherton was missing from the Texaco series, which England lost 3-0, and he was concerned about making enough runs to ensure his place in the Cornhill series. He opened with centuries against Oxford University and Durham, and there would have been another against Cambridge University had a back spasm not forced him to quit nine runs short. Atherton was intent on a new start to his England career and what better place to begin than at Old Trafford? He felt confident, positive and ready to prove that the problems of the last two years were behind him. Atherton in fact had made starts at Old Trafford, sharing opening partnerships with Gooch of 71 and 73. He was annoyed that he failed to capitalise on that. The match was notable for the first appearance in England of Shane Warne and that 'wonder ball' that did for Gatting. Gooch made 65 and 137, but no other England front-line batsman scored more than 34. On a good track, the home side went down by 179 runs. It was the beginning of the end for Gooch. He had been angry when Dexter appointed him as captain for only half the summer and had told the chairman that if things were going badly, he would not hang around. Gooch felt that, after the problems in the sub-continent, England would be best served by a united front to send the right sort of signals to the Australians. Lord Ted had different ideas, until after Old Trafford. Then Gooch was named captain for the summer. Gooch accepted, with the public proviso that his continuing leadership depended on England improving.

That was not the case at Lord's. Australia put the game out of sight with a massive first-innings 632 for 4 declared. Taylor, Slater and Boon hit centuries, with Mark Waugh making 99. England were bowled out for 205 and 365. Those were the unlikely circumstances that saw Atherton establish himself as a Test star again and force his way to the front of the queue to succeed Gooch. Atherton hit 80 on Saturday, accumulated while wickets tumbled at the other end. He was dismissed by Warne when an attempted drive rebounded off his foot onto the stumps. Smith, who became the first victim of the third umpire in a Test in England, was next-highest scorer with 22. Atherton was back at the wicket the next afternoon to play his best Test innings since the tour of Australia three winters earlier. He and Gatting took England to 173 for 1 to provide real hope of escaping, and Atherton was hitting the ball far more sweetly than the day before. He had reached 97 when he clipped Border towards the mid-wicket boundary. It did not have legs, but that did not matter – Merv Hughes was in pursuit and there were always three runs there. The problems began when Atherton set off for the third. Gatting started, hesitated and then sent him back. Before Atherton knew it, he was crawling on his hands and knees, vainly struggling to beat Hughes's throw and Ian Healy's smart take. The drama unfolded as if in slow motion as Atherton's predicament was painfully obvious for all to see. He was out for 99 and England were back in trouble. Australia's spinners completed the job after lunch on the fifth day and speculation intensified about Gooch's future as England went 2-0 down. The media, generally, were in agreement that Atherton had come of age. He had handled himself well in adverse circumstances. Hughes had given him a real working-over with ball and tongue, and Atherton had reacted with a smile or nothing at all. He also said all the right things when he met the press on Sunday night at Lord's to discuss the run-out. The fault had been Gatting's, but Atherton refused to apportion blame: 'It was a fairly disastrous occurrence, but it's no good pointing the finger at anyone. I was wearing a pair of boots which had half-rubbers, half-studs on the sole, and I slipped on the grass, the juicy bit, alongside the wicket. Once I slipped the first time, I knew I wasn't going to make it. There was nothing I could do. I wasn't nervous at all in the nineties and was thinking of still being there at the close and going on to a really big score.' There was genuine sympathy and understanding for Atherton after his efforts that day. The England chairman of selectors provoked a different response when he tried to explain the sixth Test defeat of the year: 'We may be under the wrong star sign. Venus may be in juxtaposition with the wrong planet.' Gooch had offered to resign, but Fletcher persuaded him to stay on. Gooch had made his decision, though: once the Ashes remained with Australia, he was calling time.

ATHERTON

Goochie batted magnificently at Old Trafford. The rest of us were pretty wet. I certainly felt it was touch-and-go over whether I would survive to Lord's. I knew I had to get runs there. It was a career-saving game for me – and it put me right back in the captaincy frame, especially after Gatting was dropped. McDermott was not playing at Lord's.

Run out for 99 – freak dismissal. I thought it was going for four. We both started for the third and he sent me back. I slipped, and it was all like a slow-motion dream, or rather nightmare. It's like your lace snapping or not being able to get your pads on in time – the usual recurring agonies. The run-out showed a lot about the intensity of the Australian play. The agony was that the way Gatt and I were playing, they were not going to bowl us out. Because of the winter, I wasn't thinking about the captaincy. I knew Goochie was not going to tour. At Lord's, I thought he was going to resign – I saw Ted, Micky and Fletch all talking to him. I remember showering with Gatt and him saying, 'I think we'll have a new captain next Test.'

Atherton refused to get drawn publicly into the speculation. He reminded enquiring pressmen that he had been one of the players favourite to be dropped after Old Trafford. Now, one Test later, everyone wanted to make him captain. Atherton was pleased about his runs at Lord's, but that had nothing to do with the captaincy. After almost two years, he felt part of the England Test team again. He scored another century in Lancashire's ill-tempered 111-run victory at Derbyshire. The home side were 243 for 2 with John Morris on 151 when Wasim Akram took 6 for 11 in 49 balls. Derbyshire sent the match ball to Lord's for inspection. No further action ensued, but the matter was not closed. The bad feeling between the teams exploded during the Benson and Hedges Cup final a fortnight later. Chris Adams took exception to being hit by a Wasim full toss. Umpire Barrie Meyer warned the bowler, but it did not end there – the matter was discussed in a more physical manner during the lunch-break. Atherton hit 54 in reply, but Derbyshire were victors at Lord's by six runs.

The changes threatened after Old Trafford were made after Lord's. Atherton had moved into the safety zone, but Gatting, Hick, Foster, Lewis and Tufnell were dropped. Ilott, Lathwell, McCague and Thorpe all made their Test debuts. Gooch moved down to No. 5 to accommodate Lathwell, whose inclusion appeared to have more to do with the press than the selectors. Thorpe's debut century, the first since Frank Hayes twenty years earlier, helped England to end the run of seven successive defeats. They even threatened to win on the last day, with Australia 115 for 6 at tea. England's new opening partnership did not do well. Atherton had not been happy with the bat-pad catch off Warne that ended his first innings on the Thursday, and two days later he was given out caught down the leg-side for 9. Hughes was the bowler. Atherton was reluctant to leave at the sight of Barrie Meyer's raised finger again and gazed towards Ken Palmer at square leg. Meyer initially had not checked with Palmer to see if the ball had carried. He now consulted him and Atherton was on his way. The Aussies were not happy at Atherton's behaviour and let him know in time-honoured manner. Hughes kept looking at Atherton and jabbed his thumb in the direction of the dressing-room. Atherton, in a way that was to become familiar, mouthed his disapproval and shook his head on the way off. Fletcher attempted to play down the incident: 'Atherton played a poor shot, but stood there because he thought the ball did not carry. He is fully entitled to do that.'

This incident did not affect the current thinking – the England management had identified and decided on a new captain. Gooch was convinced that Atherton was the man. So was team manager Keith Fletcher. Gatting was out of the side. That would not have prevented his promotion, but Gooch felt there was little point in selecting a stop-gap, and there had been little evidence that Gatting was capable of producing the volume of runs he himself achieved when he was captain. Stewart, through no fault of his own, was tainted with failure because of his role as Gooch's vice-captain the previous winter. His two Tests in charge, at Madras and Colombo, had ended in defeat, and he had been handed the wicket-keeping gloves again. But Gooch and Fletcher were looking at the positives. Atherton was the cricketer who could take England forward on a long-term basis. England's new captain would have to pick up the pieces of this Ashes series before facing the West Indies in the Caribbean. That intimidating schedule worried his friend at Lancashire, Neil Fairbrother: 'It would be an error to throw him in against the West Indies. Opening the batting and leading the side is asking too much. The selectors have got to give the job to someone else this winter. Cricketers don't come any more talented than our overseas star, Wasim Akram, but his first time as Pakistan captain was in the Caribbean recently. He'll tell you how tough that was.'

Allan Border gave a clear indication of the task at hand with an unbeaten double hundred at Headingley. Australia surpassed their Lord's total as he and Steve Waugh put on 232 runs for the fifth wicket. Atherton and Gooch, still down the order, took England to 158 for 3 before the heir-apparent shouldered arms to Paul Reiffel. A collapse followed and England trailed by 453 on the first innings. Following on, they were 131 for 1 with Atherton at the crease when Ian Healy appealed for a smart stumping off Tim May. It was a borderline decision. Without recourse to the third umpire, Atherton would have probably survived. As it was, Barrie Meyer took quite a time watching the replays before Atherton was sent on his way. He had batted for seven hours in the match and was now the firm favourite for the vacancy that would be created when Gooch called it a day. The Test was lost, the Ashes were gone and Gooch kept his promise: 'It is the best way forward. The team might benefit from fresh ideas, a fresh approach, someone else to look up to.'

As captain, Gooch had performed heroically with the bat, nowhere more so than at Headingley where his centuries had inspired England to victories over the West Indies and Pakistan, but eight defeats in England's last nine Tests was too much of a handicap for anyone. Dexter had not been present when the captain resigned. Gooch had telephoned the chairman of selectors to tell him of his decision and had been asked to delay the announcement for a day. But Gooch felt there had been enough speculation about the captaincy. If he left Headingley as England captain, the press would have a field day. They did – at Dexter's inability to board a plane and fly to Leeds to support the captain who had served him so loyally. Dexter's explanation was that 'I was out on the golf course. When things go badly, the golf course is a good place to be. It gets me away from the hubbub so I can have time to think. I like to think. I like a few balls. It helps me relax. I did attend the first three days at Headingley, but we usually do rather better when I'm not there. I wasn't aware that Graham was going to resign until it was too late to be at Headingley.'

Dexter then viewed the future: 'The names in the frame are obvious. Alec Stewart and Mike Atherton are the front runners from the current team. But Mike Gatting has been in the team recently and has proved a successful captain of Middlesex.' Gatting, of course, was known to have been Dexter's choice as captain in 1989 when he became chairman, but the media were not fooled. Atherton was the popular and informed choice the minute Gooch resigned. With Lancashire taking on the Australians, Atherton had planned a break in the Lake District with his girlfriend Suzie. Dexter's phone-call on Tuesday put an end to that. The new England captain turned up at Neil Fairbrother's house with a bottle of champagne: 'I have some good news.' It was not such good news for another team-mate, Graham Lloyd, son of coach David. He is the resident dressing-room bookie. To attract any business, the local lad had had to be offered at 5-4 on, very generous odds given that Ladbrokes' best price was 3-1 on. Atherton took the shuttle to London on Wednesday morning. The press conference was called less than 48 hours after the Ashes had been lost. It should have been Atherton's big moment, but Dexter, with his usual tact, managed to upstage his latest appointment. 'We were unanimous except for Dad,' he announced, referring to Alec Stewart's father Micky. 'Dad had plenty to say and he was loyal to the boy as we would have expected him to be.' The media had another field day.

ATHERTON
I felt secure with England at Trent Bridge for the first time in a couple of years. We looked a revitalised side there.

Goochie told me he was going at the end of the second day at Leeds. It was not a massive surprise by then. We had a drink at the Fox and Hounds. Now that he had made up his mind, he was much more relaxed. I didn't realise I was the man until Ted rang me up in the Lakes. I'd booked dinner and a room; I got to neither, I went round to see Harvey. I remember my heart beating a bit in bed – well, what do I do here? I was very nervous initially. I never asked what powers I had, I was never going to turn it down. I also phoned Mum and Dad. I was having Lancashire's game against the Aussies off. I'd been thinking, 'What is the side missing most? What does it need to make it successful?' That was my initial train of thought; one or two obvious questions which I couldn't answer. I had lunch with Ted and Fletch. Ted seemed an amiable bloke. He had a wide-ranging role. There was the general agreement that things were pretty bad. At my first selection meeting, one early question concerned Goochie. I was told that was totally in my hands. But as he always gives a hundred per cent, was the only one making runs and was now much more relaxed, for me it was never an issue.

Atherton was circumspect and diplomatic at his first press conference as captain: 'I see my task as getting the players to perform to their best. That's what's been lacking in the England team for the past two years. People have been talking about getting young players in the side and planning for the future. Well, the future starts now. I will take full responsibility for performances and hope to stop the rot. I'm going to be my own man – I have my own ideas. Graham Gooch carried the can for the players' performances. He is a good bloke and I felt very sorry for him at Headingley. There's a lot of nonsense talked about me not being in favour of the work ethic. I'll make the same demands as Graham Gooch when it comes to hard work. In the end, I think he was quite relieved to get rid of it. He drove me back to the team hotel during the Headingley Test and told me he was going to pack it in, which was quite a sad moment. He was very proud to be captain and gave it everything he had.' Atherton said that he had 'slept like a baby' after being told the news. Dexter admitted that five other candidates had been discussed – Stewart, Gatting, Derbyshire's Kim Barnett, Yorkshire's Martyn Moxon and Glamorgan's Hugh Morris – in a debate lasting two and a half hours. 'The two criteria,' added Dexter, 'were mental toughness and tactical awareness.' Such was Dexter's tactical awareness that he resigned during Atherton's first Test in charge. Atherton heard the news with everybody else over the public address system at Edgbaston.

Atherton was the hottest sports item for the rest of the week. Reporters went back to Briscoe Lane Infants and Junior School and Manchester Grammar. They talked to teachers, fellow students, classmates, groundsmen and mentors. Atherton had had time to gather his thoughts when Mike Selvey of the *Guardian* tracked him down the next day at Old Trafford where Lancashire were playing the Australians. Atherton was in jeans and moccasins – not totally the fault of British Airways, who had mislaid his luggage – and was pleased to be back on familiar territory in comfortable garb. The shape of things to come was predicted by the Australian spinner Tim May. He had drawn a droopy Gooch moustache on the new captain's smiling face in one of the morning papers. Atherton smiled again: 'It would be easy to be intimidated, but I'm trying not to. When things settle down, I hope I'm going to be allowed to settle on cricket matters. At the moment we are being beaten by what seems to be the better side. But the other side of the coin is that we've nothing to lose. It was there when the new side was picked for Trent Bridge, and that was converted into a decent miracle. Miracles though? I'm a bit sceptical about that. My realism isn't obscured by optimism. There's no magic wand to be waved, but we have the potential to play better than we have. I've been told my body language isn't particularly good and it's something I've got to improve on. It is just a question of bucking up and doing it. But I don't say it will be easy. Graham was actually very enthusiastic about his cricket and conveyed that verbally. Irrespective of style – and we should never lose sight of the fact that it is an entertainment – Test cricket is about toughness and temperament. It's about the Gooches and the Boons and the Borders, people who sell themselves dearly. Taking on this job was an opportunity I couldn't refuse. Now, the publicity is the downside, and it's true to say I may not be comfortable with the spotlight. But it's there and I'll cope. The job carries material benefits, and of course that's good. But make no mistake, this is about cricket. The material things are OK, but I'm not in it for the kudos, you know.'

Atherton was the 71st England captain, the sixth from Lancashire – the first for 41 years – and the 34th from Oxbridge. The last seven England captains had all made a losing start to their new careers; Atherton made it eight. It was an eight-wicket trouncing, suggesting that little had changed with the new incumbent. Atherton was bitterly disappointed. England had been undone by a wicket that appeared to suit Warne and May perfectly. John Emburey was summoned to Birmingham on the Tuesday. Atherton had no desire to bat last on this track. The new captain, as the old one had done, led the way by batting through the first one and a half sessions for 72. When he was bowled by a delivery from Reiffel which kept very low, England were in familiar territory at 156 for 6. Help came from Emburey, who played Warne more cleverly and better than most. England needed some luck. They did not enjoy it when Australia were 80 for 4 in reply to their 276 and Steve Waugh was facing his second delivery. Stewart failed to make the stumping off Peter Such. Earlier, England had gone up for a slip catch off Waugh's twin, Mark, before he had scored.

Atherton's new high profile was evident the next day. Papers reported a 'snub', claiming that England's captain had not applauded Mark Waugh's century. The Waugh twins added 153 for the fifth wicket and England were 132 runs adrift after Healy dug in. Their frustration was evident. Stewart and Thorpe were rebuked after a bat-pad catch from Hughes was refused by umpire David Shepherd. Stewart, behind the stumps, had immediately rushed to congratulate the bowler. Thorpe hurled the ball to the ground. ICC referee Clive Lloyd said: 'I will note Stewart's behaviour in my report. If it happens again, I will be taking it up with the England team.' Fletcher added: 'Thorpe showed dissent. I have spoken to him already. No further action is planned. I've also had a word with Alec. But I feel he was only trying to congratulate Such.'

In the second innings, Atherton went early when Border claimed a catch at silly point off Warne. Once again, Atherton stood his ground while umpire John Hampshire consulted with Shepherd at square-leg. Gooch and Smith prevented any further mishaps on Saturday night with England finishing 43 runs behind. Thorpe's 60 was the highlight of the fourth day, with Emburey again difficult to dislodge. England's spinner gave them a flicker of hope on the final morning, but Australia's 12 for 2 was as good as it got for Atherton. The announcement of Dexter's resignation was the only other moment in the morning session that brought a loud cheer from the Edgbaston crowd. Atherton was rather surprised to learn the news in this way. The chairman of selectors had given him no hint. Atherton bit his lip at the after-match press conference: 'I do have a reaction, but I'd like to keep it to myself.' The new captain merely emphasised his strategy for the future: 'Identify young players with two things, talent and temperament, and then show faith in them.' Dexter's record in his 'Reign of Pain', as the *Sun* described it, was nine victories and 21 losses in 44 Tests in charge. Atherton had no idea who would take over from Dexter, but was glad that the current selection-panel would pick the touring team. That way, by the time the new man arrived, Atherton would have established his credentials and style as captain. He had reckoned without Raymond Illingworth.

ATHERTON
The green seamer at Edgbaston turned out to be a bunsen. We had to send for a second spinner. We started well and thought we'd got rid of Mark Waugh. There was a huge cheer from the popular side when the loudspeaker announced Ted's resignation. I thought it was a bit odd that he hadn't told me. Like the seven previous captains, I started with a defeat. That's not a surprising statistic – changes are not made because things are going well. You dream about doing it. Then you've done it. Getting runs was a bonus, showed that I could cope with the pressures of the job a little. I didn't try to fire the boys up, it's not my style. I aimed to lead by example.

Atherton failed in his attempt to persuade Gooch to change his mind and travel to the Caribbean. But his intention to take a young squad was supported by his predecessor: 'I don't think the West Indies is a place where experience means a lot. You need people who can play a particular type of bowling.' Atherton was lucky to have Fraser fit again – Gooch had been without his most reliable bowler for two and a half years. Fraser in fact made an earlier-than-planned return when Martin Bicknell failed a fitness test at The Oval. Atherton was more confident of not being sabotaged by the Test wicket this time. Malcolm, Hick and Tufnell were also recalled, as was Ramprakash after Thorpe broke a thumb in the nets on the morning of the match. Smith had been the man dropped, but he was down with Hampshire in Swansea and Ramprakash was just across London. Atherton had been Smith's house-guest the previous weekend, and it was rumoured that the captain had the unpleasant task of breaking the news to his host that he was being dropped for the first time in 45 Tests over breakfast on Sunday morning. England's batting line-up looked formidable with Stewart at No. 6 and Ramprakash to follow. Atherton called correctly and England went on the attack. The positive attitude cost wickets, but England scored quickly and closed the day at 353 for 7. Atherton was one of four in the top six to reach fifty. Hick top-scored with 80. At one stage, England looked like batting again on the second evening as Australia struggled to 196 for 8, but Healy, not for the first time, helped the tourists past the 300-mark. England, who had been 143 for 1 in the first innings, reached 157 for 1 in the second. Gooch had passed Gower to become England's leading run-scorer in Tests when he off-drove Reiffel to the boundary just before lunch. Atherton was caught in the covers and walked off making gestures with his bat. Nothing to do with the umpire this time, just annoyance at himself for not playing the shot properly. Wickets tumbled once Gooch had gone, then Ramprakash showed his class to give England a lead of 390. In the previous 25 days of Test cricket that summer, a total of 41 minutes had been lost to the weather. Two hours were lost on Sunday. The Australians went into the final day with all wickets intact. England were perhaps fortunate to claim two of the early wickets that left the tourists at 30 for 3, but Atherton was not complaining – little had gone England's way all summer. The first England Test victory over Australia for more than six and a half years arrived just after five o'clock. Fraser, Malcolm and Watkin, as they had in the first innings, claimed all the wickets. Malcolm has rarely bowled quicker, Watkin matched his six wickets in the game and Fraser, 5 for 87 in a fairytale return, was named Man of the Match. Atherton, who had been confirmed as captain for the West Indies trip during this Test, could only watch enviously as Border was presented with a replica of the Ashes, but this emphatic victory was a real bonus in his second game. England had played with pride and passion, and it gave Atherton the clout to pick the winter squad he wanted. Also, he was now heading to the cauldron of the Caribbean not only as a new Test captain, but a winning one as well.

ATHERTON

I got Hickie back in the side and told him he would be batting at No. 3. That was to give him confidence. Actually, I didn't tell Robin Smith over breakfast that he was dropped. It made a nice tale, I know, but I told him at the ground. I assured him that if I had anything to do with it, he would be going to the West Indies. Gower was the other issue, but I went for Hick instead. My bit of luck was Angus. Ted must take the credit for that. As captain, I don't see a lot of cricket around the country. Ted thought he was ready. I said, 'If you think that, let's get him in.' Thorpe broke his thumb. Smith and Gower were in Swansea. Fletch wanted Gatting, Stewie and I wanted Ramps. We went in with Fraser, Malcolm and Watkin. They got all 20 wickets – none had played in a Test that summer. Devon bowled quick on the fourth evening. We broke the stranglehold. It was the first time Gus and I had beaten the Aussies. It was a very special day. The crowd got bigger and bigger. For a new, young captain, it was a very uplifting experience.

CHAPTER EIGHT

Back From The Dead

Atherton's first tour in charge began and ended in Antigua. The tour had looked close to collapse as it entered the finishing straight, after Atherton's young side were traumatised by Hurricane Curtly in Trinidad. Chasing 193 for victory, England's hopes of keeping the series alive there were blown away in 15 overs on the fourth evening as the tourists collapsed to 40 for 8. The next morning, England avoided matching their lowest-ever Test score, 45 at Sydney in 1887, by a single run. Atherton and Fletcher refused to condemn their 'young guns'. That public support, and private cajoling, inspired England to the first Test victory in Barbados by any visiting team for 59 years. Brian Lara grabbed the final Test glory in Antigua, but England finished with their heads held high and Atherton had proved himself a resilient leader.

Atherton was to receive a false first impression of tour selection meetings. England's captain found a panel of like minds, and a few hours later he departed with the squad that he had wanted in the first place. Dexter was leaving, but he, Dennis Amiss and Fletcher felt anyway that Atherton's youth policy was the way forward. 'When the selectors of a year ago reflect back,' Atherton commented, 'they may admit to making a mistake in not picking Gower. But when we were picking a squad for the West Indies, it seemed a little daft to try and make up for any errors that might have gone before. Having been beaten by India and Australia, it seemed to me that the best way then was to go forward – and that has to be with a young side. One with the potential to become a good Test side in two to three years' time. Neither was it entirely my own decision. All of us – myself, Keith Fletcher and Dennis Amiss – thrashed out the general policy before we sat down, and were totally in favour of a more youthful approach for this tour.'

ATHERTON

Fletch, Amiss and I were the three main selectors and we met privately before the bigger meeting. That win over Australia had given me the confidence to think I could do the job. I hope the touring squad reflected that spirit. We talked about policy first, what exactly were we looking to do. Maybe I was being rather arrogant, but I was working on the premise that I was going to be doing this job for a while.

We decided against an old hand. If Gooch had been available, he would have gone. We went for young batters who had not experienced failure against the West Indies before. I wanted guys who were going to be gutsy and up front. We left out Suchie, who had been our most successful spinner against Australia. Maybe that was a mistake with so many left-handers in their side. Lamb was the senior player considered. Gatt had come back against India and not really got a run for England for a long time. In the end, we went for youth. Basically, I got the squad I wanted.

After a Lancashire trip to St Lucia, I settled down to the twice-weekly sessions at Lilleshall. There was also a week outside at Barrington's (I'm not a great lover of indoor nets). The West Indies were still the world champions and touring the Caribbean was still the toughest assignment in cricket. I wasn't worried about my 1991 failure. I had played badly, but I had also been struggling with injury. It would not be true to say that I wasn't totally unconcerned, but I was backing myself. There's a holiday environment in the Caribbean. I don't mind that. I want a side that works and plays hard, I don't want a boring side. It's about getting the balance right. I'd get angry if players mucked around in the middle of a game.

We built up a good spirit in the first fortnight. I was ill with tonsillitis, and I don't think I went out until the tenth night of the tour. I was making myself practise in the day and was wiped out by the evening.

The West Indies Board had based the tourists in three of the Caribbean's top spots for the first five weeks of the tour. The schedule took them to St Kitts, back to Antigua and then on to Barbados. The England party worked hard and played hard. (The thousands of watching British supporters, whose presence would have curtailed such social activity, had not yet arrived.) Had such excesses been apparent on the field, Atherton would have laid down the law. He was not happy when the two opening games were not classified as first-class. That had nothing to do with the captain scoring the first century of the tour – the status and the knowledge that figures will enter the record books concentrate the minds of all cricketers. England beat an Antiguan XI by 203 runs, with Stewart and Hick also hitting hundreds. Ramprakash scored 136 in the draw with a St Kitts & Nevis XI. The Leeward Islands, who were to take the Red Stripe trophy, lost by seven wickets without five of their Test stars as Atherton top-scored with 77. His good form continued with his 30th first-class century, against Barbados, before the internationals began. It said much for Atherton's form and disposition that his disastrous series against the West Indies in England was soon forgotten and never an issue. After missing Gooch's tour to the Caribbean four years earlier, first through selection and then because of injury, the captain went into his tour with a total of 79 Test runs against the West Indies at an average of 8.75. His ability and temperament were never questioned, though.

Atherton was already suffering the traditional problems of captaining a tour in the Caribbean, even though the home pacemen had not yet bowled a ball in anger. The most ridiculous inconvenience was caused by the sunburnt head of Chris Lewis, who later clashed with Fletcher in Barbados. Atherton's comments on that lapse were unprintable. Caddick's promising start was curtailed by shin-splints, while a broken hand, sustained while batting, kept Fraser out of the first Test. Atherton prepared to lead England for the first time in a one-day international. It was only his 11th such appearance and his first for almost three years after spending 29 matches on the sidelines. But again, his role was never an issue or distraction. England's 61-run victory was built on his solid 86.

ATHERTON
Caddick's shin-splints is one of those things that happens. Lewis's sunstroke was ridiculous – his own stupidity. I don't think he was fined; I would fine him now. It caused him to miss a game. The injury to Gus was a big blow, as it kept him out of the first Test. The tour got off to a flier. The Windies had problems, there was some dispute about pay. They arrived in dribs and drabs in Barbados. We beat them well. It was one of those days when everything I did worked. Catches went to hand and I got a few runs myself.

The tour began to go wrong in Jamaica, and Atherton must take some of the blame for selection that left

England exposed. The tourists made six changes to the Test side that had won so well at the end of the summer. That Test was six months back, but those available from The Oval should have been given another chance. Gooch and Such were not on the tour, and Fraser was injured. Ramprakash, Hussain and Watkin were the trio left out from that winning side. Tufnell, too, was unlucky. Thorpe, Maynard, Lewis and Igglesden were picked after indifferent starts to the tour. Atherton admitted afterwards that England had made too many unnecessary changes (it was a mistake repeated in Australia a year later).

Not that Atherton failed England on the park. He won the toss and England were 79 for 0 at lunch. Squandering good starts had been the major problem in the first month of the tour, though, and it cost England the first Test. They collapsed from 121 for 0 to 172 for 6. Kenny Benjamin's 6 for 66 left England 234 all out. The West Indies, after being 13 for 3, made 407 with over 300 of the runs coming from Arthurton, Lara and Adams. The match was lost on the third evening when England went in again. Stewart was run out, then Walsh set about roughing up Atherton. The England captain had been warned that he would be selected for special treatment – unsettling and unnerving the opposition leader is a favourite tactic of the West Indies. It was a battle Atherton knew was coming and he relished it. Walsh had him over a couple of times; he came up smiling. Atherton's dismay at getting out was all the more acute because Walsh was all but spent when one last desperate delivery flew up and found Atherton's edge. Smith and Maynard went cheaply and the tourists finished the day over 100 runs behind the West Indies with four key batsmen gone. Hick's 96, more runs than he had scored in the 1991 series, took the game into a fifth day, but it was Malcolm, the batsman, that grabbed the headlines. He was given a real going-over by

Walsh. Richie Richardson was off the field at the time and Desmond Haynes was in charge. The umpire at Walsh's end was Zimbabwe's Ian Robinson. Atherton has no objection to being peppered with any sort of fast bowling. He can protect himself – it was no secret that Malcolm could not. The England dressing-room were incensed as Robinson took no action, even when Malcolm was hit on the backside. Robinson later claimed that he was 'about to step in'. That did nothing to placate the tourists. It was ugly and did not do cricket or the West Indies any service. Formalities were concluded 10 minutes into the final day. England's loss was compounded a couple of days later when Malcolm flew home for a knee operation.

ATHERTON

We showed our inexperience. We were 121 for 0 in the first innings, they were 23 for 3. It was either the side's naivety, or mine. We simply did not make those positions pay. The battle with Courtney did a lot for my confidence. I didn't score big runs – in fact, 28 might not seem like much. It was a torrid spell, really fast. After I was out, I went and sat behind the arm. It was quick. I think Hickie and I received as torrid and fast a spell as I have ever faced. It's a West Indies ploy to put the opposing captain under pressure. I'd given my all. I was inches from the finishing line, it was Courtney's last over. I was disappointed, but it characterised the way I wanted to bat as captain. I want to take the quick stuff up front and on the chin. I was hit on the arm. I swore at myself. 'Keep your eye on the ball.' At that speed, you're thinking of nothing. Your mind is blank. Tunnel vision. You haven't time to be distracted. It's about watching the ball. It also helps the more you play with someone – Goochie, Stewie, Robin and Hickie. It's a partnership, especially when the quicks are on. As Geoffrey Boycott said, the way to play fast bowling is from the other end. I felt for Devon. Test cricket is a hard game.

> *It's about courage and being fearless. I would never moan,
> as a batsman, about any type of bowling. I can look after
> myself. Courtney was not to blame. The umpire should
> have stepped in. Courtney was bowling to hit Devon and
> by no stretch of the imagination was he capable of defend-
> ing himself. We didn't complain afterwards, either to the
> referee or the ICC, but Devon did not get the protection he
> deserved.*

England's tour now went into a sharp nose-dive. The
Jamaican one-day international was a reasonably close
affair, but the next one in St Vincent was not. Nothing
went right for Atherton and England; even winning the
toss proved unfortunate. After much confusing information about this scenic ground, Atherton invited the West
Indies to bat – and bat. Lara's 60 came in 41 deliveries
and Richardson's undefeated 52 in only 26. The home
side's total was 313; England did not manage to get
halfway there. Atherton, who had put Lewis at the top of
the order, was left stranded on 19. It was a dreadful
display, without a redeeming feature. The team effort
improved in Trinidad with a close defeat, which cost
them the one-day series, and a five-wicket win in the final
match.

Atherton's big worries before the Guyana Test were
Smith and the wayward bowlers. Smith was England's
premier batsman with Gooch gone. Atherton had marked
himself and Smith down as the two 400-plus run guaran-
tees in his squad. The hard-hitting South African, with a
proven track record against the West Indies, was one
worry the captain was supposed not to have. The management hoped that the Test series would inspire him out
of his early-tour slump, but scores of 0 and 2 showed the
problem was getting worse. Atherton had lost Malcolm.
Fraser was fit again, but Lewis was still keeping the
physio busy. He went for x-rays on his left ankle: no one

could quite identify the problem. Lewis did face one unfortunate distraction in his home town of Georgetown when one eager-beaver journalist 'discovered' that Lewis was actually two years older than he had claimed, a fact that affected other aspects of his background. That came as a shock to Lewis, who had thought himself the son of a local preacher. He was and is. The journalist had, remarkably, found another Christopher Clairmonte Lewis. The player was relieved, but Atherton was angry at the way one of his squad had been upset unnecessarily.

Ramprakash, Fraser and Salisbury replaced Maynard, Malcolm and Caddick. Atherton led the way; his side failed to follow. England's captain was surprised when Richardson asked the tourists to bat. Walsh removed Stewart and Ramprakash with two runs on the board before Atherton added 171 with Smith and 72 with Hick as England reached 245 for 3. Atherton's 144 deserved more than a final England total of 322. His seven-hour innings was the highest there by an Englishman since Hutton 40 years earlier. One of the benefits of scoring a century at the Bourda is being added to the roll of honour on a special board in the clubhouse. Atherton's name was soon joined by those of Lara and Adams. Lara was the inspiration behind the West Indies' 556 as England's bowlers were helpless to stem the flow of runs. In the second innings, Atherton went for a duck to become Ambrose's 200th Test wicket. Stewart apart, the batting folded and the West Indies were not required to bat again. England, as had happened in Jamaica, had started brightly and faded dramatically.

ATHERTON

I was surprised when Richie asked us to bat. It was a 400-plus wicket. We were 245 for 3. I played my best Test innings that day. Had we got to 400, we would not have lost. Lara was in full flow. On that small ground, he's devastating, and our bowlers struggled. We should probably have played Tuffers here.

The tour moved on to Trinidad, home of Lara. The Queen's Park Oval has been seen as the venue for English optimism in the Caribbean in recent years. It is the one place where the spinners can play a part and the pitch offers help to England's seamers. England were staying at the Trinidad Hilton, which is built on a hillside in Port-of-Spain (the lifts take you *down* to your room) and the first English supporters had begun to appear in strength. Caddick for Igglesden was the only England change. Richardson won the toss and did the unexpected again, deciding to bat. It looked a good decision as his side reached 158 for 1. Six wickets in the final session, however, evened up the contest. Batting was not easy. Atherton dug in for 48, but England's strong position on the second evening, 16 behind the West Indies, was due to an undefeated sixth-wicket stand of 69 between Thorpe and Russell. Thorpe was on his last chance after making just 50 runs in the first two Tests (Fletcher was determined that the Surrey left-hander would come good). Having secured a lead, England bowled well on the third day to go into the rest-day with the West Indies 143 for 5, a lead of only 57.

The Guyanese teenager Chanderpaul, who had made his debut in Guyana at the expense of Trinidad favourite Phil Simmons, was the home side's saviour with a half-century. The contest turned on a 60-run seventh-wicket stand between him and Winston Benjamin. Atherton could feel the match slipping away. Chanderpaul had offered two chances to Hick in the slips on 4 and 29. Just how dispirited England were soon became obvious as they came out to try and score the 194 runs needed for victory. Atherton and Stewart walked out with 15 overs remaining. Atherton knew England could not win the match that evening. They could lose it, though. Ambrose and Walsh would have two chances to make it count: that night and the next morning. Atherton would have preferred to lose no wickets by the close, but realistically, England's captain would have settled for a couple out.

The next hour entered cricket history and West Indies fast-bowling legend. Curtly Ambrose, even by his remarkable standards, produced a devastating spell that left England in tatters. He gave the West Indies the perfect start with the perfect delivery that jagged back into Atherton's pad. As intimidating as Ambrose was, the captain's dismissal sent England into nothing less than self-destruct mode. Ramprakash went after a crazy run-out, Hick and Smith offered little resistance and when Stewart lost his off stump, England were in ruins at 26 for 5. Ambrose was inspired. Walsh sneaked in to remove Salisbury, and Ambrose collected two more that night. England's dressing-room was a scene of desolation. By contrast, the Trinidad Oval was in carnival mood. Atherton, like his squad, was in a state of shock. Events on a cricket field, especially in a Test match, generally unfold slowly. The balance of power rarely does an 180-degree turn in a matter of minutes. Atherton's hopes of winning the Test had been swiftly replaced by the harsh reality that the Cable & Wireless series was lost. It might have been better if the West Indies had finished the job that night. Instead, the last rites lasted 17 minutes on the fourth morning. The delay allowed England's captain to gather his thoughts, and Atherton gave an impressive performance in the circumstances.

ATHERTON

We needed to win. We always reckoned it would be our best chance. We played well for three days. Then Hickie dropped Chanderpaul; had he caught it our target would have been substantially lower. The whole situation would have been different. Suddenly, there were 15 overs for the Windies to bowl. I knew that while we couldn't win in an hour, we could lose the Test. Ambrose's first ball kept low, nipped back and was too good for me. I came back and sat on the physio's bed. I watched Ramps run out, shouting 'No, no' at the TV screen. An absolute hour of nightmare. When we started out, I thought we would win. We were chasing more than I would have liked, but I knew that if we got through this session, we would win. And getting through meant losing two, three at the most, wickets. It was one of those times when a captain feels totally helpless. Your top-line batsmen either have the temperament and technique to cope with such an onslaught or they don't. There was no point sending in a nightwatchman. Absolute carnage. Curtly had produced one of the great spells – sustained hostility. He hardly wasted a ball. The pitch was up and down and the batting was fragile. I'm not taking anything away from him. We talk about the fast bowlers' street-fighting qualities and how they can move in for the kill. There will be no better demonstration of that than Curtly Ambrose that evening.

Atherton was glad to be heading for Grenada before the next Test in Barbados. The squad needed to regroup, and many were in a state of shock. A repeat of the horrors of those two 5-0 West Indian 'blackwashes' almost a decade earlier had come alarmingly into focus. Less than 48 hours earlier, Atherton believed England would be back in the series, one down with two to play. He tried hard to hang on to the positive aspects of the Trinidad contest, but it was not easy. England's domination of the majority of the match had not been an illusion, but unfortunately, Ambrose had suspended reality for the time being. Atherton had no trouble fending off the inevitable questioning of the wisdom of selecting such a young squad. He had no doubt then, nor has he any doubts now, that a Gooch,

Lamb or Gower would not have made the slightest difference in Trinidad.

Atherton thought long and hard about whether he should play in the match against the West Indies Board. Eventually, he decided to sit it out. After back-to-back Tests, he felt that the need for the reserves to press a case was more important than the sight of the captain on the bridge. He now admits that was a big mistake. However devastated Atherton felt on arrival at the Coyaba Beach Resort in Grenada, his state of mind was much worse when checking out after less than four days of what the England skipper himself described as 'a pile of crap'. On top of that, the Atherton love life – which Neil Fairbrother had once announced could be written on the back of a postage stamp – was front-page news back in England. Whatever pretensions and aspirations Michael Atherton has in his life, being a sex symbol is not one of them. The headlines were a product of England's cricketing failure. With Atherton under pressure and most families and girlfriends preparing to come out for the final two Tests, journalists enquired in England whether Dr Carman would be soothing the troubled brow of the England skipper in Barbados. Thus it was revealed that Atherton and Suzie Carman, whom he had met at Cambridge University five years earlier, had decided to call it a day. This was rather old news for the interested parties, as the separation had taken place at New Year, a fortnight before England flew off. For the first and, he hopes, the last time, Atherton found himself fielding questions about his love life. He kept it simple: 'The split was a mutual and amicable decision. We've been under pressure, with Suzie in London and me in Manchester being away a lot. The relationship was even more difficult when I was appointed captain of England. There's no one else in my life at the moment.' The last part was not exactly true, but you could excuse the England captain that little white lie. He was under enough pressure without revealing that he had fallen for a stunning Guyanese girl during the visit to Georgetown.

Not that there was much love in the air after four days of inept cricket from a squad that now looked ready for the last rites. England lost by eight wickets in a pathetic capitulation. Despite the appearance of every England batsman in the squad bar Atherton, only 18 runs were mustered by the last six wickets in the first innings. England actually led by six runs after the first innings and were 146 runs in front with nine second-innings wickets left, yet in the end, the Board's victory target was only 172 after the batting collapsed in another heap. Hick scored 74 and Ramprakash 67, but Hussain's 6 was the only other innings other than 0 or 1. Thorpe was back at the hotel in bed, suffering from tonsillitis, but such was the speed of England's demise that there was no time for him to answer MJK Smith's frantic SOS. The umpiring certainly did not help, but Atherton was not looking for excuses. Yet another leg-spinner (albeit no Shane Warne), 19-year-old Rawle Lewis, had found England lambs to the slaughter with match figures of 9 for 146. The tourists travelled to the ground on the fourth morning with defeat a certainty. Atherton was much more concerned now than he had been after Trinidad. That public humiliation had required no angry words from him; this could not pass without comment. The captain laid down the law after England threw in the towel on the final morning. The contest ended with Stuart Williams hitting Tufnell for five consecutive fours. The players were left in no doubt that it was not only themselves they were letting down. Atherton also gave the team a rare lashing in print: 'Until Grenada, I had been satisfied with the motivation of the guys, but that was a bad performance. There were one or two who seemed more concerned with their own problems than with trying to save a game for England.' The only bonus of the Grenada leg was Andrew Caddick's successful proposal of marriage.

Atherton had already decided most of the issues the press were still debating when he boarded the plane for Barbados that night. Continuity was one of the cornerstones of his policy. Speculation concerned the dropping of Robin Smith, the reintroduction of Malcolm, handing Stewart the gloves and switching spinners. Atherton and Fletcher agreed that this was not the time to take chances. Neither Maynard nor Hussain had suggested at Grenada that they would score any more runs than Smith, Stewart's keeping had been poor, Malcolm had been wayward and Tufnell had been steady. So Smith stayed, Russell kept the gloves, Malcolm stayed out and Tufnell returned.

It was only after all the observations about England's shell-shocked state, and the eulogies about Lara's batting and Ambrose's bowling, had been dealt with that the small matter of the West Indies' phenomenal record at the Kensington Oval came into view. Just one defeat – against Bob Wyatt's side in 1935 with the England batting order reversed – in 29 Tests and 12 straight wins in a row in Barbados. Richardson's side were 11-8 on with Ladbrokes for a clean sweep. Atherton and England had another problem – 6,000 or so of them! That was how many England supporters had flown in for the final two Tests. Their mood was less than supportive with the series already gone, and the shambles in Grenada did little to lift their gloomy expectations.

England were back at the Club Rockley, this time with families, grannies and nannies in tow. For the first time since taking over as captain, Atherton was feeling the downside. Not about his leadership or his performance, but about his youth policy, or certain members of it. Pointing the finger was not easy: 'I had really hoped and believed that someone like Thorpe and Ramprakash would establish themselves out here. So far, that has not happened.' Atherton also felt disappointed that Hussain and Maynard had done nothing to force a way in. Like Gooch before him, the captain was discovering that if you want something done for England's cricket team, you have to do it yourself. Tufnell for Salisbury was the only change, which upset Malcolm. Having bust a gut to get fit and back on the tour, this was the Test the fast bowler felt he had to play in. Nothing Ambrose delivered in Trinidad was as fast as the barrage Smith faced in the nets from Malcolm as the Derbyshire paceman gave full vent to his frustration the day before the Test.

ATHERTON

We hit rock bottom in Grenada. Nasser and Matthew needed to bat, so I dropped out. That was a big mistake. I should have been there to give direction. The Board XI was an ordinary side by international standards. At the time, I put it down to a Trinidad hangover – I still do. We started okay and I was pleased that we appeared to have pulled ourselves together. Suddenly, there was all that fuss about Suzie and me splitting. It was the same old story. It had happened months earlier. I hadn't told anyone, because it was nobody else's business. I was astonished when the story hit the headlines; stuff about me, my lover and cricket driving us apart. All very macho and all a lot of rubbish – we parted on amicable terms. I suppose it was an indication of where my life was heading, becoming part of the public domain. The Grenada game upset me much more. We got worse and worse. I left there in a worse state than I arrived. Those games aren't easy. The Tests are the benchmark. The performance made selection for Barbados easier. Nasser and Matthew did nothing to force any changes in the batting. Tuffers proved he deserved a chance. Devon was the problem. Even one burst might have been enough to convince me, but he showed very little. Picking him would have been a bold move – but an irresponsible one, especially after his injury problems.

Atherton's team-talk contained this simple fact of life for a side 3-0 down in as many Tests: another defeat and half this team could wave their Test careers goodbye. It was time for some key participants to start repaying the faith that Atherton and Fletcher had shown in them. If they needed any more motivation than playing for their careers, their captain, their country and thousands of English supporters, there was always the growing shadow of Big Brother – Illingworth, the new chairman of selectors. The arrival of the fans also meant the appearance of the latest newspapers from the old country, and their message was that Big Brother was watching, via the satellite, in Spain.

It soon became obvious to Atherton and his team that the Grenada performance had convinced the thousands of English holiday-makers that they had flown thousands of miles to watch a cricket massacre. The island of Barbados has many compensations, but the mood among the supporters was sombre as it appeared England were beyond redemption. Atherton could not escape their dejection and disgust. Most of the 'send them home' and 'sack the lot' pleas from the more vocal element were reserved for the TV cameras – it was clear that the rum and sun were already taking their toll – yet even in the polite conversations and subdued wishes of good luck, Atherton could see defeat and despondency in the eyes of the England fans. This was something else to bring to the attention of the squad. Atherton has never been one with a great sense of duty to the fans; the 'They have paid good money to come over here and we mustn't let them down' cliché was not part of his game plan. He was more direct, telling his team that their own fans had written them off already. He was worried that some of the squad had their sights on the finishing line. For the first time on the trip, Atherton felt the tight team-unit was breaking up. That was not just down to the arrival of the families and the fans, but also to the attractions of Barbados and the proximity of the end of the tour. Those not selected here knew they had almost certainly played their final part on this Caribbean expedition and were winding down.

Such was the background to one of the most remarkable sporting upsets of recent times. Those who came to see Atherton's team buried witnessed a coming of age instead. The anticipated funeral turned into a remarkable carnival as the Kensington Oval's invincible aura was blown away and England created cricket history. In five days, the criticism of Atherton's youth policy evaporated as his young charges showed rare character, commitment and courage. It was an outstanding team performance with some fine individual displays. Barbados heralded a new beginning for the England Test team. The fact it proved to be another false dawn, Atherton believes, was due to the policies of the new chairman, who failed to attach enough importance to England's recovery in the Caribbean. All along, Atherton proclaimed that the youth strategy would take time, that there would be disasters on the way, but it would all have been a waste of time if the selectors lost their nerve and brought back the same old guns. Atherton insisted that even Gooch would have to pay a price if he wanted to return that summer. Despite his being England's top-ranked batsman, Atherton refused to consider recalling him unless Gooch made himself available for all England Tests, and specifically the Ashes tour the following winter.

Atherton was happy with the players' response at the team meeting. Grenada had been a different sort of shock to Trinidad; there was more shame attached to that Board defeat. England's players had been forced to look

inwards, not marvel at a magnificent bowling performance, for the reasons for failure. Grenada offered not a
single mitigating circumstance. But as Atherton made
plain, if they did not improve they might as well all pack
up and go home.

An important contribution the England captain felt he
could make was to win the toss. Allan Lamb, deputising
for Gooch, had done just that four years earlier. Inexplica-
bly, he asked Viv Richards to bat; England were never in
the game and just failed to hold on for a draw. Atherton
called incorrectly and cursed his luck. But the West Indies
captain put England in. Richardson's thinking, based on
the evidence of Grenada, was that England were still
shell-shocked. Atherton admitted to the TV cameras that
he would have batted, and raced off to get his pads on.
He could not believe his luck. His early performances on
the Kensington track had been fruitful, 108 against Barbados and 86 in the first one-day international. Atherton
also felt that Stewart was ready for a big score and said as
much to the English press, who were wondering whether
a new opening partner might be preferable. The England
captain's prediction proved spot-on. The pitch was fast,
but the bounce was true and Stewart was in his element,
pulling and hooking with growing confidence to celebrate his 31st birthday in style. Atherton was the rock at
the other end as the pair put on 171 for the first wicket.
The only argument was over who was angrier at getting
out. An Atherton century seemed to be only a matter of
taking care when he was caught at slip after hitting
Kenny Benjamin for successive fours. The touring captain
received a standing ovation from the largely white crowd,
whose delirium was only partly due to the alcohol. The
roar of the day came when Stewart pulled Ambrose to the
boundary for his birthday ton, his fifth for England, his
first for 34 innings and his first against the West Indies.
(With his team Chelsea having just reached the FA Cup

final, Stewart knew things were going his way.) The only part of his mission not accomplished was being there at the close – tiredness undoubtedly played a part as he dragged the ball onto his stumps. England finished at 299 for 5, and even suggestions that England had not capitalised fully on that opening stand could not dishearten Atherton. His team had their pride back. They could go out for their evening meals with some confidence and standing. Trinidad and Grenada could now work to England's advantage. Atherton did not feel the need to remind his men that the job was only a fifth done!

After being 223 for 1, a total of 355 might seem negligent. Not in the West Indies against their pace attack. They take wickets in bunches. A session might pass without much happening. Batsmen like Gooch claimed that you could sense the foot easing back off the accelerator. Yet the minute a wicket falls, the West Indies juggernaut is bearing down at you at full speed. A healthy position becomes a critical one in a matter of overs. England's 355 was largely due in the latter stages to the terrier Russell, who has never got over losing the 1990 Test there. After Trinidad, Atherton warned again of how costly catching lapses could be as England prepared to field.

It was soon evident that Atherton was not prepared to give the West Indies an inch. Haynes had driven Caddick and pottered back to his crease as he saw the ball go to the boundary. Tufnell returned the ball and screamed at Russell to remove the bails. All hell broke loose, with Atherton in no mood to give such a world-class batsman an extra life. Haynes was equally reluctant to hand over his wicket. The feeling among the fielding side was that the matter was going the way of the home player, adding to a growing suspicion that the tourists were coming second in close decisions. Atherton knew England must stand their ground, although this was a rare show of animation. Stewart, who has had his fair share of confrontations with Haynes over the years, helped calm England's fury. It was Tufnell's throw and shout that had alerted the close fielders to the run-out chance. Yet TV clearly showed that the ball had bounced back off the concrete scoreboard, although Haynes was only given three runs for the shot. England were still wicket-less, but Atherton's outburst helped inspire the bowlers, and Fraser in particular, to a remarkable second half of the day. By the close, the West Indies had collapsed from 55 for 0 to 188 for 7, with Fraser's tally half a dozen. For once, it was an England bowler who enticed bounce out of a wicket when the West Indies could not. Fraser made the ball bounce and cut away and his six victims were all caught by the keeper and the slips. It included a spell of 4 for 1 in 17 balls, and Atherton took the catches that dismissed Haynes and Richardson. Fraser was on fire and there was genuine delight among the fielders as Atherton led the celebrations at the fall of every wicket. The West Indies had looked comfortable in that opening stand, but once Richardson went, batting became much more hazardous and the crowd sensed the England bowlers now expected to take wickets.

The mood vanished on the third morning. With everyone expecting England to gain a first-innings lead of around 150, Chanderpaul and Ambrose extended their eighth-wicket stand to 71 runs. Atherton probably erred in holding Fraser back, especially as he subsequently removed Ambrose in his first over. Chanderpaul and Kenny Benjamin added another 58 runs for the ninth wicket, and Benjamin and Walsh 41 for the tenth, before Fraser collected his eighth wicket for a Test-best 8 for 75. Atherton's frustration was not helped when he dropped Chanderpaul off Tufnell. England's lead was only 51 and Atherton knew another good start was essential. They did not get it, as the captain, Ramprakash and Smith went cheaply. But Stewart and Hick both had fifties by the close and England's advantage was 222 with seven second-innings wickets left. The Stewart–Hick stand made all the difference to the state of the game and the mood of the England camp. Without it, there would have been no escaping the feeling that once again, despite England making all the running, the home side could always drag it back at the death. Atherton was pleased that while England had buckled, they had not broken. None of his team was present at the official function that night, a trip on the *Bajan Queen*. Such niceties, whether for officials or sponsors, have never been part of Atherton's game plan. The English management went, to save and show face with the Cable & Wireless and West Indies Board hierarchy. Such stiff formalities bore Atherton. The England captain feels and looks awkward at the best of times. His young team had been through much in the previous fortnight and the skipper felt they would benefit much more from a relaxing evening among friends. Manager MJK Smith was as good as gold about it. The players were exhausted after three hard days of cricket. Just to prove Atherton's point, travellers on the *Bajan Queen* were treated to the sight of the England scorer, Alec Davis, and his wife fast asleep over empty dinner-plates long before docking.

Atherton was finding life among the many thousands of England fans much easier. The hostile mood had changed; the trip of a lifetime had become worthwhile. If England could keep their nerve and the bowlers hold their line, those in Barbados this week were going to become part of cricket history. Atherton did allow himself a fleeting thought that he might enjoy the rare luxury of being able to declare an England innings against the West Indies. A few days earlier, he had not been too keen to see all the wives and families turn up just when the tour was at its lowest ebb. Believing that total concentration and commitment would be needed to produce a recovery, Atherton worried that these home comforts might prove a distraction. Now, he thought that the renewal of those ties had stopped his squad dwelling too much on the Trinidad and Grenada disasters.

Monday was a rest day, an increasingly rare luxury as the Test schedules are tightened. History was very much part of Atherton's thinking on that rest day as he lazed around the pool. The home side's 12 home wins in a row here was compounded by England's seven successive away defeats in India, Sri Lanka and the West Indies. As well as Fraser had bowled in the first innings, this was only his fifth Test back after recovering from the hip injury that had kept him out of the England side for two and a half years. The Fraser spirit was not in doubt, but the flesh was still weak from the long lay-off. Atherton knew the chance of another Fraser one-man show was slim, so he was happy for Fletcher to emphasise the need for support from Lewis and Caddick. Both had been below par in the first innings, and while Tufnell could plug away at one end, Fletcher and Atherton wanted to keep rotating the three pacemen from the other. Atherton refused publicly to set a target. Privately, it wasn't his habit either. The sight of England's target growing in Trinidad from 100 to 150 and then nearly 200 only added to his frustration at the time. Much depended on the manner of the exchanges on the fourth day. England might get past 300, but if the West Indies then fought back and wiped out the possibility of a 400 lead, such mayhem was bound to inspire their batsmen. The key, as ever, was to frustrate the West Indies, not to allow them wickets in groups and to make them fight for every one. Atherton had another reason for making sure the new batsmen did not surrender cheaply: he was sure that Stewart was not finished with the West Indies bowlers. Although the ball was beginning to keep low, Atherton felt that his opening partner was playing as well as he had ever seen him and was producing the returns that he had threatened all tour. Stewart's love of the pull and hook, especially against West Indies pace, leaves little margin for error, but his timing was spot-on in the first innings and that century had given him the confidence to play another major knock. Atherton felt no need to cajole his vice-captain; Stewart was as determined as Atherton to take full advantage of the conditions and situation.

The first session on the fourth day was a war of attrition. Stewart had added only 13 runs and Hick was still on his overnight score of 52 after nearly an hour. It was also a war of aggression. If Walsh felt aggrieved when an lbw shout at Hick was refused, he was distraught when there was no official confirmation that Stewart had got an inside edge to Junior Murray. Thorpe replaced Hick and ensured an optimistic atmosphere at lunch with England 275 ahead and no more wickets gone. An England cricket strategy against the West Indies can rarely have gone so according to plan in recent times. Phase two was now put into operation and by tea, England could not lose. Stewart and Thorpe had set a new England record for the fifth wicket against the West Indies and the lead was now over 400 after 132 runs had come in the session. Stewart surpassed his 118 with 143, only the fourth time any cricketer had scored a century in each innings against the West Indies. Such individual history lessons were wasted on Stewart. All England eyes, not just his, were looking ahead to causing a cricket sensation. When Atherton eventually declared leaving the home side a target of 446, or rather 112 overs to survive for the draw, the press box grumbled that he had been over-cautious. By the close, those private reservations had been transformed into public pronouncements of Atherton's perfect timing, with the West Indies 47 for 2 and both Haynes and Richardson troubled by injury.

Celebrations among English fans started that afternoon as Stewart made the Test safe. By stumps, the match was over as far as they were concerned. Atherton was concerned that his players not be seduced by such premature thoughts, and help was at hand. Stories began circulating of the memorable party held by the South Africans, players and all, at exactly the same venue two years earlier. That Test had not ended either, but the drink flowed the night before they returned to the Kensington Oval for the victory formalities the next morning. They would take place after the South Africans, in their first Test back after 22 years in the international wilderness, had knocked off the 79 runs needed with eight wickets left. They lost by 52 runs. Atherton went to bed knowing he could not lose. Well, almost. There was the small matter of Brian Lara, who was already at the wicket. The little man had already shown that in his case, time spent at the wicket equated to runs, and lots of them. Atherton knew that England did not have the capabilities to contain him, even though the West Indies would have to score 40 more runs than anyone else had done to win this Test. He finally consoled himself by evaluating that, even by Lara's phenomenal standards, it was going to take something exceptionally inspiring to rescue the West Indies. Atherton quietly went round his team that night, urging them to one more effort, not to worry about Lara, not to relax, to concentrate on the simple things – bowl straight and take your catches – and to remind them that, however proud and buoyant they felt tonight, it would be like a bereavement compared to what they would experience tomorrow if things went England's way.

They did. A victory by 208 runs, though plain sailing it was not. Lara did threaten, and all the more menacingly when two catching chances were not taken. The vital breakthroughs fell to the England spinners. Lara was not quite in position to pull Caddick and the ball flew in the

air high over wide mid-on. It was in the air long enough
for the catcher to make 15 or so yards backwards, and for
the crowd to identify the fielder who was about to hold
the destiny of this Test in his hands. A few seconds later,
Phil Tufnell was submerged under a grateful and relieved
bunch of team-mates. Never in doubt, but his composure
in such critical circumstances convinced most at the Kensington Oval that this was going to be England's day. The
danger of Lara winning the Test for the West Indies had
passed. Now the threat was Chanderpaul, who was well
capable of saving the match. Atherton, not for the last
time as captain, decided to give Hick an over before
lunch. Although Worcestershire use Hick's off-spin even
more sparingly than England, he has always been a tidy
bowler and Atherton reckoned that Hick would apply the
right sort of pressure at a critical time. One delivery later,
Atherton, Hick and England were celebrating the captain's perfect timing as they jumped and hugged their
way into lunch after Chanderpaul had edged the ball to
substitute fielder Hussain in the slips. Timing was everything and Chanderpaul's dismissal turned a frustrating
morning into a decisive one. Atherton kept the pressure
on during the lunch-break. Batsmen like Haynes, Richardson – although both injured – and Arthurton could all
bat for two sessions and had done so in this series. But
Atherton would not have swapped the wickets of Lara
and Chanderpaul for anything. He had identified this
pair as the greatest danger to an England victory. England's bowlers administered the last rites with a clinical
efficiency more usually recognisable among their opponents. Tufnell and Caddick were the bowling heroes,
although the West Indies' proud Barbados Test record
was finally destroyed by Christopher Clairmonte Lewis's
only wicket of the match. It was worth waiting for, as two
of Ambrose's stumps were uprooted. Ambrose signalled
the end of an era by catapulting the remaining stump in

the direction of the square-leg umpire with a lavish swing of his bat. The gesture earned him a £1,000 fine from match referee John Reid after the West Indian fast bowler refused to apologise. With another 65 per cent of his match fee missing because of the slow over-rate, Ambrose, the hero of Trinidad, had little to show for his efforts in Bridgetown.

England had achieved the impossible. Atherton had performed a sporting miracle. Yet the captain could not escape the nagging belief that England should have been heading for Antigua for a showdown, with the series tied at 2-2. Having been 'turniped' by the *Sun* just a few days earlier, Atherton had even less desire to be 'crowned' by the tabloid media now. While it would have been easier and probably wiser to go with the flow, Atherton refused to enter the press conference like a lottery winner or condemned man who has just been reprieved. Atherton resented the way his squad had been ridiculed back home and this was payback time. The hacks just wanted some inane 'glory, glory, greatest day of my life' lines, but the England captain was in no mood to play ball. For the first time, though not the last, Atherton's justification was that his input was not required to comment on and commemorate an England Test win, however historic and unforeseen, other than to pay tribute to his team and to Stewart, Fraser, Tufnell and Caddick, in particular, on this occasion. Atherton's Oval double, Kennington and Kensington, was based on steady, solid batting, inspired bowling and, most of all, a defiant team-spirit.

ATHERTON
Richie's game-plan seemed to be to do the opposite of what we expected. If that's psychology, it's lost on me. It was a pattern he adopted throughout the series. We made a good start; that was nothing new. I'd felt for a while that Stewie was due – the roar from the crowd when he pulled

Ambrose to the boundary on the first day was something else. The fans just wanted for us to fight and were delighted to see Stewie dishing it out. The crowd was even noisier when Gussie was cleaning them up. Cricket seems such a simple game when the ball is bouncing, cutting, finding the edge and fielders. It's not just the crowd that responds when Gussie is firing, the team does as well. You don't want to be the one to let him down, the one to miss a chance, drop a catch.

The lessons of Trinidad became a factor. We didn't relax, we didn't get carried away. Hickie didn't score for an hour on the fourth day. He's not used to such inactivity. Normally, he would get frustrated, but he knew we needed him there, runs or no runs. That sort of commitment becomes infectious. I declared with an hour to go. I wanted to bat them out of the game – Stewie had shown you could still play shots if you got in. I felt 450 was enough and I was happy with a couple of wickets overnight: 'We'll get Lara in the morning'. The one bad moment came when Ramps dropped a dolly from Lara. The ball came with no power. As captain, I clapped my hands and tried to appear positive. Inside, I was distraught. Was this going to be Trinidad all over again? Then Lara mispulled and Tuffers took a very good catch. That was it, we cleaned up.

I don't think I've ever come off a cricket field as emotional as I was in Barbados. Everything flooded back – Trinidad, the invincible Barbados record, the thousands of English fans, the families, the end of the whitewash talk. The press conference was a bit of a disaster. I was still uptight after all that had been written about us. However elated I was feeling, I was in no mood to be nice to them. I was a bit uppity. I shouldn't have been there, that was my feeling. I'd done my job as England captain. I'm happy to be there when England lose, to try and explain why. I expect that, I can cope with that. I honestly didn't feel the need to explain myself for winning. Getting England to

*win was why I accepted the job. That's why I do it. I later
learnt that Ambrose had been fined. That was surprising
because nobody noticed. I'll never forget Stewie's face after
that second century. Pure delight. There wasn't the same
unadulterated joy as we sat around the concourse waiting
for the flight to Antigua.*

John Paul Getty's yacht was moored in Bridgetown har-
bour. This cricket philanthropist would have loved to
play host to the England team in their hour of triumph.
Unfortunately, Grantley Adams airport was the scene of
the tourists' early-evening 'celebrations'. Time was short.
Bags, already packed, were collected from the Rockley
resort, along with camp followers, and the England officials headed off to catch the flight to Antigua. It was the
perfect public-relations opportunity for an airline company to throw an impromptu party with an English or
British connection. Instead, these heroes of British sport
were left to their own devices and spent a couple of hours
hanging around the open-air concourse with all the other
punters. The feeling among the England squad was that if
this win did not merit the red carpet and a little VIP
treatment, then it would never happen. Atherton did not
need to remind his team that the fifth Test was only three
days away, which is why the skipper wanted his players
to make the most of that evening. On the plane, plans
were made for a late-night party in Antigua, once they
had settled into the Halcyon Cove. But only a handful
found the energy.

Relieved as Atherton was to register his first Test win
as captain abroad, he was even more aware of what the
win meant to team manager Fletcher. A record of seven
consecutive defeats on foreign soil since taking over from
Micky Stewart was threatening his long-term job prospects, despite a five-year contract. Yet Fletcher was even
more reluctant than Atherton to grab centre-stage after

Barbados. One win might have vindicated Atherton and his young guns, but 11 defeats in 14 Tests as team manager were not going to be eradicated by this victory, however inspiring and memorable it might have been. Fletcher was not rejoicing because this had probably granted him a stay of execution at the very least – his pleasure was less selfish. Atherton's team had gained some necessary breathing space, leaving Fletcher confident that English cricket's youth policy would be allowed to begin the second phase of its development in the summer Tests against New Zealand.

So England and Atherton were back in Antigua, where the tour had started three months earlier. Despite the damning headlines of only a week before, Atherton felt that many of the objectives of the trip had been achieved. The Barbados victory still created a few problems for the England captain. Should he change a winning side and, perhaps, endanger the side's new-found confidence? The outstanding displays by Fraser, Stewart, Caddick and Tufnell, with support from Atherton, Thorpe and Russell, could not disguise the continuing poor return from Smith, Ramprakash and Lewis. The threat to Lewis came from Malcolm, but he was no more ready now than he had been for Barbados. The Antigua strip offers little to the bowlers except severe punishment to those who stray in line and length. Atherton's real dilemma concerned Hussain. The Essex right-hander's England career had begun in the Caribbean four years earlier, when he sustained a badly-broken wrist. Hussain did not regain his Test place until the summer of 1993, but flew to the West Indies as a member of The Oval winning side, confident about consolidating his England place. He was devastated to find himself ranked eighth among the English batsmen, an anxiety that only grew as others were exposed technically and temperamentally. Hussain felt that the poor form of others would lead to a recall in Antigua. England's captain considered the matter carefully, but felt there would be more to gain from keeping the same side and confirming his policy of team continuity than giving a one-off Test to Hussain. The Essex batsman had to wait more than two years for his next chance. Atherton had questioned Gooch's judgement in similar circumstances at Madras a year earlier. Now he found himself on the other side of the tracks as Hussain made his feelings clear.

Atherton smiled when it was suggested that the West Indies were on the run, although injury would keep Richardson and Haynes out of the final Test. For the first time in their distinguished history, a fast bowler, Courtney Walsh, would captain the Caribbean islands. Indeed, Atherton was smiling a lot more now and keen not to give his wicket away, even in a game of beach cricket at the Halcyon Cove with some of the English fans. He felt safer on the sand surface than in the nets provided for practice in the two days leading up to the Test. It is difficult to stop yourself mentally packing for home in the final week of a long tour, especially if your chances of making the Test side depend on three others going down with food poisoning. Atherton was happy that there had been little friction among the players. His difference of opinion with Hussain was about the worst of it, but the England captain was certainly not holding any grudges about a situation he was all too familiar with himself.

This was an important toss to win, especially as there was no Richardson to do the unexpected. Walsh would have had no problems bowling at England, but his cricket brain told him that batting was the only option. Caddick and Fraser gave England very early hope, but that first session was easily the best of the seven England endured as the West Indies reached 593 for 5 declared. The proceedings were dominated by Lara, who batted for 766 minutes (536 deliveries) and hit 45 fours in his innings of 375, and the most incredible scenes that greeted the leg-side flick that took him past Sir Garry Sobers' record 365. At that moment, Sobers began a processional march to the middle with a TV camera crew, while Lara kissed the pitch. Sobers had declared the day before: 'I hope he beats my 365. If he does, I will be the first to congratulate him.' It was total theatre, total chaos and totally in keeping with the West Indians' uninhibited love of cricket. Australian umpire Darryl Hair had been asked at the drinks break if Sobers could make an appearance. He refused, of course, but this amiable Aussie took no exception when his ruling was totally ignored. The least excited onlookers were the eleven Englishmen who had spent nearly 13 hours in the baking Antiguan sun trying to get this little left-hander out. Atherton was in no mood for the mass invasion, especially as he hoped to bat some time soon on the wicket that was being trampled over. Hair shrugged at Atherton's complaints, indicating that his authority was counting for very little at present.

On the easiest-paced of wickets, England's bowlers had made Lara work for his runs. The West Indies reached 274 for 3 at the end of day one with Lara on 164. The total was 502 for 4 the next day with Lara on 320, within sight of Sobers' summit. Lara had been immaculate through-out, and talk of the record had begun as early as tea on the first day. Had the rains not come on the second afternoon, Lara might have been able to go to bed with the new record already claimed. There was certainly a change on the third morning: Lara no longer looked invincible, infallible. The pressure, the strain, the expecta-tion were now evident for all to see. Much as Atherton admired Lara's talent, he was going to make the little Trinidadian sweat and work for the greatest batting prize in cricket. The closer Lara got, the more Atherton would try to increase the stakes. The England bowlers kept it tight, did not give him width and made him work for every run. Lara remained on 347 for 18 minutes, Fraser almost bowled him and Lewis delivered a maiden with Lara looking to score. It was left to Chanderpaul, just 19, to keep wandering up the pitch to tell his senior partner to stay cool and calm. Towards the end, this battle became much more a test of Lara the man than Lara the cricketer, as Atherton turned the screw. England fielders chatted loudly that Lara was in trouble and that he might never get this close again. It was not sledging, just a reminder that if he wanted the Sobers record, England were not here for hand-outs. It was Lewis who bowled the ball in the perfect spot for Lara to play his favourite shot that set off the celebrations. Afterwards, Lara revealed that he had woken up at four the previous morning in his hotel room, shaking and sweating about what he was expected to achieve later that day.

ATHERTON
The West Indies did what was expected when they won the toss for the first time in the series. We kept the same side. Nasser let me know he was pretty unhappy. It was the final straw for him on a nightmare tour. These disappointments are not too bad when you see them coming. When it's out of the blue, it's like a heart attack. Where's my name? Where is it? There's been a mistake. That's how I felt in Madras. We've all been through it. There's no way of telling someone they're out. Ramps was struggling, but I decided to keep a settled side. Nasser's face was like thunder. 'That's crap,' was his initial response. As captain, you've got to be big enough to let a player blow off steam. That mustn't get out of hand or undermine your authority. When the game starts, you expect total support. I don't want guys who don't give a damn because they are no longer part of the set-up.

Lara's innings was brilliant. Just a couple of errors in

*over two days of batting. His first false shot came on 291.
Caddick was bowling and I had taken a slip out for the
first time in the match. That's where the nick went to.
Sod's Law. I told Lara, 'It's going to be mayhem out here,
so congratulations now.' I made him sweat for those final
runs: 'Come on lads, tight on the one.' Lara said to me,
'We've played a lot of cricket together over the years.
You're making it difficult for me.' I didn't reply. It wasn't
my job to hand it to him on a plate. I remember leaning on
Judgy's [Robin Smith] shoulders for about a quarter of an
hour watching the circus. At least the delay meant we
didn't have to bat before lunch!*

Lara's 375 meant England's sole task was one of survival.
That looked unlikely for Atherton when Ambrose's first
delivery thudded into the England captain's pads as it
had done in Trinidad. West Indian umpire Steve Bucknor
was one of the slowest fingers on the international circuit,
and it took a few agonising seconds before it became
apparent that England had not made the most disastrous
of starts. Stewart and Ramprakash went cheaply, but
Atherton's century-stand with Smith enabled England to
finish the day at 185 for 2. The spotlight was firmly
focused on Lara, but Atherton had his own agenda. He
wanted the world to know that his young guns had
found their feet. Barbados would be forgotten if Antigua
was another massacre. He knew little of Illingworth,
although he was growing aware of the new chairman's
fondness for using the media to get his thoughts across.
Atherton wanted a sustained recovery from this series to
take into the first selection meeting of the new summer,
provided he was Illingworth's choice as captain.

Smith, too had plenty to play for. Fletcher used the
rest-day press conference to discuss the reasons for his
batting slump. Little over a year earlier, Smith had been
ranked number two in the world, with a Test average

over 50. England and Atherton felt they had a ready-made replacement for Gooch as England's premier international batsman. Yet Smith's previous 26 innings had produced 737 runs, with a solitary century against Sri Lanka, and he was now languishing at 30th in the world rankings. Atherton had enormous respect for Smith's courage, batting and loyalty. Yet his lack of runs in this series had been crucial, and all the more damaging to England's cause because it was a weakness Atherton had not anticipated. Just how disappointed the English management had been could be judged from the normally reticent Fletcher's views: 'He has to be aware what comes first in his life. There are a lot of money-making opportunities for players with Robin's profile, and I think this has affected him . . . By his own standards, Robin has had three poor series. Even the greatest players all had their bad patches, but this has gone on for some time now.' Smith did not have to wait for the papers to read these comments. The tabloid media rushed straight from Fletcher to find Smith on the Halcyon beach and get his reaction. His ever-present smile soon vanished when he was told that the England team manager had suggested a desire to make money was the reason for his recent poor form. Fletcher had mentioned other reasons, but there was never any doubt as to which one would grab the headlines. After a few basic words of denial, Smith stormed up the beach to find Fletcher. Whatever the merits and motivation of Fletcher's outburst, Smith's response came in the form of a record third-wicket stand of 303 with Atherton, surpassing Hutton and Hammond's 264 at The Oval in 1939. Ironically, both those Englishmen had held the record that now belonged to Lara. Smith rode his luck and was 'out' twice to no-balls before his century. He went past his previous best, 148 against the West Indies at Lord's three years earlier, and reached 175. Atherton had been content to play the junior partner. His own hundred took 78 balls more than Smith's, but it was more valuable. Atherton had begun to perceive that Smith did not enjoy being 'top dog'. First with Lamb, then with Gooch, Smith had been the classiest supporting-act in Test cricket. He flourished when there was someone else to play off. Atherton, who took his time at the crease in this series to 28 hours for his 510 runs, was the perfect foil. Happy to let Smith take his reward in the limelight, he provided the strength and foundation that allowed his partner to feel comfortable. Atherton was not being totally unselfish – Smith was an important part of his future plans, despite his recent meagre run-return.

Atherton departed after Smith with England just one run short of saving the follow-on. He edged Ambrose to Murray and needed no prompting from umpire Hair. England's captain had batted one minute short of nine hours to ensure the game was saved. That was just as well because, Smith apart, the other front-line batsmen collected a total of 72 runs. England finished the day at 442 for 6, meaning the final three sessions of the series would be relatively peaceful.

ATHERTON

It was obvious on the third morning that we couldn't win. But we had to maintain the good things from Barbados. 'Let's fight hard not to lose it' was my message. For myself, it was my aim to see us through until we had passed the follow-on target and the game was dead. Although I thought Curtly's first delivery was missing, my heart was in my mouth because it was very close. That scare made me even more determined.

England matched the West Indies total of 593 exactly, after a stand of 118 between Russell and Lewis the next day. The West Indies then batted out the final session. For the first time since he was appointed team manager at the end of the 1992 summer, Fletcher's England team had gone two matches without losing. This was a remarkable recovery by any standards, especially abroad. Atherton's England had taken two positive steps forward after three setbacks. England's captain, who was going to take a short break in Tobago, was convinced that the new chairman of selectors would need little persuading to carry on the current selection policy. Unfortunately, Illingworth had his own agenda and his own views on England's Caribbean performance. England's players never expected a heroes' welcome, but even they had not anticipated the crushing Illy-verdict headlines that greeted their arrival, minus Atherton, at Gatwick.

ATHERTON

I felt the West Indies were a stronger side. We didn't mix much, though I got on with Richie. After the Antigua Test, I went into their dressing-room with a six-pack. Generally though, they prefer their own company. I really enjoyed the Caribbean and the people. They love their cricket. It's great for team spirit with the lads round the pool or on the beach when relaxing. I like a fun-loving, easy-going lifestyle. It's a bit like university. I enjoyed that tour more than any other I've been on. I got on with the Aussies better than before in 1994-95, but it's a more hostile environment. They don't leave that competitive edge on the field. You're made to feel welcome in the West Indies. It helped that I had a good tour personally. Success breeds admiration. They know how good their fast bowlers are. If you stand up to them, they respect you.

I felt we came back on a high. We'd played some good cricket. We were poor early on, but I felt we had moved in the right direction and made real progress. The management set-up was changing and there was talk of Fletch being squeezed out. He told me that I would get on well with Illy. Fletch did a good job in the Caribbean, the lads related to him. It had been a struggle for him, losing all four Tests the winter before, losing the Ashes and going 3-0 down here. Once Illy had been made chairman, I commiserated with MJK (Smith) and thought no more about it until I got back to England.

CHAPTER NINE

The Gathering Storm

A therton was aware that Illingworth had been voicing his views publicly before the squad left the Caribbean for England. As England's captain was staying behind for a break, he kept quiet. Atherton saw no need to spoil the team's happy disposition. Also, he was conscious of having received Illingworth's comments second-hand, via English journalists who had spoken to their offices and colleagues at Lord's, where Illingworth had been on the opening day of England 'A' versus Middlesex. Atherton was wising up to the tricks of the media trade where comments are repeated out of context to provoke a response. But he certainly would have reacted if he had flown back to London and seen the headlines and the faces of his troops as they digested the thoughts of chairman Ray. As ever with Illingworth, it was not so much what he said but the way he said it and, most significantly in this case, when he said it. The timing was disastrous and it provoked a hostility among many players that remained until Illingworth quit at the end of the 1996 summer.

Whether an army returns in triumph or in disgrace, the homecoming is always emotional and no place for post-mortems. Yet, seconds after stepping back on home soil for the first time in 98 days, players had microphones shoved under their noses to answer specific accusations from the new chairman about their futures. Fraser, hero of Barbados, had to work on his fitness; Hick on his technique against the short ball; Russell, Lewis, Smith and Ramprakash on how they reacted to question marks about their England futures. As a public relations exercise, Illy's pronouncements were an unmitigated disaster. His timing, or lack of it, was uncanny and remained a problem for English cricket over the next three years. No one disputed the validity of most of the chairman's comments, but his remarks should have been made to the players concerned in private. His response to that charge was that England cricketers should be big enough to take constructive criticism. Unfortunately, it was not a fair fight. Players were not allowed to defend themselves publicly. If they did, Illingworth was down on them like a ton of bricks.

The worst aspect of the whole situation was that it confirmed everything the players had heard about the new chairman. Most knew him through his work as a BBC commentator and writer with the *Daily Express*. While not in the same league as Boycott, Illingworth was very opinionated, with many of his solutions to English cricket's problems beginning and ending in Yorkshire. Illingworth is still rated as England's best captain since the war, having led them to Ashes success in Australia in 1970-71, and should have been involved with the England management set-up much earlier than he was. He was interviewed when the job of team manager was created for Gatting's 1986-87 Ashes tour, but after studying the job description he turned it down as nothing more than a 'glorified baggage-man'. But it was a way in, and if he had been more of a politician, Illingworth could have developed his power from within, as Micky Stewart did after that successful Australian tour.

Illingworth rode into the chairman of selectors' post on the back of a county reaction to what was perceived as jobs for the Warwickshire boys, when the TCCB chief executive Alan Smith lined up MJK Smith (no blood relation) to replace Dexter. Some of the counties wanted the TCCB to put their money where Illy's mouth was. For years, he had been threatening to sort out English cricket if he was ever given the chance. Unfortunately, it was Illy's mouth that became the biggest problem. That again was the fault of the Board. Illy did not change. When his name was revealed as the successful candidate while England were in Guyana, Martin Johnson, then of the *Independent* and a former cricket reporter with the *Leicester Mercury*, ordered the tabloid media to get down on their knees and give thanks. 'Raymond,' he explained, 'is going to make your life a dream for the next few years. He's so honest and he just can't keep quiet.' The first requirement of any contract with Lord's should have been his silence. Illingworth has been an outspoken cricketer from the day he pulled on his whites (nappies, that is). His untimely tour report as England left Antigua was a clear warning about the problems to come. Even then, it was not too late for the Board to buy Illingworth's silence.

Atherton himself emerged reasonably unscathed from Illingworth's comments: 'He has a good cricket brain and we want to give him every opportunity to use it, but he hasn't captained the side that much.' As ever with Illingworth, there was a sting in the tail as he emphasised his own right of final selection by referring to the Australian system of giving the captain his team. 'Sometimes it is easier for him if he does not have 100 per cent say in who is in it.' Illingworth added that Gooch would not be considered for the summer's Tests if he was not available for next winter's tour. Fighting talk from the new chairman, but that case had been stated for months by Atherton, who already knew that Gooch would fulfil those requirements. When Gooch's change of heart became official, it appeared as if the decisive words of the new chairman had won an important battle. Honest Illingworth certainly is, but he was also a past master of playing and winning the propaganda game. His claim that 'The buck stops with me now' became a rather tame assertion in the months and years ahead, as the chairman was able to record, chapter and verse, the various reasons for failure.

It was not Illingworth's words but some *Daily Mirror* pictures which had Atherton less than amused on his return to Manchester. England's skipper had been tracked down to a Tobago hotel and photographed canoodling in the water with Isabelle. His annoyance at this invasion of his privacy was evident when he re-entered the Lancashire dressing-room for the first time. With the usual tact of a county dressing-room, the offending *Mirror* article had been photocopied so that each player had his entry for a raunchy caption competition, then stuck on all the lockers for Atherton to judge at his leisure. Fairbrother is not sure Atherton took in all the various innuendos because England's captain, after depositing them in the bin, never revealed his favourite.

Atherton's return was greeted by Illingworth's nod to carry on as captain. He was confirmed as skipper for the Texaco series and Cornhill Tests against New Zealand. This reappointment for only half the summer led some to question his long-term future under Illingworth and argue that England's progress in the Caribbean merited a greater vote of confidence, but Atherton did not regard it as any sort of slight. Illingworth claimed: 'There were no ulterior motives. In fact, I see Mike as very much a long-term captain. He's a young man and has already proved that the captaincy does not affect his game. He seemed to thrive on responsibility in the West Indies. We need stability, and I'd be looking for him still to be captain in two years' time when my term of office ends.'

Atherton's first weekend back on the county scene was dominated by Imran Khan's admission, in a new biography by *The Times* journalist Ivo Tennant, that he had used a bottle-top to tamper with the ball during Sussex's game with Hampshire in 1981. Little did Atherton imagine that such goings-on were about to affect him personally and so dramatically.

Atherton hit his first century of the season in the Benson and Hedges Cup second-round tie at Derby, a repeat of the previous season's bad-tempered final, but finished on the losing side after some sensational hitting by Dominic Cork. Derbyshire, 192 for 6, needed 89 to win with only 46 deliveries remaining. Cork was still hobbling after surgery on his left knee, but smashed 63 off 43 balls, the last a six off Lancashire's new skipper Mike Watkinson with one delivery to spare. Cork's display was not enough to convince Illingworth and his four fellow selectors: Atherton, Fletcher, Fred Titmus and Brian Bolus. The latter pair had been voted in by the counties, as Illingworth's chosen two candidates. Atherton did not need to be a mathematical genius to work out that Illingworth held the balance of power and could force through any selection he wanted. Atherton decided to wait and judge in what direction Illingworth was going at the Texaco selection meeting.

The captain emphasised the strength of England's recovery on tour and why that should be rewarded. But only six of the West Indies squad were retained, the axing of Caddick being the biggest surprise. Yorkshire's Gough and Hampshire's Udal were the newcomers in this specialist, 13-man one-day squad, which saw Gooch, DeFreitas, Reeve and Rhodes back in the fold. The biggest change from the Dexter regime, Atherton observed, was the new chairman's willingness to give a public airing to selection issues. For example, in his controversial book,

One-Man Committee, Illingworth states: 'We picked Devon Malcolm in the hope that the pitches would suit him, and anyway he would be one of six bowlers – seven with Graeme Hick – in case he didn't fire properly. As it turned out, the Edgbaston pitch was a slow nothing, so we left out Devon.' Actually, Devon had been left out five days earlier at the selection meeting.

ATHERTON

I knew life was not going to be the same for me as England captain with Illy as chairman. From our brief conversations, it was obvious that he was a shrewd judge. When I was made captain, Ted told me that I would be the main voice in selection. That's the way it worked for the West Indies tour. It was made crystal clear to me that those days were over. Still, I felt it was my duty to speak up for the lads who had battled so hard in the Caribbean. I know we had been 3-0 down, but more experienced sides than ours had been in that position and had not recovered at all. Illy and I were not at each other's throats. The change in policy was something that I was going to have to live with. I just had to get on with it as best I could. I understood Illy wanted a balanced side. We all do. But if those players are not about, you have to compromise. He seemed to forget that he was able to pick players like himself, Knott, Greig and D'Oliveira who were all world-class all-rounders. We did not have one in that category. I'd love to pick a five-man bowling attack with two spinners, but you don't play them just for the sake of it. In the end, how many times did Illy put two spinners onto the park in his time in charge?

Atherton lifted the first international trophy of the summer in a disappointing contest. England won the Edgbaston encounter by 42 runs, then Lord's was wiped out by the rain. In the Edgbaston match, the England newcomers had acquitted themselves well, although Gough picked up a side injury. He dismissed New Zealand's linchpin Martin Crowe in his first over for England and showed all the exuberance and spirit of his youth. The inswinging yorker that removed New Zealand's top scorer Bryan Young was described in *The Times* as being 'worthy of Waqar Younis'. Gough was hailed as a triumph for the Yorkshire influence, although Illingworth had not been involved when he was picked to tour South Africa with England 'A'. Udal also bowled well and collected the wickets of Parore and the New Zealand captain Ken Rutherford. The tourists never threatened England's 224 once Crowe had gone. A year earlier, 557 runs had been scored there in the Australian Texaco match on a blistering surface. There was no Test in Birmingham this summer, and after this, Atherton for one was not unhappy about that. Neither had he been unhappy when asked to bat. England's captain provided the anchor to allow Stewart, Smith, Gooch and Hick to play around him. None of them got going and Atherton's 81 from 137 balls proved to be the cornerstone of the innings, winning him the Man of the Match award from Bob Willis.

Illingworth had made public noises over the weekend about Craig White, who had become the first Yorkshire player to score a century and take a five-wicket haul in the same match for 16 years. Then, in front of Illingworth, White scored 59 and took 5 for 42 and 2 for 30 as Yorkshire beat the New Zealand tourists by an innings and 33 runs. Atherton was quickly gleaning that a Yorkshire birth certificate was as important as a good technique under the new regime. He and Fletcher found themselves in the minority in the selection meeting the following Saturday night in Stockport, where Atherton was playing. England's captain was prepared and happy for the return of Gooch and the promotion of Rhodes as wicket-keeper. Rhodes was a bubbly character and had come close to selection in the past. Gooch was still the best batsman in England and Atherton was an admirer of the Australian policy of playing three openers. Atherton, Stewart and Gooch looked as good as Taylor, Slater and Boon. England had been struggling with the No. 3 spot for years, although many felt Smith had been the ideal man to go in first wicket down in the Caribbean. The argument that Gooch should be held back for the South African series later that summer, to give a youngster a chance, was not even discussed. That left three batting spots for what Atherton perceived was England's best middle order trio – Smith, Hick and Thorpe – with John Crawley, after an outstanding A tour and an undefeated 281 in the current championship game, his choice for next man in line for a place.

Illingworth ideally wanted an all-rounder in the side. So did Atherton – but there wasn't one, or so the captain thought. Atherton glanced at Fletcher as it soon became apparent that Illingworth wanted White in the side, and that Titmus and Bolus would support that view. Fletcher argued that whoever was left out, it should not be Thorpe. After a poor start, Thorpe had grown in stature in the Caribbean and played vital innings in Trinidad and Barbados. He epitomised Atherton's young guns more than anyone else by the end of the tour. Yet he was in fact the player sacrificed as Hick's part-time off-breaks and Smith's 175 in Antigua won the day. With left-arm spinner Richard Stemp also included in the squad and Gough only missing because of his injury, there could be no denying that Yorkshire was now controlling England's cricket destiny.

Illingworth had concentrated on what had gone wrong in the Caribbean, ignoring the final fortnight of the tour, and these selections undermined Atherton's youth policy at a stroke. Illingworth's own memories of those discussions are interesting: 'Our first selection meeting was a bit of an eye-opener. I knew Atherton was a strong character, but I had not realised he had such black-and-white views about who could play and who could not. I know Brian felt the same.' Nonetheless, it was the influence of Illingworth, not Atherton, that was perceived as the major factor in this England squad by the media. Only six of Atherton's Caribbean squad had survived. The *Daily Telegraph*'s heading declared, 'England look to Yorkshire connection' – and its correspondent Christopher Martin-Jenkins was not alone in voicing these sentiments: 'The hope of a logical progression from what, in the end, was not a dispiriting tour of the Caribbean has been shattered.'

The England party assembled on Tuesday afternoon and that night Atherton was named 'England Player of the Year' at the Cornhill dinner. Fletcher summed up the judges' thoughts: 'It didn't take us very long to decide. His batting last summer against Australia was excellent, and after his leadership and batting in the West Indies, there wasn't anybody else as far as I am concerned. Michael has a lot of guts. He took a fair pounding in Jamaica and stood up to it brilliantly. He has lots of determination, wants to do well, plays within his limitations, has lots of confidence in his own ability and is a very strong character. I think he has been mature ever since he was a little lad.' England's captain squirmed at all this adulation, replying that he had 'really enjoyed taking on Courtney Walsh and relished rather than dreaded the prospect of playing in the next Test.' After claiming that his 28 in Jamaica was one of the most important Test innings in his career, he added: 'After the opening Test barrage, I opened my stance a bit if I thought another short ball was on the way, but my technique was always much the same. If you are looking forward to a challenge, it says you are thinking positively rather than negatively.'

New Zealand struggled at Trent Bridge after winning the toss against an efficient England attack that left out Ilott and Stemp. The recalled DeFreitas led the way with four wickets, with Rhodes and White making good starts as the tourists were restricted to 251. Atherton knew this series was not going to be a real test for the tougher challenges ahead. New blood could cash in on opportunities he felt his Caribbean squad had earned, and success here would tell him little about their ability to cope with an Ashes battle. There was no need to worry about Gooch, who hit a double century in England's reply. The old and new captains put on 263 for the second wicket as England posted 567 for 8 declared, the fourth time the pair had shared a stand of over 200 runs. As with Smith in Antigua, Atherton was happy to play the anchor role. Although he reached his fifty in seven fewer balls than his senior partner, he took 73 deliveries longer for the century. One of Atherton's great strengths is the way he paces an innings. He never feels the urge to lash out in desperation just because the scoring has slowed. Playing a supporting role does not cause him difficulties either.

Rain stopped play on Thursday and Saturday, the third-day shower allowing the England players to watch their rugby counterparts shock South Africa in Pretoria. The hero of England's 32-15 success was Rob Andrew with 27 points. The dressing-room fell about as Illingworth nodded approvingly, 'Well, he's from Yorkshire, you know.' Illingworth was in the dressing-room a lot. More than a lot. All of the time, in fact. Atherton had only good intentions when he said that he wanted Illingworth's influence in the dressing-room; he never expected him to set up home there for the next two and a half years. It was a serious mistake as the chairman's presence was resented by some of the England players. The dressing-room is a captain's domain, not the chairman of selectors'. It is the players' territory, a refuge where they can put their feet up and curse the rest of the world, including the England selectors and the rest of the cricket establishment. Part of the problem, though, lay with cricket's inflexible officialdom. Illingworth, rare in a chairman of selectors, likes to watch every ball – no one could ever question his diligence in that respect – and the only alternative to the dressing-room, invariably, was the committee room, where the majority of cricket thinking is outdated, ill-informed and muddled at the best of times. Illingworth, like Atherton, does not abide fools lightly, or rather at all. In that respect, the dressing-room was the lesser of two evils, although the chairman genuinely felt his presence among the players would help. The England selectors should have their own room, with a decent watching facility and all the technology available to monitor the England team's performance.

Illingworth's presence signalled the exit of the side's spiritual adviser, Andrew Wingfield-Digby, a Dexter 'appointment', from the dressing-room confines. The headline writers loved that: 'Illy kicks God out!' Illingworth had been asked earlier in the season by the TCCB's Alan Smith if he wanted Wingfield-Digby's help. Illingworth declined, but no one at Lord's thought of telling the good-natured chaplain, who had always tried to be as unintrusive as possible. The team chaplain was not the only casualty of the new regime. Mobile phones were to be switched off during the hours of play. It was added to the list of 'Illingworth's new rules', although the move was initiated as much by Fletcher and Atherton. Sunglasses also appeared on Illingworth's 'no-no' list, although the chairman's main complaint was about them being worn when they were not needed.

Atherton declared 45 minutes into the fourth day, after DeFreitas had completed a quick-fire fifty. England's 567 for 8 was the highest total at home in a dozen series against New Zealand. Play carried on into a fifth day, although Atherton took the extra half-hour on Sunday to try and finish things off, only for Parore and Hart to extend their eighth-wicket stand to 100 minutes by the close. Atherton was again pleased with his bowlers, especially DeFreitas who was making the most of his recall. The skipper himself took a brilliant reflex catch at silly point to dismiss his opposite number Rutherford. Atherton was not perturbed by not being able to seal the win on Sunday night, although the weather is always a worry. Formalities were completed half an hour before lunch the following day.

An England win is usually a cause for national celebration. Not this time. The victory by an innings and 90 runs could not even find a place on the back of sports pages, as that little Trinidadian left-hander had frustrated Atherton again. Not satisfied with the highest score in Test cricket, Lara hit an undefeated 501 for Warwickshire against Durham in Edgbaston to hold the same record in first-class cricket.

Atherton was pleased that, despite the disruptions to his West Indies squad, his new team had blended together well. Gooch (Man of the Match) and DeFreitas (nine wickets) justified their recalls, while Rhodes and White made impressive debuts. Atherton's sixth Test century was his third in five months. As with Gooch, the captaincy was proving a spur to his individual form. For once, it was Atherton's opposite number who was facing the captaincy flak. Atherton could only concur with Rutherford's remarks: 'I am under no illusions. When you aren't performing as a team, the captain is the one who is accountable.' Rutherford also showed Atherton that a touch of humour, especially in times of crisis, can have a relieving effect. One journalist asked if he found it personally distressing to be leading this ship. Rutherford just laughed. 'Did you say ship or sh . . .?'

Whereas Dexter had always provided a healthy comic

foil – although his clowning occasionally brought personal media ridicule – to the seriously minded Gooch and Atherton, Illingworth's stone-faced routine was not played for laughs. The new chairman was honest, far too honest, and far too open. No one was expecting him to lie, but much would have been better not said. Illingworth has strong views on just about every cricketer and cricket subject. After the Edgbaston Texaco win, Illingworth had assessed England's performance as 'seven out of ten'. At Trent Bridge, he was asked for his marks on this innings victory. Illingworth replied that he had given up that practice, then added, 'I don't ever give 10, I can tell you that.' It was an opportunity to be more generous to a side that had bounced back from being demolished for 46 with two Test wins and a draw. Even New Zealand's cricketing knight, Sir Richard Hadlee, felt that 'perhaps an eight-out-of-ten performance would be merited'.

Atherton was concerned about England's bowling as he joined the other selectors on the next Saturday night at the Cobham Hilton. Ilott had joined the growing injury-list that also included Caddick, Lewis, Cork, Gough, McCague and Bicknell. Malcolm, in his first Test after that knee operation, had shown little form at Trent Bridge. Illingworth's time since the first Test had been spent watching Yorkshire again. Despite witnessing tantrums from Stemp that earned the left-arm spinner a £500 TCCB fine for misconduct, Illingworth felt no need to punish him twice and he remained in the squad. So did Malcolm. The one enforced change was the recall of Paul Taylor for Ilott. Atherton felt the atmosphere was much more relaxed at this meeting. That was no surprise. England's captain had seen which way the Yorkshire wind was blowing and it was even stronger after the Trent Bridge success.

The foundations of the Illingworth–Malcolm conflict,

which dominated much of the 1995-96 South African tour, were laid the day before the start of the Lord's Test against New Zealand in 1994. Malcolm was informed that he would not be playing, so might as well make his way to Cardiff for Derbyshire's county match. This was an interesting move by Illingworth, who had made these comments on selection before the Trent Bridge Test: 'We never really thought we would play two spinners, but I am a believer in keeping all options available regarding the balance of the side. I have seen too many Tests where the captain, after seeing the pitch on the morning of the match, wishes he had picked someone else.' It was an unprecedented decision and a dangerous one. England's cricketers, fast bowlers especially, have appeared the most fragile of sporting bodies in recent years. It was Atherton who told Malcolm; it was Illingworth who made the decision. It sparked the resentment that Malcolm felt about the way Illingworth felt about him. Malcolm did not leave Lord's quietly. The press, as surprised as Malcolm was by his early departure, caught up with their prey around the back of the Warner Stand. Had it been a court of law, most of the questions would have been struck from the record by the judge as clearly leading the witness. In the world of newspapers, any affirmative response to 'Do you feel humiliated at being told to leave the England squad the day before the Lord's Test?', even a simple 'Yes', becomes 'I've never been so humiliated in my life!'

The fuss did not bother Atherton or affect the team build-up. Thursday's papers were full of Malcolm's exit, but by then the bowling decision occupying the captain's mind was whether England should play Taylor or Stemp. Taylor was the eventual choice, but the Northants left-arm quick failed to make an impression as the England attack was made to look ordinary by Martin Crowe. Fraser had taken a wicket in his first over, but it was a rare moment of English celebration as New Zealand ended the day on 316 for 4. Atherton tried six bowlers before lunch, including Gooch. Illingworth's enforced five-man bowling policy was exposed as flawed if you did not select a strike bowler in the unit. Atherton shuffled the attack around and Hick became the seventh bowler used. Unfortunately, Taylor was nervous and Atherton had nothing out of the ordinary, apart from DeFreitas, at his disposal to remove someone of the class of Crowe, once he was established on a typically placid Lord's pitch. The Kiwis were transformed. Even when Crowe went for 142 early on the second day, the final four partnerships added more than a hundred runs between them to reach 476.

Atherton felt his team's overnight 94 for 1 would give England the chance of batting for most of Saturday and Sunday to make life uncomfortable for the New Zealanders on the Monday. As it turned out, it was England and Atherton who would endure an uncomfortable three days, with defeat only being averted by the dogged determination of Rhodes. England's problems began on the Saturday morning when they added just seven runs for the loss of Atherton, Gooch and Smith. That began nine sessions of survival. Atherton's competitive instincts were evident when White was adjudged run out as England battled to save the follow-on. Umpire Steve Bucknor called in the third umpire, Roy Palmer, for an adjudication after White had raced to beat Dion Nash's throw from long leg. Atherton went inside the Lord's dressing-room to watch the TV replay and was astonished when, after watching the incident from two angles, Palmer let Bucknor know that White was out.

Atherton was not alone in thinking that the two replays were inconclusive and the run-out too close to call, in which case the batsman should have been given the benefit of the doubt. Atherton immediately went to the umpire's room and asked Palmer if he had seen any replays that had not been shown on TV. Palmer replied in the negative. Having checked his facts, Atherton felt justified in making an approach to match referee Clive Lloyd, and the pair returned to see Palmer. This visit lasted longer and Atherton would not comment on the incident. Atherton's concern was not whether Palmer had been right or wrong. He felt that, at a crucial time for England, not enough time and care had been taken over a decision that could have had serious consequences in terms of the eventual result of the match. Atherton was right. Later in the day, TV replayed the incident frame-by-frame. With White's bat just making the line, which is not in, it was just possible to see one of the bails rising out of its groove. The law states that a bail must be removed completely for the wicket to be broken. Atherton had made his point. Palmer had used his umpiring judgement, not the TV technology, to make his decision. There is little point in calling for replays if the third umpire is going to make decisions the same way he would out on the field.

Things were certainly going Nash's way. After a knock of 56, as well as running out White he took 6 for 76. His final victim at the end of the third day was Such, who with Rhodes had taken England past the follow-on. Rhodes batted three and a half hours for his undefeated 32. Atherton felt England would now save the game. The Lord's pitch would not crumble and he did not believe that England could bat as badly again. They did. Despite DeFreitas reducing New Zealand to 29 for 3 the next morning, the tourists made steady progress after that and declared an hour before stumps on 211 for 5, setting England a target of 407.

That total had been reduced by 56 runs without loss by the close of play, but any winning thoughts vanished when Nash removed Atherton and Gooch in the third over of the final morning. It was a serious blow to England's chances of survival as that pair were England's best anchors in a storm. Stewart's century saw England through the first two sessions, and Rhodes was Horatius on the bridge after tea. The last hour arrived with New Zealand requiring three wickets but Rhodes held on after bad light forced Rutherford to withdraw Nash from the attack. Rhodes had been warned several times for time-wasting, although Rutherford admitted he would have behaved the same way in similar circumstances. Atherton absented himself from the England balcony during the final minutes to shower and change: 'There's not much you can do in the dressing-room.' Atherton is not a great watcher, but makes sure he is there at the important moments. As exhilarating as Rhodes's fighting resistance was, England's captain was unhappy with almost every-thing over the five days – 'We were sub-standard in all departments' – and he again wondered why Lord's seemed to inspire tourists more than the home side. England's three victories in the previous 16 Lord's Tests had included two against Sri Lanka.

Atherton headed for home, where the final Test against New Zealand was going to be played. The selectors met at the Manchester Copthorne Hotel on Saturday night. Atherton felt that with the summer divided between two series, serious discussions about changing the batting line-up should take place at the end of the New Zealand leg, although he had already decided that Crawley was the next man in, ahead of Thorpe, as far as he was concerned. The bowling was analysed much more on a Test-by-Test basis. Everyone was pleased that Gough had proved his fitness. He was included instead of Taylor. Malcolm was also left out, along with Stemp who was replaced by Salisbury. Again, the England selectors were rolling the dice. Salisbury had taken five Worcestershire wickets the day before. Illingworth claimed that Stemp's disciplinary appearance at Lord's the following Tuesday had influenced the selectors – not from a behaviour point of view but from a logistical one (especially if he did not play and had to travel to Canterbury for Yorkshire's next match). Both Illingworth and Atherton were angry that an incident that had occurred before the second Test had not yet been resolved by now.

Atherton won the toss and batted, becoming the first Lancashire player to lead England in an Old Trafford Test since Archie MacLaren in 1902. He nearly marked the occasion with a century on the first day. England finished on 199 for 4 with Atherton undefeated on 96. The majority of batsmen, even Test stars, will look at the clock and the overs and make a conscious effort not to be stranded a few runs short of a landmark overnight. Atherton is not one of them. Each ball was treated on its merits and his sleep not disturbed for a second by the thought of the four runs needed for another England hundred. The Old Trafford crowd was not happy with England's slow progress. At tea, the total was 114 for 4 before Atherton and White added 85 runs in the final session.

Atherton was not happy at the reality of Illingworth's idea of collective responsibility among the England selectors. The issue was Salisbury, who was left out. The press were informed that it had been the captain's choice. A brave move, considering the respective records of spinners and fellow-selectors Illingworth and Titmus. But the captain had not gone out on a limb. Titmus and Fletcher, as well as Atherton, wanted Such. Bolus did not mind; only Illingworth wanted Salisbury ahead of Such. England's spinner bowled a total of 10 overs in the Test. Atherton did not argue that he had preferred Such, but what was this information doing in the public domain on the opening day of the Test? It was no big deal and there was no big row. Yet the chairman of selectors had made it known that he had not got his way, and the inference from his comments was that the England captain had. Not true – it was a clear majority decision by the selection panel, even if the final veto belonged to Illingworth. After battling away for 367 minutes, Atherton was not pleased to be quizzed about the choice of spinner. He was learning that life with Illingworth was not quite as simple as this plain-speaking Yorkshireman made out.

Atherton did not last long after completing his seventh Test century on the Friday morning. South African umpire Barry Lambson's unfamiliarity with the Old Trafford wicket was evident as he raised his finger for Nash's lbw shout, to a delivery that would have bounced over the stumps with six inches to spare. The day belonged to DeFreitas and Gough, with bat and ball. The pair added 130 in an eighth-wicket stand that was never dull, then each grabbed a couple of wickets that evening, Gough the scalp of Greatbatch in his first Test over, to put England well on top. New Zealand were all out for 151 before lunch on the third day, trailing England by 231 runs. Atherton had no hesitation in enforcing the follow-on. England had only bowled 57.3 overs and Sunday was a rest day (the only one of the summer) because of the Wimbledon men's final. England's bowlers had reduced the Kiwis to 132 for 5 just after tea on Saturday, but the home side were not to take another wicket until Tuesday morning. The New Zealand heroes were Martin Crowe, Parore and the rain. Less than 19 overs were possible on Monday and the weather ended the series at 3.20 on Tuesday afternoon. DeFreitas took the awards for Man of the Match and the Series. His 21 wickets and 44.69 batting average reflected a remarkable comeback. New Zealand's survival in this final Test was due to Crowe, as Atherton observed a world-class batsman with a bloody-mindedness to match his own. Crowe had gone into the Test with flu, and a course of antibiotics had given him the 'runs' during England's innings. After popping off a couple of times, Crowe was told by the umpires that New Zealand would not be allowed a substitute. Atherton had reminded them that Crowe had been selected despite his condition, and they would have to live with that. Such a hard line is cited as evidence of the decline of sportsmanship in cricket. Yet, Atherton believes New Zealand took a chance on Crowe and had to face the consequences. But the tourists' gamble paid off. Without Crowe's 17th Test century, England would have won the series 2-0, not 1-0.

ATHERTON
It was a quiet first half to the summer. The one-day series was disappointing because of the weather. We got Crowe out cheaply in the first Test and won at a canter. The selectors left the final bowling spot up to me. Daffy had been swinging the ball in the nets. That choice paid off. The only personal disappointment was being 101 not out overnight and getting out first thing the next day. There was a big one out there. Goochie saw it and filled his boots. Lord's was a poor all-round performance, I had wanted Devon to play, but was out-voted. Bumpy [Rhodes] saved the game for us. He batted well all summer and didn't miss a chance in two series. But for the weather, we would have won at Old Trafford. We hadn't set the world on fire, but the first half had gone well. I wasn't happy with the decision to field just five batters, but it was working, so who was I to argue? I knew the South Africa series would be a far tougher test of our resources and resilience. I never imagined it would be such a personal examination of the England captain's capabilities.

Atherton was a winning captain at last, and had a future: Illingworth had announced that Atherton was the man to lead England against South Africa in the second half of the summer. Nobody was surprised, other than at the chairman's delay in making the announcement. As ever, there was a sting in the tail: 'If he does well, he'll do the winter tour.' Atherton was already taking a view over his own position with regard to Illingworth. He could look after himself. Illingworth wanted you to respond, to bite. Atherton was going to concentrate on his cricket and his captaincy. Unfortunately, the England captain was about to plunge himself into one of sport's greatest controversies, and he could only grab the helping hand stretched out to save him – Illingworth's.

CHAPTER TEN

Soiled Forever

Although Michael Atherton is no angel and he has never pretended to be, this fair-haired young Lancastrian carries an air of innocence about him. Midway through the summer of 1994, little had disturbed the public perception that here was someone who had wandered along his plotted path to the England captaincy without a hair out of place, a bead of sweat appearing, or breaking into a trot. Even his undoubted untidiness had a schoolboyish charm about it, the comic-book hero with his shirt hanging out of his cricket trousers and his cap at an angle. Everyone knew there was steel in his stance, though. The nation had grown to respect his resilience and fortitude in the face of adversity. Even with regard to England's selection battles, Atherton was gaining sympathy as the underdog, a victim of someone who never missed an opportunity to remind the world he was his young captain's elder and better.

That squeaky-clean, whiter-than-white image was blown away for ever in one sensational weekend at Lord's. Atherton's life has never been the same since. A few relationships and friendships with officials, former cricketers and media men have not been repaired. His actions divided the cricket fraternity; so did reactions about what the consequences of those actions should be. Yet despite there being such firm and entrenched views on both sides, his behaviour that Saturday afternoon remains one of cricket's great unsolved mysteries, a sporting *Marie Celeste*. What the hell was England's cricket captain doing in full view of the television cameras? Questions about why he misled the match referee are much easier to answer and understand: Atherton panicked. What is not in question is that the TCCB handled the matter with all the confidence and sureness of touch of a blind surgeon wearing boxing gloves. No less memorable than those pictures of Atherton rubbing dirt on the ball are those of England's captain being fed to the media lions a few minutes after his side had just been bowled out for 99 and lost a South African Test by a record margin. The public did not know that Atherton's act of contrition had been organised largely without his consent or consultation. The Atherton 'dirt-in-the-pocket' episode was a mess, from start to finish. As the dust settled, Atherton was not the only person with his reputation soiled.

Atherton and England were already in trouble at Lord's before the match became of secondary importance on Saturday afternoon. Atherton knew it was time to make some important decisions about England's batting as he drove down from Blackpool for the selection meeting at the Manchester Copthorne Hotel. It was no secret that Hick and Smith had been fighting for their places during the New Zealand series, nor that the next men in line were Crawley and Thorpe. Whatever else was discussed and decided, Atherton was going to stand his ground on Crawley. He wanted him in the side. Who should go? Once again, the presence of White dictated that two senior batsmen could not be dropped. The selectors agreed that on form and cricketing judgement,

Smith had been the bigger disappointment over the past year. The problem was that this was the one match Smith had waited his entire Test career for – facing the country of his birth, now readmitted to the international scene, at the home of cricket. It seemed his destiny and the perfect final chance. Yet the panel agreed that this was not the time to let emotion sway their judgement. Now the arguments centred on the merits of Crawley or Thorpe. Both were in good form, although Thorpe had outplayed Crawley and Lancashire with a magnificent 145 in the second round of the NatWest Trophy at The Oval ten days earlier. It would have made sense to play both at Lord's, especially as Illingworth mentioned that White was struggling with sore shins. But the chairman would not revert to the six-batsmen policy. That may be why he let Atherton win the battle over Crawley. The panel was locked at 2-2, with Fletcher on Atherton's side, as the meeting went on until midnight.

The selectors spent so much time deciding who should be in the batting line-up that there was later confusion over the order. Titmus and Bolus were sure it had been agreed that Hick would come in first wicket down. Atherton believes that the choice was left to him. His view was that Crawley should bat where he felt most comfortable, and the newcomer chose his normal Lancashire spot, No. 3. The consequence of this was that England's most senior batsman, Gooch, was moved down the order. It was an astonishing decision. A new Test bowler does not get the new ball and choice of ends; such privileges have to be earned. Atherton knows only too well that nothing in the English system prepares players for the demands and rigours of Test cricket. Crawley's confidence was admirable, as was his desire to meet the challenge head-on. Yet no other country in the world would have handed a newcomer their biggest problem batting-spot, especially if it meant shifting their most experienced batsman into unfamiliar territory after nearly two decades at the top of the order. It has been a mistake oft-repeated in Atherton's time as captain, largely on his three major tours abroad. Robin Smith should have batted at No. 3 in the Caribbean in 1994 and in South Africa in 1995-96; Gooch should have been in the top three in Australia in 1994-95. England's batsmen, more than any, need time to adjust to the highest level. The Australians and the West Indians, even with much tougher first-class systems, realise that new talent needs learning-time down the order. Crawley was not the first to make a false start to his England career because too much was asked too soon.

Peter Such was the other selection casualty, with Shaun Udal brought into the Test squad for the first time. This time there were no arguments on the first morning about Salisbury's appearance, with Udal 12th man. South Africa were making their first appearance at Lord's for 29 years and Atherton knew he was in for a tiring day when Kepler Wessels won the toss. The South African batting was uncomplicated and determined. Wessels hit a century, but England's captain was reasonably happy with an overnight score of 244 for 6. The game began to drift away from England on the Friday morning as South Africa reached 357, but the real trouble began when the South African bowlers extracted more out of the Lord's wicket and conditions. Atherton was one of Allan Donald's five victims as England fell to his pace and Fanie de Villiers's swing. The follow-on target was passed with seven wickets already down, and South Africa were batting before lunch on Saturday with a first-innings lead of 177. The tourists continued to make slow, unspectacular but steady progress. That was the match situation when one of the biggest controversies ever to affect an England cricket captain sent the nation into turmoil.

Midway through the day, BBC commentator Tony Lewis was watching live pictures of the England skipper and told viewers: 'It looks like Michael is giving the ball the Aladdin's Lamp treatment.' No one could argue with his description. Atherton was working on the ball, as he was fully entitled to do. What caused the phone lines to jam the switchboards at the South African Broadcasting Corporation in Johannesburg, and eventually set Lord's buzzing, was that Atherton was not working on the ball with his fingers alone. The television pictures clearly showed England's captain removing something from his right-hand pocket and rubbing it onto the ball. The substance was dirt, and Atherton was attempting in the humid conditions to keep one side of the ball dry to help Darren Gough's reverse swing. Viewers in England were behind those in South Africa as the cricket was sharing BBC transmission-time with horse racing, but the word was soon out. Reporters headed for the pavilion, seeking reaction from the third umpire, the match referee, the South African camp and the England captain when he came in for tea. Atherton escaped the mob. The management got a message onto the field, via Gooch on the boundary, telling the captain not to talk to anyone when he came in at tea as there was some ball-tampering trouble. Gooch relayed the message, adding: 'It must be their ball, ours is doing **** all!'

True enough. A look at the scoreboard with the tourists approaching a 300-run lead with only two second-innings wickets down did not suggest any messing with the ball by England. The umpires were contacted by walkie-talkie and told to keep checking the ball. Umpire Bird told Atherton and confirmed that the umpires were satisfied that its condition had not been altered. By the time Atherton came in at tea, Illingworth had studied a video-tape of the incident and told the captain there might be a problem. Atherton did not see the TV pictures at tea-time and was not particularly worried. He felt that stopping South Africa running away with the Test was a far more pressing matter. By stumps, the tourists were 372 runs ahead with six second-innings wickets left, but few in the press box were concentrating on the match situation. Those pictures were pretty incriminating, and ball-tampering had been cricket's biggest story of recent years. Modern technology at newspaper offices allowed papers to take the pictures off the television. Only one burning question had to be answered: 'What had England's cricket captain been up to?' At this point, the TCCB and the ICC combined, foolishly believing that the matter could be resolved without any explanation being given to those millions who had watched Atherton's actions.

Atherton realised the situation had become serious at the end of play. Illingworth asked him what he had been doing. Atherton explained that he had put dirt in his pocket with the intention of keeping the ball dry. He turned out his pocket to show there was nothing else there. The chairman seemed happy with that. The words fitted the pictures and it was a practice he was familiar with. Meanwhile, match referee Peter Burge had spent the final session watching video-tapes of the incident. Atherton was told not to leave the dressing-room and England coach Fletcher remained with him. Burge's first discussions were with the umpires, Dickie Bird, Steve Randell and Merv Kitchen. They confirmed that, despite frequent examination, they were satisfied that the condition of the ball had not been altered. Then Atherton was summoned with Fletcher and asked to explain his actions, with the TCCB's public-address announcer, Alan Curtis, operating the video. England's captain, without prompting, had taken his trousers with him. Atherton and Fletcher were asked to leave while Burge talked to the umpires again and made his decision. A quarter of an hour later, Atherton walked through the Grace Gates, only pausing to say: 'Everything is fine.' The waiting press corps were still in the Lord's pavilion, waiting to be addressed by the TCCB's media relations manager Richard Little, who read out Burge's statement (the ICC regulations do not permit the referee to do so). The journalists were stunned by what they heard: 'The match referee has investigated, under Rule 4a of ICC procedures, unfamiliar action taken by the England captain when handling the ball during the afternoon session. Consultation with the umpires and an inspection of the ball confirmed that there was nothing untoward. I also confirm that no official reports were lodged by any parties. I have accepted the explanation given and no action will be taken.'

That was it. An explanation, but no explanation. The general public could whistle for any further details. At this precise moment, Atherton's future as England captain became a national debate. The most staggering fact of this incredible day was that the TCCB and the ICC genuinely believed the matter was now officially closed. Illingworth had already left the ground before knowing the matter had been resolved, a strange decision by a chairman of selectors who knew his captain was on the carpet. Atherton might have been fined or suspended that night. Illingworth bumped into Burge later that evening, who told him he had accepted Atherton's explanation.

ATHERTON
It had all come as a complete shock. Even when I came off at the end of the day, I wasn't particularly perturbed. I showed Illingworth my trousers and told him everything. I didn't think I'd done anything wrong, that's why I took my trousers into the meeting with Burge.

I can't deny that I panicked in there. If I had knowingly done something wrong, I'm sure I would have been better prepared. Suddenly, I wasn't sure. I had not cheated. But had I contravened the laws? I wasn't totally truthful.

Why? It was very much the atmosphere of the head-master's study and Burge is a fairly stern bloke. I was not totally honest with him, but I didn't feel I was withholding any evidence. He did not ask to examine my trousers. After he had asked about the resin, he asked me if I had anything in my pocket that could be used to alter the state of the ball. I didn't, but I know that I wasn't answering his enquiry as completely and fully as he expected, or as fully as I could have. I didn't think it was crucial, but if I could change anything in the whole affair, it would be that moment. That's my biggest regret.

Atherton slept well enough, but the Sunday papers proved a rude awakening. Few suggested that the affair was over and much was made of the clumsy way the incident had been investigated and generally handled by the cricket authorities. The game's most respected commentator, Richie Benaud, writing in the *News of the World*, started his comment piece with: 'Has everyone in this cricket world gone bonkers?' His view was that 'the cricket authorities have a duty to their public to make that explanation public, for the benefit of this and other cricket countries. People paying their money at the turnstiles and watching on television and buying newspapers keep the game going, along with those who play club cricket and engage in other aspects of the game.'

Illingworth was much more worried than the captain on Sunday. He had become aware that when Burge made his adjudication, he had not known about the dirt in Atherton's pocket. Burge did know now, probably from his meeting with Illingworth the night before, and he was not a happy ICC referee. That, and the newspaper reaction, left Illingworth in no doubt that he had to take pre-emptive action. While Atherton was trying to save the Test, Illingworth was attempting to rescue his captain.

Illingworth admits that he instigated Atherton's way

out, although England's captain was left looking far more guilty after that chaotic televised press conference. Atherton was presented with a *fait accompli*. England were one wicket away from a massive Test defeat when Illingworth told him he was being fined on two counts – a) having dirt in his pocket and b) failing to come clean with the match referee – at £1,000 a time. In addition, the England captain would present himself for a press conference about the matter at the end of the day. That was the price of hanging on to the England captaincy, Illingworth maintained; Atherton was never given the opportunity of taking his chance and riding out the initial storm. Illingworth states in his book that 'we had to sort it out to show the world we meant business.' It had been a very long time since England showed the cricket world it meant business. Illingworth had spent the day acting like a sporting Henry Kissinger, brokering deals, hammering out statements and trying to find an acceptable solution, and did not watch a ball after lunch. It was obvious that the England chairman of selectors, not Fletcher, should have been present at the Saturday night enquiry. The bottom line is that Illingworth made a deal with Burge: Illingworth would fine his captain and the ICC would take no further action. That is exactly the type of behind-the-scenes, corridors-of-power compromise which Illingworth has always claimed is so damaging to cricket.

The 'dirt-in-the-pocket' problems aside, Atherton's day was not going well. It had begun with England's captain walking down the pavilion steps with his hands in his pockets. It was a deliberate gesture after a lot of mickey-taking by his players as they pored over the Sunday papers in the dressing-room. (The laughing had stopped by the time of the press conference that night, and Atherton thought it sensible to deny it had been a conscious act.) South Africa declared at lunch, setting England a victory target of 456 runs, or more realistically, five sessions to hold out for a draw. England did not even manage to last two, and were bowled out for 99 in 45.5 overs. Atherton was first to go, Crawley's footwork was exposed again, and the rest of England's batting collapsed, this time to McMillan and Matthews.

When it became obvious that the match was not going to go into Monday, Illingworth should have postponed the 'dirt-in-the-pocket' press conference until the following morning to give Atherton a chance to recover from the 356-run defeat and gather his thoughts. Illingworth claims he was trying to protect the captain, yet it was obvious that Atherton was in no fit state to deal with a public trial by television, or answer questions about his very integrity and a matter that had largely been taken out of his hands over the previous 24 hours. Few sporting personalities have ever been so publicly humiliated on and off the field in a single day. Atherton, reeling from the worst defeat of his England captaincy, entered the library at the top of the pavilion at Lord's and could have no doubt that he was about to fry in the hot seat. The press had been waiting for half an hour, and the TV arc lights and humid weather had turned the library into a sauna. EW Swanton later commented: 'I never remember a Test being played in England in such stifling heat.' That room has never been so packed. The press conference went out live on the BBC's *Sunday Grandstand*, and Atherton quickly realised he was in the witness box again.

Illingworth was first up: 'In discussing this incident with Michael Atherton this morning, he told me that he had dried his fingers with some dirt in order not to dampen the ball. After giving the matter some consideration, I decided that this matter should be resolved and put to rest as quickly as possible. I took into account that the match referee Mr Burge was unaware of the full facts, that there had been no alteration to the condition of the ball and that no artificial substance had been used. He used dirt to dry his fingers. Taking this into account, I have decided to fine Michael on two counts. Firstly, for using dirt. Secondly, for giving incomplete information to the match referee. He is to be fined £1,000 for each count, £2,000 in total. As far as I am concerned, this matter has been dealt with and is now closed.' This statement had taken most of the afternoon to compose and had been altered several times.

Atherton read out the prepared statement before the press grilling started:

> Having spent some time looking at television footage and discussing it with Ray Illingworth, I felt the sooner I explained the situation the better. Yesterday evening, I was asked to attend a meeting with Mr Burge, and after that, he issued a statement that he accepted the explanation I gave and that no further action would be taken. In my explanation, I did not present all the facts. I am here to explain what I did and to answer any questions. As you are aware, we use sweat to get bruises out of the ball and then rub to maintain the shine. It was very hot and humid out there yesterday, your hands get wet and this in turn dampens the ball when you handle it. You all saw me reach into my pocket, dry my fingers with some dirt in order not to dampen the ball. Whilst I told Mr Burge that I put my hand into my pocket to dry my fingers, I did not tell him I used the dirt to dry them; therefore my response to his questioning was incomplete. I would like to add that at no time in my career have I ever used substances to alter the condition of the ball. I would like to apologise to Mr Burge and the South African team. I hope everyone accepts my apology.

The statement had TCCB double-speak written all over it

– 'therefore my response to his questioning was incomplete'. Such clumsy and unnatural language only alerted the media to ask further questions. That statement, as with Burge's, was never going to satisfy an enquiring mind. It had all the hallmarks of a rushed and botched job. It soon became obvious that Illingworth's desire to sort the mess out quickly had only made matters worse. One thing he should have realised is that these controversies have a life of their own. Public opinion and reaction play a major part in the outcome, who goes and who stays. Illingworth's insistence that Atherton would not lose the job – 'There is no threat to his position' – was perceived as a challenge to the country's morals. The view from the crowded library at Lord's that night was that Atherton's future as England captain would now have very little to do with the wishes of the chairman of selectors.

The interrogation began. When asked why he did not use a towel to dry the ball, Atherton replied, 'I did not have one.' He gave the sort of uneasy performance in front of the cameras that had cost Nixon the US Presidency to Kennedy. Illingworth sat behind the captain, who showed little stomach for the fight, especially as he became increasingly aware that the matter was not going to end here. What did rouse him were the suggestions that his actions were those of a cheat. 'People can say what they like,' Atherton retorted. 'I've explained the situation and that's the truth. I don't want the label of "cheat" on me. That is why I have come out and made this statement. I don't want it to fester. My conscience is clear. I have never worked on the ball, or used an illegal substance to change its condition in my life. To be honest, I was completely nonplussed with all the fuss on Saturday night. I don't believe I have damaged the image of English cricket.' The press felt that the £2,000 fine was a small price to pay for the England captaincy, but that was not Atherton's doing.

ATHERTON

The mickey-taking in the dressing-room was the main reason I walked out with my hands in my pockets. By the evening, that was something I could not admit to. I was out early in our innings, but took no part in the discussions. I was aware things were kicking on. With eight wickets down, I was called in to the committee room. I was told what was happening: I was being fined. I would be making a statement to the media at the end of the day. I did not know it was going out live. Goochie reassured me this was not a resigning issue. I have always been fairly laid-back about ball-tampering. I have always thought there's a difference between ripping the ball with bottle tops and a bit of seam-picking and scratching, which is obvious to detect by the umpires. That is still very much the opinion I have today.

The watching millions on television and Joe Public now became Atherton's judge and jury. As with all English institutions, the suggestion of not playing the game – 'It's just not cricket' – sent the country into a frenzy of moral indignation. Atherton left Lord's hoping but not believing that the worst of his ordeal was over. The affair had left the cricket domain. Atherton's character and integrity were about to be pulled apart, even by some he considered to be close and loyal friends. He might not have enjoyed it, but while he was at Lord's, Atherton knew he was fair game. As he left Lord's on Sunday night, he had no doubts or worries about carrying on as England captain. But over the next 48 hours, Michael Atherton was on the verge of quitting, after less than a year in the job.

Cricket's officialdom was not finished with him. On Monday, Burge issued a statement which could hardly have been intended to secure Atherton's future or lay the matter to rest:

> On Saturday, my attention was drawn to action taken by the England captain when handling the ball during the afternoon session. At tea, I consulted the umpires, Dickie Bird and Steve Randell, and they assured me that the condition of the ball had not been altered in any way. Nonetheless, after viewing television replays, I again inspected the ball after play and discussed the matter further with the umpires. Although no report was lodged, I held an investigation with Michael Atherton and the England manager Keith Fletcher, with the umpires present. At the investigation, Atherton did not state that he had dirt in his pocket to dry his fingers. On the basis of his remarks and that there was no evidence of the ball's condition being altered, no action could be taken by me. Prior to last night's media conference, copies of the statements by Atherton and chairman of selectors Ray Illingworth were given to me by the TCCB. I have now carefully considered Atherton's statement. The action of having dirt in his pocket in order to dry his hands was foolish in the extreme and cannot be condoned, particularly when done by a Test captain. Law 42.1 says that captains are responsible at all times for ensuring that play is conducted within the spirit of the game as well as within the Laws. The fact that Atherton has misled an ICC referee by not giving a full and frank disclosure when given the opportunity to do so concerns me more than anything else, because of the effect on the image of cricket. I have noted that the TCCB has imposed a fine of £2,000 on Atherton. He has also apologised to me for withholding information and I have accepted that apology. I

consider this fine and the resultant publicity and public scrutiny of the England captain is a sufficient penalty in the circumstances and I do not intend to take any further action.

Thank you, Mr Burge. Light the blue touch-paper and retreat. It should certainly not be the role or the responsibility of the ICC match referee to hang any cricketer out to dry publicly.

Sports pages and more were full of what the *Daily Mail* called 'The Atherton Affair'. Newspapers organised phone-ins about whether Atherton should carry on as captain. The *Sun*, in its own inimitable style, gave away 20 packets of what it called 'Athers Soil – It Keeps You Dry'. The same paper that Tuesday had Geoff Boycott declaring: 'Michael Atherton should quit as England captain right now – before his life is ruined.' That was not news to Atherton. Boycott had rung him several times the previous day and told him the same. Pressure was now on cricket pundits to predict the outcome of this controversy correctly. Would Atherton resign? His fate was back in his own hands for the first time since Saturday night. The mood on Monday night and Tuesday morning was that Atherton could not possibly weather the storm, especially as the BBC was now screening new footage of Saturday's goings-on. Cricket correspondents were encouraged by sports editors and editors to call correctly. A simple enough choice. The problem, as ever, was the consequences of getting it wrong. Simon Heffer, the *Daily Mail* political columnist, reveals the correspondent's dilemma: 'I have been a fierce opponent of John Major as Prime Minister. I have felt many times that his position has been untenable, but I never once wrote that he should go or called on him to resign. *My* position would have been untenable if I got it wrong and he stayed. It's a call you can only make once, and you must get it right.'

So, if you wanted Atherton's head, you had to be prepared to put your own neck on the block. On Tuesday, the sensible call was that Atherton would go. The story and furore showed no sign of abating, and the understandable reaction would be for Atherton to give it all up: does anyone need all this hassle just for the privilege of leading the England cricket team? The BBC's cricket correspondent, Jonathan Agnew, felt the time was right to stick his rather long neck out: 'In my opinion, Atherton was attempting to alter the state of the ball.' Agnew's call for the captain to resign was also publicised on the back of the *Daily Express* with the headline, 'Why Atherton has got to go.' The problem with Agnew's pronouncement was that it was dressed in 'Dear Deidre' rhetoric: 'Mike Atherton's position as England captain has become untenable this morning. I say that with a heavy heart because Mike is a nice guy who has proved himself a talented and dedicated skipper in the heat of the battle.' Certainly Agnew could have been a more understanding friend, but it would do wonders for the BBC man's career if Atherton went after his public pronouncement. And on Tuesday, that was a reasonable shout – and although Atherton did not follow his advice, Agnew's profile was raised considerably by his role in the affair.

The ICC and the TCCB, through Illingworth, had twice tried to declare the proceedings closed. Yet nearly everyone had an opinion and wanted to express it. The Board's chief executive, Alan Smith, responded to questions about Atherton's suitability for the winter tour to Australia: 'It hasn't helped his cause. That is a matter for Ray and his fellow selectors to think and talk through. The condition of the ball wasn't altered. If it had been, I'm sure Mike would have been for the high jump – and quite rightly too!' Brian Close, sacked as England captain for time-wasting when leading Yorkshire a quarter of a century earlier, knew the score:

'Atherton can live with this – if the Establishment let him.'

Atherton was going to decide his future in the very place where he had accepted the England captaincy a year earlier. He was not running for cover. The trip to the Lake District with Isabelle, who had flown over from Guyana for a holiday, was a scheduled break. Lancashire were out of the NatWest Trophy and were not playing in the next round of championship matches. Atherton was not daft enough to go home. He had been warned that his Didsbury flat was besieged by reporters and TV crews and there were cameras outside his parents' house. He needed to be back on home territory. Lord's and the TCCB had been protective for their own sakes. Lancashire were much more concerned for the welfare and future of one of their own. Not a single TCCB official made contact with Atherton after Sunday night. The next conversation Atherton had with Alan Smith was two days before the next Test at Headingley. The Board could not and should not have been ignorant of Atherton's plight. He was their responsibility as much as Lancashire's. Atherton had been appointed by Lord's to lead England in the South African series. That situation had not been affected by the events of the past weekend. Atherton was not the Lancashire captain, yet the county showed far more consideration and care. The support and professionalism of Bob Bennett and his Old Trafford back-up played an important part in Atherton feeling able to carry on.

Atherton had been at Lord's on Monday morning for a photo-call which included the England and South Africa teams. The mood was a lot less jocular over the incident than it had been the previous day. His team-mates were well aware of the seriousness of the situation. Atherton collected his kit and headed for Manchester with Isabelle before setting off for the Lakes. Sunday morning's experience had put him off newspapers for the time being and not a single one was bought or looked at during his holiday. Atherton, realising that the affair would not go away, wanted to come to a rational decision about his future as England captain. His mobile phone was rarely quiet on the drive up the M1 and M6. Gehan Mendis, who lives nearby, warned him that his flat was surrounded by reporters. Atherton rang a friend and arranged to stay at the Mottram Hall Hotel that Monday night. He dropped Isabelle off there and went to Old Trafford, where the players were holding a barbecue. It gave him a chance to return to his roots and check out the mood of his team-mates, including Fairbrother. Atherton stayed for about an hour. That evening, he took Isabelle out for dinner at the Prestbury White House. They set off for the Lakes on Tuesday morning and stayed in Cartmel for a couple of days. David Lloyd turned up, pretending that he was just passing through and this was a remarkable coincidence. Atherton knew otherwise, but was grateful for the support and thought. He does not recall it as a particularly traumatic time and remembers enjoying himself just pottering around. He spoke on the phone to his dad, Jon Holmes, Bob Bennett and Neil Fairbrother. The message Atherton was getting back was, 'Don't resign if you don't feel you have done anything wrong.' His dad did not want him to stand down for the wrong reasons. By Tuesday, Atherton had decided that he would carry on as captain, if possible. Resignation would be an admission of guilt, and Atherton would be known forever as the Test captain who quit because he was caught ball-tampering and cheating. That left another matter to be resolved: 'Would all the fuss affect his ability to do the job?' Atherton sought the advice of Fletcher, Gooch and Steven Rhodes on this point. He knew the pressure at the Headingley Test would be enormous. After he told Bennett of his decision to carry on, they discussed easing that pressure by holding a 'clear-the-air' press conference at

Old Trafford on Friday. Atherton had already rung Illing-worth and told him he would be at Saturday's selection meeting in Leeds.

Atherton had been determined to ignore outside pres-sures as he considered his future. The national debate carried on regardless. As Tuesday came and went with no resignation, Wednesday's papers decided that he was likely to stay after all. With Atherton in hiding, Illing-worth was the daily contact with journalists: 'I'll back him to the hilt. Only I have the power to decide whether he goes or stays, and I'm determined to stand by him. In my opinion, he has been punished for what he has done. The matter was dealt with swiftly and now it's finished. Mike will definitely join the other selectors to pick the team this weekend.' An interesting view on the matter came from the former Pakistan captain Imran Khan: 'I know what he is going through and I hope he can cope with the pressure. Ball-tampering has become a major issue and the problem is, nobody understands what it is.' Another ex-Pakistan cricketer, Intikhab Alam, was not quite so understanding: 'Atherton has been caught red-handed. He has to be replaced. Can anyone be as stupid as to go onto a pitch with dirt in their pockets? Dirt can be anything. He must have had something else. I would like to know what precisely it was he had in his pocket. It's now up to the TCCB and ICC to investigate this further.' The last time the country had been in such a state of moralising over events on a cricket field had been after Mike Gatting's famous clash with umpire Shakoor Rana in Faisalabad in late 1987. The same questions about the decline and destruction of the very fabric of English life were being argued over by all sections of the community. MPs felt obliged to comment, happy that sleaze had moved from the Commons to Lord's, briefly. A *Times* leading article ended with the view that 'He should be replaced.' The Headmasters' Conference condemned his actions. The team's former spiritual adviser, Andrew Wingfield-Digby, wrote to the *Daily Telegraph* under the heading, 'Atherton and the hypocrites'. The editor of *Wisden Cricketers' Almanack*, wrote in the 1995 edition: 'There was a tidal wave of public emotion in which almost everyone, from the cricket correspondent of the BBC to people who had never seen a match in their lives, demanded Atherton's resignation.' The English people are very good at moral indignation; it has become a national pastime.

One of the more rational voices belonged to Ian Wooldridge. Writing in the *Daily Mail*, one of sport's top columnists observed: 'I feel sorry for the South Africans. They ride in under a new banner of miraculous political evolution, pull off a staggering victory and are left to drink their own champagne while their English cricket hosts engage in one of those periodic bouts of Calvinism which are as hypocritical as they are inept . . . If he loses his job, it is not merely being cashiered from the regiment. It is being branded forever as the man who disgraced England. That, for me, is the ultimate hypocrisy. Maybe Atherton may eventually have to take them to the High Court. Try convincing a jury that someone cheated like mad and still lost by 356 runs.'

Wednesday's *Sun* printed pictures of the South African fast bowler Allan Donald also working on the ball during the Lord's Test. They, too, looked highly suspicious. Donald admitted he was horrified when he saw them and felt a certain sympathy for Atherton's plight: 'I couldn't believe it when I saw them. They say the camera doesn't lie. But it does. On the basis of those pictures alone, I looked guilty. If the press had seen those before Athers', it might have been me in the hot seat. I can assure you that I wasn't trying to alter the condition of the ball.'

The tabloid media had been on Atherton's trail since Sunday night. The first pictures of the England captain appeared in Friday's *Sun* under the heading, 'Seams Like a Nice Girl Athers' as he and Isabelle were getting into his Peugeot 605. They headed back to Manchester on Thursday. His own flat was still under surveillance, so Atherton rang Mendis, who had a spare flat. Atherton spent the next few nights there in Wilmslow.

Friday's press conference was the next hurdle. Atherton knew he could not afford a repeat of the Lord's debacle. He met with senior Lancashire officials including Bennett, on Thursday night to discuss the options and the best way of presenting his thoughts on the events of the previous week. The key figure at John Brewer's house near Preston that night was Eddie Slinger, a barrister by profession. Slinger gave Atherton as thorough a grilling as he would receive the next day. He was cross-examined. Had he ever done this sort of thing before? Many times during matches? Any other time? The answer to all these questions was yes. Then came 'Why?' When he was bowling, Atherton regularly put dirt in his pocket to dry his hands. Atherton admitted that he had not told the referee the whole truth. That required an apology. The group got to work on the statement. It had become a complex issue. The words had to be his. Every issue had to be covered. The group never thought the Friday press conference would halt the affair in its tracks. Originally, Atherton was going to hold two press conferences, one for the TV cameras, the other for the written media and radio. The reason for this was that he did not want the TV lights in his eyes again. The memories of that Lord's press grilling will be with him for ever. He was eventually persuaded that this was not an ordeal he should go through twice in one day. His every word would be dissected. A slightly different answer to a similar question would only create more confusion. Ironically, the opening questions would be delivered by the BBC's cricket correspondent, Agnew, who three days earlier had called for Atherton to resign. His comments and the realisation now that Atherton was staying provided an immediate indication of what a difficult position Agnew had placed himself in. In a magnanimous gesture, Atherton called Agnew into one of the offices before the press conference and told him that, while he was aware of what he had been saying, he (Atherton) had no intention of carrying it on: 'It seemed a good idea at the time. He just told me about these sleepless nights he'd had over it. He was in a far worse state than me.'

The reaction to the Old Trafford press conference was rather muted. As with most cases in law, the Atherton affair all boiled down to intent. Atherton summed up the dilemma, which was not going to end with his statement here: 'There are those who are going to believe and those who have doubts. At the end of the day, only I know. That's why I decided not to resign. I think the players are behind me, but obviously my integrity has been undermined in the public eye. That is something I have to try to rebuild.'

The press conference was as packed as Lord's, but not as hot, as Atherton walked in smiling, wearing an England blazer and tie, with a cup of tea in one hand. Bob Bennett introduced chief executive John Brewer before Atherton read out a written statement, which Slinger had checked:

During the last few days, I have had the opportunity to reflect upon the issues raised at last Sunday's press conference and some of the comments which have been made about me. It has been a difficult time. I have been strengthened by the support I have received from senior officials of the Test & County Cricket Board, from Raymond Illingworth, from many fellow professionals, and from my club here at Lancashire. Throughout my career, I have never had any interest in winning cricket matches other than in accordance with the rules and spirit of the game. I respect the values of integrity and fair play which are at the very heart of sport, and I hope that my career to date has reflected those values. I am conscious of the criticisms which have been levelled against me, and I am anxious to put the record straight and clarify anything which remains unclear.

Last Sunday, I explained the reason for putting my hand in my pocket to dry my hands on some dirt or dust which was there. I had picked up this dirt 10 or 15 minutes before the televised 'incident' during an over bowled by Darren Gough. I had picked up the dirt from an old wicket a short distance away from the Test pitch, and in full view of anyone who was watching me at the time. What I did could be seen by umpires, players or spectators. As I have said, the incident which has come under scrutiny occurred about two or three overs later, when I put my hand in my right-hand pocket to dry it on the dirt or dust which was there. When I took my hand out of my pocket and placed my fingers on the ball, it was not with the intention of altering the condition of it in any way. There was dust in my pocket and on a couple of occasions, as the television pictures highlighted, I had dust on my fingers and wiped it on the ball. My mind was solely on keeping the ball dry and ensuring that sweaty hands had not dampened the ball. This is the full truth and complete truth of what happened. There was no other substance in my pocket and at no time did I attempt to unlawfully alter the condition of the ball. As you are aware, the umpires have confirmed the ball was not damaged at any stage, and I am concerned to think that my actions have been misinterpreted.

I have expressed my full apologies to the match

referee, Peter Burge, for my foolishness in not telling him of the dirt in the pocket. Thinking back to that meeting, I gave my responses without considering the consequences and believing that I had done nothing improper, but not wishing to raise suspicions about my actions. I cannot turn the clock back, but I fully accept that on this occasion I was thoughtless and should have given him the full picture. I have apologised to Peter Burge and that apology has been fully accepted. I have always taken pride in my own honesty and integrity, and while it is for others to judge, I would like to think that my cricket career so far has reflected those principles. I repeat that at no time during my career have I cheated or attempted to cheat, and nor did I do so on this occasion. I am now anxious to turn my full attention and efforts towards the responsibilities as England captain, particularly preparing for the second Cornhill Test match which begins at Headingley on Thursday. I remain fully committed to the cause of English cricket and, having been as open as possible about the issues raised during the Lord's Test match, I do not intend to say anything further on the subject after today's press conference.

Atherton's statement was full of lawyer-speak and the expected courtesies. The TCCB had in fact offered no support to him since Lord's, and precious little then. The use of the word 'dust' on his fingers, not 'dirt', was deliberate. There was still confusion as to whether rubbing dirt on the ball to keep it dry was altering its condition. As with Sunday's press conference, Atherton had to deal with questions after his statement. 'I did take my trousers to the meeting with Burge. He asked me if I had resin in my pocket; I replied, "No". He asked me if I had any other substance; I replied, "No". That is where I made my mistake. I was thinking of other substances such as iron filings, vaseline or lipsyl. I totally regret that I did that. We all make mistakes in life. It's just unfortunate that mine are magnified.'

Atherton let slip a smile when he explained: 'I wanted to let the dust settle. I finally decided that I would be resigning for the wrong reasons. I would be going not because I had committed a crime, but because of press furore. My prime concern was whether I would be strong enough to lead the team in a Test. I think I am a fairly strong character and strong enough to come through this. I certainly hope the Headingley crowd will get behind the team. As for me, I don't quite know what to expect. But I won't do it again – that would be foolish.' Not surprisingly, Atherton has stuck to that promise.

ATHERTON

All through the whole affair, I could not understand the enormous fuss it was causing. I'm not saying I didn't treat the matter very seriously. After Sunday night's press conference, I left in no doubt as to the precarious position I was in. But questions in Parliament, the Headmasters' Conference, The Times *leader, a national scandal – I ask you. What was going on? I have never taken myself that seriously. I felt isolated at times. I appreciated the help and contact I got from friends and family. I felt I was coping well, but every little helps. The more serious consideration for me was whether all this would impair my ability to do the job of England captain. Fortunately, it didn't and hasn't. When I went into the office with Agnew, he told me he had taken a moral stance. That seemed to be what a lot of people were doing.*

I was close to going on Monday and closer on Tuesday. I felt my position had been undermined. My sole intention was to clear my mind and do the right thing. Had I done anything wrong? My answer has always been NO. The people who didn't believe that then, won't believe it now. I'm sorry. There's nothing more I can say. The great danger is that you get carried away by all the mayhem. What I can say is, there is nothing that prepares you for going through an ordeal like that.

Three years on, the cricket authorities have done little to clear up the ball-tampering regulations. Did Atherton do anything wrong that Saturday afternoon? Dirt is not an artificial substance and he was trying to keep one side of the ball dry. He was not 'altering the condition of the ball', because the umpires did not report him. They are the final arbiters on the condition of the ball. An ICC referee would not have a legal leg to stand on in court if the umpires were prepared to swear that the condition of the ball had not changed. It is not an offence to have dirt in your pocket and rub it on the ball to keep it dry, as you can with sawdust, another natural substance. If a bowler attempts to alter the condition of the ball and fails, is he guilty of ball-tampering?

The second half of Atherton's fine concerned not telling the whole truth to the match referee. Had Illingworth been present, as he should have been after conducting the England dressing-room enquiry, the situation would not have arisen. Burge's questioning was also flawed. Having asked the England captain whether he had resin in his pocket, then asked if he had anything else there, the obvious implication was 'anything else that should not be there'. That Burge did not examine Atherton's trousers, which had been brought in voluntarily by England's captain, showed the amateur extent of the interrogation. Atherton did himself no favours by not revealing the presence of the dirt. He panicked, as anyone who felt himself innocent might have done when accused of one of cricket's most serious crimes.

'Everyone will be remembered for something – and this

will be my epitaph,' proclaimed Atherton at the end of the most frantic week of his life. The fact that this has not proved correct suggests that when everyone came to their senses, most realised Atherton's crime was nothing more than a minor misdemeanour, at the very worst.

CHAPTER ELEVEN

In The Gutter Press

Atherton arrived at the Ladbroke Hilton on Saturday night still overwhelmed by the events of the past seven days. His own problems had dominated his thoughts, but since Friday's press conference Atherton had tried to focus on the reasons for England's thrashing in the Lord's Test. The home side had managed a total of 279 runs in the match. Crawley had struggled and Hick had failed again. There were injury worries about White, Gough and Fraser. All three bowlers were selected, subject to fitness, and Joey Benjamin was brought in as cover. Thorpe was added to the batting line-up in case White was not fit. Illingworth, Bolus and Titmus confirmed what they thought had been agreed before the Lord's Test: Hick would bat No. 3, with Crawley dropping down to No. 5 or 6. Gooch was put back at the top of the order, with Stewart making way. In the end, White pulled out with a shin stress-fracture, leaving Atherton with the exact six-man batting line-up he had wanted at the start of the summer. Salisbury had not bowled well at Lord's, and the panel felt that Tufnell had paid his dues over his turbulent private life. He was recalled.

While Atherton was confident that the events since

Lord's would not affect his authority or standing in the England dressing-room, the reception from the Leeds crowd was another matter. The Red Rose and the White Rose have been adversaries for centuries, and Atherton felt that if the general public judged he was wrong to hang onto the captaincy, nowhere would they show it more than at Headingley. The two-day build-up with the team helped ease his tension. The morning of the match, though, found him apprehensive as he knocked up. His only cricket since Lord's had been a Sunday match against John Paul Getty's XI at Wormsley when Atherton appeared for the Cambridge Quidnuncs.

Atherton was aware he had never entered a Test match as mentally under-prepared as a batsman, but Heading-ley offered another big problem. More than any other Test ground in England, captains wonder about batting there if they win the toss, as the pitch and conditions often favour the bowlers. This Headingley track was damp, and batting would be difficult in the first session. Atherton has rarely faced many bigger challenges. He was determined not to duck out, but he worried as he walked out to toss up with Wessels whether that desire was clouding his cricket judgement. Was the sensible decision to insert the opposition? Wessels did not call correctly, Atherton took a deep breath and announced that England would bat. As he walked out with his old partner Gooch for the first time in nearly a year, the crowd gave him a great reception, the first real public reaction to his decision to stay on as captain. With that hurdle overcome, all Atherton had to concentrate on now was the attack of Donald, de Villiers, Matthews and McMillan that had destroyed England a few days earlier. Atherton has never dug as deep as he did that day, not even during his two-day vigil at The Wanderers 18 months later. How he got through the morning session, he still cannot imagine. Gooch's presence at the other end gave him a familiar landmark to focus on for the first three-quarters of an hour, before Gooch edged the ball to second slip. Hick was still there at lunch. So was Atherton – two hours at the crease, 19 runs to his name. He was on 28 when McMillan took a superb overhead right-handed catch to dismiss Hick. England 84 for 2, and Atherton needed help. It came in the shape of Thorpe, who made a mockery of his early exclusion, took the attack to the South Africans and brought Atherton to life. The captain's fifty came in 123 balls, Thorpe's in 60 as the pair put on 142 runs for the third wicket. Thorpe had gone by the time the Headingley crowd waited for the fairytale ending. Atherton had already endured two narrow squeaks on 99 when a slower delivery from McMillan now had him driving a fraction early and the bowler took the return catch. The groan could be heard all the way to Manchester as Atherton turned and reluctantly headed for the pavilion. His disappointment did not last. As the manner and magnitude of Atherton's effort sunk in, the crowd rose as one to give England's captain an even noisier and emotional ovation than the one nearly seven hours earlier. Atherton's 99 matched England's total in the second innings at Lord's and was his second such Test score in 14 months. You could discuss Atherton's character all you wanted in bars, newspapers, the Houses of Parliament and the Headmasters' Conference. Out in the middle was the real man and the cricketer that day: stubborn, single-minded and as tough as they come.

Human and hurt, too, as he was to show in an end-of-day press conference more emotionally charged than those at Lord's and Old Trafford. There, finally, England's captain cracked. He should have followed his first instinct and not appeared. But he had been in defiant mood all day and saw no reason to change now, except into a T-shirt bearing pictures of the legendary England openers Hobbs and Sutcliffe. In front of him were many who had written that he should no longer be captain of the England cricket team. He did not give them what they wanted. Of course, this was probably the most remarkable innings he would ever play in his life, but all they got from Atherton was the verbal equivalent of the straight bat that had frustrated South Africa for most of the day: 'I was no more determined to get a hundred today than I always am when playing for England. My priority was to put the side in a strong position.' The press wanted the blood, sweat and tears, the triumph out of adversity. Atherton would not play ball. He was just doing his job. There had been enough emotional outpourings over the past fortnight. Finally, though, he gave way to the resentment that had been building up since Lord's: 'A hundred would have been the best answer to the gutter press.' Atherton repeated the phrase. David Gower might have got away with a crack like that; Atherton did not. It came from the heart. It was also foolish. Atherton knew that before Jon Holmes told him off, but did not care. He was not going to pretend that all had been forgiven. It had not, on either side – that was obvious from the way the tabloid press tore into him again the next morning. Some correspondents who had supported him felt let down; others pointed at a leader losing control. The reality was, this had been the most emotionally draining day of his sporting life. At the end of it, England's captain gave the first public sign of the enormous strain he had been under since Lord's.

Atherton has always found refuge among his team and in the dressing-room. They gave him support the next day by scoring 477 for 9, the highest score conceded by South Africa since their return to international cricket. DeFreitas took the wickets of Gary Kirsten and Hansie Cronje with the third and fourth deliveries of Saturday morning and South Africa were soon 105 for 5. That was as good as it got for England. Peter Kirsten became the sixth-oldest batsman to score a debut hundred, and with help from Rhodes, McMillan and Matthews, South Africa got within 30 runs of England's total by Sunday lunchtime. Hick's first Test century in England and another splendid innings from Thorpe allowed Atherton to declare for the second time in the match and set South Africa a target of 298 from a minimum of 60 overs. The tourists closed on 116 for 3, maintaining their 1-0 advantage into the final Test at The Oval. England had recovered well after Lord's, but Atherton was disappointed. South Africa had been down, yet once again England's bowlers could not knock the tail out. The exuberant Gough, especially, had got carried away on the fourth morning, going for 153 runs in his 37 overs. England's batsmen had shown they could cope with the South African attack, especially as Donald was struggling with an infected toe; the bowlers could knock over South Africa's top order. Atherton realised that what was needed for The Oval was someone who could blow away the tail. Just as White's injury had allowed him to play the six batsmen he wanted at Headingley, the final Test would give him the opportunity to press for the bowler Illingworth had discarded before Lord's, Devon Malcolm.

ATHERTON
There was so much media attention. That would have been a great hundred – it was still a bloody good 99! I felt the comments Burge made before the match were out of order. He showed he was not an experienced match official.

I don't know why I went to the press conference, I should have learned my lesson at Lord's. I was still feeling pretty sore. My mind was still slightly scrambled. I would defy anyone to go through that and not feel bitterness in the short term. The alarm bells didn't ring with 'gutter press'. If I'm totally honest, I didn't give a stuff after the week I'd had. I recently saw an interview with Bob Willis on the balcony after the famous Headingley victory when he took 8 for 43. The papers had been suggesting that he should have been dropped. He was raving! Now I know exactly how he felt.

The captain paid a heavy price for Malcolm's presence: Fraser was dropped. Benjamin's local knowledge and ability to swing the ball won the vote for the fourth fast-bowling place. Illingworth had a blind spot about the Middlesex seamer. He felt Fraser's body language was negative and defeatist. He could not have been more wrong. Fraser's familiar kick at the ground when he strayed in line or direction, the hunched shoulders, the hands on hips, were genuine gestures of how much he cared for England and how hard he was trying. Fraser was also a good friend of the captain, and Illingworth was beginning to wonder whether Atherton's loyalty to the bowler had more to do with friendship than form. The chairman had got it wrong again. Every captain needs a fast bowler he can depend on, at any time, in any situation, even when a game is dead and the pitch is offering nothing; someone to throw the ball to in times of stress, frustration and despair. Merv Hughes was that man for Allan Border, Atherton's was Fraser – nothing less than total commitment, and a match-winning bowler when the conditions were favourable. Fraser had not been at his best during the summer, but that was hardly surprising after a 32-month lay-off from international cricket. He had been back in the England side for less than a year, producing match-winning performances at the Ovals, Kennington and Kensington. He was slowly building up the stamina that had made him such an effective member of England's attack, but his first full England summer back, alongside his county duties, had taken its toll and Atherton saw the benefits in cutting short Fraser's England duties to allow him to recover for the Ashes tour: 'Gus looks tired, but if it was left to me, he would be a strong part of the England set-up for years to come.' Illingworth had other ideas.

Atherton's hopes that his brushes with officialdom and the media were over for this series were dashed on the second morning of the Test. England's captain knew from Burge's Monday statement at Lord's that the match referee would jump on him given the slightest encouragement. Burge had summoned a meeting of managers, captains and umpires before the Leeds Test to remind them of their responsibilities. Burge then made public his words to Atherton: 'I told him if he sneezed at 11am, he will have double pneumonia by 6pm. The eyes of the world will be subjecting all the players to extra scrutiny. The incident at Lord's detracted from the South Africans' victory and from the fact that, this incident apart, there was no trouble with the players' behaviour. I've had trouble in various parts of the world, but the conduct of the teams at Lord's was impeccable. As far as I'm concerned, Atherton has apologised and the matter is closed. Mike starts with a clean sheet.'

If Atherton had felt there were a few old scores to settle with the press at Headingley, at The Oval it was Burge's turn. As at Lord's, despite no complaint or report from the umpires, Atherton was hauled before the ICC match referee. The informal mood of Lord's had gone. Burge read out the charge and Atherton was asked how he pleaded, 'Guilty or not guilty.' England's captain looked at Burge. This was payback time. The charge against Atherton was dissent. After being given out lbw first ball, there was little doubt that Atherton was not in agreement with umpire Ken Palmer's decision. The implication from the way he held his bat up and shook his head was that the ball had nicked his bat before thumping into the pad. Disappointment, yes. Dissent, no. The incident did not attract particular interest in the press box, but in Burge's eyes, Atherton had 'sneezed'. The 'double pneumonia' dose was a fine of half his basic match fee, £1,250.

For the third time in a month, Burge issued a statement on England's captain: 'Michael Atherton did show dissent at umpire Palmer's decision by indicating the ball hit his bat and shaking his head after leaving the crease. I consider this to be clearly in breach of Code 3 of the ICC code of conduct and Law 42.1 of the Laws of Cricket. Decision: Fined 50 per cent of his match fee and severely reprimanded.' Atherton had been done. While there was renewed speculation about his future, Atherton did not join the debate this time. He felt it was a set-up job from the start to finish. Once again, the umpire's authority was undermined. He is supposedly the sole judge of fair and unfair play. Neither umpire on the field, Palmer or Steve Dunne, felt, when questioned by Burge, that Atherton was guilty of dissent, though the third umpire, Alan Whitehead, did not agree. The investigation descended into farce when Burge attempted to prove the charge of dissent with the use of video evidence. When that proved inconclusive, despite many replays, he persisted in his view and informed Atherton that he had seen gestures not captured on camera and those had convinced him that the batsman was guilty of dissent. Illingworth thought it was ridiculous and told his captain to forget about it.

Atherton could have been forgiven for beginning to feel persecuted. After 26 years of doing little wrong, he appeared to have done little right over the past month. Misfortunes come in threes, they say, although Atherton's Headingley and Oval problems were a direct consequence of the Lord's affair. He was in good enough spirits not to cancel his appearance at a *Wisden Cricket Monthly* dinner at Greens in St James's, but the Saturday morning papers were full of speculation about his future again. This time, though, Agnew did not feel justified in commenting when questioned on the *Today* programme. No one was suggesting that the dissent fine in isolation was a hanging offence. It was the cumulative effect of a turbulent month which had seen Atherton in conflict at every turn. In the cold light of day, Atherton was beginning to wonder whether it would be possible for him to continue to function effectively as the marked man he now believed himself to be. The dissection of his every move since Lord's was not something that he would put up with long-term. But they say the darkest hour is just before dawn, and so it proved in Atherton's case. By Saturday night, he and England were revitalised.

That Saturday was a remarkable one for English cricket and some of its leading exponents. While Fletcher spoke with Atherton in the captain's room, Gooch gathered the rest of the team in the dressing-room. The former captain explained that the best way of keeping their current leader and showing their support for him was by performing on the field of play. Lancashire's Bob Bennett had got the first plane down from Manchester. He had been out to see *The Phantom of the Opera* and returned to see the Ceefax headline announcing: 'Atherton fined again.' Bennett watched the headlines and then called Atherton to see if he wanted him to come down. Atherton said he was okay, but Bennett felt this was potentially more dangerous to his position than Lord's. Bennett rang Fletcher. The coach thought Bennett's presence might be helpful. Bennett had already decided that. Atherton saw him there before the start and waved. They talked later – Atherton knew what Bennett's support meant.

The Test was evenly balanced that third morning. A belligerent, unbeaten eighth-wicket stand of 59 in eight overs on Friday night from DeFreitas and Gough had regained much of the initiative for England, but the home side were still 49 runs adrift of South Africa when play started. The one significant moment of England's brief time at the wicket that morning came when Malcolm was hit on the helmet by de Villiers, first ball. 'You guys are history,' is what Malcolm is reported to have said under his breath to the concerned South African fielders. Revenge is a dish best served cold. At the end of the day, Malcolm had the sixth-best Test bowling analysis of all time and South Africa were a beaten side – though it was actually Illingworth's rejection of Malcolm at Lord's and his subsequent isolation, not de Villiers's delivery, that fired the Jamaican-born fast bowler into action that afternoon. Atherton helped, too. He had raced off the field on Thursday evening, after a wayward late spell by Malcolm, and given the fast bowler a few blunt words on his return. The tourists lost their first three wickets for one run and never recovered. Malcolm bowled a total of 99 balls in the most devastating spell by an England bowler since Jim Laker's performance at Manchester in 1956. Malcolm looked set to emulate Laker's feat of collecting all 10 until Gough took the eighth South African wicket. England were left needing 204 for victory after Malcolm demolished Donald's stumps to finish with 9 for 57 and came off the field waving his England cap in triumph.

It was an emotional day in the England dressing-room. Attention first centred on Atherton, as Gooch urged the team to get behind their captain. Malcolm was next, as the impact of his achievement hit him. England's victory target was similar to Trinidad, and the openers went out in similar circumstances with 16 overs, one more than in Trinidad, to survive that night. As in Trinidad, the game was effectively over by the time the teams left the field, only this time it was Atherton's team which was in charge. Gooch was the catalyst as England reached 107 for 1 by the close. Frustrated by his dropped catch, he launched into the South African bowlers. The openers put on 56 in just five overs before Gooch was bowled by

Hands well down the handle and straps flapping, a six-year-old Michael Atherton (*above, left*) demonstrates the forward defensive and determined look that have frustrated the best bowlers in the world. But there were days before then (*above, right*) when he was caught without a bat in his hand.

Dressed up to celebrate graduation from Cambridge, with his proud mum by his side.

After his false start in the 1989 Ashes series, Atherton made his mark in the first Test of the 1990 summer with 151 against New Zealand at Trent Bridge (*above, left*). The Gooch–Atherton opening partnership had a fruitful summer and here they take a break (*above, right*) during their stand of 225 against India at Old Trafford (*both Patrick Eagar*).

Atherton on his way to his first England Test century abroad, at Sydney in January 1991 (*Allsport/Ben Radford*).

The series against the West Indies in 1991 was a torrid time for Atherton (*above*). Here he edges Patrick Patterson to Carl Hooper at Edgbaston (*Patrick Eagar*).

A visit to the Taj Mahal with his friend Neil Fairbrother was one of the rare highlights for Atherton during the 1993 tour of India (*Allsport*). Atherton's Lord's agony later that summer, (*below, left*) run out for 99 against Australia, in fact saw him installed as favourite to take over from Gooch as captain (*Patrick Eagar*).

Atherton in charge. Atherton discusses options with veteran spinner John Emburey at Edgbaston in August 1993 on his debut as England captain (*right*). That Edgbaston Test was lost, but the next was won by 161 runs at The Oval (*below*), England's first victory over Australia since Melbourne, December 1986 (*both Patrick Eagar*).

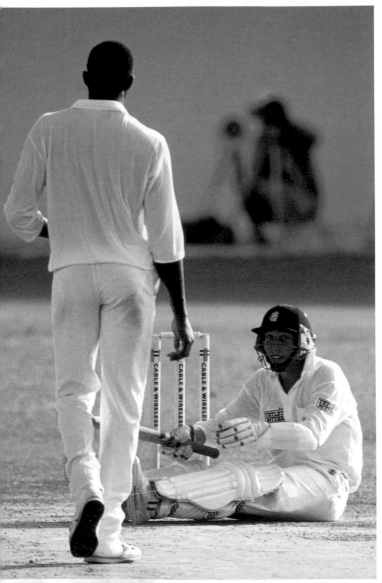

Atherton down but not out as he faces up to the challenge of the West Indies fast bowlers, and Courtney Walsh on this occasion, in the first Test of the 1994 series at Sabina Park in Jamaica (*Patrick Eagar*).

South African highs and lows. The famous TV picture (*above*) from the Lord's Saturday in 1994 against South Africa that began one of the biggest cricket controversies in recent years and plunged Atherton into a month of turmoil (*Patrick Eagar*). It ended when he was fined for dissent at The Oval by ICC match referee Peter Burge for his actions (*right*) after being adjudged lbw (*Allsport/Adrian Murrell*). The delight and determination of Atherton are there for all to see after his heroic and match-saving 185 at The Wanderers in December 1995 (*Allsport/Graham Chadwick*).

Atherton and Illingworth *(right)* at Melbourne during the tempestuous and troubled 1994-95 Ashes tour, they were together in charge for 33 Tests *(Patrick Eagar)*.

The Ray Illingworth era ended with Atherton's first success abroad as captain. The squad *(left)* celebrates taking the series at Christchurch, where Atherton was named Man of the Match for his 94 not out and 118. But, a month earlier, the outgoing chairman of selectors had written off the team and captain he had worked with for three years *(Patrick Eagar)*.

Matthews. Gooch was still depressed by his fielding lapse earlier in the match and voiced doubts about going on the Ashes tour. Atherton quashed Gooch's suggestions that now was the time to retire. Atherton and Hick carried on the attack and England finished the job 19 minutes before lunch on Sunday. This was in every way as invigorating as The Oval victory over Australia the year before, and a great way for Atherton to celebrate the anniversary of his first Test win in charge and the end of the most turbulent month of his sporting career.

The Sunday papers had continued the speculation about his future, but those discussions were pushed down the page by Malcolm's exploits. Illingworth had announced the Texaco squad to face South Africa a day earlier, then explained that the selectors would delay naming the Ashes captain for the winter by two days. 'We're putting no pressure on Mike – I don't want any more problems. We initially planned to name the winter captain on August 23, but now we will do it during Thursday's one-day international. If Mike has any reservations, then he has a few more days to think things over. He is okay at the moment, but everything's a bit up in the air at the moment and that's one of the reasons we are waiting until the one-dayer.' There was another reason: Mike Gatting. Atherton was under no illusions about the fact that Gatting was Illingworth's alternative choice as captain. Atherton had felt it at the start of the summer, Illingworth had picked Gatting as his successor during the Lord's crisis and Gatting was back in the England dressing-room for The Oval Test when Gooch had injury doubts. In a strange way, the sight of his rival a few feet away helped him through that week.

Atherton was named as captain for the Ashes tour on the morning of the first Texaco match in Birmingham. England took the one-day series 2-0, batting second on both occasions. The South African coach announced afterwards that he thought Atherton's side were a good bet for the 1996 World Cup.

ATHERTON

The lbw at The Oval was unfortunate – I got a big nick – but that's neither here nor there. I was disappointed and showed it. Look at most of my dismissals and you'll see me shaking my head and talking to myself. During the afternoon, I was told the referee wanted a word with me. Why? Who's in trouble? Me! I was going to be done for dissent. That was beyond me. I went in with Stewie. The charge was read out. We watched some video action which showed nothing. The two standing umpires were happy. Then the goalposts changed. I was told that I was in trouble for something that Burge had seen that wasn't on the video. It was an incredible month. I had never seen myself as controversial. Illy was supportive at The Oval – he said it was nonsense. These were remarkable weeks – I was just trying to hold my game together. It certainly made the captaincy more difficult.

CHAPTER TWELVE

Ashes To Ashes

England's Oval victories over Australia in 1993 and South Africa in 1994 had encouraged Atherton to believe that his team would mount a serious Ashes challenge. The tour turned out to be a disaster – every bit as feeble a campaign as the previous three. England went 2-0 down in as many matches for the fourth successive Ashes series and the second successive winter trip. That effectively ended the contest. England suffered dreadful luck with injuries – six additional players were called up – and the form of several stars of the summer dipped, none more so than the wicket-keeper Rhodes. Soon after the tour, team manager Keith Fletcher was sacked and Illingworth, now English cricket's first-ever supremo as team manager and chairman of selectors, kept Atherton waiting again before confirming him as captain for the start of the West Indies series. Illingworth had appeared in Melbourne before the second Ashes Test and stayed long enough to show that the rift between chairman and captain was growing.

Atherton, unlike Illingworth, has always kept the secrets of England's selection meetings and dressing-rooms. By contrast, Illingworth's frequent revelations often seriously undermined the captain's authority and position. Such disclosures usually came after an Atherton preference had failed to produce the goods. For this tour, though, Illingworth stood firm in the selection meeting. The chairman refused to budge or bow to his captain's pleas over the final batting and bowling spots. It is clear that the seeds of England's Ashes failure were sown in that meeting at the Copthorne Hotel in Manchester on the opening day of September. Atherton's troubled South African series had seriously weakened his influence and position, and Illingworth called all the shots with regard to Ashes selection and policy. (Atherton also remembers that the chairman had not been happy when he failed to identify Illingworth as the last England captain to regain the Ashes in Australia on *A Question of Sport* earlier in the summer.)

Illingworth's selection and policy, however, were shown to be flawed. He chose three out-and-out quicks to exploit Australia's fast and bouncing wickets, but the quarter of a century since his successful tour had slowed the Australian pitches considerably. The fastest by far was Perth, where the final Test was to be played. Atherton was happy to go along with Illingworth's feeling that Joey Benjamin would swing the Kookaburra ball. It was over the final bowling spot that battle lines were drawn. Atherton and Fletcher wanted Fraser; Illingworth, Titmus and Bolus insisted on Martin McCague to back up the pace of Malcolm and Gough. Atherton was not impressed. When Malcolm returned home from the West Indies tour for his knee operation, the management had checked on McCague's availability. His general fitness was not good, but not as poor as his tour report from the A team visit to South Africa. Illingworth ignored it. He would not budge, and England's captain was forced to abandon a bowler he trusted and relied on.

Atherton was keen to take Gooch, despite his mediocre

second-half of the season. No one had come near to handling Shane Warne as well as Gooch during the 1993 summer. Atherton did not feel he was deviating from his 'young guns' policy by including the 41-year-old veteran on such a major expedition. Atherton's reservations arrived with Illingworth's choice of Gatting for the final batting place. True, Gatting had enjoyed a successful county season, but he had not made any significant contribution with the bat at Test level since 1988, the year he was sacked as England captain. After being banned a year later for leading a rebel tour to South Africa (the five-year sentence was cut when South Africa were readmitted to the ICC), Gatting had been recalled for the 1992-93 tour to India, but his reputation as one of England's best players of spin was not reflected in his runs against Kumble or Warne, and he was dropped after the Lord's Test in 1993. Illingworth had made no secret of the fact that Gatting would have taken over as England captain if Atherton had not survived the summer of 1994. However, Atherton saw no place for him in Australia. He wanted the final batting spot to go to one of the youngsters, Hussain or Ramprakash. Atherton's thoughts were not only about investing in the future. The big grounds of Australia would be no place to hide two veterans, especially two who no longer fielded close to the bat. Illingworth claims it was not anticipated that the pair would play together – in which case, Atherton thought it made even less sense to take someone of Gatting's years and experience as back-up. But the chairman was adamant. Atherton would go to Australia without a bowler he treasured, with a batsman whose best days were behind him, and with a strategy based on outdated and inaccurate information.

The omission of Fraser was the big talking-point when the Ashes squad was announced. The Middlesex bowler found out watching the live Sky TV broadcast from Old

Trafford. As Illingworth moved alphabetically from DeFreitas to Gatting, Fraser's worst fears were realised and he reacted angrily to not being told beforehand. Illingworth claimed that had not been possible as the meeting, which also included picking the 'A' team, did not finish until after midnight. There were also suggestions that Atherton should have made the call. It was another botched job by Illingworth. Fraser was the only person left out that most people expected to be in. He deserved a phone-call, and it should have come from Illingworth. If the chairman overrules the captain, only he can explain the reasons properly to that player. There was little point in Atherton offering consolation – Fraser and the rest of the country knew that it was not the captain's decision to leave him behind. Only Illingworth could explain. England's management and communication left a lot to be desired, but Illingworth was not finished with Fraser. He fined him £1,000 for speaking out without permission and threatened to have him removed from the tour stand-by list.

Atherton toed the party line at the Ashes press conference. His support of Fraser had been well documented before the selectors met, and Illingworth made it clear that, unlike last winter, this was the chairman's squad, not the captain's. Atherton was still optimistic that the side could build on the summer and compete with the Australians. Illingworth may have dominated the selection meeting, but when England boarded the plane in October, Atherton and Fletcher would be back in charge.

ATHERTON

The selection of the Ashes squad was the final proof that it was no longer the captain who had the final say. Illy was the main influence. After all I'd been through in the previous weeks, I wasn't really in much of a position to argue. The points we argued over have been well documented. I felt that one senior player was enough. It had nothing to do with Gatt being a threat to my job, although I knew Illy was keen on him. Goochie was on top of his game physically. I knew he would cope with the rigours of Australia. It's not just a question of going out to bat, you have to look at the other requirements. As for Gus, it had nothing to do with friendship. I knew that he could do a job for England in Australia. Illy, for some reason, thought he was a negative influence. Nothing could be further from the truth.

Perth is the first stop for England's cricketers these days. The net facilities are good and the city offers a relaxing start to the Ashes tour. However, Atherton's hopes of a quiet build-up were quickly dashed. The Australian press were waiting for him. In a preview article with Martin Johnson of the *Independent* before the West Indies tour, published on 4 December 1993, Atherton had said: 'The one who really got up my nose was Steve Waugh, who spent the entire series giving out verbals – a bit of a joke really, as he was the one bloke on either side who was wetting himself against the quick bowlers, and there he was, standing under your bat ribbing you all the time.' (Johnson had misquoted Atherton. The England captain actually used the word 'crapping'.)

Those comments were saved for nearly a year and reprinted as England's cricketers were in the air. Atherton had questioned the courage of one of Australia's own, in a country where manliness is regarded as more important than godliness. The comments were certainly indiscreet and only recalled by the journalist after a dinner in Manchester because the conversation had been recorded. Atherton's defence to an aggressive Australian press corps that he could not remember making the remark was not far off the mark. He tried to repair the damage as best he could, expressing the hope that this Ashes contest would be fought out on the cricket field, not in newspapers: 'One or two recent series have been fairly bad-tempered. We are here to play good cricket. We are not here to start a sledging war, but, let's be fair, the Aussies have been pretty good at dishing it out. We don't see the need for it. Yet equally, we are not going to let them walk all over us.' The sledging problem had already subsided, with the new Australian captain Mark Taylor publicly declaring that it would not be part of his game-plan.

This first published skirmish was nothing to the crisis Atherton and the rest of the England management faced after a few days in Perth. Tufnell spent a night in a psychiatric ward after losing control in his hotel room as he was struggling to cope with what was happening on the other side of the world. The tour management considered bringing out a replacement, but the doctor would not confirm he was 'unfit' to continue. Fortunately, the incident was hushed up and did not become public until the team were back in England four months later. The England management were on the phone to Lord's, discussing what to do, when Tufnell appeared at the door, can of beer and cigarette in hand. Tufnell was fined and warned that any repetition would mark the end of his tour and the end of his Test career. Atherton was worried that the circumstances that caused Tufnell's outburst had not changed, and the management kept a close watch on him until his wife flew out with the other families to Melbourne. Apart from the one bad night in Newcastle, Tufnell was back on an even keel.

Atherton felt that four first-class matches were sufficient preparation for the opening Test, which would begin in Brisbane a month into the tour. England, without skipper Gooch, had never recovered from the three-day defeat there four years earlier. This time, Atherton's best laid plans were beset by a trio of misfortunes, one of which could certainly have been avoided. As in 1990-91, he lost his opening partner early on. Stewart broke a finger in Perth facing White in a practice match and did not return until the match before the first Test. Many felt that Atherton–Gooch was the better opening combination anyway, but before the team left England, it had been announced that Gooch would bat at No. 5, primarily to counter the threat of Warne. Once again, Illingworth's management style had created a misunderstanding. He had asked Keith Fletcher to find out if Gooch was happy batting there. The message came back that he was. When Illingworth arrived in Melbourne, he learnt differently. Gooch had told Fletcher he would bat anywhere if it served England's cause. The 'happy' aspect was never discussed. Illingworth complained that if he had known that, the switch would not have been made, but there would have been no misunderstanding in the first place if the chairman had been in direct contact with the player himself. Gooch, after hitting 129 in the festival opener at Lilac Hill, scored 38, 68, 50, 101 and 50 at the top of the order going into the first Test. Atherton kept to his pre-tour promise and Stewart opened in Brisbane. Gooch moved down to No. 5, where he was to find himself batting with Gough and DeFreitas trying to save the Test. The Australians could not believe it. Captain Mark Taylor confesses he was baffled by the tactic: 'Goochie had scored a hundred before he came in to bat. We could see him playing every ball in the pavilion. It was obvious to everyone that he hated hanging around waiting to bat. He had been in such good form. We were delighted to see him come in down the order and be stranded with the tail. It was a strange way to treat your best batsman.'

Atherton had no control over the two setbacks that occurred in the week leading up to the Test. As England left Hobart to fly to Brisbane, he lost his main strike-bowler. Malcolm went straight to a doctor after checking into the Sheraton Hotel and was diagnosed as suffering from chickenpox. He was out of action for a fortnight. Fraser, who had positioned himself in Sydney coaching and playing grade cricket for Western Suburbs, was soon on a plane to Brisbane. Tempted as he was to strengthen England's wayward bowling, Atherton felt duty-bound to pick from the original squad, as Fraser was only on stand-by. It was a point of principle Atherton maintained throughout the tour, even when Rhodes was struggling and Russell was sitting around twiddling his paint brushes. Atherton was not happy with England's batting or bowling form. The tourists had beaten South Australia but lost to New South Wales in a dismal performance at Newcastle. Atherton laid into his bowlers at tea-time on the third day: 'It was pretty shabby stuff. The bowling was crap and the fielding was worse, and as captain I felt responsible. It was time to let everyone know they were letting themselves down. You cannot ask players to be better than they are, but what I demand is that they are as good as they can be. What I say in press conferences is not necessarily what I feel.' It was Fletcher's turn to assess England's form in the next match, against an Australian XI. 'Pathetic,' was how he described the bat-ting after England were forced to follow on. With Illing-worth out of sight and out of mind, for the moment, Atherton and Fletcher decided that they would play six front-line batsmen in the Test. Stewart scored a century in Tasmania to confirm his fitness, so the choice for the final place was between Gatting and Crawley. Gatting had been left out of the Tasmania game and Atherton had been Crawley's champion during the summer, but the man who had led England to victory at Brisbane eight years earlier was chosen. That meant that the two players Atherton would not have taken to Australia, Gatting and McCague, were in the first Test line-up.

The most serious disruption to England and Atherton's

well-being before the first Test had nothing to do with injury or form. Once again, England's chairman of selectors sent his players a public message that was hardly likely to improve their spirits. Illingworth had spoken on-the-record at a Sports Writers' Association lunch in London three days before the Test. Not only did he rake over all the dirt from the summer, he gave his views on what he thought had gone right and wrong on the Ashes trip so far. The journalists had a field day. It was reminiscent of Illingworth's comments when the team arrived back from the West Indies. This was another public relations disaster, which disturbed England's build-up. Atherton ignored it as much as he could, but wondered why the chairman could not keep his mouth shut at such crucial times. In his book, Illingworth said that 'My reported answers were twisted, and given a different slant from what was intended, to a degree I have never experienced before.' He realised the problem and was soon on the phone to Atherton trying to repair the damage. Atherton had a faxed copy of the thoughts of chairman Ray pushed under his bedroom door. The content did not surprise him; he was more concerned about the effect they would have on his team. Illingworth's remarks included how he had saved the captain from the sack by fining him at Lord's; complaints about selection on the tour, the captain's failure to ring him in Spain and Fraser's call-up: 'If Mike puts him in the side, I'll ring him to tell him what I think.' An aside about Fletcher – 'He's the team manager, isn't he? He nicks a few catches in practice' – might not have been intended for general consumption but should never have been made. Atherton wondered if Illingworth knew how damaging his repeated outbursts were to England's morale. Was the Lord's affair not closed? Illingworth had made that plain at the Sunday night press conference. Four months down the road and it seemed that the chairman never missed an opportunity to remind everyone that Atherton owed his job to him.

In the team-meeting prior to the Test, Atherton emphasised that the Ashes challenge could be over before it began if England had a bad first Test, bad first day, bad first session, bad first few overs. Allan Border's side had grabbed the initiative when David Gower elected to field at Headingley at the start of the 1989 series, and rarely let it go over the next 17 Tests against England. The team's form had been poor and scratchy. Forget that, Atherton told them. Look at Gatting's side in 1986-87, the team that 'couldn't bat, couldn't bowl and couldn't field'. They went into that series with a dismal record in the state games but, inspired by Ian Botham's 138 at Brisbane, they retained the Ashes.

The two teams attended a Benson and Hedges reception two nights before the Test down on the Brisbane waterfront. Atherton was not impressed with the comedian and, at the scheduled end of the proceedings, led most of the team back to the hotel. Such formal and official functions are a chore for him. The Australian squad were much more relaxed – Warne and others stayed on to chat to Gooch and Gatting. The Aussies then moved on to City Rovers, a well-known Brisbane nightspot, and let their hair down before the battle began. England would have been well advised to do the same. The tension and apprehension in the England camp were all too evident at the Gabba nets the following morning. Crawley looked disconsolate at being left out, while McCague was feeling and showing the pressure of spearheading England's attack. Atherton would like to have told his team, 'Relax, go out there and enjoy it.' He could not. Too much was riding on this first confrontation.

All Atherton's warnings went unheeded after he had lost the toss. The first day ended with Australia 329 for 4 and in the driving seat. Taylor and Slater belted DeFreitas and McCague's first four overs for 26 runs. The pattern was set; Australia were in control. Gough celebrated the birth of his son Liam with the wickets of Boon and Bevan. The rest of the England bowlers had a dismal day. Taylor was run out and Gooch ended Slater's magnificent knock of 176. Atherton was devastated.

He was in a similar state at the end of the second day. After dismissing Australia for 426, England were reduced to 133 for 6 with the captain still there on 49. McDermott was the destroyer, finishing up with 6 for 53 as England stumbled to 167 all out. Atherton did not take his pads off – Taylor would surely have no hesitation asking England, 259 runs adrift, to follow on. That request did not come; Taylor wanted Warne and May to bowl last on the Gabba wicket. He had enforced the follow-on in Pakistan a month earlier and failed to win in Rawalpindi. Whatever Taylor's reasons, Atherton could not believe it. Tufnell took four wickets and Australia ended the third day on 194 for 7, 453 runs in front. England's final target was 508 to win or 11 hours to survive. Once again, the squad were pestered by utterances from the chairman. 'Sort it out with common sense,' was Illingworth's public message to Atherton. 'I can't do anything about it from over here. It's no use me grumbling about things. It's up to those on the spot. I'm disappointed it hasn't gone right so far, but that goes without saying.' Illingworth still said it, publicly. Atherton was dismayed when those comments were relayed to his players.

He was much more optimistic on the final morning. England were 211 for 2, with the not-out batsmen Hick on 72 and Thorpe on 66. Atherton and Stewart had both fallen to Warne before going to watch the action from behind the arm on the high TV gantry. As the third-wicket partnership developed, England's openers bowed to one of cricket's superstitions and refused to move. They were still there at the close of play. Atherton had been praying for a miracle – he was halfway there. If England could hold out, the threat of Warne in the series would appear greatly diminished and Taylor, still looking for his first win as Australian captain, would be heavily criticised for not enforcing the follow-on. It was a big 'if' which disappeared into fantasy when Warne removed both overnight batsmen early on. Gooch and Gatting were the last hope, but Gatting was exposed by the pace of McDermott for the second time in the match, and the folly of batting Gooch at No. 5 was exposed when he turned down a single to protect DeFreitas from facing Warne and was out next ball, sweeping, to become Healy's ninth victim of the match. Half an hour later, it was all over. England were 1-0 down after a 184-run loss, Taylor had his first Test win and Warne was the Wizard of Oz again with a Test-best 8 for 71. His figures on the final day were 6 for 27 off 25.2 overs. This had been Atherton's worst-case scenario. 'I am devastated to lose this game,' he admitted. 'Before the match, I said how important this match would be because in the last three series, the side which has won the first match has won the series. Warne is the best bowler from either side. If you go out there believing he is going to get you out, you will struggle. You have got to believe in yourself.' England's batsmen had spent hour after hour watching videos of Warne bowling, trying to familiarise themselves with his bag of tricks. It did not work. Perhaps they had been hypnotised by the endless videos. Rather than watching Warne in his pomp, they would have been better off seeing Gooch and Cronje, among others, giving him a hard time.

The rest of Atherton's year was an unmitigated disaster as England's batting, bowling and fielding were exposed. They lost to the Australian Cricket Academy and Zimbabwe and then to Australia in the Melbourne Test. The Ashes challenge had virtually evaporated. The biggest problem with losing the first Test in Australia is that afterwards, the emphasis switches to one-day cricket. England's biggest humiliation came at the North Sydney Oval as the Academy beat them twice over the weekend. The Sunday defeat was worse than the Saturday: England's 245 for 7 was passed with six wickets and nearly seven overs to spare. Four days later, Zimbabwe beat England by 13 runs under lights in Sydney. Atherton, who had missed the win over Australia 'A' two days earlier because of his bad back, found himself less of a media target than Fletcher. The England team manager was 'kangarooed' on the back of the *Sun*, with the heading 'Hop it Fletch.' After two one-day internationals, England had still to beat Zimbabwe. Atherton, while knowing these games can be something of a lottery, realised that supporters back home were in no mood for excuses. So when the TV replays showed that Zimbabwe's Man of the Match Grant Flower should have been given run-out on 26 – umpire Darryl Hair ignored England pleas to bring the third umpire into action – Atherton refused to grasp at such flimsy straws. England's injury situation was getting worse. McCague had departed with a stress fracture of the shin and Fraser was now a full member of the squad. White had a side strain that ruled him out of the second and third Tests. Benjamin's chickenpox was wrongly diagnosed as shingles. Mark Ilott appeared briefly, without playing, because of fitness doubts over Gough, DeFreitas and Malcolm before flying out again to join the 'A' tour. The one-day matches highlighted England's fielding problems, with Atherton attempting to man the outfield with Gooch, Gatting, Crawley, Fraser and Tufnell. Physio Dave Roberts had instigated a 'Lard League', which was based on the squad's body fat. Benjamin and Malcolm were the leanest, with Gatting, Fletcher and Crawley at the bottom.

England flew to Brisbane and then drove up to Toowoomba to face Queensland before the second Test. The

Sun had printed the hotel's number and asked its readers to fax Fletcher – or Keith the Kangaroo – with their views. Fletcher and Atherton were furious. There was no justification for the pages of abuse that were shoved under Fletcher's door. Atherton helped inspire England to a 37-run victory with a brilliant catch at mid-wicket to remove Matthew Hayden after the Queensland openers had put on 231 chasing 352 for victory. Tufnell took 5 for 71 as the home side collapsed in 18.2 overs. Gatting's timely undefeated double-hundred kept him in the Test side ahead of Crawley for Melbourne.

As Atherton flew into Melbourne, Illingworth was on a plane from England. Typically, the chairman gave a press conference before speaking to the tour management. 'The players have to knuckle down,' he told journalists. 'The one thing people back home won't tolerate is players who don't appear to be giving everything. Sloppy fielding is one example. There's no excuse for it and I won't accept it.' Atherton could not understand why the chairman had not waited until he had spoken to him and Fletcher. It appeared as if Illingworth had flown out with his mind already made up. Atherton sat next to Illingworth at the pre-match dinner and discussed the best way to play the Melbourne Test. The match started on Christmas Eve, with Christmas Day the rest day. Atherton called correctly and invited Australia to bat on a damp wicket. Australia's 220 for 7 at the close suggested England's captain had done the right thing. Atherton felt the Australians should have been bowled out in the day. The final total of 279 was no disaster for England, but the last-wicket stand of 57 by Steve Waugh and Fleming emphasised that the tourists had not made the most of the opportunity, and England's response, 212, left Australia in control again.

Atherton felt let down, not by his batsmen but by the umpiring. England's bad luck began with the first ball after lunch when Stewart's finger was broken again, this time by McDermott. Hick was then given out caught-behind off his pad by the Australian umpire Steve Randell before Atherton and Thorpe carefully added 79 runs in 33 overs. Both fell to Warne and umpire Steve Bucknor. Atherton was adjudged lbw to a leg-break which turned before hitting his pad. Then Thorpe fell to a bat-pad catch at silly point. Replays suggested only the pad had been in contact with the ball. The dressing-room was not a happy place. England were 124 for 3 and Australia, the tourists believed, had not taken a wicket. Those decisions, coupled with the fact that Steve Waugh had escaped a confident lbw shout from Gough first ball, left England believing this was anything but a fair contest. Gatting also departed to Warne that night, and Atherton had little doubt that England had been hard done by at 148 for 4.

When Gooch was caught and bowled by McDermott off the first ball, a full toss, the next morning, England's resolve collapsed. Australia were 237 ahead at the end of the third day with only three second-innings wickets gone. Taylor declared on 320 for 7 leaving England 120 overs to survive or 388 to score. The slim chances dwindled to almost nothing when Damien Fleming removed Gooch and Hick in his first two overs. Atherton was determined to fight it out. After 73 relatively untroubled minutes, he was given out caught down the leg-side off McDermott, again by umpire Bucknor. The captain's slow departure suggested Bucknor had got it wrong again. The TV replays confirmed this, showing the ball connected with nothing but pad. The final day, or rather 12.5 overs, was a complete embarrassment as England's last six wickets fell for 13 runs. Stewart, with nine injections in his broken finger, was undefeated on 8 as England were bowled out for their lowest total in an Ashes Test for 35 years. Warne, with 20 wickets for 200 runs in two Tests, completed the first Ashes hat-trick for

90 years. Australia's margin of victory was 295 runs.

Illingworth's prediction that the tour was now in danger of becoming a 'shambles' only stated the obvious. Atherton knew there was little point in bemoaning England's bad luck with decisions – this was not the place for making excuses. He himself suddenly copped much of the flak. The captain was accused of being too defensive when Australia were batting. The Test was over, heavily lost, and England had to win three out of three to take the Ashes. Respected commentators like Geoff Boycott went about tearing apart every one of Atherton's bowling changes and fielding placements.

ATHERTON

Brisbane was a disastrous start, just what we had tried to prevent. But you can talk all you want, it has to be carried out. We bowled so poorly on that first morning. Losing Devon was a big blow, but that doesn't excuse others from failing to come up to scratch. It wasn't just the bowlers – getting dismissed for 167 on that wicket was criminal.

The toss at Melbourne was a difficult decision. I did not like putting Australia in, knowing that Warne was around to bowl at us in the last innings. We weren't in a bad position at the end of the first day. I hate making excuses but we really got the rough end of the stick. And I took a lot of the stick as the captain. I didn't have the best of games, I'm happy to admit to that. Ian Chappell said that I had lost faith in my bowlers – I had. The field placings were indicative of that. I set fields to how they were bowling. Illy confessed to me that it's a captain's biggest headache when bowlers are wayward in difficult situations.

Atherton had real problems as the team flew to Sydney. Stewart was definitely out for the next Test; Gooch, Gatting and Hick were not batting well; Rhodes was keeping abysmally; Malcolm had taken 1 for 144 at Melbourne and DeFreitas had lost his form of the summer. Gough was about the only saving grace, and it was his enthusiasm and exuberance in the Sydney Test which rescued the tour from disaster.

Atherton and Fletcher decided the players would be better served taking a day off after the traumas of Melbourne. Most just relaxed around the hotel and slept, although a couple made their way to Bondi Beach as sightseers. Some of the media decided that this was an unacceptable way for the team to react to an embarrassing Test defeat. The complaints about the Gooch fitness-regime were forgotten as this England squad were savaged for lazing around on beaches when they should have been hiding their heads in shame. Even Gooch's view that England would have gained nothing from netting fell on deaf ears. As usual, Illingworth did not help matters: 'It's amazing to me in two or three months how things have drifted. It's not my job to fix up net-practices. It's their job, and it's up to them to do it. It's their jobs on the line, not mine, if they don't do the business. Michael believes if people have a job to do, they should be capable of doing it as professionals. That is correct in thinking, but it doesn't always work out quite as simply as that. You sometimes have to do other people's jobs for them and remind them of their jobs.'

As far as the series was concerned, England had to win at Sydney to keep any Ashes hopes alive. The reality was different: Atherton could not afford another defeat like Brisbane or Melbourne. He won the toss, batted and was still there when Crawley joined him after an hour with the score at 20 for 3. The Manchester Grammar and Cambridge pair added 174 before four wickets went down for four runs in the final 40 minutes and England finished the day at 198 for 7. Atherton, who coped better than anyone with the swinging ball, scored 88 before

McDermott bowled him with one that nipped back. The captain's overnight hope that England might get to 250 for once proved wildly pessimistic as Gough, aided and abetted by Fraser and Malcolm, swashbuckled England to 309. Gough, showing no fear and total enjoyment, gave Atherton genuine hope, not just in the match but for the rest of the winter and beyond. Before he went out to bat, Gough had told Sky TV commentator Mark Nicholas to 'fasten his safety-belt because I intend walloping the ball'. His 51 came in 56 balls. With Malcolm clubbing Warne for two sixes and racing to a Test-best 29, the England dressing-room was transformed and Atherton was desperately disappointed when rain ended play for the day after lunch. Gough's one-man show continued the next day as Australia were bowled out for 116, after being 65 for 8. Gough's figures were 6 for 49. He returned to the dressing-room to take a phone-call from the 'Bodyline' hero Harold Larwood, whom Gough had visited with Gooch in his Sydney bungalow. There were also congratulations from Ray Lindwall. Atherton admired Gough's dash: 'You need characters like Gough in the dressing-room – but if you had more than one they would drive you up the wall.' The third day ended with England 90 for 1 after Gooch became the latest to be mystified by umpire Bucknor raising his finger.

Atherton declared the next afternoon, setting Australia a winning target of 449. His team were on top and in charge for the first time in the series. Unfortunately, the mood in the England dressing-room was not as buoyant as one might have expected. The problem was that Atherton's declaration had left Hick stranded on 98. Hick knew a declaration was imminent, but showed little urgency in reaching three figures, and when he played three successive deliveries back to the bowler, Atherton called them in. The captain was merely putting the team ahead of the individual, but Hick was stunned and angry, and stormed off. Atherton's decision had been made with the best intentions. If Hick had been on 38 or 138, no one would have disputed that this was the time to declare. Why should 98 make it any different? When the team gathered in the dressing-room before fielding, however, Atherton realised he had made a big mistake. At the very moment he wanted the mood to be upbeat and unifying, you could cut the atmosphere with a knife. Hick did not say a word to his captain for the next 48 hours, even when Atherton made a special journey to Hick's hotel room that night to try and resolve the matter. This was a situation Atherton had not encountered before. He admits that he had seriously underestimated the effect his decision would have on team morale. Whatever the reasons, England failed to take a wicket that fourth evening and Australia started the final day at 139 for 0.

The wicket was a good one and Atherton was well aware that Australia had the batsmen to chase 310 on the final day. He kept it tight in the morning session, with 67 runs coming off 31 overs, without taking a wicket. The England dressing-room was not happy to see replays which showed that Taylor had been run out. Despite protests from the fielders, once again umpire Hair had not felt the need to consult the third umpire. Australia's hopes of chasing the target were ended by a heavy storm that lasted until an early tea was taken. Officially, only seven overs were lost, but the conditions had dramatically changed in the bowlers' favour. Australia collapsed from 280 for 0 to 292 for 7, largely due to the efforts of Fraser. Atherton was forced to take off his fast bowlers because of bad light, and May and Warne held out for a draw. The two batsmen had almost left the arena when Atherton informed the umpires that the minimum 15 overs had been bowled within the hour. The pair returned to face four deliveries from Tufnell before England's captain finally conceded defeat in his bid to regain the Ashes. He kept his disappointment to himself, keen to congratulate his team on picking themselves up from the Melbourne debacle and keeping the tour, though not the Ashes, alive. After the umpiring experiences of the past fortnight, however, Atherton felt the time was right to make a few points: 'If the technology is available, it should be used. I'm not bitter about it and whether Taylor was in or out, I'll be mentioning it in my captain's report. When the umpires walked off, I couldn't understand it and threw my cap down. I knew there was a few minutes remaining. The umpires then checked their notebooks – it was all a bit of a farce. They should know the rules.' Gough was named Man of the Match, but Fraser was the player with the biggest smile. The Middlesex bowler had taken four wickets in 13 balls to raise England's victory hopes and give Illingworth a first-hand demonstration of his capabilities.

ATHERTON
I made the Hick declaration for the right reasons. But it was wrong, because it deflated the atmosphere in the dressing-room. That certainly was not intended – you live and learn, but I was disappointed it had such an effect.

They then attacked the target. I ran out Taylor, but the third umpire was not called. Afterwards it rained and Gus nipped in. It drizzled all through the last day so in the end, I had to bowl the spinners. I couldn't complain; it was the weather that had helped get us in a winning position.

Fraser was one of many who enjoyed a belated celebration of England's recovery in Brisbane, where the tourists had flown for the next stage of the Benson and Hedges World Series. The whistle-stop nature of modern cricket tours allows the visitors little time to wind down or regroup. Whereas teams travelling round England finish a game in Birmingham, board a luxury coach and check into their Manchester hotel less than two hours later, elsewhere in the world, moving between venues is a guaranteed day out of your life and stamina-sapping. Atherton gave an interview to Peter Hayter of the *Mail on Sunday* and asked to see a copy of the article before it was sent.

England beat Zimbabwe by 26 runs the next day in intense humidity at the Gabba. Dehydration problems started early and Atherton's first request for a glass of water came before the end of the first over. Thorpe was England's mainstay with 89, but needed hospital treatment for heat exhaustion. The England bowlers completed the job, a tough one in the conditions, to give the side a realistic chance of making the finals, and Atherton headed for Melbourne hoping to put his feet up for a couple of days before meeting Australia under lights at the MCG. The article by Hayter ended all that.

Under the heading 'Atherton Bid For Power: I should pick the England team, not Illy, says captain', the selection of the England cricket team was again the topic of the day. It was a row with Illingworth that Atherton could have done without. The chairman was soon on the phone from Sydney to arrange a meeting when the party returned there. It was a rare outburst from Atherton about the way his youth policy had been betrayed. It came at an emotional time of the tour and was a minor blemish compared to the regular outpourings from Illingworth that breached selection confidences and had a serious effect on team morale. Atherton was annoyed with the distraction just as his team had got back on their feet. That improvement was reflected in England's first win over Australia after 12 weeks out there, achieved after Gough broke down delivering his first ball as Taylor's team chased 226 for victory. Gough, after a scan four days earlier had failed to show any problem, was carried off and out of the tour with a stress fracture in his left foot. Earlier, he had belted 45 runs in 49 balls. Now, as he bounded in to bowl, he collapsed in a heap in his delivery stride. The Yorkshire fast bowler had emerged as England's symbol of hope for the future. Atherton rallied his troops as Gough was cheered and chaired off – the Australians admired Gough's bulldog spirit. Fraser took his place and led the way with 4 for 22 – including the wickets of Taylor, Slater and Steve Waugh to leave Australia 19 for 3 – in his 10 overs. The home side never recovered and were bowled out for 188, a tremendous achievement considering England had been left with only three front-line bowlers. Atherton was as pleased with the commitment and team spirit as the result. Back in Sydney, Illingworth wanted to know about the Hayter article. Atherton felt England had more pressing matters, like their injury crisis. Fairbrother was now with the party and Chris Lewis, playing in grade cricket in Melbourne, had replaced him as a substitute fielder at Melbourne. The only two members of the party who had not appeared on the sick list were Gooch and Rhodes.

ATHERTON

I've never felt or said that the captain should be in sole charge. I wanted the captain to have a say. Certainly my reservations about two of the final picks for the Ashes tour had proved to be correct. I wasn't jumping around saying, 'I told you so.' I was being honest when I said that I felt some of the selectors were out of touch at their age. I knew that Illy would defend his choices. I just felt the modern game had moved on. But I was happy with my input in selection.

In the end England failed to make the World Series finals by 0.01 on the net run-rate, leaving the two Australian teams to play among themselves, after Fraser needed three off Paul Reiffel's last ball and managed only a single. They arrived back in the dressing-room to be told that they would be leaving for Melbourne the next morning on their way to the Victoria game in Bendigo in five days' time. The England players had had enough. They had a few days off and they wanted to spend them in Sydney. The schedule, with the lows of the Melbourne Test, the rejuvenation in Sydney and the trek to Brisbane, Melbourne and Sydney again, left them needing a break if this recovery was not to be short-lived. Fletcher was surprised at the hostile reaction of his players, believing he was acting in the best interests of the team. Player power prevailed and they enjoyed a couple more days with the families.

Atherton spent some of that time in discussion with Geoff Boycott for a series of articles in the *Sun*, with the paper's cricket correspondent John Etheridge operating the tape recorder. It was typical Boycott, full of typical Yorkshire arrogance. Atherton would close his eyes and wonder if he was listening to Trueman, Close, Illingworth or Boycott. The tape included Atherton's interjection: 'Can I say something?' Boycott: 'No, let me finish.' Once again, Boycott brought up the 'dirt-in-the-pocket' affair and criticised Atherton for not resigning, or at least offering his resignation. Boycott now maintained the TCCB would not have accepted it.

Illingworth had scarcely recovered from the return journey to England before *he* was back in print, despite what he had told the tour management in Sydney after the *Mail on Sunday* row: 'They denied they were criticising, so I did the best thing possible under the circumstances to defuse the situation. I told them I would not say anything more in public about the matter, and would leave all future quotes to them.' Fat chance. Illingworth told *Sun* readers, 'This habit, this modern trend of not shaving makes me angry. I sorted it out when I was chairman, but it crept in again. Since I've returned home, the trend has returned and the captain is the worst culprit. He's going to be clean-shaven this summer, I can tell you. There is a tour manager and a team manager and it is difficult for me to cross the line without stepping on somebody's toes. But I have to have a word.' No one could argue with that last sentiment.

England's injury problems went from bad to worse in Bendigo. Stewart's first game back ended when he was hit on the finger again. Ironically, the vice-captain had been dropped in the gully the previous delivery. England's batting took a further knock when Hick was ruled out of the rest of the tour with a prolapsed disc after scoring his 80th first-class century. Fairbrother travelled early to Adelaide for treatment on his damaged shoulder, but never recovered. Lewis joined the party and Mark Ramprakash was sent for from the 'A' tour in India. Atherton and the tour selectors sat down to pick from a depleted party that included only five fit batsmen. Atherton conceded that England went into this fourth Test with a side that would never have been picked out of choice. Gatting, who had been lined up for the chop since the Brisbane Test, had to play. So did Rhodes, scorer of 23 runs in three Tests. He was actually promoted up the order. Lewis went straight in as part of the five-man bowling attack.

Atherton felt strangely confident as he won the toss. The Adelaide Oval is one of the best batting surfaces in the world and there were far worse places to enter a Test with only five front-line batsmen. Gooch and, especially, Gatting both came good, while the captain added a determined 80. Gatting's century, after half an hour on 99, was his first at Test level for eight years. With England's line-up, it was no surprise that a promising 286 for 3 translated into an average 353 all out. Australia led by 41 runs on the third evening with five wickets down. Malcolm and Fraser wiped out the tail for another 25 runs before Thorpe and Crawley took England to 220 for 6 with a day to go, a lead of 154 runs. Atherton now felt that England's enforced selection might work in their favour. The Adelaide track was still a good one, but his bowlers would give Australia a run for their money if the home side were chasing anything over 200. Whatever happened, Atherton would attack. The Barmy Army were in town and making a lot of noise. The captain felt that no one could complain if they went down fighting. DeFreitas signalled England's intentions right from the start by blasting 68 off 57 balls, including 22 off a McDermott over. This was not slogging but brutal, clean hitting. England added 108 runs in less than 19 overs, Atherton had a lead of 262 and the Australians were batting before lunch. The captain told the team that they must not worry about losing. Winning was all that mattered today.

No Australian wickets had fallen by lunch and Atherton turned his attention to Malcolm. He reminded him of The Oval in 1993, how some of the best batsmen in the world had danced to his tune; of The Oval a year later against South Africa; of Brisbane and the chickenpox, how misfortune had denied him the chance of starting this Ashes campaign and how costly that had been for England. This was his chance to set the record straight. Taylor was first to go, slashing Malcolm to slip. Sixteen deliveries later, Australia were in tatters. Boon gloved Fraser hooking, Tufnell took a great catch as Slater hooked Malcolm, then Steve Waugh was beaten all ends up by Malcolm's next ball. Tufnell removed Mark Waugh, then Lewis got in on the act. When he dismissed Warne and McDermott in the over spanning tea, the home side had slumped to 83 for 8. However, his gesture to the latter – showing him the way to the dressing-room – earned both him and Atherton a reprimand. The fall of Australian wickets stopped for two hours as Healy and Fleming kept England at bay, but Lewis broke the stand and then

Malcolm ended the contest in England's favour with 35 balls remaining. England had won by 106 runs, a remarkable achievement with such a makeshift side. No one could complain about Atherton's negative attitude now. 'Days such as this make it all worthwhile. This is a moment to rank alongside any I've experienced in cricket. I'll remember it for a very long time. And I'm going to get drunk tonight. Tomorrow, we're visiting a vineyard, so I'll probably get drunk again.' It's unlikely that he sobered up in between. The Barmy Army party started at the Adelaide Oval and carried on in town through the night. Atherton joined in the celebrations and singing, but only as part of the chorus. It may be his Barmy Army, but Atherton's voice has never been heard in a solo. A good man knows his limitations. Special T-shirts were already being printed to celebrate the success in Adelaide.

The Ashes had stayed in Australia's possession when England could not force a win in Sydney. The series was still alive, though, and victory in Perth would give England a share of the spoils. To recover from a 2-0 deficit would be a rare achievement: the only England captain this century to manage it was Len Hutton in the Caribbean in 1953-54. Atherton had a problem – he was running on empty. 'Not much petrol left in the tank' had been a favourite phrase of his predecessor Gooch. Atherton was mentally, physically and emotionally exhausted. The Perth Test would be his 16th in charge inside a year. His team had recovered well in the series against the West Indies, South Africa and now Australia, as well as beating New Zealand. He had been churned through the media mill for a month after the 'dirt-in-the-pocket' affair and that notoriety had remained. The change in the selection policy and Illingworth's regular public utterances had also taken their toll. There had been hardly any time in the previous 12 months for England's captain to wind down. The non-stop, high-profile job of leading

England's cricketers against three of the best bowling attacks in the world had left Atherton drained.

Atherton had hoped that the farewell Test appearances of Gooch and Gatting would inspire the tourists to one final effort. England battled hard, but folded on the fourth evening when Taylor declared. The target was 453 to win, 104 overs to survive. But England were finished at 27 for 5 overnight and the Test careers of Gooch, setting a new record for England appearances, and Gatting were over. Atherton survived to the 12th ball of the final morning, when again he was caught down the leg-side by Ian Healy off McGrath. The captain's scores of 4 and 8 were a disappointing end to a series in which he averaged over 40 without managing a century. England, despite another spirited knock from the newly arrived Ramprakash, were bowled out for 123 and lost by 329 runs. The night before, Atherton had sat slumped in a chair in the Sheraton bar, as worn out as any of his team-mates can remember him. He revived after a drink with some of Australia's cricket legends, the Chappell brothers and Dennis Lillee. England's captain was not fed up with the job, although he did not feel the same sense of optimism that had consoled him at the end of the West Indies tour – Illingworth's arrival as chairman had dismantled much of the foundations that had been laid down there. Illingworth's selection policy for the tour had backfired. Gatting (Adelaide apart) and McCague had failed dismally; Rhodes, White and DeFreitas had faded dramatically after strong summers. Illingworth and Atherton could not be blamed for the ridiculous run of injuries that had even left the physio Dave Roberts with a broken finger and cost them Malcolm, Stewart, Gough and Hick at vital times. Atherton was disappointed because the team spirit had never reached the levels of the Caribbean.

ATHERTON

*It had been non-stop; I was wiped. I didn't feel we had
progressed. That can be a great comfort at the end of a
tiring trip. The policy of the previous winter had been
abandoned. We hadn't replaced it. The injury problems
made things very difficult, with players coming and going.
After that great win at Adelaide, I had high hopes of
levelling the series in Perth. Australia won and the 3-1
scoreline reflected their domination. The big fields exposed
our limitations.*

Atherton had again proved himself a resilient leader in
adverse circumstances. The flawed game plan, to blaze
away with a pace-attack on supposed quick, bouncy
wickets, had not been his. The omission of Fraser, again
not his decision, was a glaring mistake. Illingworth's
belief that Gatting was good enough to compete at Test
level, let alone be a possible captaincy contender, was
exposed as nonsense. Gooch and Gatting were now history, so Atherton's young guns were back in play, especially after Ramprakash's impressive late entry. Atherton
was looking forward to an uneventful break before the
West Indies. Once again, England's captain had reckoned
without Illingworth and the men at Lord's.

CHAPTER THIRTEEN

Illy's The Boss

Atherton was enjoying the delights of Neil Fairbrother's benefit golf trip in Florida when he learnt that Keith Fletcher had been sacked. Atherton was disappointed. Fletcher had been a great help to him, especially since being appointed captain, and Atherton never had to ask for his support. The England captain often wondered why Fletcher unselfishly took so much stick when it would have been easy for him to apportion blame elsewhere.

Fletcher's quiet, low-profile style was in marked contrast to the man who now assumed sole responsibility for running the England team, Ray Illingworth. The chairman had returned from Australia and met with the TCCB's chief executive Alan Smith before heading for his Spanish apartment. His experiences in Australia had led him to believe that their chairman of selectors should manage the England side abroad. There was no love lost between him and the current tour manager, MJK Smith, whom he had beaten for the chairmanship a year earlier. Illingworth identified a decline in the dressing-room spirit and believed that to be the fault of the captain and the two managers. Even in England's moment of triumph at Adelaide, Illingworth claimed Atherton was partly at fault for Lewis's gesture to McDermott, and was annoyed there had been no public words of criticism about Lewis's behaviour. As with the captain's stubble, Illingworth was placing importance on minor matters. England, who Illingworth had long complained had shown no fight, had won an historic victory with a cobbled-together team that had been competitive, aggressive and inventive. A month earlier, the tour was heading for disaster. The Test performances in Sydney and Adelaide proved that Atherton's team had the stomach for a fight. Now Illingworth was concerned about appearances, just as the powers-that-be had been at the end of the India and Sri Lanka tour. The answer to many of England's cricket woes appeared to be presenting captains Gooch and Atherton with razors. There was another problem relayed to Smith by Illingworth: 'I told Alan that I thought a lot of it sprang from the fact that nobody seemed sure what Keith Fletcher's role was.' There was no talk of sacking Fletcher, but Smith agreed that someone should speak to Fletcher officially. It was no surprise when Smith left that task to Illingworth. Other forces were at work over Fletcher's removal. One of the prime movers was Dennis Silk, chairman of the TCCB. Silk, a former headmaster, had also been in Australia and was unhappy with the lack of authority emanating from England's team manager.

Illingworth returned from Spain two days before a special meeting of the executive committee was held at Lord's on 6 March. MJK Smith and Illingworth both made reports on the tour. When the tour manager realised the way the meeting was going, he came to Fletcher's defence in his absence, concentrating on the disruptive effect of the many injuries. Illingworth left to appear on ITV's *Sport in Question*. The executive were understandably concerned about clutter of management and responsibility in the England set-up. The system, with a chairman of selectors, tour manager and team manager, was of their own making, but they wanted it streamlined and Illingworth had already indicated his willingness to take sole charge.

There would have been no problem with Illingworth taking over the role of England manager on a full-time basis and Fletcher becoming the coach. Fletcher was halfway through a five-year contract and would have accepted the change or, rather demotion, in responsibility. Silk, though, among others, wanted a sacrifice for the winter losses and Fletcher was the fall guy. The practicalities were ignored (now there was no one to run England's practices and nets) and that was it – Illingworth was now England's first cricket supremo. Little responsibility for the winter mess had ended up at the door of the man who had declared: 'The buck stops with me.' Few in the press were surprised that Illingworth stayed so free from blame, although many believed that the seeds of failure had been sown by him at the tour selection meeting. His man-management, too, had done little to revive England in mid-tour. The Board, as out of touch as ever, had put Illingworth in a unique position of responsibility with the England players, a group whose dislike of his outspokenness outweighed any respect they had for him as a cricket thinker.

Fletcher was told of his fate when he rang Lord's from his skiing holiday about another matter. Otherwise, Fletcher, who had been sacked as England captain with similar compassion 13 years earlier, would most likely have learnt of his demise from the press. Atherton returned from the States and was summoned to a meeting with the new supremo at a secret location off the M62. The pair argued their corners about the tour problems, with neither giving ground. Illingworth concluded that he saw no reason to change the captaincy. The sting in the tail was that he would not commit himself until the selectors met at Edgbaston during the Warwickshire versus England 'A' match in the middle of April. Atherton was not surprised; it was Illingworth's style. The most powerful man in English cricket since Lord Harris's days would have been giving a clear indication of intent as well as demonstrating his new status by naming Atherton as captain there and then, but the new supremo let Atherton dangle for nearly two months before confirming him as captain for the first part of the West Indies campaign. It merely served to widen the gulf between the players and Illingworth.

Illingworth lost one of his supporters on the selection panel when Bolus was replaced by David Graveney, full-time secretary of the Cricketers' Association, but this did not change the balance of power. With Fletcher gone, Illingworth now chaired a four-man committee and with his casting vote needed only one ally. Titmus had not been happy with Atherton's observations about three of the five Ashes selectors being over 60. Graveney, the new boy, saw little reason to change a captain who had served England so well under intense pressure. Yet, at his first meeting, the mood of the senior men seemed to be that Atherton should be replaced. The politician's side of him emerged when he suggested another Illingworth meeting with Atherton, in the presence of another selector. Illingworth was surprised at the press reaction when he revealed during the England 'A' game that the summer captain would not be named for another 10 days. So much for England's dynamic new cricket supremo. It was the sort of dithering management of which Illingworth had been so critical in the past. Atherton wondered whether he should take pre-emptive action – maybe that was what Illingworth wanted. His Lancashire teammates echoed the widespread media view that Illingworth was indulging in an unnecessary game. Illingworth made great play of getting things right to take on the West Indies. Yet, without a captain in place, little strategy or planning could take place.

Atherton was already concentrating on the job in hand. When he was in Illingworth's company in cricket conversation, he felt a real affinity with the last England captain to regain the Ashes abroad. But out of sight was never out of mind in Illingworth's case. His almost daily newspaper thoughts about the captaincy were a constant reminder to Atherton that he was supposed to feel uncomfortable about being in limbo. Atherton perceived it as no more than a minor irritant.

Graveney joined Illingworth at Lancashire's home Benson and Hedges Cup tie against Leicestershire for the meeting he had proposed with Atherton. England's captain joined the two selectors for a meeting that would decide Atherton's future. Graveney was taken aback as the pair began arguing about the public utterances of the other during the winter. The slanging match ended when Graveney asked the simple question: 'Do you both think you can work together?' An even simpler 'Yes' resolved the matter. Illingworth harped on about the captain setting an example in appearance and dress, although Atherton had yet to make the connection with England's cricket problems. Illingworth's recollection of the meeting is worth recalling: 'I told Mike that I wanted him to open the batting and captain the side. I didn't want him involved in the politics that invariably go with the job – that was *my* responsibility. I also did not want him making public statements, other than at press conferences before and after each Test. He took everything on board, and left the room while we made our minds up. It didn't take long because, as I have already said, I was never of a mind to change – unless Mike did not see eye-to-eye with what I thought were common-sense suggestions.' So why the seven-week delay? In fact, the press had to wait a further five days. They were summoned to Headingley the following Sunday for the midday announcement that Atherton was in charge for the Texaco series and first three Tests. Illingworth made the news public while Atherton, who had scored his fifth Roses century two days earlier, was on the golf course. No one from the TCCB had checked to see if England's captain would be at the ground at the time. Having spent so much time ensuring that the new supremo and captain were as one, it was typical folly to have Illingworth and Atherton holding separate press conferences. Fortunately, the pair told the same story. The new England campaign was underway at last.

Illingworth's new team was completed with the appointment of John Edrich and Peter Lever as the batting and bowling coaches. Illingworth also talked to Geoff Boycott, but the level of Boycott's involvement and remuneration proved too much of an obstacle. Atherton knew Lever well and had been part of his teenage squad a decade earlier. Lever, like Edrich, had been a member of Illingworth's Ashes-winning squad.

At the Regent's Park Hilton, Atherton joined the other selectors to choose the Texaco squad. The new group were out within an hour. Dominic Cork and Allan Wells were promoted from the 'A' tour, with Peter Martin edging out his Lancashire colleague Glen Chapple.

The Texaco series was a triumph for England and Atherton. The West Indies were easy winners of the first match at Trent Bridge, which was carried over into a second day because of rain. The team moved to The Oval for the 1,000th one-day international. Atherton held the England innings together with 92 as he and Hick put on 144 for the second wicket in 28 overs. The home side finished on 306 for 5 in 55 overs, a record score against the West Indies. That was attained due to a typical Fairbrother flourish at the end and Dickie Bird not calling for the third umpire when TV replays showed Fairbrother had been run out. Lancashire's day was complete when Martin, on his debut, took 4 for 44, including the wickets of Campbell, Adams and Lara in his first four overs. Junior Murray's defiant 86 kept England on their toes, but the home side levelled the series with a 25-run success.

The West Indies captain Richie Richardson went against expectations at Lord's and asked England to bat, though this was a more marginal decision than at The Oval. Atherton took 27 deliveries to get off the mark. After he turned the ball through mid-wicket for three runs, another 17 balls went by before his next run as Ambrose tested him to the full in a hostile opening spell. Slowly but surely, all the resentment, hurt and neglect of Atherton's three-year exile from England's one-day squad found its release in one of the most remarkable limited-overs innings at Lord's, or anywhere else. Atherton hit his maiden one-day century on his way to 127. As he grew in confidence, England's captain displayed such inventiveness and courage in his shot-selection that comparisons with the great IVA Richards in his pomp were not unreasonable. There could be no greater tribute. Atherton hit 14 fours, and a pulled six off Bishop. He left Lord's to a standing ovation. Those spectators had no doubt about his one-day worth, nor that here was England's leader and inspiration. By biding his time and holding his tongue, Atherton had answered Illingworth's doubts and messing-about in the most emphatic fashion. Cork made the early inroads into the West Indies line-up and the tourists never threatened – Atherton lifted the Texaco Trophy by virtue of England's 73-run victory. He was named Man of the Match and England's Man of the Series, as he had been against the West Indies four years earlier.

Illingworth's wider brief included trying to produce pitches that suited the home side's strength. That happens everywhere else in the cricket world, but Lord's had always been paranoid about pitches and any outside interference. Illingworth met the six Test groundsmen with TCCB officials at the start of May. He wanted even bounce with the grass taken off both ends to help the spinner earlier in the match. Fitness was another of Illingworth's concerns after the Australian debacle.

Atherton was happy to leave such areas of responsibility to Illingworth. The selectors met to choose the side for the first Test at Headingley at the Copthorne Hotel in Manchester. Much of the discussion centred on Stewart and who was going to keep wicket – Rhodes had lost form with the bat and gloves in Australia. Russell was an option, but Stewart would give the side the five-man bowling attack Illingworth wanted. News of Tufnell's visit to the psychiatric ward in Perth had become public and his tour report ensured another spell on the sidelines, so Richard Illingworth was recalled. So was Robin Smith after his shoulder operation. Gough was also fit again.

The selectors made things more complicated than was needed, however. If the plan was for Stewart to keep, all the selectors had to do was choose an alternative opener in case England did not bat first. Smith was preferred by Atherton and Graveney, but there was no need to set that choice in stone. Afterwards, Illingworth revealed he was uncomfortable with the arrangement, though he did not suggest how it should have been resolved. When Richardson won the toss and again asked England to bat, there was nothing to prevent Atherton and Stewart walking out together, but Stewart's job had been handed to Smith. Such inflexibility was a hallmark of the Illingworth–Atherton style.

Illingworth's influence was obvious as Fraser was left out of the final line-up, with the untried Martin given preference. Only four men – Atherton, Thorpe, DeFreitas and Malcolm – remained from the side that had beaten

Australia in Adelaide two Tests earlier. The West Indies had arrived after losing at home to the Australians, their first defeat in a series for 15 years. After England's convincing win in the Texaco Trophy, Atherton planned to keep the pressure on the tourists. Robin Smith was a proven performer against quick bowling, an obvious replacement for the elder statesman Gooch, and Atherton felt Ramprakash, who had made his debut against the West Indies four years earlier, had shown in Perth that he could make the big time at last. Atherton's own failure against the West Indies on their previous tour of England was now a distant memory. England's captain had coped better than most with the Caribbean pacemen on their own territory in 1994.

Atherton stressed, not for the first time, the importance of starting well in the series (or, more to the point, not starting badly). England had to keep the West Indies down – the task would become doubly difficult if the visitors regained their confidence and swagger, especially with Brian Lara's fondness for English bowling. Once again, Atherton's words went unheeded. England's captain led the way with 81, starting his innings seven times because of the weather, but his mastery was emphasised by the struggling batsmen at the other end. It was confirmation that Atherton was at the top of his game. At one stage England were 142 for 2, but Atherton was out to the final ball of a rain-affected day with England now 148 for 4. The next day, the home side were dismissed for 199. The feared West Indies opening pair of Ambrose and Walsh took 1 for 106 in 30 overs – the damage was done by the supporting act of Ian Bishop and Kenny Benjamin as England's batting folded. The West Indies were in front at the end of the second day. Lara took 24 off Malcolm's opening two overs after the Derbyshire fast bowler had removed Hooper with his first ball, and the absence of Fraser proved costly, especially after Gough strained his back. The tourists suffered from a late-order collapse similar to England's, as the last seven wickets added just 66 runs. The West Indies lead was 83 and discretion should have been the order of the day as England went in again. Instead, Smith and Stewart were out cutting, and Hick pulling. Atherton edged Walsh to the wicket-keeper. Thorpe's 61 was the only redeeming feature. The West Indies had a day and a half to score the 126 runs required to take a 1-0 lead in the series, but discretion was not part of their game-plan either: Hooper and Lara belted the necessary runs in 19 overs. Hooper hit four sixes and nine fours, Lara eight fours in his 48 runs which took 40 balls. The end for England came swiftly that Sunday. The problems with the batting line-up continued as Smith scored 22 runs at the top of the order and Stewart managed 6 with the gloves on.

Atherton had problems of his own as he prepared for the Lord's Test. England's four-day defeat gave him a day off before heading to Worcester for the Benson and Hedges Cup semi-final, where Hick hit a century in the home side's 261 for 6. Lancashire were coming a poor second at 169 for 7, needing 93 off the final 11 overs, before Pakistan's Wasim Akram came to the rescue with 64 off 47 deliveries. Atherton could only watch in wonder and envy that England did not have such a talent to turn matches on their head. Lancashire made their fifth Lord's final in six seasons with four balls to spare. The rest of the selectors joined him at the Diglis Hotel, and the captain played down worries that he would not be fit for Lord's after his back problem forced him to move down the batting order to No. 8 and then withdraw completely from the championship contest that followed in Worcester.

The other concern was still Stewart and his role in the side. Illingworth had been at Worcester for a couple of days and discussed the situation with Atherton. Illingworth wanted Stewart to open and keep wicket. Atherton knew the Surrey captain preferred opening to keeping and was loath to do both jobs. Once again, Illingworth delegated when it would have been simpler for the man in charge to find out for himself. It would also have made sense for Illingworth to explain to Stewart the dilemma the selectors were in. Instead, Atherton made the call and reported back that Stewart did not want to open and keep. That started three days of confusion which was largely due to the England manager failing to run the show as he had indicated he would. The selectors chose Rhodes ahead of Russell, dropped Malcolm and brought in Cork, who had taken a career-best 9 for 43 for Derbyshire during the Headingley Test. Jason Gallian won the vote over Nick Knight as cover for Atherton.

Illingworth's assertion that Stewart's unwillingness to open was the basis of the selection did not go down well with the player himself, and Stewart let batting coach Edrich know that was not the case. This news was relayed to Illingworth on Sunday. There had been obvious confusion in the original question – Illingworth now had the correct information, and the answer he wanted. The logical step now would have been to pick up the phone to Stewart and sort the matter out, with no mediator to muddle the message. The difference between 'Would you open and keep?' and 'Do you want to open and keep?' had affected England's whole selection. Illingworth should have spoken to Stewart, then discussed the matter with Atherton and the other selectors that night. Instead, Illingworth waited until the squad had assembled at Lord's on Tuesday before chatting to Stewart, and his late switch provoked a major outcry. Both Atherton and Graveney, who drove to London early on Wednesday morning to discuss the matter, had been worried about the public reaction to a late change. Rhodes was told and Atherton revealed the change to the press at the eve-of-Test lunchtime briefing.

The media had a field day. Many had been sceptical of Stewart fulfilling both roles as a matter of principle, anyway – his batting average was halved when he took up the wicket-keeping gloves. The sight of a dejected Rhodes excited the photographers and infuriated the journalists. It was obvious to everyone that the lines of communication had got tangled again. Some misread the situation and saw the switch as another example of Illingworth showing who was boss. Quite the reverse was true – it was because Illingworth had *not* acted in a dictatorial fashion that the situation had arisen in the first place. Atherton's only concern was that England should give themselves the best possible chance of beating the West Indies at Lord's. Some papers had Atherton near to quitting. The origin of that story was traced to Lancashire, though Atherton denied – and still denies – any such intentions.

Atherton's rather passive appearance throughout the whole wicket-keeping affair was due to his own fitness problems. His back was as bad as it had been since his operation. A scan led to two injections in the hot spots, a remedy he next employed at the start of the Zimbabwe tour. Atherton realised that defeat at Lord's would probably cost him the captaincy, and the home of cricket is not exactly England's favourite hunting-ground. Atherton won the toss, so there was no problem with Stewart opening and England's line-up looked far more competitive. Thorpe and Smith took England to 185 for 3 before, again, the last seven wickets went for under 100 runs. It might have been worse but for a 50 stand between Cork and Martin. Fraser restricted the West Indies to a first-innings lead of 41, taking 5 for 66 off 33 overs with the sort of accuracy and penetration which had been sorely missed at Headingley. At the end of the second day, the West Indies coach Andy Roberts criticised the pitch as being ' deliberately under-prepared'. The consequence to

Roberts was a reprimand from referee John Reid; the consequence to the West Indies party was a mistrust of a wicket that was not really that treacherous.

The game swung England's way on Saturday evening. They were 51 for 2 when Thorpe lost sight of a Walsh beamer and was struck on the helmet. Thorpe spent that night under observation at St Mary's Hospital in Paddington. Smith and Hick rescued the situation with a stand of almost a hundred before Hick was bowled by Bishop just before the close. Smith, who voiced his fear that failure here would end his Test career, curbed his attacking instincts and dug in on Sunday. Ramprakash completed a pair in the first over on the fourth day, but Thorpe, Cork and Gough gave Smith's effort enough support to put England in the driving seat. Lara was again the threat overnight, as the West Indies needed another 232 runs for victory with nine wickets remaining.

Atherton was pleased with the spirit in the dressing-room. The courage of Smith and Thorpe, the exuberance of Cork and Gough and the pride of Fraser and Stewart was proving a powerful blend. The mood on the final morning was positive. There could be no legislating for the genius of Lara – Atherton knew that better than most – but as he led England out, the captain felt that his team had the will and the equipment to win. Cork won the war with the best figures, 7 for 43, by an Englishman on his Test debut, but it was Gough and Stewart who triumphed in the crucial battle. Lara had reduced the deficit to under 200 when he edged Gough and Stewart took a spectacular left-handed catch. Thorpe was still groggy. His replacement, Paul Weekes, took catches to remove Arthurton and Murray. The West Indies were eight down at tea. By then, the crowd inside Lord's had risen to 10,000. Atherton was about to take Cork off when Ambrose hit the ball to extra cover. Two balls later, it was all over. Cork's lasting memory of that victory moment was the sight of the England captain jumping up and down: 'That made me realise how important this was to him. I had never suffered at the West Indies' hands. He had.'

As with most of Atherton's Test wins as captain (this was number six), it had emerged out of adversity (Trent Bridge against New Zealand was the exception). He now set the record straight on the controversy leading up to the match:

The press obviously had a field day after the strategy had been changed, but once we started practice on the day before the Test, everyone knew where they stood. I was happy with the situation, as I tried to point out at the pre-match press conference. Rumours started, including the one that I had had enough and was about to give up the captaincy in protest. I've simply no idea where this particular story came from – it smacked very much to me of Chinese whispers. The fact is, I'm more than satisfied with the extent of my input, and Ray is good to have in the dressing-room. The key to the win was on the final day when we discussed who should bowl from which end. I had a chat with Ray and we decided that Darren Gough should bowl from the Pavilion end. He might go for a few, but the slope would help his swing against the left-handers. As the bounce was uneven from that end in the first innings, we thought we should try our two tallest bowlers. But the pitch had eased and Angus Fraser looked a bit innocuous. I tried Peter Martin, but it didn't take too long to work out that he was struggling for rhythm. Whereas on the first morning of a Test match I might have given both bowlers a few more overs to get it right, there was no time to mess about – the time had come for Dominic Cork to have a go. He bowled magnificently, but we still had to make sure we kept it tight at the other end. That was where Fraser, in particular, and others, including Richard Illingworth when I put him on to give Cork a breather, played their part to perfection.

Atherton would have liked his winning troops to enjoy the spoils of victory, but any celebration parties were ruled out as England's best cricketers dispersed for county duty the next day. It was nothing important – the first round of the NatWest, when the counties take on the minnows. Shared experiences – the before and after, as well as the during – are an important part of building team-spirit and unity. Unless England win in less than regulation time, there is no opportunity to party. Few would have denied that England cricketers deserved the odd glass of champagne after the events of Lord's. Yet, less than two weeks later, Atherton and his heroes were forced to run the gauntlet of angry and dissatisfied supporters in Birmingham after the shortest Test match in England since 1912.

This time, Atherton and Illingworth were as one: England had been undone by the Edgbaston pitch, not the West Indies. Atherton had hoped to capitalise on the Lord's win, as well as the West Indies' falling morale. Richardson's side had just suffered their heaviest defeat ever against county opposition at Hove. On top of that first loss to an English county since 1976, Winston Benjamin had been sent home in disgrace. It was at this point that Boycott delivered his definitive verdict on the West Indies in the *Sun*. 'Lara is burnt out and Curtly has lost his fire, so let's roast the wobbling Windies!' Wrong again. It was the West Indies who left Birmingham rejuvenated, with England trailing in the series again and three of their players with broken bones. The only argument was whether Atherton or Illingworth was the more annoyed that English cricket had shot itself in the foot again.

The first hint of trouble came at the selection meeting in Manchester. Titmus had taken a look at the Edgbaston pitch on the way up. His description of the wicket as 'funny-looking' was not accompanied by any real concern. The selectors moved on to Ramprakash – the promise of Australia had faded and Illingworth felt he was too intense. Crawley should have been the next man in, but the worries over Stewart and the opening slot led to a compromise and Jason Gallian was chosen. Atherton's attitude to the bowling attack was rather conservative. He stuck with Martin, although his figures for the series were 5 for 195, in preference to Malcolm, despite Edgbaston's fast and bouncy reputation.

Illingworth had been caught out again by delegating. His heart sank when he saw the Edgbaston wicket for the first time. It was tailor-made for the West Indies fast bowlers and too late to do anything about it. Illingworth had the groundsman Steve Rouse on his hands and knees trying to give the thick tufts of grass a haircut. The sight of Illingworth, a recognised expert reader of pitches, in such a panic did little to instil confidence in the England camp. The ends of the wicket were bare. Bowlers like Cork were not sure how it would play. They had a sneaky suspicion that these worries about the wicket would work in the tourists' favour. They did. England's fate was sealed by the first delivery of the match. Ambrose's looseners landed just short of a length and flew past Atherton and over the wicket-keeper's head to the boundary. Atherton's worst fears were realised (the sight of a grinning Ambrose was as frightening as the pitch). In the event, neither Atherton nor Ambrose lasted long. England's captain, obviously unsettled, edged the fourth ball of the day to the keeper; Ambrose lasted until his eighth over when a groin strain ended his bowling participation for the match. Thorpe got a brute of a ball that exploded off the pitch. He was the exception, along with Smith who grafted for the cause again. England's batsmen, in the main, were done in the head as much as by the pitch. They were dismissed for 147, snooker's maximum break, in 44.2 overs. The first day ended with the West Indies on 104 for 1.

Atherton joined some players and pressmen for a drink in the Prince of Wales. He was furious about the wicket and could not believe that England's campaign had been sabotaged in such a way. Atherton rarely complains or becomes animated. If he does, it must be serious. He probably should have kept those thoughts to himself until after the match. Illingworth and Atherton should have focused on the players, not the pitch, at Edgbaston. Illingworth should have checked the state of the wicket much earlier than two days before the match. Having discovered it was sub-standard, the manager and captain should have joined forces in a damage-limitation exercise. Good pitch, bad pitch, funny-looking pitch or just plain ugly pitch, this Test match had to be played and England were going to have to make the best of it. Unfortunately, the mood from the start was one of surrender and capitulation. It was a test of raw courage and few passed.

The West Indies reached 300 thanks to an uncharacteristic knock by Richardson, who was dropped by Atherton in the slips. England's position was made terminal on Friday night. Memories of Trinidad were revived as England came out to bat again with 17 overs remaining, although Ambrose was less of a threat lying on the treatment couch. Walsh darted one through Atherton's defence and the home side were soon 26 for 3. Stewart and Gallian, still to appear, both had fractured fingers. Stewart never made it and Richard Illingworth had his knuckle broken as England, 89 all out, finally surrendered by an innings and 64 runs at 12.18pm on Saturday. The huge crowd, who had booed the batsmen off, spilled onto the playing area, some to abuse Atherton and Illingworth, others to eat their picnic lunches and play cricket. Others queued to demand their money back. They were offered half, or a half-price ticket for next summer's Test against India. The West Indies fast bowlers had given England's batsmen a real pasting for 78 minutes. Umpire Ian Robinson showed the same tendencies that had left Malcolm unprotected and bruised in Jamaica eighteen months earlier and much of the bowling looked intimidatory, but the public and press were in no mood for excuses, either about the pitch or the bowling. The captain and supremo had to run a gauntlet of angry fans to get to the press conference. 'You're a disgrace – it's time to go, Atherton. And Illingworth, too!' screamed one irate spectator who had to be led away by security guards. Atherton called it the worst Test pitch he had ever encountered. 'The players tried hard and did their best, but the pitch was diabolical. To my knowledge, what the England management asked for out of the pitch was even bounce and some turn at the end. Unless I was seeing things, I didn't see either of that out here. Curtly ran in to bowl the first ball of the match to me. It was just meant to be a loosener, but the ball just flew off the wicket. His eyes almost popped out and he smiled. He couldn't believe his luck. What's so annoying is that the West Indies came here under a cloud. But that very first delivery blew the clouds away.' Illingworth and Warwickshire blamed each other about its state. Like England's batting, the situation was an unsightly mess. Only one thing was certain: the West Indies had regained the advantage in the series. As Mike Selvey of the *Guardian* observed: 'A small fortune has been lost to the coffers of Warwickshire and the TCCB, but that is nothing compared to the damage, physical and mental, that had been perpetrated upon Atherton's side.'

Atherton and England had an extra week to recover

before the Old Trafford Test. The counties did not give the bowlers much of a chance to put their feet up. Like most of his side, Atherton turned out for his county in the Sunday League the next day when a one-run defeat against Northamptonshire cost the Red Rose the chance of going top. It started a week of one-day cricket for the England captain. Lancashire completed the cup double over Worcestershire with Atherton hitting 70 in a record opening stand of 140 with Steve Titchard in the four-wicket NatWest win. Three days later, Atherton put Lancashire on the road to another triumph in the Benson and Hedges Cup final at Lord's, falling seven runs short of a century in a total of 274 for 7. Kent failed by 35 runs, despite a sensational century from Aravinda de Silva. The Lancashire celebrations were as noisy and riotous as ever. A change was always as good as a rest for Atherton when Lancashire were at Lord's.

Illingworth joined Atherton at Cheltenham for the game against Gloucestershire. The England injury situation meant several changes. Stewart's broken finger opened up the wicket-keeping issue again, Nick Knight was given his chance and John Crawley was recalled, along with Jack Russell and Craig White. The spinning choices made the headlines. Atherton's county captain, Mike Watkinson, was given his first chance on his home patch and John Emburey, a few weeks short of his 43rd birthday, his 64th. The 13-man squad was reduced when Gough complained of foot problems. Officially, he was passed fit, but England were never going to take a chance. Once Atherton decided that both spinners would play, the inclusion of Russell meant that one of the batsmen would have to go to accommodate White. The choice was between Hick and Crawley. Atherton felt that Hick had had his chance. Illingworth agreed – he thought that, like Ramprakash, Hick was too intense and wound-up about his batting. The news left Hick in tears.

Edgbaston had played havoc with England's Test team – less than half the side remained from Birmingham. England fielded a totally different bowling attack from the opening Test in Leeds.

Despite the injuries, however, the side did not have the makeshift look of Adelaide and Atherton was surprised and delighted to discover that the spirit resembled Lord's rather than Edgbaston. It was as if Birmingham had never happened. The squad were going to treat it as a fluke result on a fluke pitch. The plan was to carry on from where England had left off in the second Test. Atherton would have batted if he had won the toss. He did not, and the West Indies, with Lara in confident form, were soon coasting at 86 for 2. Then Fraser removed Adams and Richardson in his last two overs before lunch and the contest was transformed. England's fighting spirit was best demonstrated by Crawley, who took a spectacular running catch from square leg to remove Hooper. That gave great satisfaction to the champion of the previous winter's Lard League – Crawley, more than any other cricketer, had taken aboard the lessons of the Australian tour. There was plenty to celebrate at Old Trafford. Watkinson took his first Test wicket, Cork his first catch and Russell his 100th. The West Indies were bowled out for 216. The only disappointment on the first day was the last-ball dismissal of Crawley, bowled by Walsh not playing a shot. The champagne flowed in the Cornhill tent that night as the sponsors celebrated their 100th Test; England had enjoyed a rejuvenating day.

Atherton knew that Friday's first session would be crucial. Any sign of an Edgbaston hangover and the West Indies fast bowlers would exploit it. He was prepared, mentally and physically, for the inevitable going-over. His old adversary, Walsh, was seven wickets short of joining the 300 Test wickets club. One ball struck Atherton just above the heart. Umpire Dickie Bird has his faults, but standing by and watching intimidatory bowling is not one of them. He stepped in where many others would have looked away, and warned Walsh. Atherton took all that was thrown at him and carried on batting in his normal unobtrusive way. He was desperately disappointed to nick Ambrose to Murray three short of his fifty. Atherton was the only England casualty before lunch, a session that brought them over 100 runs. The captain had set the example and his team batted and battled all day. Another 100 runs came between lunch and tea – Smith was the only loss. Thorpe hit four fours in an over off Kenny Benjamin but was denied a century by Bishop. England led by more than 150 runs on Friday night and the tail increased that advantage to 221. Fortune was with England, especially Cork. He hit his maiden England half-century after dislodging a bail when he set off for a run in the first over of Saturday morning. The threat that night, once again, was Lara. The tourists had lost three wickets and still trailed. Lara was the key.

Sunday belonged to Cork, then Lara, and finally Russell and England. Cork took the first England Test hat-trick for 38 years in the first over of the day. Contest over – the West Indies were 60 runs adrift with four wickets left. But Lara had put the tourists 62 runs ahead when he was the ninth man out after marshalling an almost impossible situation brilliantly. He scored 85 runs of the 122 added after Cork's hat-trick. Memories of Trinidad were beginning to flash across Atherton's mind, and those nightmares were not helped by a last-wicket stand of 31 from Ambrose and Walsh. Atherton rushed off to the dressing-room to get padded up. England would win, he assured his team, if the batsmen remained calm and positive. The plan half worked. England reached 39 for 0 with Atherton and Knight in little trouble. Then the crisis: Atherton was run out, the West Indies sensed an opening and England were suddenly 48 for 4 with a fifth batsman, Smith, on his way to hospital with a fractured cheek-bone. Russell joined Crawley at the wicket. The England dressing-room he had just vacated was in a state of flux. Bowlers, who had changed, were unchanging at speed. Batsmen, unpadded, could only watch and hope. The calmest man in the ground was Russell. His 16 months out of the side had only sharpened his appetite for the fray. Bishop, especially, was bowling for all he was worth. Russell knew that he had to keep the scoreboard moving. If England became becalmed, they would lose. Russell is not pretty to watch. He is effective, though, and rarely more so than on that afternoon at Old Trafford. He and Crawley saw England all the way home to a six-wicket victory. The series was levelled, England were heroes again. Atherton was more satisfied with this victory. England had been in control from the first morning, no mean feat after the experiences of Edgbaston. The selection had largely been determined by injury. The team had fought every inch of the way and won a Test in which Lara had batted magnificently and scored 232 runs.

England's fighting spirit had caught the imagination of the sporting public. The series was set to bring in record receipts as Atherton prepared for a fight to the finish. The Board's delight did not extend to offering the players any financial reward; when the contracts for the South African tour went out, the fee was the same as that paid for the Ashes trip. Atherton was not alone in thinking that this was shoddy treatment. After he had gauged the feeling among the squad, the captain went to Lord's with his begging bowl to ask for more. The TCCB, used to players' grumbles about remuneration, have rarely had such a direct approach. They could not plead poverty, nor deny that a substantial increase in revenue was due to England's form against the West Indies. An extra £2,000 was added to the tour fees, hardly an extravagant gesture.

With two Tests to come, Atherton felt England had the beating of the West Indies. They had twice come from behind. The tourists were now missing three key personnel – Ambrose, Hooper and Adams. Lara apart, the West Indies batting had looked fragile. England's captain was bitterly disappointed to lose Robin Smith for the rest of the summer. Smith needed an operation to repair his broken cheek-bone. Stewart was struggling to play any part in the series. Richard Illingworth told the selectors that he could play, although his broken finger had not healed. Gough was not available, despite removing Atherton at the start of the NatWest quarter-final at Headingley. Yorkshire's victory, three days after the fourth Test win, ended Lancashire's cup interests for the season. Atherton had enjoyed a good run for his money. He had placed a substantial bet on Lancashire winning the three one-day trophies at 250-1.

Atherton was playing against Sussex at Lytham when the selectors met to pick the Trent Bridge squad. Allan Wells, who had hit a century in front of Atherton the day before, and Mark Ilott were the replacements for Smith and Gough. Emburey made way for Illingworth. Certainly, Atherton's participation in the Trent Bridge Test was in the lap of the gods until he woke on Thursday morning. His back was troubling him again. Hick had the same problem. Yorkshire's David Byas was called up as cover, while Russell was nominated as the man who would lead England if Atherton's condition did not improve. Hick had told the press that he wanted a chat with Illingworth about being dropped at Old Trafford. England's boss admitted that he had not spoken to Hick at the time because he was so upset. A word of explanation over the next few days should have been his next move. Hick was given the opportunity to prove himself ahead of Wells on the morning of the Trent Bridge match after Atherton confirmed his fitness.

It was soon obvious that this was a batting strip no self-respecting batsman would want to miss. It was the Nottinghamshire groundsman Ron Allsopp's last Test match. He had built up a reputation that, if not the best groundsman in the country, he was the one most able to prepare the surface he wanted. Such glowing testimonies had been part of the pre-match build-up. There was real disappointment in his admission afterwards that his final offering was lacking in pace and bounce. Atherton, after winning the toss, dug in with Knight and the pair were still together at tea. The progress had been slow and unspectacular, as the England captain had planned. Atherton realised that on this pitch – and with no Ambrose – batting was going to be as comfortable as it ever gets against the West Indies. It had been over 70 years since an England opening pair had batted through a whole day. England lost the plot a little after tea, finishing the day on 227 for 4. Atherton had completed England's first century of the series before being run out for a second successive time, on this occasion by Dhanraj with a direct hit from mid-on. Hick, like Atherton, overcame his fitness doubts to score a century on the second day, but what was more impressive was the way he had conquered the doubts about his form and temperament. With continuing support from the tail, he helped England to 440. It should have made the game, and England, safe. Brian Lara had other ideas, and Atherton was mightily relieved when he was caught down the leg-side just before Saturday's close of play. Lara had upped the tempo of the whole match.

Illingworth was later critical of his captain and his bowlers: 'A combination of poor seam-bowling and indifferent handling of the bowlers by Mike gave Lara the opportunity he wanted to destroy us, and he did just that.' England's bowlers did bowl too wide and short to Lara. There was no way Atherton could plug the gaps under those circumstances. Atherton's supposed neglect of Craig White was at the heart of Illingworth's complaint: 'I thought the captain did him no favours at all. He did not seem to want to put him on, no matter the trouble Lara was piling up for us, and he didn't bowl in the first 70 overs. That was silly, and when he came on he went for 30 in five overs. You might argue that's why he wasn't put on before, but whatever confidence he might have had was wiped out by not giving him a go earlier.' White was playing in his sixth Test and had taken just eight wickets, with his best being 3 for 18 against New Zealand over a year earlier. He had been very much Illingworth's pick after the Caribbean tour. White had been brought up in Australia and Atherton had little doubt about his capabilities, especially as a batsman. Yet despite gaining his cricket education at one of sport's hardest schools of knocks, White lacked confidence and self-belief, and it showed. Atherton was engaged in a damage-limitation exercise that Saturday in Nottingham. Richard Illingworth eventually bowled 51 overs, his return of 96 runs being more crucial than his four wickets. That was a great achievement considering his finger had been broken again as nightwatchman on Thursday night. Mike Watkinson had turned the ball on Friday evening, and the spin attack did the bulk of the bowling with Cork and Fraser in support. Even Hick only bowled four overs. England's front-line fast bowlers were going for twice as many runs per over as the spinners. Atherton saw no need nor benefit in exposing White's bowling to Lara on this pitch to any great extent.

The West Indies innings ended midway through Sunday and England finished the day on 111 for 2, extending their lead to 134. A draw looked inevitable. Atherton had found a new opening partner, John Crawley, after Knight had been hit on the head when fielding close in. He was detained overnight in hospital. England hung on to head

for a showdown at The Oval only after a gutsy, undefeated tenth-wicket stand of 80 between Watkinson and
Illingworth. Had Sherwin Campbell not dropped a 'sit-
ter' off Watkinson at mid-wicket, the tourists would have
faced a target of 213 to win off 50 overs. Atherton was still
concerned that England rarely seemed able to bat well
twice in a match; no side should be in trouble after
scoring 440 on the first two days of a Test. At Trent
Bridge, without Ambrose and with Bishop and Walsh
carrying injuries in the second innings and an inexperi-
enced spinner in Dhanraj, England had wobbled. Lara
presented a different problem. His runs came at such a
lick, promising positions all too quickly became precarious ones.

Nevertheless, Atherton was optimistic about The Oval.
The wide open spaces and the fast bouncy wicket would
suit Lara, true enough. The Oval, though, had become
England's favourite Test ground in recent series with
famous wins over the West Indies ('91), Australia ('93)
and South Africa ('94). Two of England's match-winners
from those successes, Devon Malcolm and Phil Tufnell,
were recalled to the squad. Gallian, whose broken finger
at Edgbaston had given Knight his chance at Old Trafford, came back when Knight suffered a similar injury.
White was left out of the squad and Wells made his debut
at the age of 33. The interest in this Test reached epidemic
proportions; players had never known such demand for
tickets. The public wanted a fight to the finish.

Much of the pre-match discussion centred on the fact
that The Oval pitches during the summer had not been as
bouncy and pacy as in the past. Paul Brind was following
in the footsteps of his groundsman father, Harry. As at
Trent Bridge, the wicket did have the final word and the
series ended in a rather flat fashion. England again batted
first and scored over 400 runs before Lara turned the
game on its head on the Saturday. This time the West

Indies amassed an enormous first-innings lead and the home side had to bat out the last day. Atherton started to wonder whether winning the toss for the fourth time in five Tests had been a good call when Ambrose's second delivery rose sharply and thumped into his ribs, but it turned out to be a rogue delivery – The Oval wicket never behaved as badly again. Atherton, on the final day, became the fourth batsman in the match to fall in the nineties.

Wells, after 15 years on the county circuit, had fallen to his very first ball in Test cricket after tea on Thursday. Watkinson became Walsh's 300th Test victim the next day. But the highlight of the match was Lara's 179 from 206 balls on Saturday. That took his tally in the second half of the series to 583 runs. Towards the end of that knock, Atherton had no alternative other than to dispense with all close catchers. The only times the left-hander looked in trouble were when he tried to lash his first ball from Cork and when a direct hit from Watkinson would have ended his innings at 30. England trailed by 106 at stumps on the final day with Gallian, Crawley and Thorpe gone, but England's captain was determined not to surrender. His disappointment at falling short of a century was nothing compared to his annoyance at failing to see the job through. Furthermore, he was just a dozen runs short of 500 for the series. His average of 40.66 was only good enough for sixth place in the England listings behind Watkinson, Hick, Russell, Smith and Thorpe, who was the only person other than the captain to play throughout the series. England used 21 players, as the injury problems of the Ashes series continued through the summer. Cork was the find of the series, taking 26 wickets in his five Tests. Fraser was the only other bowler to collect more than 10 wickets.

Atherton, after a turbulent year, had emerged stronger and wiser. The West Indies manager Wes Hall chose him ahead of Cork as the England Man of the Series. Hall, familiar with the crippling and cumulative effect of pace, felt the England captain had led from the front, 'taking the fire of the West Indies pace bowlers unflinchingly. He was the defining difference to the result of this series.' The fightbacks at Lord's and Old Trafford had instilled a renewed spirit in the dressing-room. It was obvious, too, that Illingworth and Atherton were more as one. Atherton's performance, as batsman and captain, had made a mockery of Illingworth's indecision at the start of the summer.

CHAPTER FOURTEEN

Captain Courageous

England's first official cricket visit to South Africa in 30 years went the way of Atherton's other trips abroad in charge. Unlike the series in the Caribbean and Australia, this tour started well and ended badly. The poor finish created an impression of a disastrous expedition – that was not the case for the first 10 weeks. The trip fell apart in January. The deadlocked Test series ended in three dreadful days at Cape Town, then England embarked on a one-day roller-coaster that took them back around South Africa. After a short break in England, they headed for the World Cup in the sub-continent. It was England's dismal one-day form that soured all judgements about the whole winter.

Relations between Atherton and Illingworth deteriorated again. The merit of having the chairman of selectors in sole charge on tour was never really tested. Illingworth was simply too old for the task. His touring experiences were a quarter of a century old. That was light years away from cricket's modern schedules. His cricket brain and spirit were still willing; the body was not up to it. The tour began and ended with Devon Malcolm in the spotlight. He was at odds with the management from the minute England boarded the plane. The Malcolm affair became a *cause célèbre*, as the arguments about his treatment rumbled on throughout the entire tour and also had repercussions for Illingworth in his final summer in cricket. The manager's relationship with his players broke down at the end of the Cape Town Test after an amazing outburst in the dressing-room. After the World Cup, Illingworth stepped down as boss. He remained chairman of selectors for the summer, but Lancashire's David Lloyd was appointed England coach.

Atherton's own winter reflected England's fortunes. He became a national hero after defying South Africa's bowlers for nearly 11 hours to save The Wanderers Test. New Year's Day saw the captain hopeful of his first series win abroad. Three days later, England were beaten. A couple of months later, the doubts about Atherton's future as captain were no longer confined to outsiders. He returned from England's World Cup shame, went into hiding and travelled to Jamaica with Lancashire in April to decide his future. It was apparent that three consecutive failures abroad – four if you separated South Africa and the World Cup – had taken their toll. Personal glory was all very well. The realisation that his team was still only competing with the rest on an occasional basis was beginning to wear him down.

The tour selection meeting had been much less confrontational than the previous year. If there were errors in the balance of this squad, they were collective ones. Atherton and Stewart, who had not played for 10 weeks, were the only openers. Smith, too, had missed the second half of the summer. Thorpe and Hick had enjoyed successful series against the West Indies, so the remaining two spots were between Knight, Gallian, Ramprakash, Crawley, Hussain and Wells. Crawley had scored only 100 runs in his three Tests, in which batting conditions were the best of the summer as England scored 437, 440 and 454 in the first innings. Ramprakash remained the enigma. The Middlesex right-hander had taken Illingworth's advice after failing at Headingley and Lord's. He had returned to county cricket, piled on the runs, scoring 2,258 including 10 centuries (three doubles), and finished top of the first-class averages with 77.86. But would that count for anything when he returned to the England team? Knight had proved himself a determined competitor in his two Tests and would have given England a third opener, while Atherton had mentioned Hussain's name several times in meetings during the summer. The Essex batsman had recovered from his neglect in the Caribbean and disappointing form of 1994 to score over 1,800 runs and six hundreds. Illingworth, though, was not a fan. The selection strategy was to take the seven best batsmen. The final two places went to Crawley and Ramprakash.

As for the rest, Russell, Watkinson and Richard Illingworth had all proved their worth in the summer. Cork, Malcolm, Fraser and Gough were joined by Ilott and Middlesex's Richard Johnson. Malcolm, Gough and Johnson all had to prove their fitness. When Johnson failed to do so, he was replaced by Martin. England's World Cup squad would be named nearer the time. Three extra players – Dermot Reeve, Neil Fairbrother and Neil Smith – would join the squad towards the end of the South African Test series.

Atherton had hoped England could enter the Test series without any of the distractions that had hampered the Ashes challenge. Not for the first time, he had reckoned without the verbosity of Illingworth. The team flew out to headlines proclaiming Illingworth's 'One-Man Band', as the chairman explained: 'I'm not against the principle of selection committees. It's different in England when we are picking from 200 players, but we're down to just 16 on tour and I don't need any help. Of course, I will chat with Mike and vice-captain Alec Stewart, but I will have the overall say. I have been in the game a long time and would back my judgement of players against anyone's. Against the West Indies last summer, there were a couple of times when I felt I was persuaded not to follow my gut reaction. For instance, I wanted to play leg-spinner Ian Salisbury at Old Trafford and I was not happy using Robin Smith as an opener. I don't think I will make those mistakes again.' Typical Illingworth, and so unnecessary. At a stroke, it opened up all the old wounds of disharmony between chairman and captain. As usual, Atherton did not react adversely in public: 'Raymond wants to have the last say. I'm happy for it to be that way, but I don't think he's going to ignore whatever I have to say. Our relationship has progressed to a level where we get on extremely well.'

That was not all. The 'Boycott–Illy tapes' ran for three days in the *Sun* – starting the day before England left for South Africa. As the two Yorkshiremen considered the problems of English cricket, most of the blame was laid at the door of Atherton and his team. The England players felt aggrieved and the captain was not too pleased with the headline on the first article: 'Atherton is so stubborn, inflexible and narrow-minded.' Illingworth's criticism was bad enough. What also stuck in the throat was that Illingworth, who was paid for his *Sun* pieces, had banned the squad from writing newspaper diaries and columns during the tour.

England's arrival in Johannesburg was greeted with torrential rain and warnings about one of the most dangerous cities in the world, even though the squad was staying in the plush suburb of Sandton. Representatives from the British Embassy and the security forces advised Atherton's team of the dos and don'ts (hiring cars was out in the car-jacking capital of the world). The pre-Test exchanges were dominated by Mandela and Malcolm.

The South African President flew into Soweto during a warm-up game there, giving the authorities seven minutes' warning. The match was stopped and the teams lined up to meet the President. He stopped when he reached Malcolm: 'I know who you are – you're the Destroyer,' referring to Malcolm's nine-wicket haul at The Oval. Mandela, as ever, had the perfect phrase for the occasion and headline. But Illingworth was no slouch himself in finding the words that had journalists scribbling madly. Like Mandela, his mind was on Malcolm. England's Jamaican-born fast bowler had become the centre of attention, especially when the squad visited the Alexandra township. South Africa's cricket boss, Dr Ali Bacher, had persuaded Illingworth over dinner that Malcolm must play at Soweto in the township's first ever first-class game.

There is no doubt that all the adulation and attention did have an effect on Malcolm at the very time when Illingworth and bowling coach Peter Lever wanted to work closely with him. Plans to refine his action before the tour had been delayed because his knee had required keyhole surgery after the West Indies series. But even before he became the centre of attention, Malcolm was reluctant to change. He arrived in South Africa worried about his fitness and was in no mood to mess about with his action. That reluctance, plus his new-found superstar status, worried Illingworth far more than it did Atherton. Malcolm's laid-back manner had always annoyed the chairman. The sight of Malcolm, feet up in the dressing-room, listening to his Walkman was one with which Illingworth was never comfortable.

Malcolm did take the first wicket of the tour with his fifth ball in the warm-up match against diamond millionaire Nicky Oppenheimer's XI. His troubles began in earnest the day after, when he failed to turn up to watch the evening session as the tourists beat East Transvaal under lights. Atherton was not happy with Malcolm's excuse (working in the gym). He warned him against any repetition and said the matter was closed. But the press got to hear about it and that gave Illingworth and Lever the opportunity to debate the matter openly. The motive behind the England management washing their dirty linen in public was never made clear. Illingworth was aware that the media would make a meal of the situation, but if it was intended to shame Malcolm into action, it failed miserably. Atherton wanted no part of it; whatever the rights and wrongs of the management's request or the bowler's behaviour and reluctance to change, this public controversy would do nothing for England's morale or Test preparation. Malcolm had destroyed South Africa at The Oval the previous year. He was one of the most feared fast bowlers in the world. Now his confidence had been dented and undermined before a ball had been bowled in anger. The politics and psychology of such tactics were lost on the great British public. Malcolm was taken out of the Soweto game on the third morning to travel with the resting bowlers to Centurion Park for a work-out. When the final day of the Soweto game was abandoned because of rain, Illingworth and Lever held an impromptu and unprompted poolside press conference at the Sandton Sun. The intention appeared to be to give Malcolm a public lashing, hoping he would respond. Instead, it was perceived as an unnecessary public humiliation of a sportsman who was prevented from defending himself. Illingworth told the press: 'At the moment, he wouldn't frighten you, never mind the South African batsmen.' Lever added: 'He has just one asset – pace. That apart, he is a nonentity in cricketing terms.' Illingworth later denied that the word 'nonentity' had been used. Several journalists' notebooks and tape-recorders tells a different story. Illingworth also claimed that the press conference had been instigated by the media. It had been Lever who had told the press that Illingworth wanted a word with them. The press joined Illingworth by the pool; he lay back on a sun-lounger, took his top off and used it to cover his head. Most of the talking was done by Lever, with Illingworth lifting his shirt off his head to make the occasional comment. The initial press reaction afterwards was: 'What was all that about?' A look in the notebooks soon provided the answer – private cajoling was not working and it was time for a public dressing-down for England's fastest bowler. Public pressure did mount up – not on Malcolm, but on Illingworth and his management style. Atherton sat back. He had little option. England's captain was left to try to repair more internal damage caused by the supremo's forthright style. Illingworth admitted that Malcolm was now history as far as attempting any changes to his action was concerned: 'Devon is now one of six seamers. He must show me he is one of the best three or four to get in the Test side.' So much for making sure the team's main strike-weapon was in a positive frame of mind for the Test series.

ATHERTON

I was surprised when Devon didn't pitch up at Springs. He was the only one who did not make it. He said he had been working in the gym. I just said, 'Come in future.' That was the beginning and end of it as far as I was concerned. I could see the frustration that Illy and Plank [Lever] were feeling over Devon. He can be a very frustrating sort of bloke. He's always been fairly negative to advice. The main point for me was that all this should have happened behind closed doors. All sides are going to bicker and fall out. I would just prefer that it happened in private in my team. Everything was making its way to the press. A minor problem suddenly becomes a major one, the matter gets out of hand and everyone's taking sides. It's all so destructive. The press had changed a lot since Illy's day. Maybe he manipulated them in the past. You can't these days. The last thing you need on a tour is to engage in a battle that has nothing to do with the opposition.

The batting problem going into the series was Robin Smith, struggling to regain form after his operation. Atherton missed the second tour match in East London to give Smith another opportunity – a three-ball duck was not the response the captain wanted. Rain was England's other problem; it even followed the tourists to Kimberley. Thorpe, who had flown back to England because of his wife Nicky's unsuccessful pregnancy, rejoined the squad there. At last Illingworth had a few public words of encouragement for Malcolm, but it was too little, too late, especially when South Africa's coach Bob Woolmer joined the debate: 'We're much better prepared now to deal with Devon's pace. We are both mentally stronger and technically superior. I don't think Devon is in the same shape, either in form or fitness, as he was that day at The Oval.' No one could argue with that after the first few weeks in South Africa.

The home side were looking after their star fast bowler rather better. Allan Donald was spared Currie Cup duty and took a look at the tourists when they faced South Africa 'A'. The expert press-relations training was obvious when Donald was asked his thoughts on the series:

As far as we're concerned, Atherton is the crucial figure. He has proved himself to be one of the best batsmen in the world. He has the patience, technique and guts to play the anchor role and just loves to bat and bat and bat. There is no doubt that the first Test will set the pace for the whole series, so it is vital we get at him early. If you have a captain who leads from the front and from the first ball, it can pick everyone up. You can go a lot of places from there. On the other hand, because he is so vital to the way England perform, we know that if we can dismiss him cheaply, it will be a great psychological blow for us. Just before the tour to Zimbabwe, we got together at our training camp to plan a strategy for bowling at Atherton. We studied tape after tape of him batting against the West Indies last summer and spent a lot of time discussing various techniques. Atherton is a very good back-foot player who knows his limitations and works within them. He has his own style and it works. I don't want to give too much away, but I feel we have done enough homework. Now is the time to put our plans to the test.

Perfect. Respect, not unqualified, for an opponent of proven world class, with suggestions that he might have weaknesses which could be exploited.

England's weakness against spin was evident again when Paul Adams helped the 'A' side to a six-wicket victory. Match figures of 9 for 181 in his third first-class outing represented a remarkable achievement from the 18-year-old left-arm spinner with the curious action. England's batting highlight came from Malcolm with 48 not out, including six sixes. Illingworth had a few harsh words to say about and to the batsmen as the squad headed back to Sandton for the opening Test. England got a taste of the match conditions when they attended a pre-series dinner at Centurion Park, which was about to become the 76th Test venue. By the time the team coach headed back to their hotel, the ground was under water.

Centurion Park had a reputation for being one of the fastest wickets in South Africa (though recent Currie Cup games had been dominated by the spinners). When England arrived in South Africa, it was inconceivable that Malcolm would not play on such a surface. Illingworth, though, had talked himself into a corner and Malcolm had not produced the figures to provide an escape route. Malcolm rarely did. He was a match-winner of the loose-cannon variety, with the ability and speed to make life uncomfortable for some of the world's finest batsmen. The Malcolm debate continued right through to the morning of the match. No one was surprised when he was left out.

By close of play on the first day, it was South Africa's fast bowlers, all five of them, who dominated the discussions. After Hansie Cronje won the toss, that attack had been blunted by the combined efforts of Atherton and Hick. They rescued England from 64 for 3 at lunch. Atherton was at his most stubborn, especially when dealing with Shaun Pollock. The son of the South African chairman of selectors, Peter, and nephew of batting legend Graeme, was making his debut. He was easily the pick of the home bowlers, displaying real speed and hostility. Pollock had a reputation for being quicker than he looked. The previous summer, this Natal fast bowler was reputed to have hit 17 batsmen. Many had been attempting attacking shots. Atherton soon joined that club. England's captain was hit three times on the helmet – by Pollock, Donald and McMillan – and once needed attention from the England physio. Those blows only increased his resolve. There was none of the smiling through adversity that had been part of his West Indies strategy. Having been identified by Donald as England's linchpin, Atherton was going to play out that role. Any sign of surrender or weakness would cost England dear. Pollock ended Atherton's five-and-a-half-hour vigil when another short ball caught the shoulder of his bat and headed to gully. Atherton had set his sights on seeing the day through. His job was done, though. England held the initiative over South Africa, who had gambled and lost on the opening day. The home side expected more from a wicket that Illingworth was surprised to see being watered before the Test.

Hick's contribution was just as important. If Atherton had a reputation against fast bowling, so did Hick – he was the batsman who could not cope; whose footwork, temperament and technique were exposed by speed and bounce. This was Hick's fourth Test century and easily the best. It was the first time he had responded with a really big score when England desperately needed it. Hick reached 141 the next day as England progressed to 381 for 9, thanks to another fighting fifty from Russell. Atherton's plans to give South African batsmen an uncomfortable hour were abandoned after thunder and lightning left Centurion Park under water again. It began a frustrating three days for the England captain. Most of it was spent in the dressing-room playing bridge with Illingworth, who kept complaining about the level of noise emanating from the team's ghetto-blaster. When it became clear that time had run out to get a result, Atherton wanted his bowlers to at least gain a psychological edge over South Africa's batsmen. The stumps were in and the umpires on their way on the final afternoon when the rain came down again. England's first Test in South Africa for 29 years was abandoned as a draw. At the press conference, Atherton was asked, as someone who comes from Manchester, about the wisdom of playing Test matches at Centurion Park. England's captain smiled. It did not reflect his mood. South Africa had made a big mistake with their attack, but had escaped because of the weather. The continuing rain also accentuated a growing problem for the tourists – lack of match practice, especially on the bowling front. The team had one match, against Orange Free State, before the second Test in Johannesburg.

That was switched to two games – one three-day match and a Sunday limited-overs contest, with Dr Bacher's approval – to help ease England's worries. Atherton's practice was cut short when he went for a duck. Smith's and Ramprakash's poor form continued; Crawley was exerting real pressure for a place. But Illingworth had promised Ramprakash two Tests, and Atherton, too, felt it would be unfair to discard him after one innings. Smith's poor start increased the management's reluctance to move him to the trouble-spot of No. 3 and let Ramprakash come in down the order. As in the Caribbean, the selectors were to pay dearly for not putting the most experienced batsman in the toughest slot.

Atherton, whose bridge games partnering Illingworth against Ashton and the team doctor, Philip Bell, were now a part of the daily routine, was pleased to see a newspaper report that suggested England's top players should come under the control of the TCCB. The treatment of England's fast bowlers by the counties after the three-day Test defeat at Edgbaston contrasted sharply with the pampering Donald was enjoying from his employers. South Africa's premier fast bowler, after his break before the Centurion Test, sat out the three-day game against England. It was a flat wicket, and the South African management saw little advantage in putting Donald through his paces and, perhaps, allowing the tourists to gain a little psychological edge. On Sunday, he retired from the fray after three expensive overs. Atherton revealed he had no doubts about the benefits of such a system:

It would be better for the England team if the Board had full control of international cricketers. They could then decide which coaches the players would work with when necessary, what medical treatment they should receive if injured, and what fitness programmes they should undertake for the best preparation for Test cricket. Most importantly, they could decide how much cricket individuals ought to play between international matches. Generally, they should have control over the welfare and whereabouts of the players, all for the maximum benefit of the national side, without interference from the counties. The county grind is one of the main reasons why we do not produce as many quality pace-bowlers as we should. Bowling day in, day out, simply knocks too much out of them. There are times playing non-international cricket when I really have to force myself. I would be lying if I said there weren't occasions when I was not 100 per cent focused. It is hard work to forcibly build yourself up to play.

Atherton's motives on the Saturday in Bloemfontein were purely selfish and geared towards the second Test. The Free State match became a meaningless contest and meaningful practice as England batted the home side out of the game. The team relaxed at another *braai* (barbecue) back at the hotel that night. This time the chefs were not local, but Fraser and Hick. Atherton felt the squad were much more together than in Australia, more reminiscent of the Caribbean. Towns like Bloemfontein and Kimberley had little nightlife to offer other than middle-of-the-road restaurants, and the quality of South African wine improved most meals. Malcolm's participation, or rather non-participation, in the Test series was still the main topic of interest among the media. The general feeling was that if he was not selected on another fast surface at The Wanderers, he might just as well pack his bags and head for home. He had done little at Bloemfontein to suggest a change of heart by Illingworth, but the pitch at The Wanderers gave the first hint of a Malcolm recall. From first sight, Atherton and Illingworth felt that asking South Africa to bat was a real possibility. That led to

Malcolm's inclusion, not the other way round. The absence of any world-class spinner among the opposition eased any worries about batting last.

The South African dressing-room, committee-room and Wanderers stands were all astonished when the home side were inserted, and it looked a grave mistake when South Africa reached 211 for 2 after tea. But Cork, England's only steady bowler, Malcolm, with two wickets in four deliveries with the new ball, and Russell's five catches hauled South Africa back to 278 for 7 by the close. Chasing 332, Atherton was bowled by Donald as he shouldered arms. At that pace on that wicket, it was a marginal error of judgement as it clipped the off-stump, but a rare one nonetheless from the England captain. England reached 109 for 2, but the final eight wickets only added another 91 runs. The trouble started when Thorpe received a poor decision from umpire Karl Liebenberg, but that did not excuse the collapse or spinner Clive Eksteen's figures of 3 for 12 from 11 overs. South Africa were in control, a position they more than confirmed on the third day. With two days remaining, England trailed by 428 runs and South Africa were still batting. Atherton knew England were in real trouble. The situation would have been much worse if South Africa had not come off for bad light as McMillan laid into Malcolm and the new ball. Atherton had noticed that the South Africans' fear of losing was their strongest motivation as regards strategy. Abandoning the attack on the third evening was indicative of that. Atherton had tried to make South Africa struggle for runs all day, but the shackles came off when England took the new ball. McMillan belted Malcolm for two huge sixes and England suddenly looked weary. Yet when the light was offered to the batsmen, off they came. Every minute Atherton could keep England in the field on the fourth day was a minute less for them to survive. Survival was all that was left; Atherton has always been a realist.

As South Africa batted on for another hour and a half to allow McMillan his century, England were left to negotiate five and a bit sessions, not six. Atherton believed they had an escape route, but the fourth day ended with England on the edge – the last two recognised batsmen were at the crease. Had a fifth wicket fallen, England would have been finished. Nearly all hopes rested with the captain, defiant on 82 not out. Disappointingly, Ramprakash, Thorpe and Hick had contributed just 21 runs. Ramprakash lasted two balls and walked off knowing it would take a miracle to get him back in this series. Atherton had a quiet night, but not before meeting up with Ian Botham. A challenge was issued after Botham had heard that the over-forties, a club he had recently joined, could no longer cut it in the drinking stakes, according to Atherton. If Atherton was still batting at the close of the Test, Botham would be ready for a 'cane and coke' contest. That suited England's captain. Anything to increase the competitive atmosphere and environment.

It is probable that Atherton would have been a drunken wreck even without Botham's influence. England achieved the impossible and drew the second Test, with Atherton playing what Illingworth described as 'the greatest innings of all time'. The bare facts – 185 runs, 645 minutes and 492 balls – convey the magnitude of Atherton's effort in the direst of situations. His steely determination did not waver for a second. His emotions were kept in check until the moment Cronje conceded defeat and offered Atherton a handshake. England's captain raced off the field, stopping to embrace Russell, who had kept him company for over two sessions, and ran to the England dressing-room in triumph.

Russell, who had also set a new Test record for a wicket-keeper with 11 victims, played a crucial part in the final stages. He had batted for a similar time in Barbados in similar circumstances during Gooch's tour. On that occasion, Ambrose took the new ball, breached Russell's defence and broke his heart with a delivery that shot along the ground. England lost the Test, and Russell had never been ashamed to admit that the pain of that memory had not diminished over the years. He told his captain, in the plainest terms, that he was not going through all that again. It was the perfect combination in a desperate situation. The South Africans were not going to wind these two up or divert them from the task in hand. Atherton was solid as rock, and just as animated. Russell, on the other hand, cannot keep still. The proverbial jack in the box, Russell is just about the most annoying and frustrating batsman in the world to bowl at, especially in circumstances such as these. He made only 14 scoring shots in his 276 minutes at the wicket.

Atherton was England's Horatius on the bridge. He had begun the thought-process of batting to save the game on Saturday night, hoping to lose no more than a wicket a session on the fourth day. When Smith departed after 75 minutes of the last day, Atherton knew Russell was England's final chance. The captain had just reached his ninth Test century after being missed by Gary Kirsten at short leg off Donald (Atherton was intent on making history, but not as the first Test batsman to be dismissed three times on 99). The contest might have been over before lunch if Merryck Pringle had not dropped a return catch from Russell. South Africa were made to pay for those lapses. No chances were offered between lunch and tea. Atherton, who had reached 4,000 Test runs at the same time as his hundred, passed his previous highest score, 151 against New Zealand at Trent Bridge in 1990. He added 40 runs in that session, Russell eight. Atherton sensed South Africa's growing frustration as he passed Denis Lindsay's 182, the highest Test score at The Wanderers. Cronje's last desperate throw was the new ball.

Seventeen minutes later, South Africa's captain conceded defeat and England's draw.

After Gooch-like resistance, Atherton showed Gooch-like understatement at the press conference. Illingworth was not so restrained: 'This is difficult for a Yorkshireman to say to a Lancastrian – but that was one of the great innings of all time. Mike and Jack Russell were tremendous.' The adjudicator made them joint Men of the Match. Atherton: 'This is the most satisfying innings of my career. A game was there to be saved – and we did it. My motivation was simple. We had to save the game. I owed the lads one after shoving South Africa in to bat and I found a good man in Jack. It was a case of maintaining 100 per cent concentration. I took it ball by ball, hour by hour, session by session.' Russell reflected the effort that had gripped a nation: 'We played every ball as though our lives depended on it.' Illingworth's praise for his captain seemed strange after the way he had treated him earlier in the year: 'Mike is a man who will always play better captaining a side – and that is a good reason to keep him in the job.'

Atherton's ordeal was not over – the Botham challenge could not be avoided. England's captain had a head-start on the former all-rounder after the dressing-room celebrations. Botham soon caught up and the pair were not a pretty sight at Vertigo's in the early hours. As with Russell during the day, Atherton had found his perfect soul-mate for the job in hand. Dark glasses were the order of the following day as the squad flew to Cape Town, then travelled by coach to Paarl. The members of the squad not suffering from hangovers had merely delayed the inevitable. The lunchtime barbecue organised by a local winery ensured that the celebrations lasted even longer than Atherton's historic innings. The team were not kidding themselves. They knew it was the captain alone who had enabled them to get out of jail. South

Africa had escaped at Centurion Park because of the weather. At least the tourists had drawn in Johannesburg through their own efforts.

Atherton planned a break in Paarl, one of his better tactical moves. There are vineyards and wineries at every turn. He and Fraser headed off on a tour to taste the local grapes. The game against Boland meandered nowhere. A match against New Zealand had been abandoned here a year earlier because the wicket was too dangerous. The only danger this time was boredom. Illingworth cracked his head against the concrete pavilion-wall on Saturday afternoon when the plastic chair he was leaning his back on snapped, and decided he had had enough. The game would end a day early to allow a one-day game on the Sunday. Atherton returned to the hotel with his supper after his first-ever day's fly-fishing with tour manager John Barclay. The captain was not too happy to hear that he was required for duty the next day. Ramprakash and Cork had also been called back from Cape Town. Atherton responded with 77 as England won by 74 runs.

The squad flew to Durban for the third Test. England's bowling attack would have to be changed because Gough had damaged his hamstring in Paarl. No one expected the wholesale changes to the line-up that were announced on the morning of the match. Martin, Ilott and Illingworth came in for Gough, Malcolm and Fraser. The only predictable switch was the swapping of Crawley for Ramprakash. Atherton felt sympathy for Ramprakash's plight as a struggling, talented performer but as England's captain his patience had run out. England had needed South Africa to fight for every wicket in The Wanderers second innings – Ramprakash had emerged as a lamb to the slaughter and departed two balls later when Donald put him out of his misery. Atherton knew at that moment that it would take exceptional circumstances for Ramprakash to play any further part in the series. The management had done the right thing by the player in giving him two Tests. Now it was Crawley's turn, or so it seemed.

The rain settled the third Test, as it had at Pretoria. Only 32 minutes' play was possible on the final three days. In over a century of Test cricket, South Africa had only lost 11 full days at home because of the weather. Five had been washed out on this tour. Cronje won the toss and batted. England looked in trouble when the openers reached 54 for 0 after an hour, but Illingworth and Martin reduced South Africa to 89 for 5 before Rhodes and McMillan retrieved the situation to 139 for 5 when the rain came. England were set fair on the second day until a last-wicket stand of 72 between Donald and Pollock took South Africa to 226. During that partnership, Crawley tore his hamstring. Jason Gallian was soon on his way from the 'A' tour in Pakistan. Atherton was caught in the gully cheaply, and as in the first innings at The Wanderers, England crumbled without their captain, finishing the day at 123 for 5. Hick and Cork added another 29 runs in two spells on the third day, but that was it. Even a ball-tampering story involving Craig Matthews failed to excite. Atherton had never known a Test series or a tour like it. It was as if he had been in South Africa for a lifetime. All the squad, batters and bowlers, first-choice and reserves, were short of match practice. Already, the final Test in Cape Town was looking like the best chance of breaking the deadlock. Port Elizabeth was a good batting surface and the weather was still unpredictable.

Atherton found out the same was true of England's batting line-up in the fourth Test. He had to dig in again after Stewart, Gallian and Thorpe all went cheaply. Atherton had batted two minutes short of five hours when the South Africans went up for a catch down the leg-side. Paul Adams was the bowler, and the ball clipped Atherton's pad on its way to wicket-keeper Dave Richardson.

Atherton was not unduly alarmed until he saw umpire Cyril Mitchley raise his finger. His anger was not at his own misfortune; this umpire's decision could prove extremely costly at a crucial time. Atherton stood stunned for a few seconds. No one was in any doubt – least of all Mitchley – about what England's captain thought of the decision. He walked off slowly, glancing in the umpire's direction, shaking his head. It was as much dissent as his departure at The Oval against the same opposition a year before. A plastic chair at the dressing-room door received the full force of Atherton's frustration and bat. The locals treated that as front-page news: 'Blazing Atherton smashes chair.' His fears about England's precarious position were well-founded: they were soon 200 for 7. Russell and Illingworth saved the follow-on.

Atherton found himself in disagreement with Mitchley again as England fought back in the field. He was handi-capped because Ilott was out of action with a thigh strain. Martin and Cork reduced South Africa to 69 for 6, but any sort of a partnership was a problem to Atherton with South Africa already having a 165-run first-innings lead. When Kirsten and Pollock added 66 runs for the seventh-wicket, England's captain decided to adopt the leg-theory tactic. It was not 'Bodyline', but it was not cricket accord-ing to umpire Mitchley. Although Cork's bowling outside the leg-stump was not illegal, Mitchley warned Cork that he would call a wide if he persisted and informed Ather-ton. Mitchley's justification was Law 42.2: 'Umpires are the sole judge of fair and unfair play.' Atherton knew that not to be the case after his experiences in 1994. He tried to plead his case. A bowler short, he was trying to win a Test match. All to no avail. Mitchley signalled a wide to a delivery that was 18 inches outside Pollock's leg-stump. (How Atherton must have wished Mitchley had been the umpire during Heath Streak's last over in Bulawayo a year later.)

The final day began with England 20 runs towards a victory target of 328. Atherton was intent on being positive. Once again, he discovered that South Africa's fear of losing was stronger than any desire for victory. England's 42 runs in the first hour was nothing more than a steady start, but it was enough for Cronje to take fright. Most of the close catchers were removed, two men were positioned on the leg-side boundary and the off-side was packed. The tourists' batting collapses at Johannesburg, Durban and Port Elizabeth should have persuaded Cronje to keep England interested. The South African captain had bowlers to keep it tight if necessary and young Adams to exploit any nervousness in England's lower order. Once Cronje set his sights on Cape Town, the England captain had little option but to do the same. Stewart, after Atherton departed soon after lunch, made sure there was no panic in the England camp as the Test petered out. Atherton was astonished at the press conference to find out that he, not Cronje, was being blamed for the deadlock and tame finish by the South African journalists. The SA *Sunday Times* put him on the front page with the headline 'Spoilsport' and a giant picture of Atherton yawning. The article, by a respected cricket journalist, Colin Bryden, was just as damning: 'While Hansie Cronje's conservative field placings contributed to the draw, it was Atherton's performance which killed the match.'

Atherton felt the series would go England's way as the squad flew to Cape Town that night. South Africa had failed to press home the advantage in the two Tests that had gone the distance. Cronje was reluctant to gamble or take a risk. Atherton was not going to err on the side of caution in his quest for the series. Cape Town had all the makings of a giant party. The England party, now swelled to 64 with all the wives, girlfriends, children, mums, dads and nannies, booked into the Cape Sun on New Year's

Eve. Most of England's cricket fraternity seemed to be in town. For the other side, President Mandela was photographed with Adams and told Cronje's team: 'The whole nation is behind you.' The stage was set for a winner-takes-all shoot-out.

Atherton did gamble, and lost. Cronje's cautiousness, backed with a seven-batsmen line-up, won the Test and the series. Illingworth claimed that Malcolm 'cost us the Test'. His four wayward overs with the new ball certainly had a devastating psychological effect on the team. Just as damaging, though, were the totals of 153 and 157 from the tourists. Apart from the opening day and a half of the series at Centurion Park, Atherton's heroics at The Wanderers and the last-day defiance in Port Elizabeth, England's batting was all too easily knocked over by a disciplined South African attack. That made Atherton's decision to enter this crunch Test with only five recognised batsmen all the more bewildering. South Africa played seven. Malcolm and Fraser, who were not staying for the one-day games, were recalled, having hardly bowled since the second Test, while Watkinson made his first appearance of the series. Illingworth explained the selection: 'I always want to go in with five bowlers and so does Mike Atherton. But it's not been possible because our batting has not been consistent. Now we're backing them to score enough runs. We always try to be positive and win games. I'd be silly to have any other philosophy. Now I want to bat first, score 450 and see how South Africa cope with that sort of total.' Atherton won the toss to enable England to carry out the first part of the plan. Unfortunately, they finished 297 runs short of Illingworth's target 40 minutes after tea. Only Smith, at last filling England's problem spot at No. 3, provided any resistance. Atherton went after 25 minutes without a run on the board, one of Donald's five wickets. Cork's two successes for England in the final session were the only

moments of consolation. It was a sub-standard performance on a lively pitch. It seemed that if the captain did not
show them the way, the rest of the England batting
line-up soon got lost.

The mood in the camp was downbeat that night. Atherton did not believe England were out of it, but they were
again playing catch-up cricket. He was convinced that the
South Africans would cave in under pressure. On the
occasions things had not gone Cronje's way, the tension
had shown – but apart from Centurion Park, England had
been unable to sustain that pressure. Atherton warned his
players to stay calm on the second morning. Any sign of
panic or surrender would convey itself to the crowd and
the South Africa batsmen. His bowlers responded magnificently. Kirsten was the only wicket to fall before
lunch, but runs were at a premium. South Africa's 125 for
3 was transformed to 171 for 9; only 38 runs were scored
between lunch and tea. Runs and wickets became precious commodities. South Africa's lead was 18 runs with
one wicket remaining. England had clawed themselves
back into the Test and the series inch by inch.

Atherton now took the new ball, believing it to be the
most likely way of removing young Adams, and threw it
to Malcolm, the Destroyer. England's iron-Mike grip was
loosened for the first time in hours when an unnecessary
shy at the stumps by Cork went to the boundary. Those
four Malcolm overs almost broke Atherton's heart. Two
leg-side deliveries cannoned off Adams' pads and down
to the fine-leg boundary. In all, 26 runs came from those
four overs. The spell was broken. Adams and Richardson
surpassed Pollock's and Donald's last-wicket stand in
Durban and added 73 runs in cavalier fashion, the best
partnership of the match. Atherton could not believe it.
South Africa's lead was 91. Just as importantly, their
spirits had soared as England's had plummeted.
Malcolm's direction was lamentable. Straying down the

leg-side was inexcusable. He was an easy target. Atherton commented: 'We had a bowler who had bowled 10 overs in the day and was fresh. He had the new ball and there was a rabbit coming in at No. 11. Draw your own conclusions. When South Africa lost their ninth wicket, we just needed to knock over their last man with the new ball.' Atherton was distraught and furious, as angry as he has ever been on a cricket field as he saw three months of hard work go down the pan in a horrendous half-hour. Donald made Atherton's misery complete when he had England's captain caught behind with two overs remaining. It was obvious that the events of the day were still playing on Atherton's mind. He would have been better off staying in the dressing-room. Illingworth had seen how upset Atherton was at the end of the South African innings, and his first thought was to let someone else open. He did not press the matter. That was a mistake. This was an occasion when Illingworth should have followed his instinct and used his experience for the sake of his captain and his team. Atherton was in no state to judge the situation rationally. Moving down the order would not have been a sign of weakness, just expediency. Atherton would have best served England when he had recovered mentally and emotionally from his last-wicket ordeal. To lose their captain and inspiration that evening was a body-blow for England.

Atherton's Cape Town ordeal was far from over. The next day was the final one of the series as England lost by 10 wickets. All the frustrations of the tour came bubbling to the surface as Atherton returned to the dressing-room after the presentation ceremony. England's fight for survival had been severely hampered by controversial umpiring decisions that cost them the wickets of Smith, Hick and Thorpe. The Thorpe run-out dismissal led to a £600 dissent fine for the South African captain Cronje. The television replays were clear: Thorpe was out by a metre to Hudson's throw and Adams had knocked into the stumps first. But home umpire David Orchard, officiating in his second Test, had given Thorpe not out without calling for the third umpire. As the TV replays were shown around the ground and in the sponsors' boxes, a great groan went up. That told Cronje that Orchard had called it wrong. The Code of Conduct does not allow players to pressure the umpire for a TV replay, but Cronje evaluated that the removal of Thorpe was worth whatever penalties the ICC might impose. The South African captain drew out a television screen with his hands in front of Orchard. The umpire was aware he had got it wrong. The crowd's reaction told him Thorpe was out. Orchard consulted with fellow umpire Randell, the third umpire was called in and Thorpe was on his way. England's last six wickets fell for 19 runs. South Africa took just over an hour to knock off the 67 runs that earned them all the spoils.

The drama was not finished. Atherton was getting used to enduring presentations abroad as a losing captain, but his patience snapped when it was announced over the loudspeaker that England would play a 50-over game against Western Province on Saturday, the scheduled fifth day of the Test. It was not only news to the crowd, but to Atherton and his team. Illingworth had given his agreement to satisfy those who had bought tickets for the final days. It showed Illingworth's complete lack of understanding of the pressures on the modern international cricketer. England had just lost a Test series and were about to embark on a seven-match one-day series as preparation for the World Cup. A few days' break would have been far more beneficial to body and mind. It was not the first time Illingworth had made decisions without consulting his captain. When Atherton got back to the dressing-room, he wanted to know what was going on. That was the signal for Illingworth to lay into the captain, the team, the batsmen and Malcolm – 'You bowled crap and probably cost us the Test match.' The outburst ended with Illingworth going red and starting to choke. Some of the players thought he was having a heart attack. He gulped down some water, told them he wanted volunteers for Saturday's match or he'd choose them himself, and stormed out. A losing dressing-room after a five-Test series is no place for a post-mortem. England's hopes had been dashed in three days.

England had suffered similar humiliations on Atherton's tours before, and recovered. Yet the effect of this defeat lingered and festered for the rest of the winter.

ATHERTON

I felt going in with five batters and going for the win was the right thing to do. It was a calculated risk. I felt at Durban and Port Elizabeth that we had lacked that killer punch. Fresh legs might do it for us. South Africa had not been batting brilliantly as a unit. The tour boiled down to a crazy 40 minutes – 40 minutes in a tour of three months! I knew it was happening. All that hard work disappearing in a flash. We had battled brilliantly to get back in the game. Devon had bowled well at The Wanderers – really sharp.

When it looked as if the ball was swinging at Durban, we made wholesale changes. That was my decision. Illy backed me up. I felt those changes were vindicated. I don't know whether I would have been better not coming out on that second evening in Cape Town. It's my style to confront situations, not run away. But that was as wound-up as I've ever been on a cricket field. Not making it through to the close was probably inevitable. At Headingley in 1994, I was in a state – numb after 10 days of harassment. At Cape Town, the blood was boiling.

Atherton felt worn out. The batting and bowling coaches

had long gone. Illingworth was not up for much physical activity at his age. The captain found himself landed with a much-increased workload, as if leading this inconsistent bunch was not enough of a task. The England party had become something of a travelling circus. The families were a distraction during the final two Tests in South Africa. It is not so much the wives and girlfriends but the young children, which means nannies, grandparents and carrycots. (The solution in Zimbabwe the following year was to impose a voluntary ban. At least that way the wives were not blamed for England's whitewash in the one-day series.)

There was much coming and going towards the end of the series. England's one-day experts arrived, while several members of the original Test squad flew home. Some were leaving the England set-up for the last time, according to Illingworth. With his usual impeccable timing, his verdict on almost half his squad was that their Test futures were bleak to say the least. Only one of the seven, Alec Stewart, played international cricket over the next 12 months.

CHAPTER FIFTEEN

One-Day Disaster

England's build-up to the World Cup started with that
makeshift game against Western Province. It set the
tone for the next two months and 13 one-day internationals; England made a disastrous start, recovered to a
winning position and then threw it away. They lost by six
runs to South Africa on the same ground three days later:
'We did pretty well to lose that,' was Atherton's verdict
after the last seven wickets had fallen for 50 runs. 'We
bottled it. There was panic. We conceded 17 extras,
dropped Shaun Pollock and batted poorly at the death.'
Man of the Match Atherton and Hick brought England a
brief respite after floodlight failure at Bloemfontein two
days later to overcome South Africa for the first time after
86 days in the country. The remaining fortnight was a
nightmare and England came home in complete disarray
– the tourists went from bad to worse, losing at The
Wanderers, Centurion Park (without Atherton), Kings-
mead, Buffalo Park (chasing a target of 129) and, finally,
at George's Park in Port Elizabeth, the city Atherton had
left with such high hopes 24 days earlier. The seven
matches were supposed to prepare England for the World
Cup; they ended up seriously damaging the squad's

confidence, as well as confusing the strategy and selection. Before the end of the one-day series, *The Times* led the sports pages with the view: 'Atherton must stand aside for the World Cup.' The comments were not made by the paper's cricket correspondent. 'Something seems to have died within Atherton during this bizarre two-week travelling circus. It is, one might hazard, his affection for limited-overs cricket,' claimed writer Simon Wilde. 'It might be reborn one day, but not before he leaves South Africa on Monday, nor in time for the World Cup. Atherton has never been well suited to one-day cricket, either intellectually or temperamentally. He rarely eschews orthodoxy or embraces innovation. The same could be said of his captaincy.'

Atherton, and more especially Illingworth, had also to cope with a renewal of the Devon Malcolm controversy in the final week of the tour. England's fast bowler had returned home and given his side of the story to a national newspaper. The initial article claimed racial discrimination, though this was later denied. It was a strange accusation considering Malcolm had won £50,000 damages before the tour from *Wisden Cricket Monthly* after an article suggested that black players were less committed to England. Malcolm also claimed that 'Illingworth would rather have lost the series than see me do well.' Atherton regarded the whole matter as unnecessarily damaging because of the public element. Both Illingworth and Malcolm had gone running to the press, and for that reason Atherton had little sympathy for either. When the TCCB did not take action against Malcolm for breaching his tour contract, the captain was as astonished as Illingworth. Atherton believed that Malcolm would receive a ban, as he had been warned of the consequences of going public before he returned home.

Atherton had less than a fortnight at home before heading off to Pakistan to prepare for the World Cup.

He was being positive about England, three-time losing finalists, recovering in time. The seven-match limited-overs series in South Africa had made ridiculous demands on the tourists' stamina after a five-Test series. Once they started doing badly, the whole exercise became counter-productive. Atherton received confirmation that Lancashire had awarded him a benefit in 1997. He sought out businessman Bob Wilson, who had been Neil Fairbrother's benefit chairman, for advice. The commercialisation of these events, however well-meaning, horrified Atherton.

Atherton knew that England's opening game against New Zealand was critical. It was important to show there was no South African hangover. The week leading up to the tournament was dominated by Australia and West Indies' refusal to travel to Sri Lanka after a terrorist bombing there claimed more than 80 lives. Those matches were eventually awarded to the home side. England were hampered by injuries to Smith and Cork during the practice week in Lahore, and there was confusion about who they could bring in as replacements. The preparation was also disrupted by two tiring trips in four days to attend the opening ceremony in Delhi, which cost a fortune and was a shambles. Atherton's team were not alone in rating the whole exercise a waste of time.

England were in Group B, the weaker section, and the schedule was also in their favour. After New Zealand, the next two opponents were the ICC qualifiers, the United Arab Emirates and Holland. Beating those two alone would almost certainly guarantee a place in the quarter-finals. Atherton wanted more. Scraping through, after all that had taken place in South Africa, would not be good enough. He was happy with the team spirit, but then he rarely had complaints in that area. The captain emphasised the need to do the basics well, to be sharp and alert in the field. His words went unheeded as England lost their opening match by 11 runs.

Thorpe put down two catches right at the start. The life he gave to Nathan Astle, who had been playing league cricket for Illingworth's club Farsley for the past two years, cost England exactly 100 runs. Two more catches went down, Atherton and Cork being the other culprits. England were fortunate that New Zealand's 228 for 9 was not considerably more. Atherton played over an inswinging yorker in the second over, but Stewart and Hick provided the platform for victory. The innings started to go wrong at 144 for 3 when Fairbrother called Atherton (acting as Hick's runner) for a risky single. The captain hesitated for a second and Hick was out for 85. The run-chase fell apart. Some questioned Atherton's decision to put New Zealand in, Illingworth avoided collective responsibility: 'Whether we got it right or wrong, I don't know. It was Mike's decision – ask him about it.' The captain was happy to confirm he would do the same again, adding: 'I can't fault the batting or the bowling, just the fielding.' He was desperately disappointed that the South African malaise had travelled via England to the sub-continent. Atherton wanted his squad in high spirits as they embarked on the two-day journey from Ahmedabad to Delhi to Karachi to Peshawar for the game against the UAE, who had lost to South Africa when Gary Kirsten hit a World Cup record 188 not out. England saw off the UAE with 15 overs to spare. Craig White damaged rib-muscles and was replaced in the squad by Dermot Reeve, who many felt should have been in the original party and some believed ought to have replaced Atherton as England's one-day captain.

Internal politics gave way to international ones when the *Frontier Post* accused England of bribery after their attempt to practise on the square to be used for the Holland match. The allegation came under the heading,

'Englishmen At It Again.' Holland were beaten by 49 runs as Hick scored a century in a stand of 143 with Thorpe. England were still experimenting with the batting line-up: Atherton was at No. 5 and Neil Smith was Stewart's opening partner. The schedule was working against Atherton now. With England sure to go through, they continued to mess about with the line-up to try and get it right for the knockout stages. A more sensible strategy would have been to decide on a settled side and let that team use the games against South Africa and Pakistan to prepare for the quarter-final. Illingworth revealed that he had wanted Atherton to open against Holland – somehow the man who claimed he was going to call all the shots during the winter was letting the captain have his way. These instances were generally only given a public airing afterwards by Illingworth if they did not work out: 'We did a lot of messing about in South Africa and, frankly, it didn't teach us a great deal. Now we have to play our best team and, yes, I know what it is.'

Illingworth's use of the royal 'we' helped spread the responsibility, but Atherton was the only person to blame for the row that blew up after the 78-run defeat by South Africa. England's captain has never been at his best in after-match press conferences. Uncommunicative and uncomfortable is the style. When Atherton was asked could he speak up, he replied, 'No.' These occasions can be tortuous on the sub-continent as local journalists struggle with their English. Atherton overreacted by responding to Asghar Ali's stuttering question with, 'Will somebody remove this buffoon?' Relations between England and Pakistan had been rocky since the Gatting–Shakoor Rana flare-up nine years earlier (and the subsequent ball-tampering rows) and this was the first time England had been back. It was Atherton at his worst and brought the glare of publicity when the team needed it least. Atherton's apology was about as meaningful as

Gatting's in 1987. 'At yesterday's press conference, after the match against South Africa, I am sorry if I caused offence to a local journalist and local journalists during questions.' Illingworth gave short shrift to questions about replacing Atherton as captain: 'A change of captaincy is not an option. Michael was picked to lead the side in the World Cup and that is his job. If I am in charge next summer, he will be captain. I cannot foresee a situation where I stay and he goes.' A glowing testimony from the man who had made him sweat for the job the previous summer.

Whether it was because of the fuss over his 'buffoon' remark or another poor display against South Africa, the pressure of the situation suddenly hit Atherton: 'I am fatalist about the captaincy. I hold it dear and I don't want to be stood down at the end of the World Cup, but I know it's quite likely to happen if we continue to play as we are. Once the bandwagon starts to roll and people start calling for the captain's head, it's very hard to stop it. I am not going to drop myself – in fact, I haven't even thought about it.' It even made news when Atherton missed a presentation after a practice match at the Karachi Gymkhana Club because he was stuck on the toilet. Richie Richardson and the West Indies briefly took the pressure off Atherton and his team by losing to Kenya by 73 runs in Pune. It was the cricket World Cup's greatest giant-killing act, putting the West Indies' qualification in doubt. But on the same day that the West Indies Board met to decide Richardson's future, he hit an undefeated 93 to lead them into the quarter-finals with a win over Australia. Richardson had already faxed his resignation – the Board were to dismiss coach Andy Roberts and manager Wes Hall. Meanwhile, Atherton was back in the runs against Pakistan as he put on 147 for the first wicket with Smith. All 10 England wickets then fell for 102 in 21 overs and Pakistan sailed past the target, with England's old adversary Javed Miandad at the crease.

England finished fourth in group B and were matched with Group A winners Sri Lanka in the quarter-finals. That might have looked a favourable draw before the tournament. Not now. Sri Lanka had proved themselves the outstanding team of the group stage; they made full use of the fielding restrictions in the first 15 overs by blasting away. In their final qualifying match, Sri Lanka had set a one-day record with a tally of 398 for 5 against Kenya, De Silva top-scoring with 145 off 115 balls. England's bowling attack, further weakened because of Cork's absence with a knee injury, had shown no signs of being able to contain such fluent stroke-makers – DeFreitas was experimenting with his off-breaks in the nets as England prepared. It was now clear that Illingworth's bowling selection was flawed. Atherton needed reliable bowlers to concentrate on line and length. With little help from the pitches, bowlers who attacked and strayed were a real handicap. Those bowlers had little margin for error in the quarter-final after England reached 235 for 8 in the allotted 50 overs. DeFreitas, batting No. 5, top-scored with 67. Atherton had to gamble, and Richard Illingworth opened the bowling. His first 12 deliveries went for 27 runs. Jayasuriya hit the fastest World Cup fifty, off 29 balls, and Sri Lanka won with 10 overs to spare. They were ambling by the finish. The Sri Lankans went on to win the World Cup in style, overcoming India and Australia, and were worthy winners.

That was little consolation to Atherton as he fielded the inevitable questions. 'It's time to go home and reflect – I have 10 days before Lancashire's pre-season tour to do that. I would like to stay on and I'm prepared to fight my corner, but I'm not going to hang myself if I lose the job. If they don't want me, I'll walk away and enjoy my retirement.'

ATHERTON
*Everyone blamed Cape Town for what happened after-
wards. Not me. That wasn't the reason we failed. It was a
combination of a bad itinerary, planning and fatigue. The
South Africa one-day schedule was ridiculous. Once we
were on the slippery slope, that was it. We made too many
changes. It was nonsense to say that we were downbeat
about the World Cup. The competition is played every
three or four years. That might be the only one I ever play
in. It was important to me. We practised hard in Lahore,
but the damage had been done. There was an underlying
lack of confidence and it was shattered when we lost to
New Zealand. That's how fragile it was. A couple of
catches went down and we were struggling. There is a
clear divide between home and away as far as the England
cricket team is concerned.*

*Again, I didn't handle myself too well at a press
conference. I used the word 'buffoon' – that's someone
who's playing the fool. I never intended to be insulting or
rude. But those occasions can be pretty trying and chaotic.
We had just lost a match. All I wanted to do was change
and get back to the hotel. I never saw it as much of an
issue.*

CHAPTER SIXTEEN

Old Trafford Connections

England's summer was one of regrouping and recovering after the winter's one-day disasters. The 1996 season was dominated by four personalities and two controversies that had nothing to do with current events on the field. The legacies of the Illingworth–Malcolm dispute rumbled on all summer before England's chairman was cleared of bringing the game into disrepute. The main skirmish was between Ian Botham and Imran Khan, who did battle in the High Court. Atherton was just one of many from the world of cricket to be subpoenaed and have his day in court. The verdict, in Imran's favour, was the biggest cricket upset of the summer. Away from the witness box and back in more familiar surroundings, Atherton's England won the first Cornhill Test series and lost the second. Both Texaco series went to the home side. Much was expected of the Ackfield Report, but it was yet another document on the future of English cricket which offered little revolution and more crippling compromise.

Illingworth and David Graveney were the two nominations for the post of chairman of selectors. Illingworth claimed this was not a fair fight. He cited his old adversary, MJK Smith, as part of the Warwickshire executive that was pulling strongly for the younger man. The matter was further complicated by Graveney's position as general secretary of the Cricketers' Association. Devon Malcolm had been seeking the Association's advice over the TCCB's threat of disciplinary action over his newspaper comments. Illingworth retained his job after Graveney withdrew before the postal ballot. Surrey – 'People forget that ours was not a pro-Graveney vote; it is an anti-Illingworth vote,' insisted chairman Mike Soper – and Warwickshire, two of Graveney's supporters, were angry at his late withdrawal, which left no time to promote another alternative. Graveney's change of mind reflected a possible conflict of interests over pressure of time, disciplinary actions against members of the Cricketers' Association (CA) and dealing with the media while wearing two hats. This conflict was confirmed towards the end of the year when Graveney again expressed an interest in succeeding Illingworth. It was resolved early in 1997 by altering the chairman's terms of reference to remove the disciplinary aspect.

With Illingworth confirmed as chairman of selectors, the spotlight moved on to the new coach. John Emburey had enjoyed a successful tour with England 'A', but the doubts about Atherton's willingness to continue were a big boost for the other candidate, Lancashire's coach David Lloyd. The choice was made in the TCCB's usual quaint way of dealing with such matters. For a start, the TCCB's chief executive and chairman did not speak directly to the candidates – the chief executives of Northamptonshire and Lancashire, Emburey and Lloyd's respective employers, were the go-betweens. The basic deal was £20,000 for a summer's work, much less than the pair were already getting, and the summer was the extent of the Board's commitment. The applicants were being asked to consider giving up a three-year or four-year contract, and take a drop in salary with little security, to take the most important and prestigious coaching job in England. The TCCB executive met to discuss the candidates on a Tuesday and wanted an answer by Friday. That yes or no was not to accept the job, but to confirm they wanted to put their names forward for consideration. Emburey wanted the job, but not at that price – especially as he already knew the majority of the counties would back Lloyd. The Atherton preference and connection were obvious and swayed support in the Lancastrian's favour. Another advantage was that Lloyd had not been involved in the recent in-fighting at national level. The fact that Emburey was Illingworth's declared choice also helped Lloyd. Emburey kept his dignity and Northampton job by withdrawing. The official reason was that he wanted to 'gain more experience in cricket management and coaching with his new county'. The next day, Lloyd, 49, was appointed England coach. He was in Jamaica with Lancashire and Atherton.

This news did not immediately prompt Atherton to announce his intention to carry on. He had always intended to keep his powder dry and felt no need to abandon his original timescale. Atherton wanted to see all the other pieces of the jigsaw in place, including the two new selectors. Still, it was hard to see Atherton walking away now, with such a close friend an integral part of the England hierarchy. Atherton kept quiet; Illingworth did not: 'I remain in charge until the teams are picked. The chairman of selectors remains in sole charge of disciplinary matters. I will still be spending time in the dressing-room.' About Graveney: 'He's ambitious. He wants everyone's job. As far as being a selector is concerned, I think he's in a very dodgy position.' About selection: 'It is time for one or two of the older players to go. One or two people on tour have been guilty of backstabbing. It has really annoyed me. I do know the identity of the people who have been trying to stuff me. I tend to be a bit like an elephant – I don't forget.'

Atherton was enjoying Jamaica in the company of his Lancashire mates. The first week was spent in Montego Bay. Lloyd left the party after this leg of the tour to clear his desk at Old Trafford and prepare for England duties. He had already taken the opportunity to find out the way Atherton wanted England's season to develop. If the chairman of selectors' and coach's positions were two-horse races that became canters for the winners, the rush for the two selectors' spots quickly resembled the chaotic start of the Grand National. The old guard were repre-sented by Fred Titmus, Brian Bolus and John Edrich; Derbyshire nominated Ian Botham and Kim Barnett, Graveney stood again and was joined by Graham Gooch, Chris Cowdrey and Geoff Miller; there was talk of umpire Peter Willey being included. Illingworth had his say before the voting: 'I am not going to comment on individual candidates from the nine, but there are only three or four who I think could do the job as it should be done.' Titmus dropped out well before the postal voting. Graveney was on everyone's list – the interest was the second spot. That went to Gooch (ahead of Botham and Bolus), who became England's first player-selector since Cyril Washbrook. Without having pulled any strings, Atherton was now surrounded by the coach and selectors he would have chosen himself. Illingworth's power-base had been dismantled.

The new panel met at Chelmsford as England 'A' took on The Rest. Illingworth sidestepped the captaincy issue because he had not spoken to the chairman of the TCCB. Instead, he made it clear that contrary to Lloyd's inten-tions, Botham would have no part to play in the England set-up. It was typical Illingworth, just what you would expect from a self-confessed 'stubborn bugger, deep down'. As England prepared for the Texaco series,

Illingworth was the man in the news. The *Daily Express* serialised his book, *One-Man Committee*. Unlike England's players, Illingworth's contract with the TCCB did not require him to get official permission before publication. The decision of the TCCB to investigate his comments therefore came as a surprise, especially as Lord's had decided that no action would be taken against Malcolm. That all-clear had surprised Atherton, who was in no doubt that Malcolm had breached his tour contract, whatever the provocation.

Atherton made his first public appearance of the new season at Cornhill's traditional Player of the Year lunch along with Lloyd. The pair had known each other since Atherton was 14. Atherton insisted: 'It is a fantastic appointment for England. "Bumble" will bring a sense of joy to the dressing-room. He is good fun to have around, but he is strict when he has to be and you soon learn that you can't get away with too much. He is also a modern thinker, up with the latest theories and techniques in the game.' Lloyd reacted to Atherton's 'Captain Grumpy' award: 'Michael has already identified that problem, and the fact that he acknowledged this shows he has no great psychological hang-up. He knows he needs to work on his image and body-language, to make it more upbeat, but he is a terrific lad. I don't think he is weighed down by the captaincy – it's simply that he does not like losing. I think this season he will be a much happier character. I am here to help him and the rest of the team, and if at times they think I'm crackers then I don't mind.' The Player of the Year award went to Dominic Cork. It could have gone to Atherton again but, as with Gooch, the sponsors liked to look beyond the captain and the previous year's recipient. Atherton, relaxed after his break, went off to a pub with a few of the journalists. The Jamaica trip had been intended as a relaxing holiday, but he had felt refreshed enough at the end to pick up a bat and score a century against the island XI. Another followed against Durham, his third in the Benson and Hedges Cup, which earned him his second Gold Award.

After the winter debacle, England's Texaco squad against India showed wholesale changes. The selectors went for Surrey's Alistair Brown as a pinch-hitter to try to emulate Sri Lanka's World Cup success. Mark Ealham and Ronnie Irani were the other newcomers, while Matthew Maynard and Chris Lewis were recalled. Much was made of Lloyd's Union Jack and British Bulldog style. His tennis forehand was much in evidence at The Oval as the England players struggled to catch a tennis ball. The rain prevented England from winning at The Oval after Atherton won the toss. Hick was top scorer in the home side's 291 for 9 off 50 overs. Four wickets from Lewis then reduced India to 96 for 5 before the weather closed in. The players were back at The Oval the next day, but by mid-afternoon everyone was heading up to Leeds for the second match.

Lloyd's presence allowed Atherton to ignore the outside distractions caused by the furore over Illingworth's book for once. Too often in his reign, it was the captain who had got caught up in these wrangles. England gave a performance in the field at Headingley that far surpassed anything seen in South Africa and the sub-continent. India were bowled out for 158 after Atherton had won the toss. Cork and Martin each took three wickets and there were three run-outs. Atherton flashed at a wide delivery, and Brown and Hick went for ducks as England struggled to 23 for 3. An undefeated stand of 94 between Surrey's Thorpe (Man of the Match) and Stewart won the day. The weather continued to disrupt the Texaco series as the final contest at Old Trafford was carried over to the Monday – England had faced one over in reply to India's 236 for 4 when the rain started again. It was long enough, though, for England's captain to depart, lbw to Srinath after two deliveries. The next day was dominated by a century from Brown. The pinch-hitter strategy was not conducive to England in a wet and overcast May, but Brown had not deserved some of the derisory comments his debut had provoked. His 118 at Old Trafford earned him the Man of the Match award and gave England a four-wicket victory and the Texaco series 2-0. Atherton and England looked unrecognisable from the outfit that had been bundled out of the World Cup two months earlier. Another bonus for England was the news that Sidhu had walked out on the tourists, announced his retirement and would miss the Test series. But even a combination of Sidhu, Atherton, Brown and an England victory could not knock Illingworth off the back pages. The TCCB had finally decided that he would be charged with bringing the game into disrepute.

Lloyd and Atherton had always made it clear that the squads for the Texaco and Cornhill series would be different. Atherton had phoned up Nasser Hussain, after the England 'A' captain was left out of the one-day internationals, and told him of the policy. Hussain was selected in the England XIII, along with Crawley, Knight, Mullally and Patel. The senior casualties were Stewart, England's vice-captain on the winter tour, and Robin Smith. Atherton rang Stewart on the Sunday morning to explain his demotion. Illingworth had publicly declared in South Africa that Stewart was no longer guaranteed a Test spot. By the end of 1996, he was the leading Test run-scorer in the world for the year.

Atherton's opening partner would be Knight, and Hussain was the latest remedy offered to cure England's No. 3 problems. Crawley lost the battle for the No. 6 spot to Irani, who made his debut along with Mullally and Patel. It was a frustrating time for Crawley. Two years after his debut, the Lancashire right-hander had still not established himself, but he had learnt from his mistakes. It was a measure of his desire to succeed that he worked so hard on his technique and fitness. That had earned him a recall in Durban, where the unfortunate hamstring injury ruined the rest of his winter and delayed his return for another half a year.

Atherton had more than a passing interest in the Edgbaston pitch. This was his third Test here as England captain and his team had been wiped on both previous occasions, largely, he believed, because the surface had proved tailor-made for the Australian spinners and West Indies fast bowlers. The general feeling now was that the strip was not much different from a year earlier – the big difference was that the Indian attack was nowhere as deadly as the West Indies'. Atherton would have batted, which is what Mohammad Azharuddin duly did after winning the toss. Nasser Hussain missed a catch at cover off the second ball of the Test. It was a bad start for Hussain, back after three years and one of the country's best catchers, and a bad moment for Atherton, who had often seen a simple error start a catalogue of mistakes from which England never recovered. The captain took a catch in the gully four overs later which redressed the balance. Knight then took a smart chance diving forward at third slip before hanging on to a screamer at midwicket as Azharuddin lashed at Irani. It was England's day. India were bowled out for 214 and Atherton and Knight survived to the close, reducing the deficit by 60 runs. England managed a first-innings lead of 99 thanks to 128 from Hussain, his first century for England, six and a half years after his debut in Jamaica. Atherton made 33. He was annoyed when he chased a wide delivery from Mhambrey after surviving a good work-out from Srinath and Prasad. It was an uncharacteristic lapse.

Atherton's team were almost home and dry by Saturday night. India managed to improve their first-innings score by five runs and England had reached 73 for 1, 48 runs short of victory. The highlight of the day was a magnificent 122 from Tendulkar, who found himself involved in a minor skirmish with the England captain. Atherton gets understandably frustrated when he sees some escaping punishment for misdemeanours that have brought others fines and reprimands. The Indians were flouting regulations regarding advertising on the back of their bats. England players would never have got away with that.

Nobody seemed to police England's opponents, even in England. When England's close catchers went up for an edge-behind off Lewis and umpire Shepherd turned down the appeal, Tendulkar responded to a few words from an England fielder by rubbing his forearm. Batsmen are not supposed to undermine the umpire's position in that manner, and Atherton wandered over from cover to voice his views. It was Atherton, though, who felt the sharp edge of umpire David Shepherd's tongue – Shepherd has never taken kindly to any player telling him how to do his job. At the tea interval, ICC referee Cammie Stewart, in Lloyd's presence, spoke to Atherton, who wondered what all the fuss was about. If he was out of line, then Shepherd had dealt with it promptly and fairly. Atherton could live with Shepherd's finger-wagging, but once again, the authorities had shown that the umpire was no longer the sole judge of 'fair and unfair play' on the field. Atherton felt he could not win. If he sat back, England's captain was lacking aggression and authority; yet when an incident like the Tendulkar one blew up, Atherton was criticised for displaying a ruthless streak deemed unsightly and unhealthy in an England captain.

He refused to allow it to detract from another good day for the home side. An hour into play on Sunday, Atherton was shaking hands with Tendulkar after his eighth win in 30 Tests as captain. Atherton was undefeated on 53 as England won by eight wickets. It was only his third 'not out' in 106 Test innings. Once again, Edgbaston was offering half-price tickets for the fourth day of the following year's Test. Warwickshire had reacted angrily to press comments about the state of the wicket, although they later admitted it was not all it should have been. Atherton was just delighted to be on the winning side in an Edgbaston Test for the first time in six years. He was much more diplomatic than the previous year, when he had described the pitch as 'diabolical'. The celebratory glass of champagne in his hand at the press conference negated any urge to rock the boat again.

England's selectors picked the same team for Lord's, although Stewart eventually came in for Knight who had cracked a finger on the Saturday evening at Edgbaston. The balance of power was now back with Atherton – Illingworth had suggested Yorkshire's captain David Byas for cover at Lord's; the others went for Stewart. Illingworth had problems of his own: his disciplinary hearing took place two days before the Lord's Test. Illingworth's row with Lord's and umpire Dickie Bird's farewell Test left the England side a poor third in the back-page battle. The TCCB shocked Atherton by throwing the book – *One-Man Committee* – at Illingworth. The easy and sensible option would have been to accord Illingworth the same courtesy as Malcolm by sweeping the matter under the carpet. Instead, Illingworth, despite an impassioned plea from the TCCB's chairman Dennis Silk, was fined £2,000 for bringing the game into disrepute. It was a cowardly and unnecessary act. 'The committee took into account the mitigating circumstances put before them and in particular the exceptional service Mr Illingworth has given to the game at county and international level. This resulted in a lower penalty than would otherwise have been imposed.' Illingworth had 28 days in which to appeal. Atherton did not believe Illingworth, for all his tactless public utterances, deserved such treatment, especially as Malcolm had escaped. The other downside for Atherton was that the TCCB's stance meant the affair would overshadow the whole summer.

England's captain also became an unwilling victim of Dickie Bird's tearful farewell. For all Bird's antics over the years, the undying memory for batsmen and bowlers is that Dickie has always been a 'not-outer'. Azharuddin, as he did six years earlier, invited England to bat at Lord's. Rain delayed the start and the two teams lined up to salute an emotional Bird as he walked out, handkerchief in hand. Atherton had no premonitions, but when the fifth ball of the match nipped back and thudded into his pads, he knew the tears in Bird's eyes were going to mean trouble for him. The perfect finale – the great 'not-outer' able to prove sentiment played no part to the very end. Atherton walked back ruefully. When Stewart's pads performed a similar defence, normal Dickie Bird service was resumed. The TCCB, anticipating Bird's emotional entrance, had suggested he might like to regain his composure by spending the first over at square leg. No chance.

England's day was saved by Thorpe and Russell, recently honoured with the MBE. The pair had more than doubled England's score to 238 for 5 by the close. Russell completed his second England century as the home side made 344. On Saturday, however, minds wandered from Saurav Ganguly's achievement to become only the third man and first foreigner to score a century on his Test debut at Lord's to England's penalty shoot-out against Spain in the Euro 96 quarter-final. If the officials had displayed any sense, the Test, which was hardly enthralling viewing, could have been halted for a few minutes and the penalty shoot-out shown on the giant screen. The decision was as insensitive as refusing a mobile TV camera the opportunity of recording Bird's reception as he walked through the Long Room on the Thursday morning.

The match ended in a draw, although England wobbled more than once on the final day. Atherton again survived the new ball before being bowled by Anil Kumble on Sunday evening. He had been bothered with a burst blood-vessel on his right index finger after being hit by Srinath. Russell was batting before lunch on the final day. England were 85 runs on with four wickets left. He batted for 31 overs with Irani and the danger passed. England paid a price for the draw – 45 per cent of their match fee for the slow over-rate. Atherton asked: 'Do people realise that Jack Russell performed so stoically and with such commitment during the five days at Lord's for a fee of around £450? We realise that we could have bowled our overs a bit quicker, but a fine of 45 per cent of our match fee is ridiculous. I resisted the pressure from the team to declare before the end of the match and reduce a Test match at Lord's to a farce with "over-rate" bowling. I might not next time.'

The selectors made changes for Trent Bridge. Martin was dropped; Salisbury and Mark Ealham were added to the squad. Stewart kept his place, with Knight still sidelined. The press made much of an Illingworth assertion that 'Martyn Moxon is the best opening batsman in the country.' So did Atherton and Gooch at the selection meeting. The chairman was not to be outdone – he could not find a place for either as he ran through his top five openers in the country! Considering Atherton was not in the best of form at the time, it was a less than diplomatic observation by the chairman of selectors. Incidentally, four of the five came from Yorkshire. It became a running gag. By the end of the summer, Gooch, who hit eight centuries and was the top Englishman in the averages, just managed to sneak into Illingworth's list. England's captain never made it. The England lads pulled Atherton's leg when word got out. Russell remembers seeing that steely glint in his captain's eye before the Nottingham Test: 'I knew then that it was worth putting your mortgage on an Atherton century.' Atherton came to Nottingham after a few days' break in the Lake District. For once England cricketers were not under fire for taking a break from the relentless routine. For once, Atherton was able to relax in the Lake District without being disturbed or tracked down.

At Trent Bridge, Ganguly carried on where he had left off at Lord's after Azharuddin won the toss for the third time in the series. India, 33 for 2, finished the day on 287 for 2 with centuries for Ganguly and Tendulkar. The former joined Alvin Kallicharran as the only players to reach three figures in their first two Test innings. Tendulkar might have departed without scoring – Atherton dropped a sharp chance in the gully. Hick did catch the second new ball at second slip, but Tendulkar escaped because of Cork's no-ball. That apart, England bowled and fielded well. Most pundits had predicted that the Trent Bridge pitch would come out on top. India batted for most of the second day with Tendulkar making 177 in his side's 521. The value of such a big total was evident as England's openers endured a testing final three-quarters of an hour. The biggest let-off came when Atherton edged Srinath through third slip's hands. He made India pay for their lapse and Illingworth for his verdict on England openers, batting all through Saturday for his tenth Test ton, his fourth at Nottingham. Atherton was nowhere near at the top of his game and had been in the nets early most mornings trying to find his rhythm and timing. His determination was undiminished: 'I've been hearing about a crisis in form and I shouldn't be taking matches off. Nonsense. I had one poor Test at Lord's. You get mentally tired with all the cricket we play. It's not physical.' Illingworth caught his captain's mood of defiance and announced he would be appealing against his TCCB fine.

Atherton had needed luck to survive, but made the most of it. Hussain was the day's other centurion, the perfect foil to Atherton's stickability. Stewart, for exactly 50, was the only wicket to fall on the third day (replays suggested he had been unlucky) as England reached 322 for 1. The summer's only rest day was not enough time for Hussain to recover from a blow on the finger and Atherton, who was confirmed as skipper for the Pakistan series on the Sunday, came out to bat with Thorpe. England's captain went after an hour, having added 15 runs to his overnight 145. Only Russell failed to reach 20, going for 0 as England went ahead of the Indians. Ealham marked his debut with an impressive half-century. A draw was inevitable, but England did not let the Test drift away. India were bowled out for 211, with Ealham taking 4 for 21. There was no time for England to bat again. The series was won 1-0. Ganguly took his second Man of the Match award as well as India's Man of the Series. The England award went to Hussain, who was acclaimed by Illingworth as Atherton's successor as England captain.

Lancashire were back at Lord's the following Saturday for another Benson and Hedges Cup final. Lloyd, the former Lancashire coach had been asked to resume his BBC radio seat for the two Lord's finals – that was too dangerous for the TCCB and he was banned from accepting the offer. The Red Rose's route could not have been more dramatic and exciting. The semi-final battle with their old rivals Yorkshire matched anything that Old Trafford has served up in its famous cup history. The match did not get underway until late afternoon. Yorkshire struggled after losing the toss. Michael Bevan and Richard Blakey transformed 87 for 5 to 254 for 5, with more than 50 runs coming in the last four overs. Their partnership of 167 was a new sixth-wicket record in the competition.

Gough, as he had at Headingley in the NatWest Trophy

the previous year, proved a point to the national selectors by removing the England captain, and the tie was turning Yorkshire's way with half the opposition gone for 97. Lancashire's fighting cup tradition was never more evident as Fairbrother and Hegg set about retrieving a lost cause, but they were still 90 runs short when Fairbrother was run out. Yates joined Hegg and took Lancashire to within 11 runs. The final over began with eight runs required and one wicket left. Even by Old Trafford standards the tension was extreme, especially on the Lancashire balcony. It eased when Martin had three balls to score two runs; two deliveries later it was back to fever pitch after two dot balls. Eventually, Martin got bat on ball, squirted it behind square on the off-side and took Lancashire to their fifth Benson and Hedges Cup final in seven seasons. Martin gave Lancashire another one-wicket win in the NatWest Trophy second round three days before the final. It was a great psychological boost because the victims, Northamptonshire, were also their opponents in the Benson and Hedges final.

The Lancashire and England captains opened together at Lord's after Watkinson won the toss. Atherton was two short of his fifty when he hit Emburey to mid-wicket. Fairbrother maintained the attack, with help from Crawley and Lloyd, and Lancashire reached 245. Northants reached 97 for 2 in the 27th over before the wickets started tumbling. Austin, recipient of Gooch's Gold Award adjudication, started and finished the job, ending up with four wickets. Chapple took four in the middle. Lancashire had retained the Benson and Hedges Cup and won a 12th Lord's final, and the usual raucous Red Rose celebrations began. Lancashire chairman Bob Bennett showed consideration for the losers by sending round some hot eccles-cakes to the Northants committee, and Old Trafford favourite Wasim Akram popped in, a reminder to Atherton of the task ahead. Wasim, in his second spell as captain, had brought Pakistan over to England for a three-Test series.

Many hoped that the Lancashire combination of Atherton and Akram would ensure a trouble-free series. The England Test team had not toured Pakistan since Gatting's clash with umpire Shakoor Rana in 1987. Controversy over umpires had given way to ball-tampering allegations during Pakistan's 1992 tour of England, and that issue had not died down. Allan Lamb and Sarfraz Nawaz had already met in the High Court over it. Now Lamb was back there with Ian Botham for their libel action against Imran Khan. Ball-tampering allegations were something England's captain had been forced to live with himself for the past two years, but Atherton had little doubt that he and Wasim could keep things friendly on the field: 'My friendship with Wasim will defuse the memories of four years ago. The cricket will be hard but fair. My side won't be involved in anything underhand and I don't think Pakistan will be either. Wasim and I realise that things have gone on in the past, but it was the same in Australia last winter and he and Mark Taylor sorted out the job between them pretty well. We can do the same here.'

Atherton had plenty of opportunity to ponder England's selection for the opening Test – he had failed to score as Gallian hit a triple-century against Derbyshire at Old Trafford. Knight was fit again and included as cover for Hussain, who was spending time in an oxygen chamber to try and heal his broken knuckle. Lewis also had fitness worries with a thigh problem. He had made an impressive return to international cricket, but his critics were waiting until the end of the season before passing judgement. Salisbury was the only spinner, while Durham's Simon Brown was given his first chance. Hussain and Lewis failed their fitness tests the day before the match. England were down to eleven. Knight was back opening, with Stewart dropping to No. 3, while Brown would open the bowling with Cork. The final practice session was delayed to allow Atherton to return from appearing in the High Court. Lloyd arrived back from the same place some time later. The pair had been sub-poenaed by Imran Khan's lawyers to give evidence for the defence, an unwanted distraction. Atherton's and Lloyd's heavy schedule was further complicated by breakfast with the Prime Minister the day before the match.

Despite these distractions, England put in 'their best day of the summer', according to the coach, on the Thursday at Lord's. Pakistan were 290 for 9, with over half those runs coming from Inzamam-ul-Haq. He reached his century with a six off Hick into the Long Room wall. The tourists had threatened at 142 for 2, but Atherton varied his attack, remained positive and kept nagging at the Pakistan batsmen. His perseverance paid off with Mullally's 3 for 14 spell in the final session. Atherton's pleas that the ball was out of shape were finally accepted by the umpires after tea. The bonus for England's captain was that this 'new' ball swung; its predecessor had not. That pleased Atherton, who had also lost the toss for the choice of balls. Lloyd revealed: 'We picked an attack for swing, yet it wasn't until late in the day that it began to happen. That shows that in the end it wasn't the bowler, but the ball, that counted.'

Atherton's Friday morning was not so fruitful. Pakistan's last pair added 50 runs in an hour and a quarter. The captain was the only England casualty before lunch, lbw to his opposite number and a delivery that hit him high. Those who felt Atherton had been given the benefit of the doubt by Sri Lankan umpire KT Francis at Trent Bridge in similar circumstances agreed that umpire Peter Willey had probably evened up the score. Atherton walked off, looking back to study a replay of his dismissal on the giant screen. Knight and Stewart fell in successive overs, Hick failed again and England were 116 for 4. Thorpe, Ealham and Russell came to the rescue, although the final five wickets fell for 25 runs. England had lacked the major contribution from a front-line batsman that would have held the innings together. Thorpe was unable to transform his 19th Test fifty into a third century. Pakistan finished the third day 215 ahead with three wickets down.

As if to mirror the High Court case, Friday's TV highlights showed Waqar working on the ball, which prompted Richie Benaud to comment: 'You see some strange things in the big city.' The fact that the BBC refused to replay the incident for journalists on the Saturday only fuelled the fire.

England's 'best day of the summer' was followed by four pretty poor ones. Wasim declared before tea on Sunday, setting England 408 to win and four sessions to survive. It was never going to be an easy task against an attack that contained three match-winning bowlers, Wasim, Waqar and Mushtaq Ahmed. For two sessions, Atherton and Stewart coped well, putting England within sight of safety. England's captain was at his most belligerent on Sunday evening. The Reader ball was changed after only three overs of England's innings, for the fifth time in the match. Then umpire Steve Bucknor warned substitute fielder Moin Kahn who had decided to chat at Atherton from silly mid-off. Atherton did not understand how a substitute for Inzamam, who had batted for three hours with a bruised knee, could be allowed. In all, Pakistan tried to use three substitutes. Wasim should have known better – all these distractions merely served to concentrate Atherton's mind on the job in hand. He was on 24 for the final 50 minutes of the session and was in no mood for nonsense. That night he dined with Lloyd and Wasim. Unfortunately, he did not heed Wasim's warning: 'You better stay in – or we'll win.' His team failed miserably to follow his example. England collapsed from 168 for 1, eighteen minutes after lunch, to defeat before a delayed tea-interval. Mushtaq claimed 5 for 26 in 16 overs after lunch. It was a dismal procession of flawed techniques and suspect temperaments. England's captain could not believe the speed at which his batsmen capitulated. He was similarly unhappy with the Reader balls and the pitch. Atherton's after-match comments were muted – he was learning – although he confessed to a 'poor shot' which started the collapse.

Atherton had to delay dwelling on the reasons for defeat and the likely changes. He headed north for another frantic Lancashire cup tie; the Old Trafford faithful were certainly getting value for money. Derbyshire were the NatWest quarter-final opponents. Atherton batted until the 58th over for his 115. Derbyshire's Australian captain Dean Jones dominated their reply. It took a spectacular leap by Fairbrother on the boundary in the 59th over to palm down Jones's 'six' and save Lancashire five runs. Jones needed a boundary from the final ball of the match, from Chapple. The off-drive brought him his century, but no Derbyshire victory: Lancashire made the semi-finals by two runs. Man of the Match Atherton was happy when the draw brought them a repeat of the Benson and Hedges semi-final against Yorkshire, who had to venture into the lions' den again.

On the same day, the Ackfield Report was published. It recommended that the national team should be looked after by an England Management Committee. (Take out the 'Management' and that was exactly what Dexter had organised for the Test team early in the nineties.) The consensus of opinion gathered in the report suggested that neither the captain nor the coach should sit on the selection panel. The Ackfield Report half listened – the coach would lose his seat in 1997, but not the captain. That changed at the start of the 1997 summer when

Atherton has worked with three England team managers during his time as captain. Keith Fletcher (*above, right* with Atherton in Barbados in 1994) lasted only halfway through his five-year contract and he was sacked after the 1994-95 Ashes tour. Ray Illingworth (*above, left* with Atherton before the disastrous Cape Town Test at the start of 1996) went from chairman of selectors to supremo, back to chairman before finishing after selecting the 1996-97 winter squad (*both Patrick Eagar*). David Lloyd (with Atherton at The Oval in 1996, *below*) was appointed at the start of that summer, a move that helped Atherton decide to carry on as captain because of their Lancashire connections (*Allsport/Graham Chadwick*).

A CAPTAIN'S LOT

Atherton takes the wheel (*above, left*) in Barbados during his first tour abroad as England captain in 1994. There were no smiles a few months later at Lord's as Atherton faced the media (*above, right*) after losing the South African Test and being fined £2,000 by Illingworth after the 'dirt-in-the-pocket' incident. Atherton is soaked by Mike Gatting (*below*) following England's remarkable victory at Adelaide at the start of 1995. Atherton meets Nelson Mandela, South Africa's president, in Soweto (*opposite, top*) at the start of the 1995-96 tour. Those winter travels end in the World Cup quarter-final defeat (*opposite, bottom*) at the hand of eventual winners Sri Lanka (*all Allsport*).

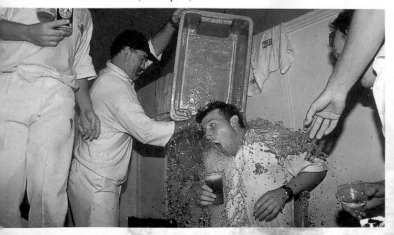

CHIN MUSIC
The West Indies have a special way of making batsmen dance to their particular brand of 'chin music'. Here Atherton shows that 'Staying Alive' is no easy business in the Caribbean as he demonstrates two ways of evading the rising ball during his first Test abroad as England captain, Sabina Park, 1994. The visiting skipper is an obvious and favourite target, and Atherton knew he would have to survive this test of fire after his poor series against the West Indies in 1991 (*above – Patrick Eagar; right – Allsport/Ben Radford*).

Even in today's hectic tour schedules, Atherton finds time for other activities. Atherton (*left*) is an avid reader, though he claims the sports pages are down his list of priorities these days (*Patrick Eagar*). Atherton (*below*) looks rather nervous of the photographers' suggestions that he should move near the edge of the Kaiteur Falls during the 1994 West Indies tour (*Allsport/Ben Radford*).

Atherton as Robin Hood (*above*), with physio Dave 'Rooster' Roberts certainly n[Maid Marion in the players' traditional fancy dress Christmas Day party during the 1994-95 Ashes tour (*Patrick Eagar*).

Fly-fishing has become a real passion with Atherton who celebrated his Christchurch Man of the Match award by landing this seven-pound brown trout (*Allsport/Graham Chadwick*).

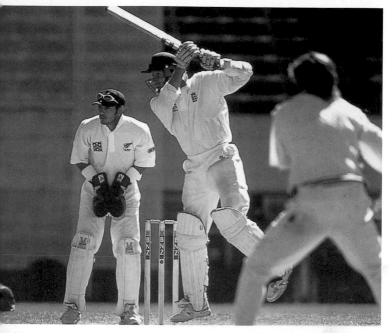

Atherton's undefeated 94 *(above)* in the first innings at Christchurch helped keep England in the decisive Test in the series against New Zealand, while his second-innings 118 helped win the match *(Patrick Eagar)*.

Victory in the final Test at The Oval helped persuade Atherton that he should lead England to the West Indies the following winter, even though the Ashes were lost 3-2 *(Sportsline/David Munden)*.

Atherton stepped down as a selector. It concluded that players should not be contracted to the Board, thus ignoring the central theme of the report: that no one in the world plays as much cricket as England's leading players. Despite the input from such recent England captains as Gower and Gatting, it was the usual mish-mash and fuddled thinking that has dogged England's ambitions for a quarter of a century.

Hick again failed to last the summer after the selectors picked the squad for the Headingley Test. That had happened five times in his six years of international cricket. Simon Brown and the injured Ealham were also left out. Brown might have been given another chance if England had not lost at Lord's, and Atherton was not comfortable with having given a newcomer only one chance. Lewis and Hussain were fit again, although Lewis did little to press his claims as Surrey captain against South Africa 'A'. Irani was back, Crawley took Hick's place and Caddick was picked for his first Test of the Illingworth era ahead of Gough, whom many felt would have caused Pakistan problems with his own reverse swing.

Pakistan's batting on the opening day was similar to Lord's. They finished on 281 for 6 with one batsman providing more than half the runs. That was Ijaz Ahmed with 141. The difference at Leeds was that Atherton had won the toss for the first time in the summer. England had already decided to send Salisbury back to Hove, so Atherton's decision meant the home side would be batting last. The captain caught Inzamam in the gully off Mullally to give England their best position of the day with Pakistan 103 for 3, and the insertion might have paid off if the tourists had slipped to 114 for 4 when Ijaz was caught by Cork off a Caddick no-ball. After inviting the opposition to bat, the merit of such a decision is judged by the time it takes to bowl them out. As Pakistan's innings lasted 15 minutes short of 11 hours, it appeared as if Atherton had blundered. Had England's bowlers, especially Lewis, used the conditions properly his gamble might have succeeded.

When Wasim found Atherton's inside edge with a beautiful delivery that cut back late and England only 14 runs towards Pakistan's total of 448, England's captain wondered whether another disaster was imminent. The fire-alarm bells ringing around the dressing-room area on his return would have only increased his concern. However, Stewart and Knight prevented any further mishaps that night and England had saved the game by the following evening after Stewart's 170. It marked a tremendous comeback for a player who, to all intents and purposes, looked finished after the winter tours. The TV cameras had panned to the players' balcony and caught Illingworth looking rather reserved in his applause of a batsman who had proved him wrong. It was said that Stewart's cause, in Illingworth's eyes, had not been helped by Surrey's support for Graveney at the start of the summer. Luck brought Stewart back, in the shape of Knight's finger injury, and Stewart rode that luck for all it was worth in 1996.

Knight was Sunday's hero with his maiden Test hundred and Illingworth, annoyed at press reports that Stewart's century had not been acknowledged with enough enthusiasm, jumped on a chair and waved his arms frantically for the benefit of the press box next door. Typical Illingworth. Untypical England, as they posted 501. Pakistan batted out the final day and the highlight was a second Test wicket for the leg-spin of Atherton just before the close. It was his first delivery for 50 Tests. The victim was Wasim Akram, who was adjudged lbw by Bucknor after playing no shot. Wasim admitted: 'I'll have to live with it for the rest of my career. But I must remind Mike that I've dismissed him

10 times.' Atherton brought himself and Thorpe on to escape any repetition of the Lord's over-rate fines, which England had been trying to have reduced for most of the summer.

Ian Austin, Gold Award winner from the Benson and Hedges final, took the Man of the Match medal in the NatWest semi-final. Yorkshire were getting sick of the sight of Old Trafford and gloating Lancastrians as the home side won by 19 runs in a high-scoring contest. Atherton always enjoyed walking into a selection meeting after Lancashire had beaten Yorkshire. He was also pleased to have scored his first championship runs for over two months. A combination of Test matches, cup games and a duck against Derbyshire was the reason why the last Britannic runs Old Trafford had seen from England's captain before his 63 against Hampshire on 15 August was 80 in the Gloucestershire game on 31 May.

Atherton had won the battle with Illingworth to keep Russell as wicket-keeper for the Leeds Test. The chairman had wanted to hand the gloves back to Stewart and pick five bowlers, but the coach backed the captain on that occasion. After Leeds, Atherton confirmed his position on the Russell/Stewart situation; Lloyd did not. Now that England needed to win at The Oval, Lloyd agreed with Illingworth and Russell was sent back into exile. Atherton insisted: 'Jack is still our first-choice wicket-keeper, but this is a one-off tactical change. I'm one of five selectors and if it is the feeling of the others, I'll go along with it.' It did not work out that way. The switch lasted through the Zimbabwe and New Zealand winter series and possibly provoked Russell's controversial book *Jack Russell Unleashed*, which landed the wicket-keeper in hot water. Illingworth's backing for Stewart in the all-rounder's role sealed an astonishing transformation in his fortunes in less than two and a half months. Gooch, who had been named England 'A' coach for the pre-Christmas tour of Australia, had often used Stewart in such a capacity when four England bowlers, or the batting line-up, or both, were proving ineffective. Rarely had it anything to do with Russell's ability or form, and it was a step Atherton took with great reluctance. Russell had played in 13 Tests since returning at Old Trafford the previous July. He had guided England to victory in that match and had made significant contributions with the bat in seven other Tests, most notably his partnership with Atherton at The Wanderers, where he also took his world record 11 catches. In 13 months back in the England side, Russell had averaged over 35 with the bat, as well as taking 51 catches and three stumpings.

Robert Croft joined Salisbury as the second spinner. This was Illingworth's final home Test, and at last he and Atherton had reached some sort of compromise. Atherton had his six-man batting line-up; Illingworth had his five-man bowling attack, with two spinners.

Atherton decided to bat at The Oval. The Pakistanis were able to use the ball they preferred, the Reader, after Wasim won that toss. Atherton and Lloyd hoped it would be the last occasion on which touring sides were given that facility. The changing of the Reader ball six times at Lord's had focused attention again on England's generous regulations. England travel the globe with no say in the cricket ball that is used in foreign series. England have two manufacturers and two balls, the Duke's and the Reader. Atherton has no problem with that. All he wants is for England to decide which ball suits them better and use that. Atherton believes that England's tradition for fair play is taken too far in allowing the touring team any involvement in the process. Atherton's record of losing tosses left England harshly penalised by the system in 1996.

Caddick was the surprise omission on the morning of

the match, instead of Croft or Lewis. Wasim charged in. The Pakistan captain was six wickets short of entrance to the 300-club, and he had not forgotten Atherton's moment of triumph at Leeds. The first ball of his second over reared up into Atherton's shoulder and bounced away for four leg-byes. It was not the easiest of mornings for the England captain, although because of Pakistan's attacking strategy, runs were not in short supply. Wasim targeted Atherton's leg stump, and was not happy when he was missed at short leg. It was left to Waqar to remove England's captain after lunch with a delivery that hit his leg stump. Crawley dominated the first day, although he was still six runs short of a maiden Test hundred at the close, completing it on Friday after rain delayed the start. England's 326, after being 248 for 4, was a poor return on this wicket. Pakistan confirmed that when England's bowling disappeared to all parts of The Oval on Friday evening. The tourists reached 229 for 1 off 56 overs to leave no one in any doubt that the gap between the sides was down to the bowling attacks. Only Croft offered Atherton any consolation. Lloyd's verdict was that 'it was our poorest day in the field. We expect discipline when we play for England, but here they were poor.'

The only excitement on a rain-affected Saturday was a spat between Saeed Anwar and Cork, who apologised to match referee Peter van der Merwe. The drama on Sunday took place before play started. Atherton was badly let down by Lewis who turned up late, offered a feeble excuse and behaved exactly as his critics predicted he would. Atherton had bent over backwards in Lewis's direction so that England might benefit from his undoubted cricketing talent. At the start of the summer, Lewis, who had moved from Nottinghamshire to Surrey, performed well in the early Benson and Hedges Cup games. That earned him a place in the Texaco squad, then the Test team for Edgbaston, where he took seven wickets, and he was England's leading wicket-taker in the India series. After injury kept him out of the Lord's Test, he took 1 for 152 at Headingley and by The Oval, Lewis was unrecognisable from the bowler to whom Atherton and Lloyd had given a final chance in May. Although he had taken just one wicket since his return in the second half of the summer, Lewis was picked for England's Texaco squad which was announced by Illingworth before the start of play in the Test on Sunday. Not for the first time on his home patch that season, Lewis was late. So late, in fact, that explanations were sought. The answers concerned his Mercedes convertible, a flat tyre and a flat mobile-phone battery – they were not reassuring. This was new territory for Lloyd, but only too familiar to Atherton. If Lewis had held his hands up, Atherton might have contested Illingworth's decision to remove him from the Texaco squad. But enough was enough, and Dean Headley was named instead. Typically, this slight spurred Lewis into one of those brilliant pieces of fielding, a run-out of Mujtaba, that only served to emphasise what a contribution he could have made to England.

Another disappointment was the form of Salisbury. The Sussex leg-spinner, bowling at the ground that became his home in 1997, could offer no excuses. The Oval wicket was turning and Croft gave him a partner at the other end. Salisbury's figures of 1 for 116, including 0 for 71 off 14 overs on Friday evening, were more than disappointing. Atherton and Stewart went to the wicket with a 195-run deficit and 23 overs to negotiate. They were still together after a hostile burst from Waqar and Wasim, with Mushtaq taking up residence at the Vauxhall End.

The next morning began with a rare show of affection: Illingworth gave Stewart a hug and 'well done' – the nearest Stewart was ever going to get to an apology from the chairman after proving him wrong. Both openers had gone by lunch. Atherton was annoyed with himself for pushing forward at Mushtaq to give silly mid-off a catch. At lunch, England were 158 for 2. Batting was more difficult than at Lord's, though, and they still needed another 37 runs to make Pakistan bat again. The last eight wickets went down for 76, with Mushtaq the destroyer. Wasim took the last two in two balls to become the 11th bowler to take 300 Test wickets. Pakistan reached the 48 target in less than seven overs and won the series 2-0. Atherton had no arguments or complaints. His side did not possess anyone to match Wasim, Waqar or Mushtaq. Three times England had to bat under pressure in the series. Twice they folded after the captain and Stewart had taken them most of the way towards safety.

The Texacos, with Hussain, Crawley and Cork (as well as Lewis) rested, offered some consolation with a 2-1 victory. The introduction of Adam Hollioake, the return of Gough and back-to-back centuries from Knight were the big bonuses. Atherton was Man of the Match in the opening match on an Old Trafford wicket that did not play as badly as it looked. After Pakistan had been restricted to 225 for 5, Atherton decided to move himself down the order to No. 3 to let Stewart open with Knight. The captain held the innings together with a watchful 65. Pakistan's two-wicket victory in the third match made no difference to England taking the Texaco Trophy. Latif hit the winning runs with two balls remaining, though Atherton was convinced his throw had run him out two overs earlier. 'All very strange,' was his comment after the third umpire, Ray Julian, had studied the TV pictures. It was denied that the umpire had pressed the wrong light button, although even the Pakistan batsman himself thought he was out and was almost back in the pavilion before returning. The doubt concerned whether Stewart had knocked off the bails before Atherton's throw hit the stumps.

Illingworth cleared his name before selecting his final England squad. His appeal to the Cricket Council was upheld, his fine and costs rescinded. The failure of the TCCB to take action against Malcolm was a factor in Illingworth's favour. Unlike Malcolm, he had breached no contractual obligations. Atherton had no desire to see Illingworth leave cricket under a cloud. Had Malcolm been brought to book, Atherton believed Illingworth should have been judged by the same regulations. All England's captain has ever wanted is for his players to be treated like everyone else in cricket. He has never been happy with an environment which has allowed his team to be criticised by those with whom they work.

The result of Illingworth's appeal and the NatWest Trophy final left the winter tour selection-panel happy in the main. The one exception was Gooch, who had stood at the non-striker's end and watched the rest of his batting colleagues collapse to 33 for 6 against Lancashire's Martin and Chapple. Essex were eventually bowled out for 57, the lowest total in a 60-over final, as Lancashire achieved a second cup double, by 129 runs. Chapple's 6 for 18 made him the obvious Man of the Match, although Crawley's 66 runs was 45 more than anyone else managed. The real victor, or villain, was the Lord's pitch. Well as Ilott, Martin and Chapple bowled, batting was extremely difficult on what should be a showpiece for strokeplay. Atherton made 4 before being bowled by an Ilott in-swinger. The next similar delivery rapped Crawley on the pad. Had umpire Shepherd reacted differently to the mass Essex appeal, the result might have been reversed.

Lancashire had two trophies and England had won three out of the four international series. After the dramas of the World Cup, Atherton and England appeared to have recovered well. The captain had found an ally in Lloyd, and Illingworth had come to the end of his term of office. England were heading off to face Zimbabwe and New Zealand – it would surely be Atherton's quietest winter in charge. Atherton did have a quiet end to the season, missing Lancashire's final two matches in the championship, won by Leicestershire. 'Certain people play too much cricket,' explained Lancashire chairman Bennett, 'and Michael is one of them. It's essential that we cut down the workload so that they can maximise their ability. We have decided to take this initiative not only to protect Michael as England captain, but to set an example that we hope other counties will follow. The longer England have Michael at the helm, the better chance our Test team have of rising up the ladder.' It was a generous gesture, not least because Lancashire won only two championship games in 1996.

Two was also the number of the first-class successes Atherton enjoyed during the summer, the Edgbaston Test and victory in Durham in consecutive matches early in June. He failed to reach 1,000 runs, his only century coming in the Trent Bridge Test. His Lancashire return was five fifties in 14 championship innings, 519 runs at an average of 37.07. This reflected a growing problem for Atherton. His *modus operandi* had changed. He no longer enjoyed a challenge, he needed one. Without the buzz, the tension, the TV cameras, the world-class opponents, Atherton was finding it increasingly difficult to motivate himself. His loyalty and devotion to Lancashire had not diminished. Unfortunately, the County Championship is no environment for those who want to be tested to the full. Atherton could only wonder at the appetite of Gooch, who took top place in the Whyte & Mackay batting awards at the age of 43, scoring eight centuries and nearly 2,000 runs.

This change was not a serious problem as long as he

was scoring runs for England, but Atherton knew the day would come when an international slump would intensify his difficulties. He did not envisage that it would happen quite so soon, or in the newest of Test-playing countries.

CHAPTER SEVENTEEN

Athers' Agony

Quiet Zimbabwe was not. Even without hindsight, it might have made sense for Atherton to take the winter of 1996-97 off. Three years of non-stop, high-pressure and high-profile captaincy had taken its toll in 35 Tests, and a refreshed Atherton would surely improve England's chances the following summer of making a reasonable Ashes challenge for the first time in a decade. Atherton scoffed at any suggestions of a rest. His reasons were simple: he was not going to miss out on facing two of the easiest international attacks after battling against the likes of McDermott, Warne, Ambrose, Walsh, Donald, De Villiers, Srinath, Kumble, Wasim, Waqar and Mushtaq! Such logical thinking turned out to be flawed. During the cold winter months, the calls for Atherton to quit reached a crescendo, and on this occasion it was not because of his involvement in any controversy. For the first time, the reasons were cricket ones and the belief that England would be better off with a new captain. Those demands intensified as Atherton struggled to emerge from the worst batting slump of his career. He and England left Zimbabwe in low spirits. Domination in the Tests, but no victory. The public humiliation came in the one-day matches, a 3-0 drubbing, England had not only played poorly; they had toured badly, incapable of reacting to one of the most hospitable cricket countries in the world. The watching new chairman, Ian MacLaurin, and new chief executive, Tim Lamb, of the new English Cricket Board expected better. The pressure was certainly on Atherton and England as they moved on. Any repetition in New Zealand and Atherton was history. The captain was the first to acknowledge this.

Atherton did rediscover his batting form in the first Test in Auckland, yet that match only increased speculation about his future as England's leader when the tourists were frustrated by New Zealand's last pair. For the second time in three Tests, England had been one ball away from victory. The critics piled in, not least Illingworth. Three weeks later, Atherton was a national hero once more after wins at Wellington and Christchurch gave England the series 2-0. Atherton had travelled from the West Indies to Australia to South Africa to Pakistan to India to Zimbabwe to New Zealand to find success abroad as England's cricket captain. The contest was decided when his century inspired the tourists to successfully chase over 300 runs for only the second time in England's history. The captain was defiant to the end. His press conferences had been a battle all winter, and the touring party decided to boycott the press's Christmas panto in Harare because of the tone of much of the coverage being sent back home. Such a siege mentality, however understandable, is rarely attractive or productive.

Atherton's relationship with certain sections of the media has been uneasy since Lord's 1994. Outside the confines of those official conferences, Atherton was as approachable and co-operative as ever. Inside, he was as stubborn as he had been at the crease in the Johannesburg Test, and saw no reason to lower his guard at the end of the New Zealand series just because of the turnaround in his and England's fortunes. It is a battle Atherton knows he cannot win, yet he will never come quietly. Those confrontations were ironic because the 1996 season had ended with rumours that Atherton would abandon the dressing-room for the press box permanently – there was speculation that he might become the cricket correspondent of the *Sunday Times*. Unsure as he is of his future beyond cricket, few imagine that such a watching brief would appeal to Atherton. Zimbabwe also highlighted his growing problem with his back, which he has conceded is more likely to finish him off than any hostile bowler or vitriolic report.

The team's problems began before they left England. Cork, who had split from his wife Jane during the summer, pulled out of the Zimbabwe leg of the trip because of domestic troubles. His withdrawal, a few days before England flew out, came as a surprise to everyone, including Atherton – Cork had given no hint of any problem during the training week at Barrington's in Portugal at the start of November. It was decided not to replace him in the 15-man party. That left Mullally, Gough, Silverwood, Caddick and Irani as the quick bowlers. Caddick had played one Test in two and a half years, Gough had not played Test cricket for 18 months, Silverwood was uncapped and Mullally was a newcomer from the 1996 summer. Irani was not looked upon as a front-line bowler. Tufnell was recalled to join Croft. Russell was included, but was immediately deposited on the sidelines. The six batsmen that had finished the Test summer were taken.

Lack of options caused England problems in Zimbabwe. Cork's withdrawal had made it a party of 14 and a couple of days into the tour, England were effectively choosing from 13. Atherton knocked on Russell's hotel bedroom door to impart the news that England's wicket-keeper dreaded and expected: Stewart would be continuing in the all-rounder's role. That would definitely apply to the Zimbabwe leg of the trip and probably New Zealand as well. Atherton has never enjoyed such moments, especially involving those whose attitude and ability he respects deeply, such as Russell and Fraser. The captain was feeling poorly himself. His back had been playing him up before he left England, and plans for him and physiotherapist Wayne Morton to work on the problem had been curtailed when Atherton went down with a virus just before setting out. The first net session took place without flu sufferers Atherton and Caddick, as well as Thorpe who had delayed flying out in order to be at the birth of his son.

England's first weekend set the tone for the six-week tour. The first one-day game was abandoned through rain after the Districts XI made 198 for 9. Stewart made the first century of the tour in England's 211 for 5 against the President's side. That did not prevent a five-wicket defeat. Atherton lasted two balls, the first bringing a big shout for a catch behind. The touring media latched onto a local magazine which was headlined: 'Captain Grumpy comes to Zimbabwe.' England's captain was described as a miserable sledger. The team were called bad-mannered and narrow-minded. Zimbabwe's coach Dave Houghton attacked the tourists for not socialising after Sunday's defeat: 'They may have been disappointed, but I can't believe they couldn't find an hour to stay for a drink with our players, and to meet the local people. What's the point of going back to the hotel to brood?' Zimbabwe may be the newest Test country, but it is still very much a colonial environment and such old-fashioned customs are foreign to today's cricket stars, especially those from England whose workload is the heaviest in the game. Atherton felt such criticism was unfair as they were never invited.

His problems with the media had surfaced even before the tour began. After Dean Headley had taken 11 for 98 in England A's victory over South Australia, it was reported that the bowler hoped he had proved a point to the England captain who did not think he could move the ball away from the bat. Atherton was not happy with the inference. He let tour manager Graveney know that he had made no such judgement. Headley, who had taken Lewis's place in the Texaco series at the end of the summer and expected a place on the senior tour, was warned by the TCCB about making public statements. Some felt it was an overreaction, but Atherton was getting fed up with England's cricket problems, real or imaginary, being chewed over in public by the participants. No sooner had Atherton landed in Zimbabwe than Illingworth was reminding everyone of the 'day I saved Athers's skin' in the *Sun*. Little of what Illingworth said or thought was new. That did not reduce Atherton's annoyance. There would be no holding Illingworth now he was back on the 'outside' – not that the chairman had shown much restraint during his two and a half years as part of the England set-up.

Battle-lines were drawn after England crashed to defeat against Mashonaland. The touring batsmen struggled to cope with the conditions and England lost by seven wickets with more than a day to spare. In both innings, four front-line England batsmen had departed before the scoreboard reached 30. The fact that the Sussex rookie bowler James Kirtley caused much of the damage did little to ease England's suffering. Atherton had troubles of his own; his back was getting worse, not better. He could not even touch his knees and the problem was affecting his batting as he failed twice. The after-match press conference took place on one of the temporary stands. Atherton hates excuses, and was not pleased that the

329

press had found out about his visit to the local hospital for a scan on his back. He refused to discuss the matter, other than insisting that his back was 'fine'. England were 'still a bit rusty' and had not underestimated the opposition. Physio Morton was more forthcoming: Atherton's bout of influenza and diarrhoea had meant that the pain-killing tablets taken for his back had not been in his body long enough to work. (Atherton had another reason for being less than concerned about his own welfare or England's loss of a first-class match. His back-scan had taken place in the local trauma unit. The England captain could not believe the number of road-accident victims that were brought in. He saw one youngster with terrible injuries and heard a woman was dead on arrival.) Atherton was not trying to mislead journalists when he claimed his back was fine without knowing the results of the scan. He was in familiar territory, and had correctly anticipated that the problem would need to be remedied by injections into two 'hot spots'. In the midst of his back troubles, Atherton pointed out that he was the only ever-present in the England Test team over the past three years.

The captain was angry that his squad was being criticised for not getting out more (socially, that is), a rare complaint after the activities of some England touring sides of the past. The modern England cricketer is a closeted creature; the mediocre first-class system does not force him to be otherwise. By the time they make the Test team, most are too set in their ways to change. Atherton was selected for particular scrutiny in a *Sunday Times* article, headed: 'Atherton finding his burden unbearable.' It began a running battle between journalist Graham Otway and Atherton and Lloyd that lasted until the final press conference in Harare when Otway told Atherton, 'See you in court.' It was an unseemly personality clash for a quality paper to get involved in. The *Sunday Times* was without a cricket correspondent after Robin Marlar's retirement, and Otway, who had joined the paper after *Today* closed a year earlier, was bidding for the post. Although Atherton had been touted for the same job at the end of the summer, it was very unlikely that England's captain was ever a serious contender.

Atherton got back to business and surprised everyone by playing in the one-day win over Matabeleland in Bulawayo. The tourists followed that up with a win in the first-class fixture. Atherton went off fishing, with high hopes of a successful winter. A trip to Scotland with John Barclay at the end of the season had produced his best day with the rod, his haul of five salmon prompting many calls on his mobile phone. The fish in Zimbabwe were not as accommodating and he failed to catch a thing. Runs were equally hard to come by. Atherton was out for 4 at the Bulawayo Athletic ground on the first morning. Wandering round the field afterwards, he took great pleasure in bidding 'good morning' to several journalists who had arrived late and missed his knock. Despite the rain, England beat Matabeleland by 114 runs. Knight scored the opening first-class century of the tour and Gough took a career-best 11 for 141 in the match.

The real trouble began in the first one-day international. England were bowled out for 152, and though the bowlers and fielders battled hard, the damage had been done. Zimbabwe won by two wickets, their third success in four meetings between the two countries. After the fuss of the Mashonaland defeat, this was the first chance for cricket supporters back home to see what was really happening. It made depressing viewing on Sky. The pitch was not easy and England were asked to bat. They reached 124 for 4, knowing that a total near 200 would be enough. They failed to get near it, or even use up all the overs. Atherton made 23 after taking 35 balls to get off the mark. He was lucky to escape being run out on 15 as the

third umpire's television had broken down. Zimbabwe
looked in trouble themselves at 106 for 7, but skipper
Alastair Campbell, Heath Streak and Eddo Brandes saw
them home. Once again, the cricketers who play more
one-day matches than anyone else in the world had
performed like novices. However praiseworthy their
efforts in the field after the batting collapse, it was not the
way Atherton wanted to go into the Test series. With no
Cork, Irani's bad back, Russell surplus to requirements
and Caddick out of favour, England were picking from 11
for the first Test. That meant a Test debut for Yorkshire's
Chris Silverwood, who had impressed England's bowling
adviser Ian Botham, a recent arrival.

None of the England bowlers impressed on the first
morning, however, after Atherton lost the toss on the
occasion he went past Peter May's record of 35 consecutive Tests as captain. The tourists conceded 109 runs
before lunch after Gough had taken a wicket in his
second over, his first wicket at Test level since Lord's in
1995. At tea, Zimbabwe were 200 for 3. That they finished
the day on 256 for 6 was largely due to Croft, who bowled
one spell of 12 overs for seven runs. Atherton had seen it
all before – England repairing damage that had been
caused by nothing more than failing to put the bat or the
ball in the right place. They repeated the exercise on the
second day as Zimbabwe reached 376, and Atherton's
misery was made complete when he was lbw playing
back to Paul Strang. That was the penultimate ball before
tea. England went in at 40 for 1 and never came out again
because of the rain. Hussain and Crawley hit centuries to
give England a first-innings lead, and Tufnell and Croft
made the breakthrough on the fourth evening: Zimbabwe
were five wickets down and led by 77 runs. On the final
day, England's regular morning sickness left the tourists
needing 205 for victory off 37 overs. That is an easy
enough Sunday League target; not so in the first-class

game, with no fielding restrictions and bowlers able to spear the ball down the leg-side with no penalties. At the halfway mark, England were 106 for 1. Atherton had raced off the field when Silverwood took the final Zimbabwe wicket to dispel any thoughts that he might move himself down the order.

Atherton chopped onto his stumps, then Knight and Stewart got moving. Zimbabwe's tactics were bewildering. Instead of making England take chances, there were five or six singles offered every over. If Campbell had attacked, England would have gone for their shots – but after three or four wickets, the tourists would have had to shut up shop. Stewart's departure at 154 slowed England down, and the last over started with 13 runs still needed. Heath Streak was the bowler. Knight hoisted the third ball over square leg for six. Five to win. The next ball was just inside the popping crease. Knight could not reach it. Umpire Ian Robinson did not move. Knight and England needed three off the last ball. Knight thought he had given it enough to reach the cover boundary. It didn't, and he was run out going for the third. Scores level, but no tie, the first time that had ever happened in a Test match. The fun was not over. Lloyd, who had been pacing near the sight screen in the last overs, had a verbal altercation with some supporters as he made his way back to the pavilion. The England dressing-room was not a happy place, and Lloyd's frustration made it worse. Botham appeared to try and calm things down. Many of the younger tourists were not sure how to react. Some sense of normality was eventually restored and England wandered into the Zimbabwe dressing-room for a drink.

The final act of this incredible day came at the press conference. Lloyd's ill-advised 'we murdered them' quote was always going to rebound on him. The coach later admitted that a cold chill went up his back when he said it. Meanwhile, Atherton and the *Daily Telegraph*'s Martin

Johnson were having a staring contest of their own. England's magnificent effort got lost, and Atherton's and Lloyd's frustration was understandable. That one extra run would have taken a lot of pressure off the whole squad, who had responded positively to a stiff challenge. Nor was Atherton happy to find out that his report on the umpiring would be going to one of the men standing in the Test, Zimbabwe's chief administrator Ian Robinson. Away from the press conference, Atherton wandered up to Johnson's hotel room at the Bulawayo Hotel Inn and apologised. The England captain moved down to the bar and the matter was settled over a beer. The day before, Atherton and Stewart had wandered over to the press tent to inform the assembled journalists that the players had voted not to attend the media's panto on Christmas Day. That invitation to lunchtime drinks and the journalists' show is a long-standing tradition. It may have terminated during Atherton's reign. Christmas Day was disrupted by the weather. The players had intended to practise in the morning, but it was put off to the afternoon. The squad had flown to Harare via Victoria Falls. Atherton, Lloyd and Barclay did not make it. One of the pilots was ill, so they gave up their places and drove for five hours to Harare. Craig White, who had flown in from the 'A' tour as cover for Irani, was already there.

White went straight into the side of the Test starting on Boxing Day. England's bowlers had struggled in the Bulawayo morning session; England's batsmen made a day of it at the Harare Sports Club. From 50 for 1, the tourists finished at 137 for 9 as batsman after batsman committed suicide by lashing out. Atherton lost the toss again, but he and Stewart dogged it out after Knight was caught down the leg-side. Stewart had already tucked his bat under his arm when Campbell dropped a dolly. It should have been a timely warning. Instead, it began a period of madness. Atherton started the rot when he drove at Guy Whittall. His feet were still not moving and this time Campbell made no mistake. Only Crawley showed any patience and fortitude. The most telling figures came from Whittall, who took 4 for 12 in 13 overs. Little more than a part-time bowler and partnership-breaker, Whittall was made to look dangerous and deadly. The England batsmen had been told, warned and advised not to attempt driving on this surface and in these conditions. Like moths to the flame, they predictably perished; Lloyd had some harsh words. Crawley, with help from Tufnell, took England to 156, the ease with which Tufnell batted emphasising the batsmen's failure.

That sort of total normally puts a side on the defensive for the rest of the Test. England turned the match round on days three and four. The frequent rain-storms prevented Zimbabwe gaining any momentum with their innings. England restricted them to a first-innings lead of 59 just before Saturday's close, with room-mates Gough and Croft taking seven of the wickets. There was still time for Atherton's misery with the bat to continue. He was snapped up by Campbell again, this time off Streak, for a single off the third ball he faced. His total tally for the series was 34 runs, and for once, it was the responsibility of the other England batsmen to do something for their captain – defeat here would be Atherton's death-knell. Stewart led the way with his first century as England's wicket-keeper, and the tourists finished with a lead of 136 runs with Stewart and Thorpe still at the crease.

The final day was abandoned because of the rain and the Test series was drawn 0-0. Atherton declared: 'We would have won both games given five days of good weather.' Zimbabwe's captain did not quite see it that way: 'For them to say they outplayed us is truly astonishing. Why can't they just admit that there have been two good games of cricket between two evenly matched sides? In the 22 Tests I've been involved in, this has been the easiest series of all. We've spent most of our time playing in the sub-continent where even the likes of Australia and South Africa get beaten. What happened to England the last time they were in India and Sri Lanka? Four-nil, wasn't it? It's about time they got rid of their superiority complex. This "we murdered you and you know it" business is frankly monotonous. They're clutching at thin air as far as I'm concerned, and conning themselves into thinking they've played well. There's not much between ourselves, England and New Zealand among the minnows.'

This stance certainly gave the final two one-day internationals an extra edge. There were no arguments at the end – England had been well and truly stuffed, with all the old failings exposed. Zimbabwe were bowled out for 200 on New Year's Day. More rain reduced England's allowance by eight overs and the target by 16 runs. At 137 for 3, Atherton, Crawley and England were coasting. But as so often happens, England got lost in the middle of an innings. Merely keeping up with the run-rate does not allow for the inevitable fall of wickets. With Thorpe rested, England had no one after Atherton, batting at No. 5, to adapt to or work a situation. Irani got bogged down and Crawley lashed out in frustration. There was nobody capable of pulling the match out of the fire. The tourists finished six runs short: Zimbabwe had the one-day series. The downpour the next day suggested little hope for the final match. Lloyd was desperate for it to clear to give England the chance to salvage something after New Year's Day: 'We got ourselves into terrific positions three times and we still managed to throw it away. We bottled it. It was rabbit-in-the-headlights stuff, and if they are really professional players, they should be right up for this game after I let them know what I thought. If the language was fairly strong, they'll just have to live with it. Our problem is that we have too many off-days.'

Lloyd was spot-on, as his charges demonstrated the next day. England were back on the front pages after losing their fifth one-day international to Zimbabwe in six starts. The hero was the chicken-farmer Eddo Brandes, who took his country's first international hat-trick. At one stage, England were 77 for 8 chasing 250 for victory. This was England's second-heaviest ever defeat, a margin of 131 runs. The Harare Sports Club was in party mood. 'We murdered them' had returned to haunt Lloyd and England. Brandes's hat-trick was no end-of-innings mop-up. His victims were Knight, Crawley and Hussain, with an almost unplayable delivery (Atherton, the next man in, admitted he was out of his chair and on his way before the ball even reached Hussain). The five England ducks and general capitulation led to mass hysteria. The Conservative MP Terry Dicks called for the tour to be abandoned. The Ladies cricket captain Karen Smithies called for Atherton to go.

The pressure was certainly on Atherton. He was determined to see the winter through – but had already made up his mind to quit if the New Zealand leg went the way of Zimbabwe.

CHAPTER EIGHTEEN

Back From The Brink

England could have returned home for a short break after Zimbabwe. Atherton had been offered that choice a year earlier, but he saw little point in coming back for a few days. The captain found himself being blamed for the 'wives ban' and the players not practising between the end of the season and flying to Zimbabwe. That was not true. Atherton had not been happy with the travelling circus that accompanied the team round Cape Town, but he was aware, as one of the few single men within the squad, that such a ban would not really affect him, so the final decision was coach Lloyd's. Atherton explained the problems to him, the advantages as well as the drawbacks. Lloyd wanted the players' full attention and decided that families would not be encouraged to come. Quite a few were unhappy. In Australia, the England players had understood the need to focus on the Ashes, but this was now the third Christmas in a row away from England. When the 1992-93 Indian tour was delayed to start a couple of days after Christmas, it was part of a general move to allow the players to be at home at that time of the year. The Ashes tour was supposed to be the only exception – the exception had quickly become the rule again. Lloyd was also the one who wanted the players to get away from cricket at the end of the season, as from November 1996 through to August 1997, the schedule allowed little respite for England's top players, especially the captain, who had just entered his benefit year.

New Zealand was 'make or break' for Atherton. Other than Lord's in 1994, the previous crises surrounding his captaincy had not been as serious as the headlines had suggested; most could be put down to the games Illy played. This was different. His position was fast becoming untenable. The combination of poor form and poor results had not affected him before. Through all of England's troubled tours, Atherton's form had held up, better than before he was captain. Atherton's need for runs in New Zealand was almost as essential as his need for victories, Test ones. The experiences of Zimbabwe meant that he could not afford any mistakes. Some felt his days as leader were already numbered. Atherton never did, though he had no doubt that he was on borrowed time: one slip in New Zealand and the game was up. His batting slump was Atherton's biggest worry. Hard as he tried, his feet were still not moving. Failure to score runs against New Zealand might cost him more than the captaincy. Atherton grafted and battled as never before. Then, just as he was emerging from his batting nightmare, Danny Morrison denied England in Auckland and the pressure was back on. The captaincy, not his batting, was now the big issue as a nation's frustration boiled over. Everyone, as in the 'ball-tampering' saga of 1994, had their say about what was wrong with England and Atherton. Illingworth led the charge.

Atherton took a deep breath for what he knew could be the final battle. He won at Wellington and triumphed at Christchurch in emphatic fashion. As gracious as Atherton tried to be in victory, there was no escaping his 'ye of little faith' gaze. England's captain had 'dogged' it out all winter. It had been a war of attrition for him, a real slog. At times, Atherton was going nowhere. The team was not responding and it seemed that nothing could bring them a Test victory. The rain almost frustrated them in Wellington, and England wobbled on that final afternoon in Christchurch after Atherton had been on the field for over four days. Even the fish had not been biting – three months away and not a single nibble at that stage. But the rain held off at Wellington and the team held their nerve at Christchurch. England were home and Atherton was safe. The very next day, a 7lb brown trout did something that no other fish in three continents had done since that Scottish salmon the previous September: it bit on Atherton's fishing-line. After dangling himself all winter, Atherton was back in business.

However bad England felt when they left Harare, they were a lot worse by the time they landed in Auckland. It was a nightmare journey that could have been largely avoided if they had taken the direct flight from Harare to Sydney the following day. Cork was waiting for them. England's all-rounder had some explaining to do to Lloyd, after failing to appear for two fitness sessions. The matter was resolved quickly. The first New Zealand press conference saw Lloyd defending his captain over whether immediate resignation was the only honourable course for Atherton.

ATHERTON

The ITN reporter, Michael Nicholson, arrived fresh from England armed with newspaper cuttings (and an editor's brief, no doubt) and championed the cause of the English follower in our press conference on arrival in New Zealand. He, of all people, having spent more time than most in war zones, should have remembered to bring a sense of perspective. But no, carried away on a tide of public

emotion, he proceeded to embarrass himself and our hosts.
Cricket is a sport. It is a sport we try to play as well as we
can, but one in which one side wins and one side loses —
and at the end of it, nobody dies and we usually share a
beer over the result. I do feel I would be letting down the
team if I stood down halfway through the job. If you run
away every time you face problems in life, you won't solve
or achieve anything.

The headline writers had another field day when Atherton took part in Danny Morrison's benefit match. England's captain belted the ball to long-off, where the catch was confidently taken by one Emily Drumm, a member of the New Zealand ladies team. Atherton had the good sense and good grace to walk off beaming. He did not mind the 'wicket maiden' or 'caught by the short and girlie' cracks. The day after the *Sun* declared that 'Atherton even flops with a woman', England's captain gave the paper's cricket correspondent John Etheridge a couple of exclusive interviews. For all the Captain Grumpy tags, Atherton gives freely of his time to members of the media.

England turned out at New Plymouth sporting new cricket shirts. The TCCB had ceased to exist on 1 January. The old logo was out. The three lions – very prominent during Euro 96 – and the ECB were in. The Tetley Bitter logo had also changed. (Much had been made of the company's announcement during the Zimbabwe tour that they were withdrawing their sponsorship of the England cricket team. In fact, the decision had more to do with a takeover and change in marketing direction, but England's results certainly gave Tetley's departure real impetus.) The rain prevented England from batting after the NZ Academy had been bowled out for 201. Atherton's form leading up to the first Test was as bad as it had been in Zimbabwe. He lasted 14 balls at Palmerston

North as Stewart and Hussain scored centuries and Tufnell took 5 for 58 as England won by an innings and 113 runs, Atherton lbw for 7. Next time out at Hamilton he was lbw for 5 in the last Test dress-rehearsal, after Northern Districts had been bowled out in a session for 69. Atherton's total of first-class runs since leaving England was 114 in 10 innings, his batting average all too easy to calculate. He was working hard, maybe too hard. Finally, the bowling machine in the indoor nets was put to work overtime to get the captain's feet moving properly. Atherton did not duck the issue when England batted for a second time requiring 35 for victory – he had everything to lose if he had been dismissed a second time. The captain's 12 not out in England's 10-wicket victory will probably be quickly forgotten, but it was a major step forward and proved he was still up for the fight.

The New Zealand Test series brought Atherton and ICC match referee Peter Burge together again, but the former Australian batsman was less confrontational than he had been prior to the Leeds Test in 1994. His diplomatic remarks suggested that he, too, had learnt from that month of turmoil two and a half years earlier: 'I've got no problems with Mike. He's got some ticker, and Australians like that.' Likewise, Atherton had no desire to get involved with an ICC referee at this time. That would finish him off. The England team had been particularly vocal in their support of Atherton, but while such words were reassuring, they had to be translated into action. On the first morning at Eden Park, Atherton was let down as badly as he had been in Bulawayo, as England's bowlers failed to capitalise totally on the moisture and movement in the pitch. Again, as at Bulawayo, the day's final session saw a vast improvement, although Gough's dropped catch off Cairns, which would have left the Kiwis 220 for 6, proved costly. That morning session was as bad as

Atherton can remember it. He won the toss and put the opposition in for a third successive time in New Zealand. The one surprise in the England line-up was the absence of Croft. Cork, who had been struggling with a bad back, came in and Mullally was still preferred to Silverwood. After less than an hour, Atherton had tried out all five of his bowlers, some from difficult ends. The ball was swinging all over the place, but the tourists could not find the right spot to put it. Mullally's opening six overs produced three runs. Figures do lie. The New Zealand batsmen did not put bat to ball because they could not get bat to ball way down the leg-side. Mullally was the most culpable, though not the only culprit – Stewart had a finger dislocated diving like David Seaman to try to stop a wild delivery from Gough. Atherton had believed that the chances of New Zealand getting through to lunch without losing a wicket were as remote as hearing Illingworth whisper: 'No comment'. His bowlers were dreadful. Bryan Young and Blair Pocock came in for lunch with the score 72 for 0.

The pressure was back on Atherton. What was he doing letting the Kiwis bat? The home side should have been bowled out in two sessions. Lloyd admitted that he skipped lunch: 'I don't know what was said at lunchtime in the dressing-room. I stayed away and let the captain and players get on with it. I had nothing to say to them.' By tea, New Zealand were 193 for 2. Atherton kept a calm disposition throughout, arms folded and chewing. He was also biting his lips. Any public display of the frustration and annoyance he was experiencing would have only added to his problems. He simply could not understand why an attack that had been performing so well could lose it so completely in advantageous conditions on such a big occasion. The Gough lapse emphasised a lost opportunity – Cairns went on to make 67 in an 118-run sixth-wicket partnership with Stephen Fleming, who hit

129 – though Gough's bowling was the only consolation in New Zealand's 390.

Knight was lbw cheaply, but Atherton and Stewart ensured that England suffered no major mishaps on the second day. Atherton was not at his best, but it was a vast improvement. The feet were beginning to move in the right places. The determination, of course, was undiminished. England had reached 200 and Atherton 83 before he was caught and bowled by Dipak Patel after an attempted drive was parried by Justin Vaughan at short mid-on. England's captain was back in the runs. It was not enough for him. He was furious at having missed out on a century. (The odds on an Atherton hundred had been 16-1. He told his friends and colleagues to get the bet down.) Atherton was happy to play second fiddle to Stewart, who dominated England's innings with 173, the highest score by an England wicket-keeper. It was Stewart's fourth century against New Zealand and took him into double figures in all Tests. Thorpe carried on the good Surrey work with 119 as England's 521 gave them a lead of 131. Tufnell's removal of Fleming was the most important of England's three successes on the fourth evening.

New Zealand started the final day 75 runs short of making England bat again. Victory for the tourists looked a formality at lunch as the home side went in at 105 for 8, still 26 runs behind. Most watching Sky or listening to *Test Match Special* back home went to bed at this point, half an hour before midnight, confident that England's first Test win abroad for two years was in the bag. Those same viewers and listeners could not quite believe the news the next morning that England had failed to win. Atherton could not quite believe it either. The morning session had gone well, perhaps too well. After a steady start, the Kiwis had collapsed from 88 for 3. Parore ran out his captain, then madly charged Tufnell and was stumped. When Patel was lbw to Mullally to the last ball before lunch, the England celebrations had a finality about them. The tourists were one ball away from certain victory when Gough yorked Simon Doull 37 minutes after lunch. New Zealand were 11 runs in front when Morrison, the man with the record number of Test ducks (he was selling 'Danny Duck-Callers' as part of his benefit season), joined Astle. Atherton was slightly more animated than on the first morning, but no less distressed as Morrison batted for two and three-quarter hours to deny England. Astle, 102, and Morrison only came off after Germon declared with the game safe: New Zealand's lead was 117 with seven overs remaining. It was New Zealand's third century last-wicket stand and the 13th in all Tests.

Unfortunately for Atherton and England, the general perception back home, confirmed in the media, was that New Zealand had not saved the Test, England had thrown it away – the tourists had batted too slowly on the fourth afternoon, Atherton should have crowded Morrison and experimented more on the final afternoon. His batting no longer an issue, Atherton's leadership had replaced it in the spotlight and under the microscope. The popular image of Morrison of a rabbit because of his 24 Test ducks, however, was a false one – Atherton knew that from Morrison's days as the overseas player at Old Trafford. This New Zealander had once batted for four and a half hours in Pakistan. The Eden Park pitch was placid and Morrison saw no need to take any chances. Astle did not even try to hog the strike – of the 266 deliveries bowled at New Zealand's final pair, Morrison faced exactly half. The result was a cruel blow to Atherton, more so than Bulawayo. After picking the team up from the Zimbabwe problems and himself up for the Test, this 'failure' was a real kick in the teeth. The draw had become increasingly inevitable as the afternoon wore on, but a grim-faced England captain was still numbed by it all by the time he sat down at the press conference:

We had a great opportunity to win, but didn't take it. We couldn't take the last wicket, so New Zealand deserved a draw. We missed the boat on the first morning and dropped an important catch that evening. We played as poorly as a team as I can remember that day. With No. 11 at the crease, you know it takes just one ball, so you tell yourself to be patient and relax. That's what I told the bowlers. Now, inevitably, the players are down because we have twice seen the winning post and not passed it. It was disappointing and frustrating, but despite Morrison's reputation, I know he can bat when he puts his mind to it. From what I remembered at Lancashire, he used to block and slog and I set our fields for that. This time, though, he restrained himself.

Atherton added that he was not interested in moral victories, even though that was all England seemed to be able to achieve at the moment.

The impact of Auckland was all too evident in England's feeble performance against New Zealand 'A' at Wanganui. England were bowled out for 107 in the first innings and stuttered to a 90-run defeat before lunch on the final day. Atherton made 5 and 0. Russell, in a rare outing, remained defiant on 61 and issued a 'we were awful' verdict, much more damning than anything offered by Lloyd: 'I'm sure Bryan Young, Blair Pocock, Nathan Astle and most of the other New Zealand players have enjoyed their time off. This is not sour grapes, not whingeing. Just pure facts. Wanganui is a lovely place on the coast and the lunches have been terrific. But everyone here knows this is a park ground with no resemblance to a Test ground. I'm very pleased and proud with the way we approached this game.' The journalists did not think much of Lloyd's comments, and the way they were reported led to a bust-up with the England coach after the third Test. As at Bulawayo, Lloyd's comments were too open to misinterpretation, especially as he had made it clear that this match had come too soon after the Test. 'Proud of them' was not a sensible observation when England had lost badly to New Zealand's second-string XI. Left-armer Geoff Allott was promoted from there to the second Test team, but all attention was focused on Daniel Vettori, a left-arm spinner who would be 18 years and 10 days old when the Wellington Test started. Vettori had just left school and was waiting to attend university. His appearance against England for Northern Districts a fortnight earlier had been his first-class debut. His sudden elevation was more unexpected than Morrison's demotion: the hero of Eden Park was dropped. Another Kiwi got his chance in the second Test – for England. Caddick, after a tour almost as anonymous as Russell's, was brought in. Mullally paid for his Auckland waywardness, while Silverwood, who had taken a career-best 6 for 44 at Wanganui, had been ruled out of the rest of the series after splitting the webbing on his hand. England went back to two spinners, and suddenly they had an attack of five serious wicket-taking bowlers.

The Basin Reserve, like the rest of Wellington, can be wet and windy, and the weather provided the perfect answer to England's problems with poor opening sessions – the Test did not start until tea because of the rain. New Zealand batted after winning the toss, but Gough and Caddick soon had them in tatters at 23 for 5. Play closed with the home side 62 for 6 and they were bowled out for 124 before lunch the next day. Gough took his first five-wicket haul since Sydney more than two years earlier; Caddick was just as impressive with four. England's aggressive attitude and purpose were evident as umpire Steve Bucknor spoke to Atherton after Gough had a few words with Allott. The New Zealand bowler had been dishing it out himself at Wanganui, and Atherton did not worry too much about Gough redressing the balance. There was an obvious growing tension between the sides, later described by Lloyd as a matter of 'poking the opposition in the chest'.

England set about batting the Kiwis out of the Test. Atherton knew there would be terminal trouble if England failed to win now after this start. He made only 30, but the batting crisis was over. Stewart, Hussain, Thorpe and Crawley all got past 50, with Thorpe scoring a second successive century, his fourth for England after waiting nearly two years for his third. England then lost five wickets for 26 runs, but 383 was still a winning total. The pressure was on the Kiwis, and not only because of the match situation. Cairns was named as one of those New Zealand players who had stayed out into the early hours. A taxi driver had phoned a local radio station to complain about the time and the state of the players he drove back to the team hotel. Ball-tampering was also a factor after Paul Allott on Sky TV had commented, on his namesake: 'That's illegal. You shouldn't be doing that, and he's being very naive.' But the Sky pictures were not the ones referee Burge was looking at, and in contrast to his probing search for any evidence, video or otherwise, in 1994, Burge did not budge as the umpires had made no reports, just as they had not done at Lord's or at The Oval in 1994. 'The umpires check the ball at the end of every over. That's good enough for me,' Burge explained. 'I shall not be asking to study any TV footage.' The irony was not lost on Atherton. Nor was it in the next Test when New Zealand's Bryan Young queried a close catch and once again, Burge felt unable to act.

The Wellington weather was now Atherton's only serious worry. No New Zealand wickets fell on the third evening. Play did not start on day four until 3.15 pm and England looked like entering the final day with nine wickets still required. Then Croft lifted England's spirits and hopes with three wickets for no runs in 14 deliveries. Hotel curtains were pulled back nervously the next morning. Gough went for the kill, taking 4 for 10 in 21 balls. Knight had taken a blistering catch at second slip to remove Pocock. He also pocketed the chance that gave England victory by an innings and 68 runs. England's joy was only matched by the relief of a Test win abroad after so much heartache and heartbreak. The players, with Gough and Croft to the fore, saluted the win and the Barmy Army by spraying champagne from the balcony. The new ECB bosses, MacLaurin and Lamb, had recovered from Harare and flown out to Wellington. MacLaurin treated the upturn here as carefully as the downside in Zimbabwe. He did talk about Atherton, though: 'Mike has had a lot of pressure on him, but he is a good captain and a nice man. I have told him he will get no pressure from me. He has my full support, even in Zimbabwe when everybody was baying for his blood. If I can get my act right, I'll make Mike's life a lot easier. I have great respect for him. He's a strong character.'

Atherton went in to attend his first winning press conference in nine Tests. He was in no mood for any gushing pronouncements: 'I'm happy to have won and we want to win again in Christchurch. That's as far ahead as I'm looking. If we keep playing like that, we'll win more games than we lose. I know I've been criticised, but I wouldn't say that makes this victory any sweeter. Every Test win is sweet for all sorts of reasons.'

It was left to Lloyd to capture the mood: 'I'm particularly pleased for Michael. He is a caring captain and the way he is handling the side is improving all the time.

When he took the job, back in 1993, I said that he needed time to develop. He is developing nicely and should reap the rewards. Michael got his tactics right. Dominic Cork wasn't at his best today, the conditions were damp, the wind blustery and the ball wasn't swinging. So Athers took him off after two overs. Darren Gough came on and didn't that work well? Michael is a tough character. He never wavers, he just doesn't. The whole team is pleased for him. He has been criticised all winter, but we could have won all four Tests. I'd love to see him as captain next summer and I think we're progressing. I expect to be consulted over the appointment of skipper. Athers is a tough little sod and we need more like him.'

Such historic moments provoke historic action. At Christchurch, England fielded an unchanged team for the first time in 33 Tests and almost three years. (The last such occasion, in the West Indies, featured the last two Tests before Illingworth became involved.) England's three fast bowlers all had Christchurch connections. It was Caddick's original home, while Cork and Gough had shared a house there in the winter of 1991 when playing for East Shirley. Atherton put the opposition in for the third time in a Test on this winter tour. The captain thought that was the best chance England had of winning. He felt no necessity to try to protect England's 1-0 lead by playing for a draw. His decision went the way of the others as New Zealand scored 346, although Croft's 5 for 95 confirmed a stunning first senior tour. Then England collapsed to 104 for 5, and it was back to business as usual for Atherton, the England captain who stands alone. Alone, but firm, as his colleagues crumbled around him. The other five front-line batsmen contributed a total of 60 runs, and Atherton was left stranded on 94 with England trailing by 118 runs. He became the seventh England player to carry his bat after Abel, Warner, Hutton (twice), Boycott, Gooch and Stewart, and the third after Boycott and Stewart not to score a century. England's varied attack brought the tourists back into the game. The Kiwis went in after the third day at 95 for 6, a lead of 213. Atherton's hope was to be chasing less than 250, but Cairns forgot about his Wellington problems and blasted away, his half-century setting a target of 305 in five sessions to win. Time was not a problem, but the size of the task could be judged from the fact that only once before, at Melbourne over the 1929 New Year, had an England side scored over 300 runs in the fourth innings to win a Test. The return to form of Atherton was the main reason for the optimism in the England dressing-room. A target like that needs someone to dig in for victory. Atherton has the technique, temperament and relish for such a role.

England were 118 for 2 overnight, the late loss of Stewart having evened up the contest again. Atherton came out on the final Test morning of the winter with Caddick, who had been sent in as nightwatchman, but the key partnership was Atherton's with Hussain. England's captain reached his 11th Test ton before lunch, his first since Trent Bridge the previous July. The main New Zealand threat came from young Vettori, who was showing few signs of being overawed by the cricket company he was now keeping. The target was only 79 runs away when Atherton got a faint edge as he tried to run Astle to third man. It was 40 minutes after lunch and Atherton was off the field for the first time in the match. England's 226 for 3 became 231 for 6 in ten minutes, with Vettori quickly removing Hussain and Thorpe. Atherton wondered whether all the hard work of the winter months was going to evaporate in less than an hour, as it had in Cape Town, but Crawley and Cork, confirming a more responsible attitude to his batting, saw England home. They had become the 13th Test side to get past 300 in the fourth innings and win. Atherton had won a series abroad as captain for the first time. After 34 Test runs at an average of 8.50 in Zimbabwe, he had scored 325 in New Zealand at 108.33. This was Atherton's match. As New Zealand's stand-in captain Fleming revealed: 'One way of stopping Atherton is to get all the other batsmen out – and leave him stranded, like we did in the first innings.' The Kiwi coach Steve Rixon went further: 'Right now, I'd give Mike Atherton anything he wants. The way he went about the job was superb and his personal input was an inspiration. They shouldn't take anything away from him.' Nor did they. When the Atherton smile goes with the Atherton stubble, the Establishment seem less bothered.

Atherton admitted how much his performance here meant to him: 'The fact that my two innings were played in winning circumstances makes them very special – more special than Johannesburg. I don't like watching in these situations, but I managed to stay out in the viewing area. But there was a little group of four or five on the sofa in the dressing-room going through about 30 packets of fags. We had a bit of a wobble in mid-afternoon, but John Crawley and Dominic Cork showed a lot of strength under pressure. This was a strong performance and I'm pleased with the way we've played throughout the series. I've said all along that our Test match form has been good this winter. We could have won four out of five Tests.'

Even allegations of Tufnell smoking marijuana in a Christchurch restaurant failed to dampen English spirits. Tour manager Barclay issued a denial, the restaurant hung out a sign saying 'Phil Tufnell must agree that Bardelli's really is Christchurch's best joint' and the matter was forgotten. Tufnell took the Man of the Match award as England won the first one-day international by four wickets. It was only England's second limited-overs win abroad over a Test-playing country in 15 matches. The batsmen walked out to the theme song of their choice. Atherton and Knight chose Oasis's 'Some Might Say'. Most of the selections were predictable. The best were Tom Jones's 'Delilah' for Croft and Lita Roza's 'How Much is that Doggy in the Window?' for Russell. England went 2-0 up in the series without Atherton, missing because of a stiff back, in a rain-affected game at Eden Park as Knight rediscovered his touch. The one-day series could have been decided in a last-ball finish in the third game. Gough, one half of the Bulawayo finale, could only scramble a bye and the match was tied. The batsmen had had problems with the light – Atherton, Stewart and Hussain were all bowled by similar looping deliveries from Chris Harris.

Atherton now felt able to confirm what had become increasingly obvious. He wanted to carry on as captain and face the Australians:

The question of the captaincy is always just around the corner because the time limit is so short. At the end of each tour, we don't have a captain until a new appointment is made. There are times when I find this irritating and the constant questioning about it helps nobody. In my view, they should appoint a captain and tell him to get on with it until he either resigns or is sacked. If he is making a mess of it, obviously he must go, but there would be great flexibility on both sides. The way the Zimbabwe leg ended for us meant I had to face certain possibilities. If we had not won in New Zealand, if things had continued as they were, I couldn't have gone on. The position would have been untenable and I would have resigned. I'd have had no choice, I'm sure. I was going through a personal struggle in Zimbabwe, badly short of runs and form, but I never allowed that to affect the way I captained the side or to get through to the players. It stood me in good stead, made me stronger for the knowledge that I could cope. I have a good grasp of situations here, largely through my confidence in the bowlers. Having two spinners of quality gives me control, and it dates back to the decision that Alec Stewart must keep wicket. A lot of people disagreed with it, but it enabled us to play our best five bowlers and was the key to the entire winter.

As usual, there was no problem knowing what was wrong with my game, it was knowing how to put it right. It was only when I had two four-hour sessions against a bowling machine in that school, the physio feeding in the balls and the door shut against anyone inquisitive, that I worked it all out. At Christchurch, I never allowed myself to think about the job. My only thought was winning the game. The captaincy can be a difficult thing to carry around if you allow it to burden everything you do. After I was out on the final day, I sat for an hour in the shower cooling down. Phil Tufnell twice poked his head in to say we'd lost another wicket. He looked terrible, ridden with anxiety, and I didn't want to come out and watch. I don't feel a burden from the job. I'm enjoying it now and like the set-up we have. It's amazing how quickly the mood has changed this winter. It has left me very positive about the future. If there was a time when the players' support for me was tested it was in Zimbabwe, and I'm grateful they didn't waver. So as long as the team maintains that faith, I would like to go on.

England failed to win the one-day series. The fourth international, in Auckland, was delayed by a day because of rain. England's target was 154 in 43 overs. They fell short by 10 runs. Knight's left index-finger was broken first ball and the tourists were always struggling. The Kiwis levelled the series with a 28-run victory in Wellington. It was a typical, flawed England run-chase. Front-line batsmen got bogged down in the middle of the innings and got behind with the rate. The introduction of Silverwood at No. 5 was a desperate measure. Atherton and Germon shared the trophy, the New Zealand captain being sacked later that day for the Sri Lanka Tests. The highlight of this final match, though, was the sight of Botham having his head shaved for charity, raising a six-figure sum. Atherton had been bowled third ball, but the Allott delivery was a no-ball. England's captain went on to make 43 before being run out. The England coach hoped that some of the one-day razzmatazz might find its way to the English summer: 'I want young children to come to cricket and be passionate about supporting their team. I also want them to have fun. The occasion sparks good banter between supporters. What's more, it's very important the players get used to the atmosphere. They will now experience it everywhere else.'

Atherton had survived his worst captaincy crisis in style. Outside the New Zealand Tests, he only scored 131 runs in seven other first-class matches in Zimbabwe and New Zealand, but already the winter was part of history. Atherton looked ahead: 'It should be a cracking summer, with Australia being the top side coming over here. All the Test matches are virtually sold out, which is great news. There were very few problem areas on this tour, and I felt a lot of players enhanced their careers during the trip. We should start in the summer with players who have played in back-to-back winning Test matches.'

Atherton returned for his benefit year with his reputation restored; Gatting joined Gooch under the new chairman of selectors, Graveney; his opposite number, Mark Taylor, was under as much pressure for runs as he had

been in Zimbabwe. Win, lose or draw against Australia,
Atherton felt he was probably nearing the end of his
captaincy reign. He feared that if England lost the Ashes
for a fifth consecutive series, it was more than likely he
would not survive as England captain.

CHAPTER NINETEEN

Ashes In The Wind

Michael Atherton's Ashes summer ended as it had begun, with a famous Test victory over the Australians, but it was not enough to recapture the Ashes. However, the 3-2 scoreline in Australia's favour suggested a more sustained English challenge than usual for this oldest of cricket trophies. That was not the case. England made a winning start at Edgbaston after whitewashing the tourists in the Texaco limited-overs event. It was a comprehensive defeat of an Australian team which appeared to have problems that might impair its effectiveness. Atherton went to Lord's to pass Peter May's record of 41 matches in charge of England, but Mark Taylor's side had regained its composure. The rain determined the outcome of that second Test, but Australia took the series, the Ashes and the next three Tests as England's confidence evaporated. Despite England's Oval success in the final match, it had been widely rumoured for weeks that Atherton would be standing down, with Nasser Hussain, Alec Stewart or even Adam Hollioake to lead England to the West Indies in the winter of 1998. Atherton, not for the first time in his career, retired to the countryside to consider his future. He turned up with

357

chairman of selectors Graveney at Lord's a week later to convey the unexpected news that he was willing to carry on. Adam Hollioake would lead England to the Sharjah Cup to give Atherton a complete break before the West Indies and a chance to work on his technique with Graham Gooch.

Atherton could not have asked for a better start to the Ashes summer. It was the manner of England's victories in the Texaco series and at Edgbaston, as much as the results, that seemed to bode so well. The Aussies were taking a pounding. Hounding a cricket captain is a regular English summer sport; it has just been a while since that target was anyone other than the home man. Australia's Mark Taylor is one of the most popular and successful Test captains of recent times. Had he been English, Taylor's position would have been secure, but Australia has always prided itself on its tradition of picking its best XI and then choosing the captain, but Taylor came to England without a fifty in his previous 20 Test innings. The poor form continued, and his bad trot with the bat was all the more obvious because of Australia's unsuccessful start in England. Atherton took little pleasure in seeing his rival suffer, although he was happy with anything that was likely to undermine Australia's team spirit. At Bristol, someone thought it would be funny to present Taylor with a three-foot wide bat. The Australian management were not amused, and made an announcement that Taylor would definitely play in the opening Test at Edgbaston. The Australian captain knew that two Tests was the extent of his allowance if the runs did not flow. Coach Geoff Marsh supported Taylor as the pressure mounted, but former captain Ian Chappell stated before the first Test: 'If Mark was mentally fit, I know he would have stood down long ago. Mark is in a classic state of denial. I don't believe he is capable of admitting that he has a problem.' Taylor was most upset by the public views of Bobby Simpson, who had been Australian coach when Taylor was first made captain. Simpson described Australia as 'strife-torn and ripe for the picking. Mark Taylor shouldn't even be thinking of playing.'

There were no such problems for England. The first Test of the post-Illingworth era was a triumph for Atherton and the new management regime. Even Devon Malcolm was back in the fold. Surrey's Mark Butcher and Adam Hollioake were promoted to the senior squad, but Hollioake had to wait until later in the summer for his Test chance. June was a glorious month for England's sporting teams. Glenn Hoddle's soccer stars won Le Tournoi de France, the British Lions travelled to South Africa and beat the Springboks and Atherton's England inflicted one of the most comprehensive defeats suffered by Australia in modern times. Atherton realised that the tourists were in turmoil, but England had often failed to exploit such positions. This time they did not fail. Seldom have they enjoyed such a perfect cricket day as Thursday, 5 June 1997. At one stage the best Test side in the world were 54 for 8 after a blistering opening spell from Darren Gough, with strong support from Malcolm and then Andrew Caddick, who finished with 5 for 50. The most telling moment came when Gough bowled Greg Blewett only to see the umpire signal 'no-ball'. Such moments have ended England revivals in the past. Gough walked back to his mark with a wry smile on his face. Blewett was not going to escape. The next ball found the edge of the bat and flew to Nasser Hussain in the gully. Atherton received a special tankard from Peter May's widow Virginia at lunch-time to mark his achievement in equalling his record. The scoreboard, showing Australia at 92 for 8, meant even more to him. Australia were all out for 118, just after lunch, inside 32 overs. Briefly, England appeared in danger of wasting their good work, with Atherton, Butcher and Stewart gone by the time the score had reached 50. Crucially, Graham Thorpe and Hussain, who had come together before tea, were still there at the close as England had gained a lead of 82 runs. The next day, rain ended play at 4.40 by which time England had advanced to 449 for 6, a lead of 331 runs. Hussain and Thorpe had carried on from where they left off. Thorpe scored his third century in four Tests, while Hussain reached a career-best 207, stating: 'It doesn't get any better than this.' Their fourth-wicket stand of 288 against Australia was an Ashes record for England, who have rarely enjoyed such domination over the Aussies in recent times. When Shane Warne finally dismissed Hussain, the touring leg-spinner's figures were 1 for 102 off 29 overs. The wicket did not suit Warne, whose usual control was missing, or Glenn McGrath, whose rhythm vanished when he tried too hard to make things happen. Australia's world-class match-winning bowlers were reduced to the role of mere mortals.

The first signs of an Australian revival came on Saturday, with a gutsy century from the Australian captain after England had finished with a first-innings lead of 360 runs. By Sunday afternoon, Australia had reached 465 for 6, an advantage of 105 runs, which not only threatened to take the Test into the final day, but had begun to get England's supporters worried. Atherton had looked to Mark Ealham to break the tourists' resistance, but his first over back went for ten runs. England's captain held his nerve. Ealham continued and collected the wickets of Ian Healy, Warne and Mike Kasprowicz without conceding another run in his next ten deliveries to end Australia's fightback. England needed 118 runs to win, with 32 scheduled overs left. Despite the early loss of Butcher, Atherton and Alec Stewart were not going to put off finishing the job until the next day. Atherton's 57 came off 65 balls and Stewart hit the winning boundary. The pair had put on 90 in 72 minutes to enable England to win by nine wickets and with more than ten Sunday overs to spare. Hussain was named Man of the Match and England had taken the lead in an Ashes series for the first time since winning at Brisbane in November 1986.

Atherton and England seemed set for the summer. Between Edgbaston and Lord's, where he would break May's record, Atherton had a busy schedule. On Friday, England's captain became the youngest cricket recipient of an OBE, arriving late at Old Trafford as he had forgotten the announcement was being made that day. Tuesday saw the launch of his authorised biography and, later, his Ashes dinner as part of his benefit year. Atherton's reluctance to focus on fund-raising activities made life difficult for his benefit chairman, Bob Wilson, especially when Atherton put a block on collections at Old Trafford during Lancashire matches. His Ashes dinner, coming on the back of that Edgbaston success, proved an inevitable money-spinner with over £80,000 being raised that evening. Over £11,000 of that came when the bat Atherton had used to perform his heroics at The Wanderers in Johannesburg was auctioned. The benefit of London as a venue for such events was reflected in the fact that his Christchurch bat – 94 not out (carried his bat) and 118 – went for less than four figures in Manchester. So hectic was Atherton's schedule that Wilson was put in sole charge of his diary so that England's captain was never double-booked. It also prevented his off-the-field activities from distracting from his cricket. A record benefit total of £307,000 showed the extent of Wilson's devotion to the cause.

England were in pole position at Lord's, ready for the kill, although the Australians had just beaten Leicestershire by 81 runs, their first win in nine matches. Lord's displayed little home advantage in Ashes Tests, as England's record of one win (in 1934) in 101 years was hardly inspiring. In 14 post-war clashes, Australia and the draw were tied at seven apiece. Lord's 1997 saw no change to England's fortunes at the home of cricket. The rain, then Glenn McGrath combined to ruin Atherton's special occasion. England came away still one ahead in the series, but many thought only the weather saved England, a belief Atherton disputes. Thursday was a complete wash-out, but Lord MacLaurin gave the press something to write about. The new chairman of the England Cricket Board was putting together his plan to revive England's Test fortunes. Ironically, the Edgbaston victory had made his task impossible. The counties were able to defend themselves by calling the prophets of gloom and doom scare-mongers, highlighted by the comprehensive beating of the best Test team in the world.

Only 21 overs were possible on Friday. It was enough time for McGrath to remove Atherton, Butcher and Stewart in 13 deliveries to leave England 13 for 3. England closed on 38 for 3 after touring wicket-keeper Healy had owned up to an edge from Thorpe's bat not carrying. Saturday belonged to McGrath and Australia as England were bowled out for 77. Bowling wicket to wicket and getting the ball to move late, McGrath picked up the best-ever figures for an Australian at Lord's, 8 for 38.

Atherton felt his bowlers could make similar use of the receptive wicket, but Australia finished the day at 131 for 2, well in control, with the weather cited as England's best hope of escape. A draw seemed inevitable with play delayed until 5.40 on Sunday, but the Australians, especially Matthew Elliott making his maiden Test century, showed commendable aggression in difficult conditions. Taylor declared on the overnight score of 213 for 7, a lead of 136 runs. It was the Australian captain who missed a relatively simple chance off Butcher when the Surrey opener had made two. That was the nearest Australia got to an early breakthrough. Butcher, fighting for his own Test survival, made 87 in an opening stand of 162 with

Atherton, who reached 77 before treading on his leg stump as he turned Kasprowicz down to fine leg. Stewart, who had been forced to hand the wicket-keeping gloves to John Crawley because of back spasms failed, as did Hussain, but Crawley and Thorpe added 64 in an undefeated fifth-wicket partnership that allowed Atherton to declare with honour. Nobody had seriously believed that Taylor's side would hand over the Ashes. Atherton's side had been given a glimpse of the Australian fighting spirit, but had lost nothing in the Ashes battle.

The action moved to Old Trafford, where attention again focused on the wicket. No captain has ever won in Manchester after sending the opposition in, but batting first was a real risk, so there were certainly some stunned faces in the Australian dressing-room when Taylor's decision to bat was announced. It was symptomatic of Taylor's ability to separate the captaincy from his own problems as an opening bat. Ian Chappell, who a month earlier had called for Taylor to step down, summed up Taylor's action: 'Batting first was the correct decision, but I'm not sure I would have been brave enough to make it.' Australia closed the first day on 224 for 7 after wobbling on 113 for 5. The stumbling block, not for the first time, was Steve Waugh, who was undefeated on 102. Atherton knew a golden opportunity had been lost. Australia should have been bowled out by the close of play. Dean Headley, becoming the third generation of that famous West Indies family to play Test cricket, was the pick of the England bowlers.

The pick of the Australian bowlers was Warne, returning to the scene of his first great triumph against England, 'the ball from hell' that bamboozled Mike Gatting and hypnotised a generation of English batsmen. England were bowled out for 162 by Saturday morning, with Warne collecting six wickets, enough to take him past

Richie Benaud's Australian record Test tally of 248 for a leg-spinner. Butcher top-scored with 51, as once again the McGrath–Healy combination did for England's captain as he attempted to hook. Butcher and Stewart, the Surrey brothers-in-law took the score to 74 before England lost nine wickets for 88 runs. Australia spent the rest of Saturday and half of Sunday grinding England down. Again, Headley-inspired, Australia's batsmen, Steve Waugh apart, had gone for a modest total, this time 132. Again, Steve Waugh reached a century, although it was the 173 runs scored by Healy, Warne, Paul Reiffel and Gillespie that really rubbed salt into the wounds.

The victory target was 469. Realistically, England had to survive 141 overs, a mountain that Atherton had climbed in Johannesburg, but there was to be no repeat. England were dead in the water by Sunday night at 130 for 5. Atherton and Butcher resisted for over an hour, but four wickets fell for 11 runs, three to Gillespie, and England, Crawley apart, seemed to lose the stomach for the fight. The numerous pitch invasions by streakers only emphasised the general frustration at England's loosening grip on the series. England lasted another 21.4 overs on Monday morning before Australia levelled the contest with a 268-run victory.

All square after three Tests was a significant improvement on the previous four Ashes series from England's point of view, but the manner of England's capitulation sent out bad vibes regarding a quick England recovery. England's captain was quick to support his team. 'I will put good money at the bookies that we have the same squad for the next Test at Headingley. We have to hold up our hands and admit we were outplayed this time. But the measure of a side is how they come back. We need to turn up in the right frame of mind at Headingley and be ready for one hell of a scrap. I am confident of my team and I'm backing them to do that.'

This Ashes series was now buzzing. Hussain had come in for some traditional Australian stick while batting, because they were not happy with his catch that removed Greg Blewett at Old Trafford. Television replays were inconclusive, but the Australians were convinced the ball had been scooped up on the bounce. After Healy's gesture at Lord's, the tourists were determined to exploit the moral high ground. Warne's one-finger gesture at the post-match presentations was all over the back pages the next day for he was a popular target for abuse and the fatboy's theme song 'Who ate all the pies?' He was seen swigging champagne from the bottle, patting his pushed-out stomach and revelling in his nine-wicket haul that had silenced those who claimed he was finished, for he knew he had put his side back in the series.

There is a natural gap in the English summer in a six-Test series between the third and fourth matches. The Benson and Hedges final gives both sides a chance to regroup. England did just that at Headingley the weekend before the fourth Test was to be played there. They held another team bonding session, similar to the pre-season gathering at Heythrop Hall in Oxfordshire. The ECB had been particularly secretive first time out and lack of information had forced the media to adopt a light-hearted and rather sceptical approach to the whole affair. That experience made the England set-up even more protective second time out. Will Carling, whose Insights company had set up the motivational courses, could not understand the cricket authorities' reluctance to be open about what was going on.

Atherton was right. The losing XI at Old Trafford were retained with Phil Tufnell again included in the squad. Many felt giving a defeated unit this vote of confidence two weeks before the next Test was over-generous, providing a comfort zone that had not been deserved. The Hollioakes, Mike Smith, Devon Malcolm and Essex's young paceman Ashley Cowan also attended the Leeds team-bonding session. Meanwhile, Atherton and the media began to drift apart again. He felt England could get back on track if everyone got behind the team, but instead the bad feeling from the previous winter resurfaced. The media felt the side's body language towards them and opponents had changed little. Despite MacLaurin's effort, which included many cricket journalists being interviewed by a consultancy firm about what was wrong with the cricket authorities, communications had not improved. Eventually, Brian Murgatroyd, a freelance journalist, was appointed ECB press officer and he certainly helped ease the tension.

Some things never change. The Headingley pitch was again the centre of attention, with the Australians claiming that David Graveney, England's chairman of selectors, had interfered in the preparation of the wicket. The strip had been changed, but that decision had nothing to do with Graveney. The greenish surface suggested that the seamers might enjoy the Headingley conditions. The switch had been made by Harry Brind, the ECB inspector of pitches, who explained that the original one had been 're-laid and after the wet weather we've had, it was bare at one end. I don't think it was up to Test standard.' The match referee Cammie Smith agreed England had done nothing wrong, but that did not dissuade the tourists that this was an attempt to neutralise Warne, especially when Tufnell dropped out early from the England squad and Gloucestershire's uncapped left-armer Mike Smith came in. Smith eventually made the side, at the expense of Caddick, a selection that became more significant as the match wore on. Difficult as his decision had been at Old Trafford, Taylor had no hesitation in asking England to bat in the overcast conditions after winning his fourth successive toss of the series.

Atherton and Butcher had reached 14 for 0 when the

rain came. The pair waited six and a quarter hours in the pavilion and would have probably preferred play to have been called off for the day. The sun appeared and England had to negotiate 31 overs. Atherton was undefeated on 34 at the close, with England 106 for 3. It could have been worse, but it might have been better if Butcher's full-blooded clip had not been caught in Blewett's midriff. Friday was the day Australia took control of the Ashes. England were bowled out for 172, with Atherton top-scoring with 41 in nearly four hours. The last six wickets fell for 18 runs with Gillespie taking 7 for 37. Atherton was not one of his victims. McGrath got England's captain again; this time Atherton connected to McGrath's leg-side delivery, hooking it straight down Gillespie's throat.

However, the decisive moment of the match and, probably, the summer came when England had removed Taylor, Blewett and Mark Waugh and Australia were 50 for 3. Matthew Elliott edged a ball from Mike Smith and it spooned gently to Graham Thorpe at first slip. It was a regulation catch in front of his face, but it slipped through Thorpe's fingers and the groan from the crowd suggested they knew how costly it was going to be. They were not wrong. Initially, Thorpe's lapse seemed irrelevant as Headley removed Steve Waugh and Australia were reduced to 50 for 4, but that was as good as it got for England. Just over three hours later, at 258 for 4, Taylor's team had one hand on the Ashes. Ricky Ponting had joined Elliott, who had reached his second Test century of the summer, while Atherton and Smith joined Thorpe on the list of those who had dropped Elliott. As Elliott had also been dropped three times in his 112 at Lord's, England were making things doubly difficult for themselves in containing this talented left-hander. Ponting reached his century before being the only wicket to fall on Saturday, with play abandoned at lunch-time and

Australia on 373 for 5. England's bowling performance on Sunday was pitiful as the tourists made 501 for 9 declared, a lead of 329 runs. That made Atherton's reluctance to use Ealham more all the more strange. Darren Gough, who bowled Elliott on 199, took 5 for 149.

An early finish looked likely when England were reduced to 89 for 4. McGrath again accounted for Atherton, this time taken in the slips. Hussain, hero of Edgbaston, had struggled since. With support from John Crawley, Hussain scored his second century of the series and saw England to the close without further mishap. England were still 117 runs short of making Australia bat again, but with six wickets left, escape had become possible. Sadly, that hope evaporated next morning when Warne deceived Hussain. England lasted until the first ball after lunch, but Australia's victory by an innings and 61 runs was conclusive and even more decisive because of the time lost to the weather. Atherton's side were 2-1 down with two to play; the 'Team England' had been exposed. All the bonding, pitch switches, selection changes could not disguise the fact that England were outclassed when competing at the highest level. The weakness of England's inadequate domestic structure was revealed for all to see, though the counties seemed more interested in sabotaging MacLaurin's blueprint for the future.

Atherton put a brave face on England's situation, but he was beginning to examine his own position, for he had been convinced that England's revival was genuine. The speed and the generosity of England's handing back of the Ashes initiative forced him to question that judgement. Atherton had another problem – his own form. He was not the only batsman having a troubled summer. Australia's Mark Waugh was struggling on pitches that made quality bowling the dominant factor. Unlike previous losses of form, Atherton, for the first time, felt the captaincy was contributing to his poor run. At this stage, Atherton had kept his own counsel and come to the conclusion that, a miracle apart (i.e. winning the final two Tests), he would give up the captaincy at the end of the series. Atherton worked with Graham Gooch before Trent Bridge, having scored just 206 runs in eight Ashes innings. His reputation as a world-class batsman has always been more important to him than the kudos of being England's leader. The decision, having been made for the time being, brought some relief as Atherton prepared for Trent Bridge, where England had to go all out for victory.

Malcolm and Caddick played for the injured Gough and Smith. The most significant change was the introduction of the Hollioake brothers. Ben, at 19, would become the youngest England Test player since Brian Close made his debut against New Zealand in 1949 aged 18 years and 149 days. That meant Stewart was back opening as well as keeping wicket, with Crawley up to No. 3. It could be argued that the Hollioakes had done little to deserve such elevation, especially with regard to their first-class record, but desperate situations require desperate measures and the pair had shown their liking for the big-time in the Texaco Trophy. A month earlier Ben Hollioake had given further evidence of this and was Atherton's choice as the Gold Award winner as Adam lifted the Benson and Hedges trophy at Lord's when Surrey beat Kent. While the selectors could be bold, MacLaurin unveiled his 'Raising the Standard' just before the Nottingham Test, which was widely seen as a cop-out.

England's last lingering Ashes hope vanished when Taylor called correctly for the fifth time in the series. Trent Bridge was the best pitch of an unpredictable summer and the Australians had first use of it. No tourist reached three figures, but the first five all got to fifty. England did well to keep Australia to 427; at one stage, Taylor's team were 311 for 3. Stewart took the game to Australia and, for a while, threatened to take it away from them with his most aggressive batting of the summer. England's hopes faded when he was brilliantly caught one-handed by Healy, who had parried an edge when Stewart drove at Warne. England's 313 was disappointing and was some way short of forcing Australia's hand, which they might have done at 243 for 4. Australia, with six wickets left, had built up a lead of 281 runs by Saturday night. The Ashes briefly came into English view with Caddick's second delivery the next morning. It reared at Steve Waugh, who could only edge it to slip. The rest of the day was an unmitigated disaster for England's bowlers and then batsmen. Healy led Australia's charge with 63 off 78 balls. Australia were out before tea for 336, with England requiring 451 to win in four sessions. That Australia did not need the final day was testimony to England's decline from the heady days of Edgbaston. Atherton went in the last of the nine overs before tea when McGrath brushed his glove. Stewart went to Paul Reiffel's first ball after the break and England fell apart. The home side's inexperience was mercilessly exposed. Adam Hollioake went back to Gillespie and his brother played no shot to Warne. Both were out lbw. The most senseless bit of cricket came from Robert Croft, who had just clubbed Warne for six, and then was enticed into trying to repeat the shot but instead chipped the ball to mid-on. Warne's face was a treat; he could not believe that Croft had fallen for it. When Malcolm fell to McGrath at the end of the day, Australia had won by 264 runs and retained the Ashes. The strength of Australia's purpose could be judged by the way they celebrated together on the pitch.

Atherton had no complaints. For the first time in his career, England had got their noses in front during an Ashes contest, so excuses about the pressure of playing catch-up cricket did not apply. In a fair fight, England's best cricketers were still a poor second against the best team in the world. The England captaincy had become a major talking point since England's Headingley defeat. The arrival of Adam Hollioake had added another pretender alongside vice-captain Hussain and former captain Stewart. After the loss of the Ashes, the *Daily Mail* carried the headline on the back page 'Dead Duck. Michael Atherton – you are charged with impersonating an England cricket captain.' Post-match questions focused on the captain's future. 'I will sit down after this series end and ruminate over it. I have always said I will know when it's time to go.' Little else was discussed between Trent Bridge and The Oval, apart from Robert Croft's spat with Mark Ilott in the NatWest semi-final. One day Croft was criticised for lying down without a fight, the next he was castigated for showing some bottle. The day before, Hussain had got plenty of press coverage for his view that England's cricketers were too soft.

Croft's aggressive behaviour was to cost him his Test place as Phil Tufnell, after a summer of waiting in the wings, was finally given his chance. Mark Ramprakash, now installed as Middlesex captain, was brought in for Crawley. But it was the future of England's captain that dominated all Test previews. The general consensus was that Michael Atherton was about to lead England out for the 46th and final time. Chairman Graveney considered the best policy was to give his captain as much space as possible. 'I intend to speak to him about that shortly, but I won't twist his arm. I know the pressures he has been under and it would be an insult to his integrity to apply any more.'

Atherton spoke briefly on the eve of the match: 'It's difficult to say whether a win here would make me more inclined to stay or not. The performance of the captain is judged on the performance of the team, which is right and proper. If the team is not performing, the captain takes the flak and I have never shied away from criticism because it goes with the territory. If any captain gets to the stage where he no longer feels he has support from the dressing-room, it's a clear indication that it's time to step down. But I'm encouraged that I still have that support. You don't want to be second guessing yourself as a captain over things like that all the time, or it would drive you crazy. I'm pleased to report that I'm not going crazy yet.'

Atherton won the toss for the first time in the series and was soon wondering why he had bothered. Deciding to bat, the McGrath–Healy combination did for England's captain again. A promising 97 for 2 soon became 180 all out as McGrath bowled magnificently to claim 7 for 76; Stewart's 36 was the top England score. Coach David Lloyd admitted afterwards: 'For the first time this season, I sensed a real lack of confidence among our players. I gave them a good dressing-down when we lost at Trent Bridge and it was a case of having to say all the same old things all over again. When we went in to lunch at 97 for 2 we had the opportunity to make the most of winning the toss, but then we started to chase the ball and against great bowlers like Glenn McGrath and Shane Warne you just can't do that. Sadly, we've seen this all before. The team let the captain and themselves down.'

The only England relief came when Tufnell removed both openers before the close. The Middlesex left-arm spinner was not finished. Six years earlier, Tufnell had stolen the show on The Oval Saturday with 6 for 25 against the West Indies. This time he was a day early, but his 7 for 66 brought England right back into the game, restricting Australia to a lead of 40 runs. Tufnell had never bowled better and this display made a mockery of his seat on the sidelines all summer. He bowled unchanged and suggested that he might make life awkward for the Australians if England could get 150 in front.

Friday night saw England 12 runs in front, but Atherton, Butcher and Stewart had gone. Atherton, who had received a series of fine deliveries, played his worst shot of the summer, edging Kasprowicz to Mark Waugh in the slips. It seemed the final confirmation that Atherton would be better off without his captaincy duties.

England reached 131 for 4 before the last six wickets fell for 32 runs, with Kasprowicz taking 7 for 36. Australia needed 124 runs for victory and a 4-1 winning margin, which seemed a formality even on a poor Oval wicket. They failed by 19 runs on the most sensational day's cricket in England since Headingley and Trent Bridge 16 years earlier. Wickets kept tumbling, but at 88 for 5 Australia appeared in sight of the finishing line. The key moment came when Healy, having crashed Caddick through the covers just after Ponting's dismissal, hit the next ball hard and straight. Caddick took an outstanding return catch; Australia were 92 for 7. Caddick finished with 5 for 42 after his most aggressive spell for England. The final wicket fell, fittingly, to Tufnell, when McGrath clubbed the ball to Thorpe at mid-off. The Oval crowd, which had been behind England all day, went berserk.

There was no way Atherton was going to call it a day in this environment, although he had told senior management and players that he had made his decision. 'It's all so emotional for me at the moment and I need a few days off before I decide what to do next. It's a very important decision for me and other people involved in the England set-up, so I hope I make the right one. Four years of captaining England home and away takes its toll. Anybody who has done it for a while will tell you that it's an extremely demanding job, both physically and mentally. It makes you think what a few months away from the hard work would do to get you fitter and stronger. That's the problem with me right now – I'm pretty jaded and I badly need a rest. The pride and commitment have never been in doubt. The only problem has been the quality of our cricket at times. This has been a poor series for me with the bat and I will have to think about that, too.'

While Atherton, excused Lancashire duty, went away to clear his head, the country debated his future. England players, the England management and the general public came to the conclusion that there was no one else, but that he would probably resign. Adam Hollioake's inexperience had been exposed in his two Tests and the two other contenders, Stewart and Hussain, gave public support to Atherton. Stewart was installed as favourite should he decide to go. Atherton had left The Oval with those at the top of the England camp declaring their full support, adding that England's captain must be left to decide his own future. England coach David Lloyd explained: 'We've all spoken to him. Now it's his decision and whatever he decides is fine by us. I think I know where he's coming from. Life goes on. Much as I want him to carry on, I love him too much to try and influence that decision if it's not right for him.'

The following Friday Atherton and Graveney appeared at Lord's to announce the outcome of the deliberations. Only Chris Lander of the *Daily Mirror* predicted that Atherton would stay and that was because he was fed up writing the opposite. Lander was spot on. The real question was 'Had Atherton changed his mind?' England's captain denied that he had ever made a decision to go. Subsequent revelations make that unlikely. During the Trent Bridge Test he told Hussain, his vice-captain, that he had had enough. At the same match, Atherton offered to step down before The Oval Test if that suited the selectors. He was happy to see out the series as captain, but it might be better to give the new captain a run-out before the Caribbean. Lord MacLaurin turned down Atherton's offer. Had England lost at The Oval, there was no way Atherton could have stayed.

While Atherton was in Devon with his girlfriend Isabelle, he considered whether The Oval victory should persuade him to stay: his team could play on their day; they could beat anyone in the world; they were behind him. The management also wanted him to stay. But he knew all that before The Oval. What had changed? Certainly, The Oval Test seemed to be final and conclusive proof that the captaincy was affecting his batting – he still shudders about the shot that got him out in the second innings.

Atherton met Graveney at the Regents Park Hilton on the night before the Friday press conference and told the chairman that it was time for a change. That should have been it if the England management had stuck to their promise to let Atherton decide his own future. Within minutes, Graveney had put coach Lloyd on the phone. Graveney knew that if anyone could persuade Atherton to stay it was Lloyd. After 20 minutes, during which Lloyd did most of the talking, England's captain bowed to the pressure. Lloyd said: 'I told him that if he resigned now, he would be putting at risk everything we had worked for over the past two years.' There is no doubt that Lloyd had played on Atherton's emotions. 'He bent my ear to some effect,' remembers Atherton.

England had talked themselves into a corner and convinced themselves that only Atherton would do in the West Indies. What exactly would Atherton be putting at risk? He might miss leading England to victory over the West Indies, who were whitewashed 3-0 by Pakistan at the end of 1997 before losing twice to Adam Hollioake's England one-day side in Sharjah. At the Lord's press conference, Atherton talked about the job being 'half-done'. 'One or two aspects of the job are not great. I would be lying if I didn't say the win at The Oval did not make any difference to my decision. I needed time to reflect and, finally, to ask myself three questions – whether I had the desire to do the job, whether I could get my batting back to its best and whether the team and selectors still wanted me. The answers were "yes". It was a big decision, but I felt I would have been walking out on a job half done. I wanted to see it through. When I took over four years ago I set out to help improve the performance of the team. I feel that's not finished yet. I don't think I've failed, but I haven't yet achieved what I set out to do.'

Graveney insists that no deals were done with Atherton, no lightening of the media duties that England's captain was finding more and more onerous. Graveney announced that Atherton would be missing the Champions Cup in Sharjah so that he could have a real rest before the Caribbean and work on his batting with Graham Gooch. That could be the end of Atherton's limited-overs international ambitions, though he has not given up the desire to lead England into the 1999 Cricket World Cup.

ATHERTON
If the England captaincy has ever got to me, it was during last summer. I've had problems before – they go with the job – but I've always felt I've coped before. I felt I was managing things in 1997, but you don't realise how the pressures are affecting you. That's the thing about stress. If it was easy to spot on a personal basis, it wouldn't be a problem. It's other people who've got it all wrong – not you. Towards the end of 1997, quite a few friends admitted that I was really hard work by the end of the summer. I didn't think so at the time, but looking back, the events of the Ashes series must have taken their toll. Does that mean I was in the right state of mind to make my decision to stay on as captain? All I can say is that I'm still happy with it and believe I've made the right choice.

Losing the 1997 Ashes is certainly my biggest disappointment as captain, especially after our winning start. Bumble [Lloyd] said after Edgbaston that we would never have a better chance. We had prepared and planned well and had outplayed the best side in the world in the first Test. The Aussies were certainly under-cooked there, but we had knocked their confidence with our display. I don't subscribe to the view that the weather saved us at Lord's. That's nonsense. The rain had such an undue influence and we batted well in the second innings. Old Trafford was the key Test match of the summer. A lot was made of Taylor's decision to bat. I would have done the same. Steve Waugh turned the game, but we believed we had him lbw before he had scored. I don't think the Ashes were won or lost in Manchester, but it's where the balance of power swung back to the Australians. People were critical of us at Headingley and Trent Bridge. I agree with the first assessment, not with the second. We failed to take our chances at Headingley, and the Aussies, as they are always likely to do, made us pay. Trent Bridge was different. We had to win that match. After Taylor won the toss and batted, we were not in a great position at the end of the first day. On the Sunday, we had half a sniff when Caddick removed Waugh, but that was it. At Old Trafford and Headingley, we had real opportunities to take the contest.

Test series are won and lost by batsmen. The 1997 summer was a difficult one for batsmen. There's no way I'd be happy with 257 runs in a six-Test series, but I never felt that I played that badly. I got a lot of good balls. Only at The Oval did things get on top of me and that was shown by my dismissal in the second innings. Mark Waugh scored only 209 runs in ten innings. Pitches were not great and there was very little defensive cricket played. Not unnaturally, with the bowlers they have, Australia played a pretty aggressive sort of cricket. There weren't many 220 for 3 days. That's not the way we play; that's not the way they play. The fans got plenty of exciting cricket. We took a lot of stick later on because of our great start. Expectations were sky-high after that. I'm not surprised; we had them at Edgbaston. We knew it; they knew it: England were on top – that's the greatest feeling I've had in my time with England.

I wasn't unhappy with my performance as skipper. The biggest mistake was leaving Caddick out at Headingley. I could have used Ealham a bit more. It's said I don't rate him. That's not true; you've got to call it as you see it. Our poorest performance of the series was at Headingley. The Aussies are a good side, they are cricket's equivalent of the All Blacks – very competitive, and you don't get many chances against them. If you fail to take those, they will give you a very hard time and you can't expect to win.

I wasn't surprised over the speculation about my future. The press have got to talk about something. Look at what happened to Mark Taylor all through the summer. It was a difficult time and I probably was affected by the pressures. My shot to Kasprowicz was symptomatic of the pressure I was under, but that doesn't last. If we had lost the last Test, the issue would have been cleared: I couldn't have carried on. But I didn't want to tie myself down with a decision about my future before the end of the Ashes series. As soon as you announce it, you are bound by it. I talked to people close to me. The gap before the West Indies tour was important; I needed time and a break. If the Australian tour, with an October departure date had been next up, I would have viewed things differently.

I can own up now to being quite stressed up by the end of the summer. You don't think you're affected, but your friends tell you afterwards. They said I was hard work and that I looked tired. One said you can always tell by your eyes – and mine looked pretty bad. In the four years I've done the job, there have been some bad times. I didn't cope with the job at the end of summer: the team was losing, I *wasn't scoring runs and there was the debate about the captaincy. However, the rest has been beneficial and I didn't head off to the Caribbean, thinking 'what have I done?'*

England's results in the Caribbean will be the ultimate jury on whether Atherton was right to stay. His only real problem before the tour came when he looked out of his Manchester flat to see his red Peugeot ablaze. Thieves had broken into another car, then set fire to it. The fire spread to Atherton's car and he watched helplessly, waiting for the fire brigade to arrive. He was most upset by the loss of his expensive fishing equipment. That apart, Atherton worked hard with Gooch and enjoyed the break from the limelight. A few had queried the mass vote for Atherton to stay. England finished the Ashes summer of 1997 more than a decade from their last success in a major Test series. The captain has normally paid the price for those failures, but Atherton has remained relatively immune compared to the head-hunting that went on for Ian Botham, David Gower, Mike Gatting and Graham Gooch. However, he is living on borrowed time. He knows it and only some major England success will inspire him to carry on much longer.

ATHERTON
My technique is always changing. I'm always fiddling about, seeing if I can improve, probably to the detriment of it all. In that way the captaincy has probably helped because there's little time to muck around with my batting. Generally, my technique is trying to bat fairly still without huge movements. Essentially, I am more comfortable on the back foot and I play pretty straight. That's always been a strength, and I have a good type of arm technique. My technique has certainly changed over the years. When I first came into the England side, I was a

very upright batsman, a bit mechanical, a bit stiff-legged. The first time it really changed was in the winter of 1989 working with Geoff Boycott. I worked very hard on some fundamental things before I went away to Zimbabwe with England A. The reason for that was I had made my entry into Test cricket, not that successfully. And, while I realised that I was promising, I had a lot of work to do. So I worked hard. It's all very well saying you've played for England, but actually I hadn't done very well playing for England in my two Tests. I wanted a long and successful international career, so I had to make some fundamental changes. That's what I did. I became lower in stance, attempting to change my feet alignment. Since then I've played pretty well most of the time and been reasonably successful.

Within that there have been patches when I have not played well, patches when I've played exceptionally well. Strangely, during my best innings – that 185 at The Wanderers at South Africa, I would say my technique wasn't great at that stage. I stayed there because I was very focused and had enough nouse to get through. In times of trouble, you forget basics. You start to think too much about your feet, your backlift, your weight and all that kind of thing. The best and simplest advice I have to give is to forget everything, just look at the ball and concentrate on playing naturally. Obviously, you can't think too much two days before a Test match, but if you get a period like I had last winter, two or three months where you've got some time, then put some work in.

I didn't play that well last summer – or that badly, either. If you have a period of two or three months away, you take stock. What's the motivation? What do I want to achieve? Is 70 games and 5,000 runs enough? Or do I want to play 100 games and score 7,000 runs? If you are still motivated and still want to improve, that's what you do, otherwise you stand still. So I spent some time

*working with Graham Gooch. Boycs' methods of coaching
are different from Goochie in that he is more critical. I
mean that in a nice way. He picks you to bits. What you
have to do is be very strong with Boycs. You have to know
what's good about your game, what's not so good and
what needs changing. With Goochie, I had opened with
him 30 or 40 times, he knew my game pretty well. It's
more a case of 'this is what you're good at, let's work at
what you're not so good at'; so there's fewer fundamental
changes.*

*Working at my game wasn't a problem before I became
captain. When you are playing county cricket and you are
not England captain, you are never sure you are going to
be picked for the next game, therefore you are looking to
perform at county level. Part of the problem when you are
captain of England is that you know you are going to be
picked and you normally come back from a Test match
mentally quite tired because it's an extra effort and therefore you get lazy about your batting and you get lazy
when you play for your county and you get lazy when you
play some non-international matches on tour when you
really should get a big score. You get 50 or 60 and say I'm
happy, I'm feeling in good nick, ready for the Test. I've
never been one for being really greedy in situations that
don't really matter, like at Spanish Town at the start of the
West Indies tour. It was a dead game and there was
probably a hundred there for the taking. I'm not saying
that I got out deliberately, but I've never really been
greedy in those circumstances. I would much prefer to be
remembered as someone who got runs when it counted and
when it was important. When you are playing and not 100
per cent focused on what you are doing, that's when you
get lazy, that's when the bad habits creep in. So rather
than play in matches when you are not focused, even one
per cent less, you are better off not playing. It's like
practice – bad practice is worse than no practice.*

I made no fundamental changes during last winter working with Goochie. I'm a pretty good player and I'm happy with what I've got. I don't see any need to be making major changes. It was a question of taking stock, re-motivating, setting some targets, some challenges, working hard on little things like balance, footwork, playing a bit more sideways on, all that sort of thing and, hopefully, getting some runs. I've played enough now to know what the mental side is all about. But the good thing about Goochie is, at his age and even having scored all those runs, the enormous enthusiasm he has for batting, the enormous enthusiasm he has for passing it on and wanting you to be the best. That break was good for me to get away from the game a little bit and to put in some work.

Certainly, captaining the side takes it out of you. If I had just been playing for the past four years, I'm sure I would have been looking forward to going to Sharjah or somewhere, if selected. I know that I'm not going to be playing until I'm 40, I don't think I'll be physically up to it. I've got three or four years left and I don't think I'll be captain for all that time. In fact, I know I won't be. But I think I've got it in me to play three or four years more for England. I'm pretty motivated now and I'm still captain. I want to finish on a high. I've still got it in me to play for England when I'm not captain.

CHAPTER TWENTY

The Captain's View

Atherton's achievements have matched exceedingly high expectations. A professional and international career was predicted at school, as was the possibility of leading his country's national cricket team. The FEC challenge was thrown down in his first year at Downing College. The inconsistent state of England's Test team and Illingworth's troubled reign have conspired to make a difficult job almost impossible at times. Atherton was appointed England captain after the team had lost eight of its previous nine Tests. The new captain had struggled back from injury, loss of form, a disappointing tour of the sub-continent and had only just re-established himself in the side. Yet, when Atherton was named Graham Gooch's replacement on 28 July 1993, the popular and widespread view was that here was the man who would pass Peter May's record of leading England 41 times. Time was certainly on his side, Atherton was 25, if he remained fit and in form; history was not. England's captains, like Gower, Gatting and Gooch, have found the task daunting and eventually, thankless. Atherton overtook Peter May's record on 19 June 1997, less than four years after taking the job and at the earliest possible date. Atherton has kept fit, despite his continuing problems with his back. He is the only ever-present member of the team during his period as captain. His form has improved. Like Graham Gooch before him, the extra responsibility of leadership has helped his own game and the side has relied on his runs more than it should. The Zimbabwe tour was the exception, when he made a mere 34 runs in two Tests. He recovered in New Zealand, scoring 94 not out and 118 at Christchurch which won the Test and clinched the series. Without it, England's Test winter would have ended in stalemate. But his form dropped again in the 1997 Ashes series on some bowler friendly wickets.

Atherton's assessment of his best Test innings varies. Normally, it is the most recent knock that has been in service of his country and team. Atherton was and still is proud of his 28 in the second innings at Kingston when he stood toe to toe with Courtney Walsh; his courage and capability against pace are not now an issue, as they were at the start of the 1994 Caribbean tour. England's new captain had to prove himself for his previous series against the West Indies had produced 79 runs from five Tests in 1991. Bad back or no bad back, Atherton had to demonstrate that he could dance effectively to this fearsome 'chin music'. Atherton lost the battle against Walsh that day, but won his war in the West Indies with 510 runs in the series, 469 of them scored in the vital first innings of matches. His name was added to the list of Test centuries scored at the Bourda in the next game, 144 in Guyana. His 85 at Barbados in an opening stand of 171 with Stewart was the first sign England could recover from Trinidad's Hurricane Curtly. After Lara's Test record at Antigua, Atherton dug in with Smith to save the game with another century.

After two centuries in the 1994 New Zealand series, the gutsiest moment of Atherton's troubled summer came with his 99 against South Africa at Headingley. For dogged determination and bloody-mindedness, nothing has surpassed that. Atherton averaged over 40 in Australia, then scored one of the most memorable Lord's one-day centuries against the West Indies. Atherton was particularly pleased to demonstrate his limited-overs capabilities at the home of cricket to those who doubted he possessed such stroke-making inventiveness. England's captain scored his side's first century of that West Indies series, again averaging over 40.

His first-day 78 at Centurion Park against South Africa was as brave and battling as his Kingston going-over. Atherton set new standards for himself and England at The Wanderers in the next Test with his match-saving 185. His 160 at Trent Bridge against India in July 1996 was his tenth Test century, accumulated when he was not in the best of form. Atherton and Stewart twice took England to within sight of safety against Pakistan. Twice the rest of the batting collapsed. Zimbabwe followed, but Atherton showed his class and determination by averaging over 100 against New Zealand, including that Man of the Match 94 not out and 118 at Christchurch. He places that performance above Johannesburg because it helped England to a win.

Atherton has also learnt to cope with the verbals. First blood went to the Australians in 1989. Eighteen months later, a withering stare from the England batsman to wicket-keeper Ian Healy in Sydney, after a claim for a leg-side catch, showed Atherton was learning how to deal with this other type of intimidation. Graduation came at Old Trafford in 1993 after edging a ball from Merv Hughes. 'Jesus Christ. You've not got any better in four ****** years!' bellowed the bowler. Atherton just smiled back. 'Yeah, yeah, Merv, we've heard it all before. No new ones?' The smile in the face of batting adversity has become the Atherton trademark. He can be knocked off his feet, but Atherton will be up quickly and still smiling. England's captain has demonstrated that really little flusters him at the crease. As with Gooch, opposing bowlers no longer waste their energy trying tricks and gamesmanship.

ATHERTON

I didn't think I would get picked way back in 1989. I didn't feel I batted as well at university as I had done in the previous two years. That was caused by slow wickets and partly by working for my degree. Then I was disappointed by the way some people reacted to my failure in the first innings – people who should have known better – questioning my technique after just two balls. My strengths are reasonable technique, good concentration and good composure under pressure. My main weakness is that certain technical things are not as they should be. In an English summer, batting five or six times a week, fluency and getting runs can get you through that – back and across with the weight and the head moving forward. When you are playing well, it all happens naturally and you just don't think about it.

The period after my back operation in 1991 was pretty desperate. Lying there on my back for one endless day after another, the thought did cross my mind that it was all slipping away. In some ways, since then, I've known my days are numbered, so to speak. Ultimately, the state of my back will have the final say in how long I play for England. I might just make the Millennium. I've prepared myself for not going any further than that. My philosophy in the 1989 debut was to turn up thinking: 'Things might go for me today, they might not. There's always tomorrow.' But what I took on board, thanks to Gooch's influence, is the realisation that that way of going about things is just not good enough. If you want to be successful, there is no alternative. You have to put in the work.

I've done better with the bat since I became captain. The

problem in Zimbabwe and New Zealand was technical. Playing against Donald, Pollock and McMillan, when I got a lot of short stuff, got me into the habit of getting square-on. That's the way to play the short-pitched stuff. I didn't mind it, but on slower wickets with the ball leaving you, it's not the best way to play. There are two things with batting, the talent and technique, which mark you out originally and the characteristics such as composure, concentration and stubbornness. I think I'm very good at the mental side of the game. That's what sees me through. It saw me through most of the 1996 summer when I played poorly for England, but still averaged 47. That was an example of mind over matter, of having sufficient mental strength to keep going. So stubbornness at the crease is a good thing. Yet I don't think I'm stubborn by nature. I'm quite prepared to listen. I don't always agree with people, but I'll hear them out. I'm the captain and have to make the decisions.

My greatest sporting experience was batting with Jack Russell at The Wanderers. The partnership was a great experience in camaraderie with a team-mate against the opposition and against the odds. Generally, though, nothing beats the winning experience. As for watching, you want the best. That's why I envy Brian Lara his talent. He's the best I've ever seen. From what I've seen on film, I would have loved to have watched Mohammad Ali in his prime.

Zimbabwe apart, most of the flak Atherton has faced during his reign as captain has centred on his style of leadership and the problems that arose from the 'ball-tampering' saga. His first four winters abroad as captain have been tough. The most enjoyable was the first, to the Caribbean. Atherton was convinced the youth policy had proved its value and the team had made real progress. Despite a successful 1994 summer, the Ashes tour was a failure after Atherton had clashed with Illingworth over selection. The remedy from Lord's was to put the main architect of that mission in sole charge with full power. Fletcher was sacked and Atherton was made to stand in the corner like a naughty boy. Atherton kept England alive in South Africa at the start of the series, but the tour collapsed in Cape Town. Half the Test party returned home with Illingworth predicting their England careers were over. The one-day series at the end of South Africa proved a disaster and England's World Cup campaign collapsed in a mire of mediocrity. After years of Illingworth saying that the top man needed full power to put England on a winning track, the winter of 1995-96 exposed this approach. A third successive losing winter left Atherton pondering his future. The arrival of a new generation, with David Lloyd as coach and Graham Gooch as a selector, persuaded Atherton to see out the Illingworth era. At the end of the Zimbabwe tour, England looked like starting the 1997 summer with a new captain as well as chairman of selectors, the captain struggling as never before to make runs. The humiliation of the one-day whitewash brought widespread condemnation of the whole England set-up, as well as the view that Atherton's position was now untenable. Atherton refused to quit midway through his winter appointment. This was not blind obstinacy. Atherton made it very clear that if he did not score runs and if England did not win in New Zealand, his reign as captain was over. It was as simple as that. Atherton has always been fond of a challenge. There is no more challenging job in England sports than trying to get the national cricket team to compete with the best.

Mark Nicholas, the former Hampshire and England A captain and now a cricket commentator, has followed Atherton's career and development closely since the youngster was his vice-captain on the 1990 A tour to Zimbabwe:

I didn't select him as the vice-captain. That was down to Dexter, Stewart and possibly Tim Lamb, who had managed an Under-19 tour with him in charge. The England selectors have been much maligned over the years, and rightly so. Yet, with Michael, they spotted someone who was young and gifted. I was a bit wary. English cricket is littered with casualties who have been given top billing too early.

I got an early example of his stubbornness. There was a selection meeting that also included Fletcher and Pringle. When we didn't agree with him, Michael picked up a newspaper and started reading it. I just ignored it. It was just him at that stage. The upside of Atherton came at another selection meeting. I said that we needed to put our best catcher at backward point. He looked up and just said 'I'd better go there then. I don't drop anything.' Of course, he took a brilliant one-handed catch and, after the celebrations, he gave me that 'I told you so' look. He has that incredible confidence in his own ability and capabilities. He has become the most important England cricketer of his time, much as Gooch did. Michael has handled a lot of things well. He's done the odd impetuous thing, like bowling three yards down the leg-side in South Africa. The issues have all been moral ones – ball-tampering, dissent when given out. I believe he's mainly got the morality right. You want the wisdom of Solomon as well as the fitness and eye of youth to do the job.

A dissenting view was aired at the end of the 1996 summer by Dermot Reeve, the captain of Warwickshire, forced to retire from the game because of injury and now coach at Somerset. Reeve's innovative style had helped Warwickshire to great success and he had been a key member of England's 1992 World Cup side. Reeve turned up at the end of England's South African tour along with several other one-day specialists. He was not included in the final World Cup 14, although he flew out after an injury to White, who had overtaken him in the reckoning. His book *Winning Ways* includes: 'England were never in the hunt during the World Cup. One-day cricket at that level had passed us by and our management team of Ray Illingworth and Michael Atherton must take the bulk of the blame for that. They were way off the pace in terms of preparation, tactical appreciation and man-management. Atherton gave no real indication of having a feel for captaining a side in one-day cricket. He had made no secret in the past that he prefers Test cricket, that one-day matches aren't important. As a result, his captaincy lacked drive, purpose and flair. Add to that his passive body language and you're struggling when the team is up against it.' He continued by saying that Atherton should have stepped down and that 'it's not as if he would have been picked on merit'. His final criticism was that 'he needed to talk to his players about their game, to lift their spirits. I said that communication with the players was poor and that Illingworth was now a laughing stock, that not many in the squad took any notice of him and laughed behind his back.'

As well as maintaining his fitness and form, Atherton had kept his head and cool. Many times when Illingworth went public, Atherton wondered whether it was all worth it. Yet, the desire to take England forward remained his over-riding concern and his refusal to deviate from that cause is further evidence of his incredible determination and single-mindedness. Atherton has never confessed to being the world's greatest cricket captain. That responsibility was just given because he was the best player in the side at school. At Cambridge, the captain had nothing to lose as the students were always outgunned. That was about the extent of Atherton's leadership experience when Ted Dexter decided to entrust the next generation of England cricketers to his care against the might of Allan Border's Australians and Richie Richardson's West Indies. It has been a battle and a struggle for Atherton to survive. Atherton has needed his wits as well as his ability. The scars are there, although there is little physical evidence of change.

ATHERTON

I'm very self-analytical and self-critical. After each day's play and certainly after every Test match, I just sit down and think, was I right to have taken the options I did? You know, I've always been a great believer in following your gut feelings and when I haven't, I've nearly always regretted it. There are moments when the captaincy is extremely hard work and there are moments when it is particularly enjoyable. In fact, the experience it brings is like no other. The emotions from the highs and the lows are what I'm in the game for and I wouldn't swap them for anything. Captaincy changes your attitude. You know that if things go wrong, people will look back and say it was your tour. My best time as captain was on the South African tour when I made that 185 at Johannesburg. After that, I was on a high and so all the captaincy decisions came easily and I made them with confidence. I prefer to lead from the front, through my own performances, so if that is not as good as you would like, you tend to turn in on yourself and I suppose, subconsciously, it affects your captaincy.

Over here we tend to get on our high horse a bit more, as the role of England captain seems to be viewed in a more rounded sense, almost as an Establishment figure and therefore someone who should be setting a broader example. Elsewhere captains just seem to be judged for what happens on the field. I never had a problem with the amount of coverage after the soil-in-the-pocket affair, just with certain interpretations of it. I hadn't really grasped the implications of being England captain. I thought it was just about getting the cricket right. I realise that the England cricket captain has to be an utterly blameless figure. If it ever got to the point where it's changing me too much, I'd consider giving it up. I'm a sportsman, not a statesman. Hate mail goes with the job, especially if the ball-tampering incident [about 800 letters] and any criticism of the Edgbaston pitch are anything to go by. My first experience of hate mail came when David Gower was not included in my first touring squad. It's really amazing that one bloke can create such emotional feelings, and it was certainly brought home to me after we left him out. I'd never had such vicious letters – maybe 150 of them stuffed into my pigeon-hole at Old Trafford – and all of them pro-Gower. It doesn't make it any easier when you are a fan, either. He was my boyhood hero, in fact. I was 10 years old, watching the TV in the lounge with my father, when Gower pulled his first ball in Test cricket for four and my dad said: 'Just look at that and learn. Look how still his head is.' Ever since he has been a fairly heroic figure for me. He presented me with my first England cap, and we have always got on well together. We both got hundreds at Sydney in 1991. His century that day was one of the best I've ever seen; it was wondrous stuff. It wasn't easy leaving him out.

My words about Edgbaston were the first time in 20-odd games as captain that I had ever made an excuse. The wicket was a 'disgrace'. If I want to make excuses, what about our injury situation in Australia. I went from Antigua in 1994 until Christchurch 1997 not being able to pick an unchanged England team. My only regular complaints are the same as everyone else involved with the

England team. We bend over backwards to be fair to the opposition. Hopefully, that situation over the choice of two ball manufacturers has been resolved. England will get the ball that suits them better. The other concern is the way we prepare pitches. After the 1996 Oval Test, Waqar came to me and said: 'Why do you always prepare pitches to suit our bowlers?' I didn't have an answer. I'm not talking about doctoring wickets – just preparing them to suit the strengths of the home side as every other country in the cricket world does.

The only times I've been really disappointed with my captaincy was during the Melbourne and Sydney Tests, where I let the pressure get to me. But, more disconcertingly, I allowed it to show to the rest of the team. At Sydney, I was just too far off the pace. A good captain is ahead of the game and I was always that bit slow. That began to get to me and I started to make decisions on what other people felt rather than being confident in my own judgement. It can be difficult at times, but like anything the more you do it, the more you come across situations you've seen before, the quicker you react to make something, or even prevent something from happening. So, just by virtue of experience, I believe I am improving. I don't believe in passing pleasantries on the field and I didn't need to go into the opposition dressing-room for a beer at the end of the day. Now I'm captain I do. The Australian tour in 1994-95 was much tougher than the Caribbean. It's harder to keep the lads together. Players do their own thing in Australia. The worst aspect in those matches was the standard of our fielding. That got me down more than anything. A high-quality fielding side lifts the bowlers, lifts the team. Unfortunately, the reverse happens with a poor side and that gets up everyone's nose.

The England captain does need some help. I am convinced that it is best coming in the form of a coach, and not a manager or supremo. Manager implies a football-style control over team affairs and tactics, which he can never have because of the changing nature of the game out on the pitch. During the match the captain must be in charge of the team. The toss, tactics, bowling changes, field placings, declarations and team talks are all the captain's sole remit. Where the coach does have a role to play is in the team's preparations, individual technical help and having a positive influence and presence around the dressing-room. It is on tour, I believe, where the coach's role in practice is more keenly felt. When players are together every day, the need for variety in practice while maintaining an intensity becomes crucial. It is on tour, also, where a coach can have more impact on a player through technical help. Day-to-day contact with any members of the squad in need of assistance is vital.

I have never had any problems with individuals. I have heard that Phil DeFreitas and Phil Tufnell have been kept out of the side at times because I don't want them. But I have never spoken out at selection meetings against a player for anything other than cricketing reasons. If we pick awkward people, it's up to me to handle them. I don't mind awkward people. Part of the game is to have 11 characters within the team. To me, cricket is the over-riding consideration – batting, bowling, fielding and attitude. That's what I look for. When you are talking to players, trying to find out their thoughts, in the back of their minds they are weighing up whether what they say might affect selection, so you are never getting the truth. I realise that the management took much flak over the wives ban in Zimbabwe. It was a no-win situation, but the truth is that the arrival of an enormous party of wives and girlfriends altered the focus at a vital stage in South Africa.

I am not besotted by the thought of having my picture in the paper every day. I find it a pain in the backside. I am not a very public person, so that side of it is difficult for me. But I am also analytical about my own performances, which has meant I have had periods of self-doubt. Losing does get you down, so does playing badly. Is it time for a new man to take charge? The lowest point of my captaincy came in those seven one-dayers in 12 days in South Africa last year. I don't peruse the various areas of the media as much now if we've done badly. That comes from advice from Manchester United manager Alex Ferguson. He explained that if it hurts when you lose, why hurt yourself twice by reading about it when you do badly. Read about it when you do well. As I've already said, I never had a problem with the amount of coverage after the 'soil-in-the-pocket', just certain interpretations of it. I'd be lying if I said there hadn't been times when I wished I'd given it away during that period. Those were fleeting moments and soon passed.

I find myself constantly having to assert how much I enjoy the captaincy and playing for England. I took this job because I genuinely felt I could make an impact on the cricket field. That's what excites me. I get slightly more for being captain, but I've always felt I don't want to milk it or make what I could out of it. Being captain of England is such a massive honour. I have a contract with Gray Nicholls and a writing contract with the Sunday Telegraph and that's all. I don't have a wife and children to support, so it wouldn't worry me from that point of view. The criteria haven't changed from the day I took the job — you can only captain an unsuccessful England side for so long. Losing gets you down; playing badly gets you down. You can't keep putting yourself in the firing line without good reason. I feel that England are a much tougher team to beat in Test matches since I took over. Not putting up a fight is a far bigger crime in my book than losing, especially when you are representing your country.

Atherton's Career Record

(to 1 January 1998)

ENGLAND RECORD

Year	Opposition	Tests	I	NO	HS	Runs	Ave	100s	50s	0s	Ct
1989	Australia	2	4	0	47	73	18.25	0	0	1	1
1990	New Zealand	3	5	0	151	357	71.40	1	3	1	3
1990	India	3	6	0	131	378	63.00	1	3	0	3
1990-91	Australia	5	10	1	105	279	31.00	1	1	2	5
1991	West Indies	5	9	0	32	79	8.77	0	0	1	3
1992	Pakistan	3	5	0	76	145	29.00	0	2	1	5
1992-93	India	1	2	0	37	48	24.00	0	0	0	2
1992-93	Sri Lanka	1	2	0	13	15	7.50	0	0	0	1
1993	Australia	6	12	0	99	553	46.08	0	6	0	1
1993-94	West Indies	5	9	0	144	510	56.66	2	2	2	3
1994	New Zealand	3	4	0	111	273	68.25	2	0	0	2
1994	South Africa	3	6	0	99	207	34.50	0	2	1	1
1994-95	Australia	5	10	0	88	407	40.70	0	4	0	4
1995	West Indies	6	12	0	113	488	40.66	1	2	1	3
1995-96	South Africa	5	8	1	185*	390	55.71	1	2	1	2
1996	India	3	5	1	160	263	65.75	1	1	1	2
1996	Pakistan	3	5	0	64	162	32.40	0	1	0	3
1996-97	Zimbabwe	2	4	0	16	34	8.50	0	0	0	2
1996-97	New Zealand	3	4	1	118	325	108.33	1	2	0	1
1997	Australia	6	12	1	77	257	23.36	0	2	0	2
	Home	46	85	2	160	3235	38.97	6	22	7	29
	Away	27	49	3	185*	2008	43.65	5	11	5	20
	TOTAL	73	134	5	185*	5243	40.64	11	33	12	49

ATHERTON: Country by Country

Opposition	Tests	I	NO	HS	Runs	Ave	100s	50s	0s	Ct
Australia	24	48	2	105	1569	34.10	1	13	3	13
New Zealand	9	13	1	151	955	79.58	4	5	1	6
India	7	13	1	160	689	57.41	2	4	1	7
West Indies	16	30	0	144	1077	35.90	3	4	4	9
Pakistan	6	10	0	76	307	30.70	0	3	1	8
Sri Lanka	1	2	0	13	15	7.50	0	0	0	1
South Africa	8	14	1	185*	597	45.92	1	4	2	3
Zimbabwe	2	4	0	16	34	8.50	0	0	0	2

ATHERTON: England's Test Grounds

	Tests	I	NO	HS	Runs	Ave	100s	50s	0s
Trent Bridge	8	13	0	160	706	54.30	4	0	1
The Oval	9	18	0	95	572	31.77	0	5	2
Lord's	10	19	0	99	608	32.00	0	6	2
Edgbaston	6	12	2	82	418	41.80	0	5	0
Old Trafford	6	10	0	131	455	45.50	2	1	1
Leeds	7	13	0	99	476	36.61	0	5	0

ATHERTON TEST CENTURIES

					Test No
1.	151	v New Zealand	Trent Bridge	1990	3
2.	131	v India	Old Trafford	1990	7
3.	105	v Australia	Sydney	1991	11
4.	144	v West Indies	Guyana	1994	31
5.	135	v West Indies	Antigua	1994	34
6.	101	v New Zealand	Trent Bridge	1994	35
7.	111	v New Zealand	Old Trafford	1994	37
8.	113	v West Indies	Trent Bridge	1995	50
9.	185*	v South Africa	Johannesburg	1995	53
10.	160	v India	Trent Bridge	1996	59
11.	118	v New Zealand	Christchurch	1997	67

ATHERTON AS ENGLAND CAPTAIN

P46	W12	L15	D18	3508 runs @ 44.40

Victories as captain

1.	161 runs	v Australia	The Oval	1993
2.	208 runs	v West Indies	Bridgetown	1993-94
3.	Inns & 90 runs	v New Zealand	Trent Bridge	1994
4.	8 wickets	v South Africa	The Oval	1994
5.	106 runs	v Australia	Adelaide	1994-95
6.	72 runs	v West Indies	Lord's	1995
7.	6 wickets	v West Indies	Old Trafford	1995
8.	8 wickets	v India	Edgbaston	1996
9.	Inns & 68 runs	v New Zealand	Wellington	1996-97
10.	4 wickets	v New Zealand	Christchurch	1996-97
11.	9 wickets	v Australia	Edgbaston	1997
12.	19 runs	v Australia	The Oval	1997

ATHERTON'S FIRST-CLASS RECORD

	M	I	NO	HS	Runs	Ave	100s	50s	Ct
1987	21	35	4	110	1193	38.48	2	4	7
1988	16	27	4	152*	1121	48.73	4	3	15
1989	18	33	3	115*	941	31.36	1	4	16
1989-90	2	3	0	122	250	83.33	2	0	3
1990	20	31	4	191	1924	71.25	7	12	24
1990-91	11	22	2	114	577	28.85	2	2	10
1991	14	23	3	138	820	41.00	3	2	9
1992	21	37	6	199	1598	51.54	5	7	24
1992-93	5	10	1	80*	253	28.11	0	2	5
1993	19	32	1	137	1364	44.00	3	9	14
1993-94	7	12	0	144	704	58.66	3	3	4
1994	16	27	2	111	899	35.96	2	4	14
1994-95	10	20	1	88	755	39.73	0	6	8
1995	18	31	1	155*	1323	44.10	4	6	14
1995-96	10	17	2	185*	731	43.73	2	5	3
1996	15	26	1	160	963	38.52	1	7	8
1996-97	10	17	2	118	456	30.40	1	3	10
1997	16	28	2	149	853	32.81	2	5	8
TOTAL	249	431	39	199	16725	42.66	44	84	196

ATHERTON'S RUNS

Manchester GS	1982-86	3463 runs @ 65.34
Cambridge University	1987-89	1493 runs @ 41.47
Lancashire	1987-	8216 runs @ 46.15
England (Tests)	1989-	5243 runs @ 40.64
England (LOI)	1990-	1727 runs @ 34.54
England (Tests/Captain)	1993-	3508 runs @ 44.40
England (LOI/Captain)	1994-	1392 runs @ 33.92
All First-class	1987-	16,725 runs @ 42.66

ATHERTON THE BOWLER

1496.5 overs   289 maidens   4733 runs   108 wickets   43.82 average
Best bowling 6/78 v Nottinghamshire at Trent Bridge, 1990

Test Bowling   2/302
Test wickets

1.	DB Vengsarkar	c&b	Atherton	33	The Oval, 1990
2.	Wasim Akram	lbw	b Atherton	7	Old Trafford, 1996

Index

N.B. Family relationships to Mike Atherton are given in brackets.